RESEARCH METHODS FOR STRATEGIC MANAGEMENT

The field of strategic management has developed significantly since its birth from "business policy" and "business planning" in the 1960s. Pioneering studies were essentially normative, prescriptive, and often based on in-depth case studies. The evolution of strategic management into a respected field of academic study resulted from the adoption of research methods previously employed in economics. Today, research in strategic management is likely to employ a mixture of methods borrowed from related and unrelated disciplines, such as political sciences, psychology, neuroscience, and behavioral economics, which can be confusing to researchers new to the field.

This book provides the reader with a broad introduction to the array of qualitative and quantitative research methods required to investigate strategic management. Throughout the book, strong emphasis is placed on practical applications that transcend the mere analysis of the theoretical roots of single research methods. The underlying result is a book that encourages and aids readers to "learn by doing" – in applying the implications of each chapter to their own research.

This text is vital reading for postgraduate students and researchers focused on business strategy.

Giovanni Battista Dagnino is Professor in the Department of Economics and Business at the University of Catania, Italy and Visiting Professor at the Tuck School of Business at Dartmouth, USA. He has authored/edited eleven books and several articles in leading management journals.

Maria Cristina Cinici is Assistant Professor of Business Economics and Management at the Department of Economics of the University of Messina, Italy.

This fascinating book is a valuable companion to post-graduate doctoral courses introducing students to the broad range of opportunities available for the study of strategic management. It offers a comprehensive overview of well established and emerging research methods in strategic management, without privileging a particular perspective or research tradition, but acknowledging the methodological richness that characterizes current research on strategy.

Davide Ravasi, *Professor in Strategic and Entrepreneurial Management, Cass Business School, City University London, UK*

This volume features novel research designs and methodological approaches for scholarship in strategic management. It provides an invaluable set of contributions on frontier topics that span quantitative and qualitative research methods. It will be a precious guide and reference source for scholars as well as students.

Jeffrey J. Reuer, *Guggenheim Endowed Chair and Professor of Strategy and Entrepreneurship, University of Colorado, USA*

Strategic management research has grown significantly in its rigor. This book makes an important contribution to this fast growing body of research, covering an impressive range of quantitative and qualitative methods and tying them to theory building and testing. The approaches discussed are carefully and methodically presented in an organized fashion. Dagnino and Cinici do a great job in making the material easily accessible and useful to researchers. I strongly recommend this book for serious scholars.

Shaker A. Zahra, *Robert E. Buuck Chair and Professor of Strategy and Entrepreneurship, University of Minnesota, USA*

For academics in the field of Strategy who aspire to undertake research that is rigorous and robust, this wonderful book is a goldmine! It brings together a host of research methods to guide the investigation and make the research journey more rewarding. This book is academically rigorous, practical and easy to read. It belongs on the shelf of every researcher exploring business strategy.

Costas Markides, *Robert Bauman Chair of Strategic Leadership and Professor of Strategy and Entrepreneurship, London Business School, UK*

This edited book on research methods in strategic management offers useful guidelines for scholars interested in designing and executing their research projects. Instead of echoing methods that are commonly taught in research methods courses, this book highlights some less popular approaches and emerging trends that can be adopted from related fields, such as psychology, linguistics, and neuroscience. The chapters review relevant literature on these research methods, provide a roadmap for implementing these methods, and illustrate their use in strategic management research. The book offers a good starting point for those interested in specializing in these research methods.

Dovev Lavie, *Professor of Strategic Management, Technion-Israel Institute of Technology, Israel*

I have been waiting this book! Of course there is a range of books on research methods but none are dedicated to strategic management and so few, if any, describe and explain practically so many methods. I am particularly impressed by the diversity of methods, the equal emphasis given to qualitative and quantitative methods and by the attention given to the increasingly popular mixed method approach. A must read.

Véronique Ambrosini, *Professor of Management, Monash University, Australia*

RESEARCH METHODS FOR STRATEGIC MANAGEMENT

Edited by Giovanni Battista Dagnino and Maria Cristina Cinici

Routledge
Taylor & Francis Group

LONDON AND NEW YORK

First published 2016
by Routledge
2 Park Square, Milton Park, Abingdon, Oxon OX14 4RN

and by Routledge
711 Third Avenue, New York, NY 10017

Routledge is an imprint of the Taylor & Francis Group, an informa business

British Library Cataloguing in Publication Data
A catalogue record for this book is available from the British Library

Library of Congress Cataloging in Publication Data
Research methods for strategic management / edited by Giovanni Battista Dagnino and Maria Cristina Cinici.
pages cm
Includes bibliographical references and index.
1. Strategic planning. I. Dagnino, Giovanni Battista, 1966- II. Cinici, Maria Cristina.
HD30.28.R463 2015
658.4'012—dc23
2015016286

ISBN: 978-0-415-50620-5 (hbk)
ISBN: 978-0-203-67661-5 (ebk)

Typeset in Bembo
by FiSH Books Ltd, Enfield

CONTENTS

FIGURES

TABLES

CONTRIBUTORS

Chahrazad Abdallah is Lecturer in Management in the School of Management and Organizational Psychology of Birkbeck College, University of London. She received her Ph.D. in Management from HEC Montreal, Canada. She has been Research Fellow at Cass Business School, City University of London, and has a particular interest in the discursive constitution and dissemination of strategic plans in pluralistic organizations (specifically, cultural and media organizations). She is currently a member of the Research Group on Strategy Practices based at HEC Montreal, Canada, and is working on organization theory in a post-industrial context and on qualitative research method.

Claudio Barbaranelli is Full Professor of Psychometrics and researcher at the Department of Psychology of the University of Rome "La Sapienza." He is the director of the Psychometrics Laboratory where, with his research group, he is conducting investigations on personality assessment and measurement, social-cognitive models, occupational health and stress, work safety and security, problem gambling, and research methods. He is author of more than a hundred articles in national and international journals, five books, and ten psychological tests.

Maria Cristina Cinici is Assistant Professor of Business Economics and Management at the Department of Economics of the University of Messina, Italy. She received her Ph.D. from the University of Catania, Italy, and was post-doctoral research fellow at Grenoble Ecole de Management, France, and visiting scholar at NYU's Stern School of Business, USA. Her research focuses on competitive strategy with a primary interest on the use of cognitive tools in the development of business models and firm capabilities, the large-firms' impact on the dynamics of high-tech clusters, and the contribution of semiotic approaches to SM field. She has authored a book, several book chapters, and research papers published in national and international journals, such as *Technovation*.

Giorgia M. D'Allura is Assistant Professor of Business Economics and Management at the University of Catania, Italy, where she did her Ph.D. and spent a post-doctoral research fellowship period. She was visiting scholar at the University of Florida in Gainesville. Her research interests regard the governance of family business and SMEs, innovation and development in firm regional networks, and the strategic management of service firms. As concerns research methods, she focuses on data collection protocols and network analysis.

Giovanni Battista Dagnino is Professor of Business Economics and Management in the Department of Economics and Business of the University of Catania, Italy, where he is Coordinator of the Ph.D. Program in Economics and Management. He is Visiting Professor of Business Administration at the Tuck School of Business at Dartmouth, USA. He is also faculty member of the European Institute for Advanced Studies in Management in Brussels, Fellow of the Strategic Planning Society in London, and Friend of the European Investment Bank Institute in Luxembourg. His research revolves around the advancement of the strategic theory of the firm with specific focus on coopetition dynamics, the role of anchor firms and networks in regional innovation and development, the relationships between strategy, governance and entrepreneurship, and the evolution of research methods in the social sciences. He is Associate Editor of *Long Range Planning* and has authored/edited eleven books and several articles in leading management journals.

Simone Ferriani is Professor of Management at the University of Bologna and Honorary Visiting Professor at Cass Business School, City University London. He earned his Ph.D. from the Management Department of the University of Bologna, and has been a visiting scholar at the Wharton School, University of Pennsylvania, and the Stern School of Business, New York University. His research interests include entrepreneurship, creativity, and interorganizational networks. His works have been published in journals such us *American Sociological Review*, *Administrative Science Quarterly*, *Organization Science*, and *Strategic Management Journal*. He has served as advisor to startups and engages in initiatives aimed to support students in the creation, development, and commercialization of innovative ideas.

Thomas Greckhamer is Associate Professor and William and Catherine Rucks Professor of Management at Louisiana State University. He earned his PhD from the University of Florida. His research interests are at the intersection of organization studies, strategic management, and research methods, focusing on theoretical and methodological contributions to as well as empirical applications of qualitative and set theoretic (csQCA and fsQCA) approaches. His research has been published in academic journals such as the *Strategic Management Journal*, *Organization Studies*, *and Organization Science, Organizational Research Methods*, and *Research in the Sociology of Organizations*, among others.

Gerard P. Hodgkinson is Head of the Behavioural Science Group, Associate Dean, and Professor of Strategic Management and Behavioural Science at Warwick Business School. An elected Fellow of the British Academy of Management, British Psychological Society, Chartered Management Institute, Royal Society of Arts, and the Academy of Social Sciences, he was the Editor-in-Chief of the *British Journal of Management* and a member of the Grants Board of the UK Economic and Social Research Council. He is also an Academic Fellow of the Chartered Institute of Personnel And Development (CIPD). His current theoretical interests center on the behavioral microfoundations of dynamic capabilities, especially the nature and role of conscious and non-conscious cognitive processes, emotion, and personality and individual differences in strategic adaptation. Other work addresses the production and diffusion of knowledge in the management and organization sciences and its significance for wider publics.

Ann Langley is Chair in Strategic Management in Pluralistic Settings, Professor of Management and co-director of the Strategy as Practice Study Group at HEC Montréal, where she obtained her Ph.D. in management. She is also Adjunct Professor at Norwegian School of Economics and Business Administration, at the Université de Montréal, and at the University of Gothenburg, and co-editor of *Strategic Organization*. She is the author or editor of six books and over 50 articles. Her research deals with strategic management processes and practices, with special emphasis on organizational change, decision making, leadership and innovation in pluralistic settings. She has a particular interest in qualitative research methods.

Gianni Lorenzoni is Professor Emeritus of Strategy at the University of Bologna and former President of Bologna Business School and AlmaCube, the business incubator of the University of Bologna. He was also Vice-President of the Italian Academy of Management. His research focuses on strategic management and organizational networks. His work was published in journals such as *Strategic Management Journal, Industrial and Corporate Change, Research Policy, Journal of Business Venturing, California Management Review*, and *Long Range Planning*.

Sebastiano Massaro is Assistant Professor of Behavioural Science at the Warwick Business School. He holds research degrees both in Management (UCL) and Neuroscience (SISSA and Trieste) and held research and study fellowships and scholarships at the Martinos Center for Biomedical Imaging, Boston University, and London Business School. His research, which among other topics focuses on organizational neuroscience, appeared in major scientific journals and received several awards.

Gaetano "Nino" Miceli is Assistant Professor of Management and Marketing Research at the Department of Business Administration and Law of the University of Calabria, Italy, where he obtained his Ph.D. He earned his M.Phil. cum laude in Marketing from Tilburg University, The Netherlands, and was visiting student at the Robert Smith School of Business, University of Maryland. His research concerns product customization, communication of creativity, copycat brands and similarity perception, visual and conceptual complexity in logo design, and structural equation modeling. He is lecturer and coordinator of the Summer Schools on Research Methods for Social Sciences organized by the University of Calabria.

Jose Francisco Molina-Azorin is an Associate Professor of Management at the University of Alicante, Spain. His substantive research topics are strategic management, environmental management, organizational structure and quality management. His research also focuses on mixed methods. His works on mixed methods has been published in several book chapters and in methodological journals including *Organizational Research Methods*, *Journal of Mixed Methods Research*, *International Journal of Multiple Research Approaches*, and *Quality & Quantity*, among other outlets. He is an Associate Editor of the *Journal of Mixed Methods Research* and a member of the Editorial Board of the International Journal of Multiple Research Approaches.

Thomas P. Moliterno is the Associate Dean of Faculty & Engagement and an Associate Professor of Management at the Isenberg School of Management at the University of Massachusetts, Amherst. He received his Ph.D. from the University of California, Irvine. His work has appeared in *Academy of Management Review*, *Administrative Science Quarterly*, *Journal of Management*, *Organization Science*, Strategic *Management Journal*, and *Strategic Organization*. His current research interests include resource-based theory, behavioral theory of the fim, strategic human capital, multilevel theory, and social networks.

Sotirios Paroutis is Associate Professor of Strategic Management in the Strategy and International Business Group of Warwick Business School, where he is Assistant Dean for generalist masters. He received his Ph.D. in Strategy and Organization from the University of Bath. He served as chairperson for the Strategy Practice Interest Group of the Strategic Management Society and currently is as officer for the Strategizing, Activities and Practices Interest Group at the Academy of Management. His research interests concern the intersections of strategy practice and process: discourse, tools and cognition, rhetoric and paradox, chief strategy officers/strategy directors, visual interactions, workshops and strategy maps, and CEO language and political capabilities.

Robert E. Ployhart is the Bank of America Professor of Business Administration at the Darla Moore School of Business, University of South Carolina. He received his

Ph.D. from Michigan State University. His primary interests include human capital resources, staffing, recruitment, and advanced statistical methods. His research has appeared in a wide range of journals spanning management, psychology, and research methods. He has also served as an Associate Editor for the *Journal of Applied Psychology* and *Organizational Behavior and Human Decision Processes.*

Damiano Russo received his Ph.D. in Management from the University of Bologna, where he has also been post-doctoral research fellow, and is teaching associate in degree courses. He is interested in the study of the relationships between identity and practices in work environments especially as concerning nanoscience and technology applications.

Harry Sminia is Professor of Strategic Management in the Strategy and Organization Department of Strathclyde Business School, Glasgow. He received his Ph.D. in Business Administration from the University of Groningen, the Netherlands, and earlier held positions at the University of Groningen, the Vrije Universiteit, Amsterdam, and the University of Sheffield. His research interests are in the area of processes of strategy formation, strategic change, and competitive positioning. He has done research on how top management team activity actually affects the strategic direction of a firm, how industries develop, but also how crucial things that take place within an industry remain unaltered over a period of time despite a strong impetus for change. He is also interested in process research methods and methodology.

Robert Wright is Associate Professor of Strategy in the Department of Management and Marketing of Hong Kong Polytechnic University. He is a graduate of executive development programs at IMD in Switzerland, and the Harvard Business School, and Fellow of the Australian Institute of Management and of the Hong Kong Institute of Directors. He is the Program Chair for the Teaching Community of the Strategic Management Society overseeing pedagogical advancements for over 3000 strategy professors in over 80 countries. He has published in the *Journal of Management Studies*, *Organizational Research Methods*, *Leadership Quarterly*, *Journal of Organizational Behavior*, and *Journal of Constructivist Psychology*. His current research involves mapping strategic cognitions from a clinical psychology perspective.

ACKNOWLEDGMENTS

After a few years of intense rumination, preparation, writing, and revising, we are delighted to pass this book for press. This is a little, but remarkable outcome. In fact, our sense is that a book dedicated to the study and application of research methods in strategic management is incredibly timely and utterly required. While we see numerous publications spreading out on research methods in the field, strategic management researchers do not have access to a single book on the key issue that is as systematic as it is handy. In fact, the project started out since we felt the need of such a book along the path of our studies.

We hope that this perception of ours might be confirmed by the book readership as well as by community acceptance not merely in the strategic management field, but in the management constituency at large as well and beyond its virtual boundaries in the realm of the social sciences.

For research methods are means to expand our understanding of the world, learning a new method is nothing else than acquiring an intellectual key to unlock the gate of knowledge. We wish that this may be the attitude of our prospective readership in approaching this volume. For this reason, we appropriate the shrewd words of the old savvy Latin saying "*paratus semper doceri*," or be always ready to learn!

At this time, our feelings momentously stretch to all the ones who have, directly or indirectly, joined us in this endeavor with different roles. Without the invaluable participation of the chapter authors and the relentless assistance of our Routledge editors, as with any other collection of essays, this book would have never come into existence. We acknowledge this fundamental condition and, as opening special mention, we wish to express our most profound gratitude to all the other seventeen expert contributors for providing their immense wisdom and vivid practical understanding of research methods, thereby wisely distilling them in their unique contributions that appear incredibly terse, much-required and astonishingly precious. We recognize each one in alphabetical order: Chahrazad Abdallah, Claudio Barbaranelli, Giorgia D'Allura, Simone Ferriani, Thomas Greckhamer, Gerard Hodgkinson, Ann Langley, Gianni Lorenzoni, Sebastiano Massaro, Gaetano Miceli, Jose Francisco Molina-Azorin, Thomas Moliterno, Sotirios Paroutis, Rob Ployhart, Damiano Russo, Harry Sminia, and Robert Wright.

We show our appreciation to the couple of our guardian angels at Routledge, Terry Clague and Sinead Waldron, that have accompanied us over the entire editorial voyage leading to the publication of this volume. Sinead and Terry deserve a particular sign of gratefulness for constantly devoting to the present editors, often on very short notice, their time, advice, and suggestions.

Other organizations and individuals merit our attention. Our home institutions, the University of Catania and the University of Messina, and especially our colleagues, in the Department of Economics and Business and in the Department of Economics, ought to be thanked for providing the suitable atmosphere to allow us to actively survive the navigation through the pretty rough waters of book steering.

The colleagues in the strategy and management area at the Tuck School of Business at Dartmouth warrant a special word of thanks for generously hosting one of the present editors in New England in spring, thereby providing the right productive environment to bestow the finishing touches to this enterprise.

Last but certainly not least, our respective families deserve the greatest admiration for bearing our absences to work the book out and for the unremitting psychological support they provided along the phases of this editorial undertaking.

Giovanni Battista Dagnino
Maria Cristina Cinici
Catania-Messina, 31 March 2015

1

INTRODUCTION

New frontiers in research methods for strategic management

Giovanni Battista Dagnino and Maria Cristina Cinici

Aims of the book

This book aims to offer a systematic compendium of research methods and approaches in the field of strategic management. In our intention, by reading this volume engaged scholarship will be placed in the favorable position to design and execute thorough qualitative and quantitative applied investigation.

In more detail, the book hunts for a harmonic amalgamation of a collection of methods in strategic management inquiry. In fact, it includes methods that have been (and are) customarily used in the field (e.g. multilevel methods, or cognitive mapping), methods that are completely novel (e.g. semiotic analysis or neuroscientific methods), less-used (e.g. structural equations modeling and multiple case method) or simply heretofore unexploited (e.g. qualitative comparative analysis and mixed methods). In such a way, we intend to tackle a critical need that every strategy researcher (from graduate and postgraduate students engaged with their theses and dissertations to more experienced junior, mid-career and senior scholars) usually experiences when he/she has to start a new research endeavor: how to make the inquiry they are carrying out as rigorous, robust and validated as possible?

Our proposed target is that the book will help researchers and scholars to become fully aware of the generous options of research methods that are relevant to current strategic management investigation, appreciate their present wealth, and find some suitable guidance in selecting the most appropriate method(s) for designing and executing their investigation activities. As it is straightforward to understand from what we have argued heretofore, we have taken the decision to discount econometric methods and single-case study methods from our selection. This choice is motivated by the fact that, while we recognize that the two categories of methods are unquestionably popular in strategic management analysis, they are at the same time widely taught in courses and seminars and it is straightforward to locate an array of good references on these traditional approaches.

The book's original contribution rests in the fact that, to our knowledge, this is the pioneering rumination of a collection of qualitative and quantitative methods and approaches in the strategy field. Consequently, the book seeks to conveniently stretch into a "practical sourcebook" for researchers keen to generate and/or test knowledge in the strategy field and its relevant sub-fields (global strategy, strategic entrepreneurship, corporate strategy and governance, management of knowledge and innovation, strategy for practice, behavioral strategy, strategic sustainability and so on).

For theories and ideas of strategy have profoundly influenced neighboring areas (Ketchen, Boyd, and Berg, 2008); the book may be valuable to researchers in disciplines that, in the current organization of management knowledge, are deemed germane to strategic management, such as organization theory, organization behavior, human resource management, international business, marketing management, and operations and supply management. It can also be beneficial to other fields of fruitful exchange with strategic management, such as contemporary history, business history, economic geography, international affairs, and political science. Drawing on the wisdom of a variety of prominent colleagues and scholars in designing, testing, and developing theories and perspectives relevant to strategic management studies, the book seeks to expose the current state-of-art as regards wise selection of research methods and perspectives,

Strong emphasis along the book is placed on practical applications that transcend the mere analysis of the theoretical roots of the specific research method. We acknowledge that judicious and rigorous scholarship can nowadays win maximum benefit *only if* methods are properly designed and applied, while methodological missteps may irremediably jeopardize the overall validity of results, thereby inhibiting the researcher's ability to properly develop knowledge and inform managerial choices. For this reason, the contributors to this volume have collectively infused a good deal of wisdom and accuracy in elucidating and illustrating each research methods in detail, supplying practical applications and useful suggestions to current and prospective investigators. For each method taken into account, the chapters will provide specific illustrations with a handful of details so that interested readership may easily realize how things work and undertake it, thereby fully embodying the method(s) chosen in their current and future work.

The underlying message of this endeavor is that the book's readership is expected to activate a *multiple virtuous cycle* of learning-by-reading in the scholars and researchers who will be reading it and of learning-by-doing in those who will find themselves applying the methodological recommendations herewith presented. In other words, by reading the book and applying to their data, contexts, and fieldworks the detailed suggestions contained in the chapters of this volume, the prospective readership are expected to gain advanced prowess on how to employ a specific method in research, thereby fireproofing the concrete contribution of this volume.

Background of research methods in strategic management

Strategic management as a field of inquiry has journeyed dramatic developments within the last three and a half decades. Rooted in early 1960s' applied management area often termed "business policy" and/or "business planning" (Andrews, 1971; Ansoff, 1965), pioneering studies in the strategy tradition were essentially normative and prescriptive in purpose. In the initial years, the main goal of strategic management was to immediately convey the required applied knowledge to business practitioners, rather than to hunting thorough knowledge for pursuing genuine scientific advancements. Under this circumstance, the appropriate widely used method for accomplishing the study's objective was barely inductive in character, e.g. in-depth case studies typically of a single firm or industry.

The field underwent spectacular growth, especially subsequent to the appearance of Schendel and Hofer's book *Strategic Management* (1979) and the almost contextual establishment of the *Strategic Management Journal* (SMJ) in 1980, and the *Strategic Management Society* in 1981. As the strategy field's stature and reputation progressively advanced within the management sphere, so did its theoretical status and empirical sophistication (Dagnino, 2012).

The desire to elevate the newly launched field to a more rigorous scientific and academic discipline compelled early strategic management scholars to look at research methods, distinct from case studies, which were able to produce more rigorous, generalizable, and practically applicable results, in the quest to unambiguously uncover the sources of firms' and industries' competitive advantage. For this reason, strategic management started to embrace the structure-conduct-performance (SCP) paradigm of industrial organization economics and emphasizing scientific generalizations based on study of broader sets of firms and industries (Rumelt, Schendel, and Teece, 1994). Consequently, in the 1980s and 1990s strategy researchers began to increasingly employ multivariate statistical tools (e.g. multiple regression and cluster analysis), with large data samples primarily collected from secondary sources to test theory. The use of these methods has quickly turned into the standard way of doing research in a large number of Ph.D. programs taught in universities and business schools and thus in strategic management research as a whole. Subsequently, depending on the research question under scrutiny, strategy scholars started to use a *plurality* of methodological approaches, such as multiple case studies, event studies and event history analysis, all the way to multi-dimensional scaling, panel data analysis, network analysis, and so on (Van de Ven, 2007).

The evolution of strategic management into a more respected scholarly field of study was, at least initially, a result of the adoption of scientific methods originating from industrial organization economics and, more specifically, from Michael Porter's (1980; 1981) transplant of the SCP paradigm in strategy analysis. Subsequently, in the 1990s and 2000s the development of the resource-based view (Barney, 1991; Peteraf, 1993) and the dynamic capabilities perspective (Teece,

Pisano, and Shuen, 1997; Teece, 2007) came to pose a major methodological (and epistemological) problem to strategy researchers. In many respects in fact the study of heterogeneous firm features required a multiplicity of methods to identify, measure, and understand firm resources and capabilities, that were purported to reside within the boundary of a firm. More importantly, the proponents of the resource-based view and the dynamic capabilities perspective suggested that each firm has distinctive endowments of resources and capabilities that in turn contribute to achieve and sustain competitive advantages. Actually, the exclusive use of research methods using large data samples, secondary data sources, and econometric analyses suddenly started to ring a bell in scholarly wisdom as they appeared to be as rigorous as insufficient, particularly when operated to examine intangible firm resources, knowledge, and capabilities (Danneels, 2002; Seth, Carlson, Hatfield, and Lan, 2009). Because of the focus on a firm's idiosyncratic resources and capabilities, the bearing and generalizability of firms' knowledge started to be put at odds (Grant and Verona, 2015).

TABLE 1.1 Path of methods used in strategic management research (1960–2010s)

	1960s and 1970s	*1980s*	*1990s*	*2000s*
Name of field	Business policy or business planning	Strategic management	Strategic management	Strategic management
Dominant frameworks or perspectives	Long-range planning SWOT analysis PIMS studies	Structure-conduct-performance paradigm	Resource-based view Knowledge-based view	Resource-based view Knowledge-based view Evolutionary and behavioral perspectives
Type of methods preferably used	Qualitative	Quantitative	Quantitative	Quantitative and qualitative
Specific technique(s) typically used	Single case study	Statistical analysis	Econometric analysis	Multiple case study Statistical and econometric analyses Discourse analysis Mixed methods Multilevel inquiry

Nowadays, these conditions have considerably changed since strategic management research of the mid-2010s is likely to integrate and contrast multiple theories and to develop more fine-grained and complex models (Priem, Butler, and Li, 2013). Hence, a forceful call has emerged for raising a more inclusive approach where inductive qualitative research drawing on basic disciplines, such as sociology, political economy, psychology, and evolutionary and behavioral economics, plays a significant role in strategic management, along with deductive approaches mainly rooted in mainstream economics and econometrics (Bergh and Ketchen, 2011; Wang, Ketchen, and Bergh, 2012)[1] (see Table 1.1).

While at the end of 1990s Hoskisson *et al.* advised that "In light of the future complexity and variety of the issues facing strategic management researchers, the methodologies used will likewise reflect a similar level of complexity" (1999: 446), recently, strategy scholars' sensitivity to research methods is suggesting that they have fragile guidance to draw upon (Easterby-Smith *et al.*, 2012). In fact, the new scenarios of the new millennium require a pursuit of the inevitable trajectory of chasing impact on both managerial practice and theory. Accordingly, the strategy field is unmistakably required to pay further attention to the practical relevance of its studies nonetheless without dethroning academic rigor. Further, somewhat mirroring the awareness of the origins, the strategic management field is expected to envelop a set of issues that were conventionally considered more pertinent to practitioners, such as strategic implementation, strategic leadership, sustainability and social issues, and regulation issues.

To sum up, we posit that a critical examination of a range of research methods that are looking at being "fully-exploited" in strategic management seems today particularly timely and required for various reasons. Actually, we report below a quartet of these motives (see Table 1.2):

(a) strategic management scholars experience today the necessity of using in their research projects an array of original methods;
(b) the inner complexity usually featuring the application of research methods;
(c) the intricacy and subtleness of applying methods in strategic management that are already in use in other fields of inquiry;
(d) the need to develop, by means of empirical investigation, academically rigorous and practically relevant insights about firms, organizations, industries and networks, as well as other promising levels of analysis, such as ecosystems and platforms.

Novelty of the book

With this book, we intend to offer four key contributions to the bulk of the existing studies dedicated to research methods. First, as we know, no collected book can be better than the combined value of the contributions it contains. This book is unique since thirteen out of the fourteen chapters it contains are original essays specifically prepared for this endeavor by an exclusive set of nineteen international

TABLE 1.2 Motivation for systematic methodological inquiry in strategic management

	Key challenges in using research methods		
(I) *Necessity to use a plurality of research methods in empirical investigation*	(II) *Complexity in the application of research methods*	(III) *Difficulties in transplanting in strategic management methods already-in-use in other fields of study*	(IV) *Necessity to overcome the rigor-relevance chasm*
Quantitative methods Qualitative methods Mixed methods Multi-level analysis	Learn methods Practice application Data availability Data reliability Measurement problem Phenomenon identification problem	Disciplinary features Context specificities Methods characteristics	TARGET: Produce impactful research grounded in sound methodological rigor (*Nothing is so practical as a good theory*)

scholars based in the USA, Asia, and Europe, who are unusually familiar to methodological issues. The authors are in fact specialists particularly acquainted in a specific methodological quantitative or qualitative subject matter, whose cumulative efforts in methods-building over the last decade have significantly contributed to shape the contours of strategic management as an accurate research field as well as a sound scholarly community.

Second, in pursuing the book's purpose we have considered the range of research methods the book covers. In this way, the book does nothing less than proposing a balanced mix of methods that are radically original and relatively novel in strategy studies. Along the book's chapters, this condition applies consistently to the domain of management investigation taken as a whole. Since other academic fields and regions (e.g. psychology, semiotics, and marketing) have successfully used a few research methods displayed in this book, we have reasons to suspect that strategy scholars will show soaring interest in knowing the functioning and applications of this comprehensive selection of methods.

Third, despite its collected nature, the book shows a high degree of coherence and consistency. In fact, the fourteen method-oriented chapters we have gathered are presented in a reliable, logical sequence that allows the reader to achieve an immediate acquaintance of the current state-of-the-art of each of the research methods. Accordingly, the book provides a particularly authoritative compass effective in detecting the research method that fits better the objectives of a specific research project, as well as in exploiting in depth the power of data.

Finally, as a highly distinctive tip, the book portrays a specific section dedicated to appreciate how it is possible to carefully design and successfully execute relevant research projects in the strategy realm, thereby allowing researchers and scholars to detect and interpret contemporary business reality.

The last few years have featured the publication of a choice of journal special issues, books, and edited volumes dealing with different aspects of research methodology in management. Nonetheless, the majority of these books have presented a discussion of research methods that is rather scattered and mainly concerned with disciplines other than strategic management. As specifically regards strategic management, from 2004 to 2014 the Emerald book series on *Research Methodology in Strategy and Management* has circulated a set of ten volumes edited, almost annually, mostly by David Ketchen and Don Bergh. The scholarly journal *Organizational Research Methods* (ORM) has disseminated two special issues devoted to methods in strategy and entrepreneurship, respectively, on "Research Methodology in Strategic Management" in 2008 and on "Research Methods in Entrepreneurship" in 2010.

Notwithstanding that, neither the ORM special issues nor the books of the Emerald series overlap with the range of research methods we selected for this book, nor its systematic assessment and spirit. Actually, the main challenge of the ORM special issue on strategic management research methodology was "to better tap into motives, preferences, and decisions of the executives charged with managing firms strategically" (Ketchen *et al.*, 2008: 652), thereby especially focusing on a range of research methods specific to discourse and cognition investigation, such as content analysis, critical discourse analysis, and management cognition mapping. The aim of the ORM special issue on entrepreneurship methodology was instead to identify the major challenges of the state of entrepreneurship research methods and to feature how it is possible to resolve these challenges (Short, Ketchen, Combs, and Ireland, 2010). The Emerald book series mixes theoretical and empirical contributions with no real purpose, in each annual volume, to distil a systematic account of research methods in strategic management.[2] For the reasons above, we can corroborate that the one we propose here is the initial systematic collection of contributions on research methods in strategic management.

Should someone ask us to itemize the criticalities of this book, we would pinpoint an explicit angle. We would bring to light the circumstance that it falls short in dealing with all the research methods currently in use in strategy investigation; explicitly to the ones that are grounded on statistics and econometric models. Actually, as anticipated earlier this is far from being the outgrowth of fortuitous judgment, but the upshot of our deliberate choice. Since a single volume has no adequate space to embrace a fully-fledged account of all the extant research methods, we had to take a hard-hitting decision. In the end, our preference was intentionally accorded to the set of research methods that, while in use in other disciplines related to strategic management (e.g. marketing, sociology, psychology, and so forth), have found no sufficient room in the strategy field.

Readership of the book

As we have previously mentioned, the book is primarily targeted at researchers and scholars that recognize themselves as part of the global community in strategic management.

The global community in strategic management is a community that, in the last decade, has undertaken a particularly rapid and sustained pace of growth. At the Academy of Management it is formally represented by the Business Policy and Strategy Division, which is the second largest of the Academy's twenty-four divisions since it counts some 5,000 members. It is also featured by the Strategic Management Society, which consists of over 3,000 members representing over fifty different countries in the world. The Strategic Management Society (SMS) is structured in a range of interest groups that encapsulate various sub-fields of strategic management, such as global strategy, strategic entrepreneurship, corporate strategy and governance, strategic management of knowledge and innovation, strategic leadership, strategy for practice, and behavioral strategy.[3] It is worthwhile noting that the SMS has recently launched an internal initiative specifically dedicated to fostering awareness of and education in research methods. Arguably, the majority of strategy scholars and researchers is intensely engaged in empirical research and strives to use the methods that are the most appropriate to carry out project design and analyze data.

An important subset of the audience above is made by the community of beginning researchers (especially graduate students and Ph.D. students), that contend with their research projects and are generally looking for the most appropriate research methods in performing their investigations. In fact, while carrying out their inquiry, researchers sense the necessity to collect data and analyze them according to specific (and possibly reliable and widely institutionalized) research methods. This is a way of achieving results that are consistent and rigorous as well as of winning legitimization in the realm of social sciences. In fact, today's university and business school tenure track career paths customarily require researchers to perform and disseminate studies based in thorough empirical research. This condition implies in turn notable investment of time on behalf of the researcher for achieving acquaintance in specific research methods and their intense practice. Accordingly, in the USA, Europe, Asia, and Oceania nowadays the vast majority of Ph.D. programs operated in universities and business schools, as wells as of graduate and postgraduate courses in management, are organized in such a way as to offer methodology-oriented courses.

The book speaks well to graduate students, junior, and established scholars engaged in organization theory, organization behavior, human relations management, international business, marketing management, and operations and supply chain management. We also believe that the book may be of interest to scholars and researchers in other social sciences (such as contemporary history, business history, public administration, economic geography, international affairs, and political science), that wish to become skilled in methods relevant to their research issues and perspectives. This conviction is rooted in two conditions. First, top-notch research in strategic management has achieved a level of methodological rigor and conceptual sophistication that has turned into the archetype to imitate by bordering fields. Second, the book shows how a researcher can move from theory to investigation, from investigation to interpretation, and eventually from interpretation to routinized praxis.

Last but not least, a significant audience is made up of consultants and practicing managers, who work in R&D and documentation departments of firms and organizations in practically all industries and sectors, as well as in a broad array of public bodies and institutions and research centers. They usually rely on practical information as a routine part of their work and look for research methods that are helpful in practice for making the best use of it.

Structure of the book

The book contains twelve unique chapters organized in four interrelated parts. Each chapter is focused on a special method expressly written for this collection, except for one. In line with the book's general purpose, that is to provide a critical discussion of research methods in strategic management, especially those that are novel or unexploited, each of the four parts of the book will pursue a targeted objective.

Part I: Testing and developing theory

Part I is made of four chapters advancing and discussing research methods for testing and developing theories in strategic management. They are essentially multilevel methods, contextualized explanation, structural equation modeling, and multiple case studies.

Part II: Analyzing texts and talks

Part II focuses on the study of texts and proposes original research methods to disclose their sense and meaning. They are discourse semiotics and repertory grids.

Part III: Novel methodological approaches

Part III highlights the benefits of research methods that strategy scholars have heretofore overlooked. They are qualitative comparative analysis and neuroscientific methods.

Part IV: Research design and execution

Part IV, one of the most distinctive of the volume, focuses on a multi-indicator approach for tracking field emergence, data collection protocol, and designing and performing a mixed-method research in strategic management.

TABLE 1.3 Structure and organization of the book

	Author/s	*Chapter title*
Introduction	Giovani Battista Dagnino and Maria Cristina Cinici	"New frontiers in research methods for strategic management"
	Giovani Battista Dagnino	"Epistemological lineage and dominant paradigms in strategic management research"
Part I Testing and developing theories	Tom Moliterno and Rob Ployarth	"Multilevel models for strategy research: An idea whose time (still) has come"
	Harry Sminia	"Contextualized explanation in strategy research"
	Gaetano Miceli and Claudio Barbaranelli	"Structural equations modelling: theory and applications in strategic management"
	Ann Langley and Chahrazad Abdallah	"Templates and turns in qualitative studies of strategy and management"
Part II Analyzing texts and talks	Maria Cristina Cinici	In search of strategy meanings: semiotics and its applications
	Gerard Hodgkinson, Sotirios Paroutis and Robert Wright	"Putting words to numbers in the discernment of meaning: applications of repertory grid in strategic management"
Part III Novel methodological approaches	Thomas Greckhamer	"Qualitative comparative analysis: fuzzy set applications for strategic management research"
	Sebastiano Massaro	"Neuroscientific methods in strategic management"
Part IV Research design and execution	Simone Ferriani, Gianni Lorenzoni and Damiano Russo	"A multi-indicator approach for tracking field emergence: the rise of bologna nanotech"
	Giorgia D'Allura	"Data collection protocol for strategic management: challenges and methods"
	Jose Francisco Molina-Azorin	"Designing and performing a mixed-method research in strategic management"
Conclusion	Maria Cristina Cinici and Giovani Battista Dagnino	"Methodological challenges in strategic management research"

In order to complement this introductory chapter with a distinctive explanation of the evolution of strategy studies in the last 35 years, Chapter 2, written by Giovanni Battista Dagnino, is grounded in the evolutionary epistemology of Donald Campbell and David Hull. The chapter presents the four dominant paradigms in strategic management and offers an interpretation of their evolutionary history intended as a history of incomplete dominances. For its encompassing flavor, this condition is seen as possibly paving the way to the application of evolutionary epistemology to the development of other management fields and social sciences.

Part I of the book, as mentioned, revolves around a range of innovative methods that may be extremely useful to test and develop theories in strategic management. Chapter 3, by Tom Moliterno and Rob Ployarth, offers researchers helpful guidance on multilevel methodology in strategic management: how it can be leveraged, how the analytical tools in the multilevel researcher's toolkit are used, and what questions cannot (yet) be fully examined with current multilevel analytical statistics. Chapter 4, by Harry Sminia, digs into the contextualized explanation methods. The chapter explains the specific methodology, starting with how a research project can be set up, to continue with the kind of data to collect and the way these data should be analyzed. Chapter 5, by Gaetano Miceli and Claudio Barbaranelli, presents the statistical theory underlying structural equation modeling and discusses its basic components. The chapter addresses the estimation of structural equation model and the tools that are key to assess model fit and measurement properties, eventually comparing rival models and testing hypotheses. Chapter 6, by Ann Langley and Chahrazad Abdallah, delves deep into qualitative research. Based on detailed epistemological foundations, it presents four different approaches to perform and write-up qualitative research in strategic management. Drawing on methodological texts and a detailed analysis of successful empirical exemplars from the strategy and organization literature, it also illustrates two relevant templates (i.e. positivist epistemology and interpretive) that turn pretty helpful to carry out research, and introduces two recent "epistemology turns" (i.e. the practice turn and the discursive turn) that merit greater attention.

Part II of the book credits special attention to the analysis of texts and talks. Chapter 7, written by Maria Cristina Cinici, digs into the applications of semiotics in management inquiry. Drawing on the early conceptualization of strategy advanced by Alfred Chandler and Ken Andrews, this chapter clarifies the value of semiotic method in analyzing and uncovering the meaning of texts. On the premise of managerial and organizational cognition applications, Chapter 8 by Gerard Hodgkinson, Robert Wright, and Sotirios Paroutis clarifies the origins of a particular technique termed Repertory Grid Technique (RGT). It also traces how strategy scholars have used the RGT in a variety of innovative ways to advance strategic management theory development, empirical research, and practice, probing into a rich variety of fundamental cognitive processes of strategy formulation and implementation.

Part III of the book is concerned with a range of novel methodological approaches. It includes two highly original chapters. Chapter 9, by Thomas Greckhamer, deals with a progressive methodology in management studies that is termed Qualitative Comparative Analysis (QCA). The chapter explains the four major applications of QCA, discusses its potential to cope with diversity and causal complexity in research, and provides researchers with appropriate guidelines to use

QCA approaches. Chapter 10, by Sebastiano Massaro, offers an array of imaginative reflections associated to employing neuroscience approaches in strategic management. It supplies a core description of the most relevant neuroscience techniques that can be applied in strategy research, thereby concentrating on the way to study firms by using brain-imaging techniques.

Part IV of the book pays specific attention to the most relevant aspects relative to the design and execution of research projects. It features three original chapters. Chapter 11, by Simone Ferriani, Gianni Lorenzoni, and Damiano Russo utilizes an original multi-indicator approach to map in real time the early stages of field emergence. By using customized search techniques, the chapter also shows how multi-indicator approaches may be developed from existing databases, as well as how the insights from multi-indicator measurement can be used to provide guidelines for research and innovation policy. Chapter 12, by Giorgia Maria D'Allura, focuses on that particularly challenging section of designing and executing research projects that is related to the development of a data collection protocol. The chapter provides a set of compelling suggestion on how to collect and analyze data in a manner that crops out outcomes that are comparable with the past ones and across different contexts. Chapter 13, by Jose Francisco Molina-Azorin, is targeted to support scholars in gaining acquaintance with mixed methods research; i.e. the combined use of quantitative and qualitative methods within a single study. The chapter presents an accurate account of extant baseline literature on mixed method research and clearly identifies under what circum-stances and in what fashion it is possible to make effective use of the mixed methods research approach in strategy studies. On the ground, of the major strands and themes discussed in the set of thirteen chapter heretofore presented, the concluding chapter written by Maria Cristina Cinici and Giovanni Battista Dagnino will interestingly gather the main glitches and difficulties that prevent the advancement of research on methods in strategic management and portray the future challenges for their further development.

At the closing stages of our editorial endeavor, our auspices go in the direction that the book readership may welcome straightaway the collective value of the research methods proposed in this volume. We also hope that students in management and scholars in other social sciences may get inspiration from reading this volume, thereby discovering a set of accurate guidance to streamline their investigation efforts in the years to come.

Notes

1   Since strategy research scope is increasingly expanding in new virgin contexts, a new intriguing appeal is recently emerging in strategic management research methods: the appeal to adapt methods and approaches to such unique contexts as for example of China and Africa (Zogah, 2014). We recognize that the plea is motivated, at least in principle, by the remarkable institutional differences actually existing between these contexts and the ones that have traditionally been the cradle of strategy studies (e.g. Europe and the US). At the same time, we also ought to consider that, since these are

to be seen as dynamically moving targets, the condition at hand might bear the flaw of wanting to chase the horse while he is racing as fast as possible to win the race.

2   Lately an annual issue of this book series has appeared about methodologies bridging the Eastern and Western worlds (Wang *et al.*, 2012). This volume encompasses some unorthodox methods that rest outside the original methods that have traditionally found room in strategic management investigation.

3   This condition somewhat mirrors the overlapping membership between the Business Policy and Strategy Division and other divisions of the Academy of Management. Actually, the four divisions traditionally sharing with the Business and Strategy Division the highest number of constituent members are: Organization Theory, Entrepreneurship, Technology and Innovation, and International Management.

References

Andrews, K. J. (1971). *The Concept of Corporate Strategy*. Homewood: Irwin.

Ansoff, H.I. (1965). *Corporate Strategy*. New York: McGraw-Hill.

Barney, J. B. (1991). Firm resources and sustained competitive advantage. *Journal of Management*, 17(1), 99–120.

Bergh, D. D. and Ketchen, D. J. (2011). Introduction: Building methodological bridges. In Bergh, D. and Ketchen D. J. (eds). *Research Methodology in Strategy and Management: Building Methodological Bridges. Volume 6*: ix–x. Bingley: Emerald Group Publishing.

Dagnino, G. B. (2012). Introduction: Why a handbook of research on competitive strategy. In Dagnino, G. B. (ed.). *Handbook of Research on Competitive Strategy*: 1–18. Cheltenham: Edward Elgar.

Danneels, E. (2002). The dynamics of product innovation and firm competences. *Strategic Management Journal*, 23(12), 1095-1121.

Easterby-Smith, M., Thorpe, R., and Jackson, P. (2012). *Management Research*. London: Sage.

Grant R. and Verona, G. (2015). What's holding back empirical research into organizational capabilities? Remedies for common problems. *Strategic Organization*, 13(1): 61–74.

Hoskisson, R. E., Hitt, M. A., Wan, W. P., and Yiu, D. (1999). Theory and research in strategic management: Swings of a pendulum. *Journal of Management*, 25(3), 417–456.

Ketchen, D. J., Boyd, B. K., and Bergh, D. D. (2008). Research methodology in strategic management: Past accomplishments and future challenges. *Organizational Research Methods*, 11(4): 643–658.

Peteraf, M. A. (1993). The cornerstones of competitive advantage: A resource based view. *Strategic Management Journal*, 14(3), 179–191.

Porter, M. (1980). *Competitive Strategy*. New York: The Free Press.

Porter, M. (1981). The contributions of industrial organization to strategic management. *Academy of Management Review*, 6(4): 609–620.

Priem, R., Butler, J., and Li, S. (2013). Toward reimagining strategy research: retrospection and prospection on the 2011 AMR decade award article. *Academy of Management Review*, 38(4): 471–489.

Rumelt, R. P., Schendel, D. E., and Teece, D. J. (1994). Fundamental issues in strategy. In *Fundamental Issues in Strategy: A Research Agenda*: 9–47. Boston: Harvard Business School Press.

Schendel, D. and Hofer, C.W. (1979). *Strategic Management: A New View of Business Policy and Planning*. Boston: Little Brown.

Seth, A., Carlson, K. D., Hatfield, D. E, and Lan, H. W. (2009). So what? Beyond statistical significance to substantive significance in strategy research. In Bergh, D. and Ketchen, D.J.

(ed.) *Research Methodology in Strategy and Management. Volume 5*: 3–27. Bingley: Emerald Group Publishing.

Short, J. C, Ketchen, D. J., Combs, J. C., and Ireland, R. D. (2010). Research methods in entrepreneurship: Opportunities and challenges. *Organizational Research Methods*, 13(1): 6–15.

Teece, D. J. (2007). Explicating dynamic capabilities: The nature and microfoundations of (sustainable) enterprise performance. *Strategic Management Journal*, 28(13), 1319–1350.

Teece, D. J., Pisano, G., and Shuen, A. (1997). Dynamic capabilities and strategic management. *Strategic Management Journal*, 18(7), 509–533.

Van de Ven, A. H. (2007). *Engaged Scholarship: A Guide for Organizational and Social Research*. Oxford: Oxford University Press.

Wang, C. L., Ketchen, D. J., and Bergh, D. D. (2012). Introduction: West meets East: Building theoretical bridges. In Wang, C. L., Ketchen, D. J. and Bergh, D. D. (eds). *West Meets East: Building Theoretical Bridges. Research Methodology in Strategy and Management, Volume 8*: xi–xiii. Bingley: Emerald Group Publishing.

Zoogah, D. B. (2014). Introduction. In Zoogah, D. B. (ed.) *Advancing Research Methodology in the African Context: Techniques, Methods, and Designs. Research Methodology in Strategy and Management, Volume 10*: ix–xii. Bingley: Emerald Group Publishing.

2

EVOLUTIONARY LINEAGE OF THE DOMINANT PARADIGMS IN STRATEGIC MANAGEMENT RESEARCH

Giovanni Battista Dagnino

Introduction

On the ground of the application of evolutionary epistemology to examine the path that strategic management studies have taken, this chapter aims to identify the dominant paradigms in strategic management and to present an interpretation of their evolutionary history intended as a history of *incomplete dominances*. The crux of the argument is that, since its founding in the 1960s, strategic management as a discipline has developed and revolved around four relevant paradigms that have been the lighthouses illuminating the work of the researchers in the field.

Over time a twofold transition in the sequence of evolutionary approaches to strategic management has emerged: from a paradigm that emphasizes environmental factors to a paradigm that looks at factors endogenous to the firm (Hoskisson *et al.*, 1999). Thus, while in the 1980s the SCP paradigm-rooted competitive approach was central, in the 1990s the interest of scholars progressively turned towards the resource-based view of the firm (Barney, 1991; Teece *et al.*, 1997; Teece, 2007) and the knowledge-based view of the firm (Grant, 1996; Nonaka and Toyama, 2002).

I take advantage of the evolutionary approach and evolutionary epistemology,[1] observed as interpretative lenses effective in grasping the succession, integration, and internal evolution of the dominant paradigms. On the basis of an evolutionary elucidation, I detect four paradigms of strategy: (a) the structure-conduct-performance (SCP) paradigm; (b) the resources-competences-performance (RCP) paradigm; (c) the knowledge-capabilities-performance (KCP) paradigm; and, (d) the evolutionary paradigm. In this chapter, I investigate evolutionary paths, logical structure, causal relationships, and main limitations of each paradigm. I eventually show the way cross fertilizations between the paradigms has unfolded. Rather than appreciating a mere paradigm succession or progression in strategic management studies, I also contend that it is possible to observe a *chain* and *intersection* among the paradigms.

In more detail, the evolutionary approach is intended in the two-fold meaning of interpretive key of strategy paradigms evolution and of evolutionary paradigm itself in strategic management. I elucidate that, in this view, the evolutionary approach embraces both the long-established biologic metaphor and also the fundamental social and relational interactions within the scientific community (Boyd and Richerson, 1985; Durham, 1991) that, together with the former, shape a coherent whole.

This chapter is primarily motivated by the condition that strategic management studies present all the key features of an academic discipline that has reached maturity at the global level:

(a) a common base of knowledge, which polarizes and solidifies in textbooks (Grant, 2005; Hitt *et al.*, 2001b; Thompson and Strickland, 2001; Saloner *et al.*, 2001), handbooks (Faulkner and Campbell, 2003; Hitt *et al.*, 2001a; Pettigrew *et al.*, 2002; Dagnino, 2012) a recent topical encyclopedia (Augier and Teece, 2013);
(b) a specialized and codified language, which serves for motives of economy of energies and disciplinary nucleation and identification;
(c) a full range of teaching courses offered at the various academic levels (bachelor, master, MBA, Ph.D.) in the vast majority of the world's universities and business schools;
(d) a critical mass of researchers and scholars, who identify themselves as strategic management students and scholars. They give life to an established scientific community, which meets in a number of international conferences and venues. Among those, we may recall the Business Policy and Strategy Division of the Academy of Management, the Strategic Management Society, the Ibero-American Academy of Management, and the European Academy of Management;
(e) an extensive community of practitioners operating in business and in managerial consulting firms who, alongside the academic community, disseminates strategy culture inside private companies and public organizations, also by means of a few particularly influential specialized journals (here, among the others, the *Harvard Business Review*, *MIT-Sloan Management Review*, *California Management Review*, and *McKinsey Quarterly*).

For the intention of typifying the epistemological lineage and logics of the evolutionary dynamics of strategy paradigms, the chapter is structured in five sections. The second section introduces the conceptual rudiments of the evolutionary perspective by examining the bases of Donald Campbell (1974) and David Hull's (1988) evolutionary epistemology and underscores the dual role of the evolutionary perspective in strategic management. The evolutionary perspective is observed as both the interpretive key of paradigmatic shift and as the groundwork for the definition of the evolutionary paradigm. The third section examines the general evolutionary dynamics at the foundation of paradigmatic shifts. Applying the premises of the previous section to our field of inquiry, the fourth section discusses in detail the evolutionary dynamics of the four dominant paradigms in strategic management. In this context, the evolutionary history of strategic management paradigms is seen as a history of incomplete dominances. In the final section, we gather the fundamental features of the last five decades' evolutionary dynamics in strategic management and point up the main advantages that the present evolutionary interpretation is able to offer.

The evolutionary perspective as interpretive key of paradigm change and groundwork to identify an evolutionary paradigm

The path of scientific knowledge in strategic management can be interpreted as an *evolutionary and coevolutionary process* (Dagnino, 2005). In this fashion, the *evolutionary epistemology* of Donald Campbell (1974) and David Hull (1988) takes center stage as the interpretive key to explain paradigm change in strategy. Evolutionary epistemology is targeted to provide an evolutionary account of the advancement of cognitive structures, by examining the development of human knowledge by engaging pertinent biological wisdom. This particular critical realist epistemology features a stream that is oriented to appreciate the succession of scientific theories or to define "an epistemology able to treat in evolutionary fashion the enlargements in knowledge, the breakthrough of limits of preceding science, and scientific discoveries" (Campbell, 1974). Under this vantage lenses, the evolution of scientific theories is construed as selection processes.

While evolutionary epistemology might not be the only practicable nor the best one, I contend that it seems the fittest to the aims of this essay. Evolutionary epistemology approach assumes the dual connotation of interpretive key of strategy paradigms evolution as well as groundwork for laying an evolutionary paradigm in strategy. In this perspective, the evolutionary outlook encompasses the biologic metaphor as well as the social interactions occurring inside the scientific community (Boyd and Richerson, 1985; Durham, 1991).

The dual role that an evolutionary approach takes on is epitomized by three fundamental characteristics reported as follows:

(a) evolutionary *enhancement*;
(b) evolutionary non-neutrality;
(c) the possibility to reconcile micro and macro evolutionary processes.

Evolutionary enhancement

Evolutionary enhancement presents a notable potential for enrichment and speed, therefore of the amplification of inclusive fitness, descending from the application of the evolutionary perspective to strategic management. Actually, the evolutionary approach is active at different levels, both theoretical and metatheoretical. At the metatheoretical level, the evolutionary enhancement allows a better grasp of paradigm genesis and development, paradigm interrelations, paradigm convergences and divergences, paradigm integrations (real or potential), paradigm filiations and speciation that occur due to the social relationships between scholars, research groups, and in and between scientific communities. Evolutionary enhancement is made possible by coevolutionary processes, that are recursive and feedforward processes.

Metatheoretical relations are termed *intraparadigm* relations when they occur between theories of the same paradigm. They are named *interparadigm* relations when they present relations external to the single paradigm, that are relations enhancing different paradigms. Evolutionary enhancement is relevant at the theoretical level, since it contributes to study and appreciate better, on one hand, the meaning, role, and application field of theories (knowledge-based theory, resource-based theory, and so on), and, on the other hand, evolutionary nature, potentiality, and speed of various categories and analytical levels (and their interrelations) that are relevant to strategic management (e.g. firms, networks, industries, individual teams and individuals).

Evolutionary non-neutrality

As regards evolutionary non neutrality, this is a property that mirrors evolutionary enhancement. As it is known, in presence of neutrality there are no significant differences in the inclusive fitness of the individual that are part of a population. Emerging variations neither add nor take away anything to the individual fitness state; they are neutral vis-à-vis the relative fitness of an individual of a species.

Since the application of the evolutionary perspective to strategy significantly affects both the degree of relative adaptive fitness of theories and paradigms as well as the development of an evolutionary paradigm, since it is able to modify considerably their evolutionary paths, we can confirm that it presents the property of non-neutrality. This does not imply that the course of strategic management (meta)theoretical developments or the evolutionary history of a paradigm may be exempt of periods of stasis or neutrality also because of the interventions of neutral mutations.

The possibility to reconcile micro and macro evolutionary processes

For its inclusive and coevolutionary nature, the evolutionary perspective supplies the possibility to subsume and reconcile, in a harmonic fashion, micro evolutionary processes, occurring within the single firm, and macro evolutionary processes, happening in firm aggregates and the economic system. In such a way, the evolutionary approach encompasses processes and relations occurring at the *mesolevel*, or the relations between and among firms that are part of the same firm aggregate and relations within the single firm. This relevant property bringing together micro and macro processes recalls *micro-macro behavior* (Schelling, 2006), a quasi virgin branch of economic literature, and the coevolution in the dynamic features of firm and industry, or *competitive organizational behavior* (Barney and Zajac, 1994) in strategic management.

The evolution of strategic management: a paradigm-based view

In this section, I wish to illustrate "the process of filiation of scientific ideas," as Joseph Schumpeter names it, or the process by which "the efforts of men aimed to comprehend economic phenomena built, improve and destruct analytical structures in a sequence without and end" (Schumpeter, 1954). One of the main tenets is that this process does not vary from similar processes that unfold in other fields of knowledge. Nonetheless, for its relative youth, the filiation of ideas in the strategy field is recent and thus not so straightforward to grasp. It seems therefore helpful to draw an evolutionary history of the dominant paradigms in our field of investigation that can effectively extend the received knowledge and support future research work.

Some years ago authors maintained that strategic management has undergone an "enchanted childhood" (Barry and Helmes, 1997). This condition has occurred because business policy and planning (the way the newly-born discipline was initially identified in the 1970s and 1980s) was taking profit of the success of *positive* and *normative* strategic planning. At that time, it was intended that "Planning could do no wrong" as Henry Mintzberg (1994) has emphatically confirmed. Strategic planning was conceived as the "long life elixir" for firms that cannot help doing without planning intended as a formal, integrated, and long-range support device. Consequently, the term strategy has landed up to banalize in a concept "good for all the seasons," the reference base on which any managerial discipline (from marketing to operations management, from finance to human resource management) wished to be connected with.

Times have profoundly changed. According to Prahalad and Hamel (1994), strategic management has travelled "the best of times and the hard of times." Hard of times because it is recognized that, in the relatively time-bounded history of the discipline, the actual ones are times of change, in which there is no single perspective unanimously shared and consistently dominant. Nonetheless, the fact that this is a critical phase leads to say that the field is experiencing the best of times. In the process of scientific research, it is in fact in these times that some strategic windows usually emerge to pave the way for significant evolutionary leaps.

As anticipated, the initial image of strategic management as a "golden boy" is now forgotten and the field has become highly critical and under dispute for the presence of perspectives in competition that tackle and cross-fertilize one another (Barry and Helmes, 1997: 429). This situation has occurred for two main reasons: on one hand, strategic management is some five decades old, or is middle-aged if we confront the field with the human beings' biological life. It is thus advancing towards a much higher level of theoretical deepening and methodological sophistication. On the other hand, the rapid socio-economic and technological developments popping up over the late 1990s and the first decade of the new millennium have superseded the interpretive framework prevailing over the 1980s and 1990s (Porter, 1996: 74).

Various authors have maintained that, under the influx of the globalization processes and the advancements in the digital and information technologies, international markets and competitive arenas have become more rapid and changeable and hence present superior competitive dynamic interactions. Can we affirm that we are living a Kuhnian phase of paradigm shift? According to some strategy contributors, the answer is certainly positive. In this vein, Young (1995) has maintained that the "old" SCP paradigm dominant in the 1980s reveals insufficient. On the other side, other scholars maintain that the model of scientific development that Thomas Kuhn proposed in the early 1960s is far from being the best way to look at the circumstances of growth and progress in strategic management (Rumelt *et al.*, 1994; Ansoff, 1987). These contributors posit that a single paradigm that is *unifying* and shared by everyone, or the typical condition of Kuhn's normal science, could not be rightly fitting a multidisciplinary field such as strategic management. If nobody can deny that the SCP paradigm has been considered from its onset as a paradigm, it is possible to ask oneself: what kind of paradigm is this one? Is Kuhn's definition of paradigm the only one available? The definition at hand, does it fit the strategy field? The answer is likely to be negative given that there are other ways, likewise epistemologically and methodologically rooted, to define a paradigm.

The meaning of the term paradigm I convey here is softer and more flexible than Kuhn's original notion and midway to Larry Laudan's (1978) research traditions. Drawing on Ceruti (1985) and Morin (1977), the paradigm concept intends to illustrate the *micro-historical standard* accepted by a particular scientific community in a given time period. A paradigm is thus a type of *logical relation* (of inclusion, conjunction, disjunction, exclusion) among a certain number of basic notions. Accordingly, more than by a single definitive paradigm the practice of research is inter-temporally characterized by heterogeneity in the fundamental ideas that are coexistent and opposing one another. Heterogeneity in fact characterizes not only the different communities and scientists, but also research perspectives within a certain community and sometimes a single independent researcher.

Consistent with the above definition, we introduce three additional paradigms in strategic management: (a) the resource-competence-performance paradigm, that has found consolidation in the 1990s; (b) the knowledge-capabilities-performance paradigm, that found confirmation in the course of 2000s; and (c) the evolutionary paradigm, that has recently succeeded to find room for establishing its own identity.

TABLE 2.1 Evolutionary sequence of paradigms in strategic management

SCP paradigm
RCP paradigm
KCP paradigm
Evolutionary paradigm

A. structure-conduct-performance paradigm

Firm behavior and industry structure are connected by means of a direct relationship that has been a central focus in industrial organization economics (IOE) for pretty long time. Emphasizing the focus on firm behavior and industry structure, IOE has been largely influenced by the work of a group of economists based at Harvard University in the 1930s. Edward Mason and his early PhD student Joe Bain formulated a framework for empirical analysis of a variety of industries, termed Structure-Conduct-Performance, that has contributed to illustrate how key aspects of industry structure relate to each other. The SCP paradigm became the dominant framework for empirical work in IOE between the early 1950s until the early 1980s.

During the 1980s, the SCP paradigm turned out central in strategic management (Schmalensee, 1985; Scherer and Ross, 1990), corroborating the analysis of the industry structure as a means to assess the competitive potential of firms (Porter, 1981). In this period, the SCP paradigm evolved from an initial shape assigning priority to the structure of the industry (*structural* approach), to a second one ascribing greater importance to firm behavior (*behavioral* approach), and finally to a third one that gives to interdependent (see Figure 2.1).

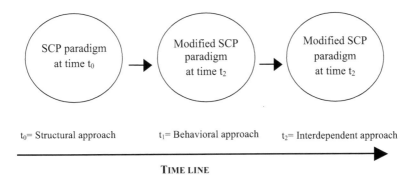

FIGURE 2.1 Evolutionary dynamics of the SCP paradigm in strategic management

Source: Dagnino, 2005: 51

Genetic and evolutionary profiles of the SCP paradigm may be better understood by briefly investigating goals, motivations, and applications of IOE. Industrial organization economists aim to offer satisficing general explanations of the economic forces operating inside industries. As Scherer and Ross (1990: 1) put it: "In its mainstream, industrial organization is concerned with how productive activities are brought into *harmony* with demand for goods and services through some *organizing mechanisms* such as a free market, and how variations and imperfections in the organizing mechanisms affect the success achieved in satisfying an economy's wants."

This statement contains three basic dimensions (equilibrium, efficiency, and equity) around which most economic and industrial policy literature revolves. The reason for the interest in the problems of industrial organization is connected to its influence in public policy so as to improve the market efficiency, well-being, and social equity. IOE has evolved in different lines of methodological development, of which the mainstream is represented by Edward Chamberlin's (1933) post-Marshallian economics. According to Chamberlin, the industry is the most important economic phenomenon for industrial development thereby crediting relevance to the extant relationship between the industry (in which the firm operates) and firm performance. Therefore, based on this perspective, in its original structural form, the SCP paradigm is deemed a fundamental research tool to understand the ways in which firms compete (Scherer and Ross, 1990).

Mason (1939, 1949) was the one who advanced the grounding of the SCP paradigm as he focused specific attention on industry structure deemed as the main driver of the firm's pricing policies. Mason's analysis digs into the industry's morphological information, suggesting a classification based on three homogeneity factors. These factors concern: (a) the economic characteristics of the product and productive processes; (b) the number and size of buyers and sellers in the market; and (c) the level of barriers to entry and distribution channels.

The structural approach tends to give a restrictive interpretation of the industry that may include only homogeneous firms in relation to the suggested factors. Bain's contribution (1956; 1968) weakens the role of conduct in favor of industry structure. The mechanism of Mason's SCP paradigm is based on the causal sequence between market structure-conduct of sellers and buyers-market performance (as Figure 2.2 shows).

Industry performance can therefore be ascribed to: (1) the industry *structure* (or market structure) – it concerns the firm size vis-à-vis market demand or the firm distribution as concerns industry size (concentration), or the presence of barriers to entry and to exit, and finally demands elasticity (Besanko *et al.*, 2000; Hay and Morris, 1984); (2) *conduct* of the firms belonging to an industry; i.e., firm's behavior – variables related to conduct concern the nature of the firm's objective function and its attitude toward rivals; and (3) *performance* that concerns outcome or equilibrium assessed in terms of allocative efficiency – it represents the outcomes the firms achieve in various industries in which they operate.

In the structural view,[2] the SCP paradigm displays a mechanistic and rather static

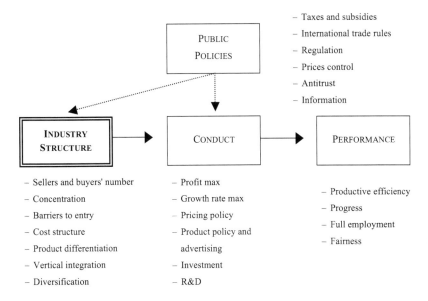

FIGURE 2.2 The structural view of the SCP paradigm

Source: Scherer and Ross, 1990: 5, with adaptations

configuration: the firms' conduct is influenced by the configuration of the industry and the industry is considered the unique exogenous variable, while performance follows conduct in a quasi-automated fashion. According to the structural approach, the firm traces back to Marshall; thus it is the "representative firm" with a standard target and without a decisive influence on the industry (Langlois, 2003: 283–284). According to this view, technology, scale economies, and demand elasticity are exogenous factors that are consequently independent, as they depend from *pro tempore* circumstances of techniques and consumer tastes. These factors establish the level of entry barriers that in turn affect the firm's number and concentration. Concentration produces firm market power thereby affecting firm conduct.

As anticipated, over time the initial version of the SCP paradigm has undergone a dual evolutionary review: (1) the first emphasizing the role of firm conduct and advancing toward a behavioral interpretation; (2) the second according to which the SCP paradigm has changed considering all three key components (i.e. structure, conduct and performance) as equally connected and interactive. This dual shift in interpreting the SCP paradigm outdoes Mason-Bain's idea of the firm as inactive or, at most, reactive actor (Jacquemin and De Jong, 1977). The first review comes in the mid 1970s thanks to European scholars from the managerial theory of the firm. The second review starting in the 1980s is related to the development of *contestable market* theory and games theoretical views to explain the emergent firm's cooperative behavior (see Figure 2.3).

FIGURE 2.3   The behavioral view of the SCP paradigm

Source: Jacquemin and De Jong, 1977: 214, with adaptations

The conduct-oriented view of the SCP's paradigm behavioral approach originates in the studies of IOE scholars that had the firm (rather than the industry) as their primary of object study. The firm is appreciated as the essential core of the entrepreneurial world, as it is endowed with a unique identity and a discretionary action power, in such way that entrepreneurial behavior is aimed to transform the environment in which the firm operates or to anticipate its structural changes. The firm does not passively fit to changes, but it creates them (Jacquemin and De Jong, 1997: 20). This strand of studies has its roots in the work of post-Marshall scholars (Kaldor, Robinson, and Sraffa) and of managerial economists (Baumol, Marris, Penrose, Sylos-Labini, and Williamson).

Stage three in the evolution of the SCP paradigm is affected by contestable markets approach and game theoretical contributions. The SCP paradigm is influenced by contestable markets (Baumol, Panzar, and Willig, 1988) in as much as it reduces the firm-size's weight and concentration in order to estimate the *efficient* industrial configuration. The latest review changes the concept of efficient market structure that turns multifaceted and multidimensional. Hence, this approach acts differently vis-à-vis the behavioral one emphasizing the transition from structure to behavior. The approach paves the way to a SCP paradigm configuration that can be defined as *interdependent* (see Figure 2.4). The study of interdependencies requires a further contribution generated by game theory. Game theory contributes to turn the SCP paradigm more dynamic as it facilitates its progress in the evolutionary pathway. It emphasizes the firm's active role; that is therefore similar to the role that strategic management has traditionally assigned to the firm. However, according to this approach, the focus is not the current industry structure, but rather its prospective configuration; i.e. the *potential* or *hidden* industry structure.

This view results from the strategic interaction between, on the one hand, firm behavioral choices and industry structure and, on the other hand, rivals' competitive strategy. Consequently, the configuration takes form in the interdependent or concurrent SCP paradigm. Figure 2.4 shows that competitive strategy choices are carried out through a cause-effect iterative process.

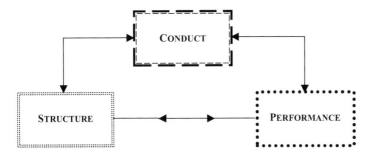

FIGURE 2.4 The interdependent view of the SCP paradigm

It is worthwhile emphasizing the role that the SCP paradigm plays in strategic management. As known, Michael Porter's (1981) competitive strategic approach is rooted in the SCP paradigm whose implementation has emphasized the juxtaposition between industry effects and firm effects. Consequently, vis-à-vis IOE, strategic management adapted the SCP paradigm to its purposes; i.e. understanding the sources of firm sustainable competitive advantage. The notion of sustainable competitive advantage regards the firm's ability to appropriate rents or returns that are above industry average.

Over the 1960s and 1970s, pioneering studies in strategic management (Ansoff, 1965; Andrews, 1971; Hofer and Schendel, 1978) proposed a strategy notion – widely known as SWOT analysis – that highlights the role of exogenous factors (related to the environment) and endogenous elements (related to the firm), to analyze the firm's strengths and weaknesses, as well as environmental opportunities and threats. While this framework has continued to be influential among strategy scholars, in the 1980s grounding on Mason-Bain's SCP, Michael Porter (1980, 1981) proposed the *enlarged competition* framework. Porter reverses the analytical framework of the SCP paradigm: strategy purpose is to develop ways that can help firm's managers (rather than policy makers) to achieve higher returns. The enlarged competition framework identifies five basic competitive forces at the industry level (barriers to entry, the existence of substitute products from competitors, bargaining power of suppliers, bargaining power of customers, and rivalry among existing firms).

These five forces determine the state of competition and profit in an industry, and by this means the relative attractiveness of an industry as a whole or of a segment within an industry. The enlarged competition model involves powerful external factors (as threat of new entrants) that transcend the rivalry and competitive interaction among existing firms in an industry. According to Michael Porter, industry structure has a crucial influence in determining competitive intensity. Competitive intensity does not depend on coincidences, but it is rooted in its basic economic setting. Porter adds: "the resultant of these competitive forces determines, ultimately, the *potential profit* of the industry" (Porter 1981: 24).

Industries have not the same potentiality, but they diverge in potential profits in relation to matched effect of the forces in that industry (market power theory).

In this framework, industrial setting and its related factors generate the "industry effect." Industry characteristics are the ones that determine strategic planning as firm profitability levels are identified as follows: the existence and importance of barriers to entry; the firms' number and size in the industry; the differentiation among firms' products in the industry; and demand elasticity for goods in the industry.

The enlarged competition model has had huge global success in strategic management literature as well as managerial and consulting applications and is therefore considered a strategic milestone.

B. Resource-competence-performance paradigm

Over the 1990s, numerous contributions started to repeatedly question the strongholds of the IOE view. Porter's five forces framework has been criticized by various scholars (Rumelt, 1991; Baden-Füller and Stopford, 1994). These critiques provided empirical foothold to the widespread necessity to outdo the SCP paradigm. Actually, empirical studies underscored that the view of the competitive contexts based on the SCP paradigm was not any longer useful to the formulation of firm strategies in the competitive environment of the 1990s, pinpointed as hypercompetitive (D'Aveni, 1994) and epitomized by temporary competitive advantages (D'Aveni et al. 2010).

Consequently, scholars felt the necessity to evaluate the firm's strategic role in inter-industry and intra-industry competition. As a consequence, strategy contributors (Barney, 1991; Peteraf, 1993; Teece et al., 1997; Nonaka et al., 2000) started offering attention to variables that are endogenous to the firm.

Researchers' main focus shifted towards a theory of the firm based on resources (i.e. the resource-based theory of the firm) and, during the second half of the decade, to a theory of the firm grounded in knowledge (i.e. the knowledge-based theory of the firm). During these years, the idea emerged that "*the firm matters more than the industry*" (Baden-Fuller and Stopford, 1994: ch. 2 [emphasis added]), and that the firm is able to transform its industry and the competitive rules of the game, turning itself into a *proactive* agent of change.

Consequently, the RCP and KCP paradigms ascribe to the firm's internal constituents the differences in performance and economic rents. These approaches stimulate the transition of competitive advantage's focus from an external view to an internal view of the firm (Hoskisson et al., 1999). The change in the sources of competitive advantage arises as a counter-reaction to the long-lasting influence of IOE in strategic thinking, but also as a consequence of the different socio-economic and technological configurations of markets and firms in the 1990s. The three following factors are considered as drivers of this transformation: (1) the changed economic conditions of the world economies in the 1990s; (2) the altered economic weights of the new geographical contexts (at the time USA, Europe, and Asia, nowadays unbalanced in favor of Asia); and (3) the globalization processes.

These drivers affected new economic conditions that were pretty different from the homogeneous and relatively stable conditions typical of the SCP paradigm. The economy of those years started to be a knowledge and service economy, characterized by the convergence of industries and increasing returns. This condition reduced dramatically the explanatory and predictive power of the SCP paradigm and inspired the need to replace it. In this sub-section, we shall clarify the emergence and evolutionary sequence of the RCP paradigm, while in the next we shall portray the KCP paradigm.

The RCP paradigm locates the source of competitive advantages in the endogenous and heterogeneous characteristics of the firms. Unlike industrial economic models that look outside the firm to explain outcomes above the average, according to the RCP approach the source of firms' rents is mainly *internal*. Rather than looking at the competitive environment, firm performance heterogeneity is due to their distinctive resources,[3] competences, and capabilities (Barney, 1995). Ultimately, it is not the industry that makes the firm profitable, but the same firm's strategic choices and intertemporal resource allocation. Consequently, there is no such factor as lasting "industry effect," but long-lasting "firm effect" (Rumelt, 1991). Firms are different and traditional elements of diversity (size, profitability, ownership structure) allow to grasp phenomena only on the surface.

In the resource-based RCP perspective, the firm recaptures relevance, character, autonomy, and its creative and innovative behavior takes on the possibility of piloting industry value. This setting enhances and reinforces the concept of strategy in such a way that resources/competences are not the passive effect of the industry structure, but the real drivers leading to development, size, technologies, and structure of the industry.

In the conceptual representation of the firm in the RCP paradigm, the second important element is related to the notion of *competence*. The concept of competence is not novel in strategy, but its function is novel (Rumelt, 1994). Richard Rumelt posits: "The idea that competence is an important element of successful strategy is not novel. However, the traditional role ascribed to competence is less central, less integrative, and less dynamic than that proposed by Prahalad and Hamel" (1994: xvi). The concept of competence draws the attention on a more dynamic firm as it refers to how to assemble or combine firm resources, until obtaining "bundles of constituent skills and resources." At the bottom of the concept of competence, there are complex mechanisms of coordination among individuals within a firm (the so-called *behavioral* elements of coordination) and among these individuals, and the services provided to customers through tangible and intangible resources.

The RCP paradigm has an evolutionary path corresponding roughly to the SCP one. The evolutionary examination of the RCP paradigm underlines how performances depend on the resources that the firm controls, while the competences are obtained through a unique and authentic recombination of resources. We identify three key formulations of the RCP paradigm: (a) the resource-based approach; (b) the competence-based approach; and (c) the interdependent approach to resources,

FIGURE 2.5   The resource-based view of the RCP paradigm

Source: Dagnino, 2005: 147

competences and performance. The resource-based view of the RCP paradigm (Figure 2.5) is the original one and has hitherto been the most followed in academic research.

According to the resource-based view of the RCP paradigm, the resources that the firm controls at a specific time are the drivers of its competences; the latter are generated by the integration and combination of resources. Competences lead to performance through their application in production processes and firm activities. This is seemingly a deterministic interpretation of the sequence of the RCP paradigm that may recall the Mason-Bain SCP approach from the viewpoint of the cause-effect relationship, because it does nothing than substituting structure and conduct with resources and competences, while the focus is centered on the firm.

A second interpretation of the RCP paradigm is the competence-based view (Prahalad and Hamel, 1990), depicted in Figure 2.6.

The competence-based view differs from the resource-based view because, to achieve a competitive advantage, it ascribes greater importance to competences and the interaction between resources and competences. The main focus is no longer on resources, but on the processes of integration and recombination of these resources that firms fulfill through competences. The deliberate construction of competences, which support several businesses, is the cornerstone of competition. Competition among firms changes its nature: it is no longer competing on products, or on access to resources, but it turns into competition on competence acquisition and development (McGrath *et al.*, 1995). Unlike the original resource-based approach, where resources bear the strategic value of grounding firm competitive advantage and performance, in the competence-based view to have

FIGURE 2.6   The competence-based view of the RCP paradigm

Source: Dagnino, 2005: 148

more resources is neither necessary nor sufficient condition for success (Hamel and Heene, 1994). Competitive advantage will accrue to firms that accumulate resources by developing competences and recombining resources in imaginative ways.

In this strand of studies, the basis of competitive success and of achieving superior performance does not require wide resources endowments, but the ability to *combine* and *integrate* resources in a unique way. The combination of resources is achieved through the application of both individual and team competences acquired and developed by firms (Sanchez and Heene, 2003): this combination occurs through strategic innovation and entrepreneurial creativity. Baden-Fuller and Stopford (1994) add: "Organizations looking to rejuvenate should realize that the winners of today's battles have often been able to overcome their disadvantages by deploying new combinations of skills and competencies." Thanks to its openness, the competence-based approach has been deemed stronger in explaining firm strategy than the resource-based *tout court*.

Finally, the interdependent view to the RCP paradigm (see Figure 2.7) is a more balanced view than the previous two, because it considers resource, competencies, and performance as interdependent.

Since it considers the three elements (resource, competencies, and performance) as interdependent, this understanding of the RCP paradigm involves no *primum movens*, no cause-effect relationship. Instead resources, competences, and performance affect each other. The interactive view of the RCP paradigm is not just a theoretical hypothesis, since via this interpretation of resources and competences we see that the RCP paradigm is able to adapt to changed circumstances in its evolutionary path. Thanks to the theoretical articulation and wide favor received, the RCP paradigm reached the status of dominant paradigm in strategic management over the 1990s and the first decade of 2000s.

While the above reasoning explains a part of competitive heterogeneity in an economic system, it is necessary to clarify the characteristics of resources and competences that enable firms to obtain a competitive advantage. These characteristics are:

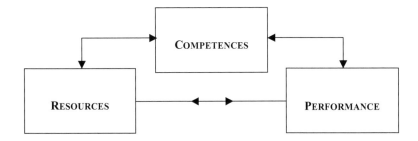

FIGURE 2.7   The interdependent view of the RCP paradigm

Source: Dagnino, 2005: 149, with adaptations

(1) Resources and competences assume a *strategic role* when they allow to offer quality products in the market and/or high product performance, or to incur costs lower than rivals. Accordingly, resources and competences are the ones that make a firm more competitive (Amit and Schoemaker, 1993).

(2) Superior performance (achieved thanks to resources and competences) should not be absorbed by the cost sustained to access resources and competences (Barney, 1986).

(3) Resources and competences ought to be available in *limited* quantities; i.e. they should be *rare*, *inimitable*, and *valuable*. Where resources and competences are available in sufficient quantity to satisfy the demand, they will not be useful to differentiate the firms from competitors and usually they do not generate rents (Peteraf, 1993: 181).

(4) Resources and competences' *durability* establishes *ceteris paribus* the "longevity of the firm's competitive advantage" (Dagnino, 2005: 152).

Resources and competences that ensure the firm sustainable competitive advantage are those that bear *strategic value*. The features required to maintain the competitive advantage are: (a) *imperfect mobility* of resources, meaning that it is not possible to transfer these resources from one firm to another with no trouble. This condition depends on the incompleteness of factors markets and their imperfections. It is possible to distinguish between totally static resources and resources with reduced mobility. The former typology of resources includes resources with ownership structure that is not well defined or that have problems with recognition and measurement (Dierickx and Cool, 1989: 1505). Other typologies of resources are firm-specific or idiosyncratic resources. They have an imperfect mobility because of the switching costs that firms ought to bear to transfer them; and (b) the presence of *barriers to imitation* or *isolation mechanisms* (Besanko *et al.*, 2000: 503) that safeguard firm rents over time. Some of these barriers are part of the institutional context and are termed as "property rights."

Internally developed resources and competences are particularly difficult to imitate because they have a remarkable tacit dimension and display social complexity. Dierickx and Cool (1989) identify the characteristics of the processes of resources and competences' internal development that are useful to prevent imitation, influencing the sustainability of competitive advantage: time compression diseconomies, asset mass efficiencies, interconnection between resource stocks, casual ambiguity or uncertain imitability (Lippman and Rumelt, 1982), and finally degree of substitutability of resources and competences.

Although in the RCP perspective the firm appears to recall the neoclassical way of thinking, there are notably few differences in its underlying assumptions. In fact, while according to the neoclassical perspective the firm remains an abstract entity (or *a black box*) condensed in a production function with cost and revenue curves, the RCP perspective makes an attempt to open the black box to understand the elements that compose it as well as how they interact in the firms' activities (Sirmon *et al.*, 2007). In the neoclassical perspective, economic actors are rational and perfect transparency of markets is assumed. Conversely, in the RCP paradigm economic actors are rational (although to a lesser extent vis-à-vis perfect neoclassical rationality), there is no market transparency, but there is *imperfect* competition, and therefore firms can influence market forces (ibid.).

In the neoclassical perspective, resources are fully transferable, while the RCP paradigm posits that there is no easy resource tradability. In mainstream economics studies, the dimension and degree of diversification have no theoretical value because, due to cost curves that are assumed to be marginally increasing, firms will not grow beyond a certain level of production. Notwithstanding that, in the RCP paradigm there is significant heterogeneity in firms' size and nature of activities, even when the economy is in partial equilibrium.

Overall, the RCP paradigm makes it possible for a firm to identify the link resources-competences-performance to generate superior rents. In the following subsection, I shall examine the emergence of a third paradigm in strategic management that, instead of the one on resources, this time is grounded on knowledge.

C. Knowledge-capabilities-performance paradigm

As anticipated, the current landscape of strategic management is not limited to the SCP and RCP paradigms. Actually, other two paradigms have emerged, such as the KCP paradigm, that I illustrate in this sub-section, and the evolutionary paradigm that will be inspected in the next one.

Because knowledge is deemed key to competitive advantage (Reus, Ranft, Lamont, and Adams, 2009), the new emphasis on various aspects, such as learning processes, the concepts of intangibility and ability, know-how and know-what, the debate on the role of routines, competences, and capabilities paved the way to the study of firm knowledge production and integration, and thus to the emergence of the *knowledge-based* view of the firm (KBV).

Dating back to the mid 1990s, the initial formulation of the KBV is based on the following statements: "knowledge is a resource," or "knowledge is the most important resource," or also "knowledge is the only meaningful resource" (Drucker, 1993), or finally "knowledge is one of the most important resources that gives a firm sustainable competitive advantage" (Grant, 1996; Felin and Hesterly, 2007).

Originating as an extension of the resource-based view of the firm, the KCP paradigm deems the firm as an entity that develops a superior capability of *knowledge protection* (Porter-Liebeskind, 1996) and/or an integration and application of knowledge embodied in individuals (Grant, 1996). Nonetheless, other influential KBV-related studies (Nonaka, 1994; Nonaka *et al.*, 2000; Nonaka and Toyama, 2002) look at the firm as an entity that has the ultimate purpose of the production of knowledge. According to Kogut and Zander (1992), the challenge in managerial theory and practice is to understand the knowledge base of each firm that gives life to a set of capabilities, which in turn are the leading sources of competitive advantage.

The development of the KCP paradigm stems from the considerations that follow. The KCP approach can be deemed a paradigm because knowledge, evaluated as an *evolutionary resource*, is able to engender and develop capabilities that have direct effects in terms of competition and profits. The evolution of the KCP paradigm shows two phases (reported in Figure 2.8):

(a) an initial evolutionary process of speciation from RCP to KCP_1;
(b) a corresponding evolutionary sequence based on Nonaka theory of *knowledge creation* in the firm considered as a knowledge-creating entity.

Consequently, the evolution of the paradigm KCP discloses an interesting branching into two sub-paradigms as Figure 2.8 shows.

The initial view of the KCP paradigm may be termed as sub-paradigm KCP_1, as it is essentially referred to *knowledge protection*. The second view of the KCP paradigm may be termed as sub-paradigm KCP_2, as it is instead creative and dynamic. While KCP_1 is grounded in economic theory, KCP_2 can be ascribed to Nonaka studies about *knowledge creation*. In the knowledge literature, the two different perspectives (KCP_1 and KCP_2) are related to the integration-protection of knowledge, as concerns the KCP_1 perspective (Grant, 1996; Porter-Liebeskind,

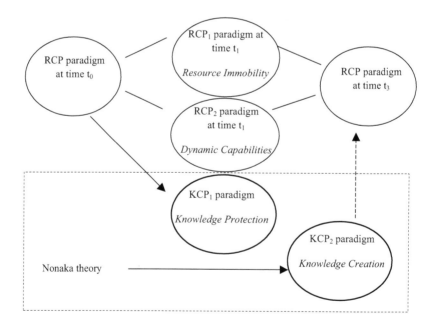

FIGURE 2.8 Evolutionary dynamics between the RCP and KCP paradigms and sub-paradigms

Source: Dagnino, 2005: 233 with adaptations

1996), and to knowledge creation, as regards the KCP$_2$ perspective (Nonaka, 1994; Nonaka *et al.*, 2000; Nonaka and Toyama, 2002). Due to evolutionary enhancement, the two KCP sub-paradigms are the result of a "speciation-adaptation" mix, which appears "unique, non-repeatable, and non-reversible" (Dagnino, 2005: 232).

The two KCP sub-paradigms are different not only in the way they locate the sources of rents (Ricardian vs. Schumpeterian), but also in the conditions under which rents are considered to be of interest to the firm's competitiveness. Accordingly, while in KCP$_1$ the firm's focus is value appropriation, in KCP$_2$ the focus is value creation.

Nonaka and Takeuchi hold that: "By organizational *knowledge creation*, we mean the capability of a firm as a whole to create new knowledge, disseminate it throughout the organization, and embody it in products, services, and systems" (1995: 3 [emphasis added]). Hence, according to the KCP perspective, the knowledge and capabilities to create knowledge are the most important sources of sustainable competitive advantage (Nonaka and Takeuchi, 1995). KCP$_1$ seconds that the creation of knowledge is an individual activity and the main role of the firm is to apply existing knowledge and to erect barriers to imitation and substitution. Arguably, this approach is essentially based on a static view of knowledge and falls short to consider the role of social interaction.

In KCP$_2$, knowledge creation is a dynamic and interdependent process, where knowledge is created and recreated through social interaction between individuals and between individuals and contexts. Accordingly, Nonaka *et al.* purport: "Instead of merely solving problems, an organization creates and defines problems, generates and applies new knowledge, to solve the problems, and then further generates new knowledge through the action of problem solving" (2000: 3).

In this perspective, knowledge is dependent on the circumstances of *time* and *place*. Therefore, knowledge is context-specific because, in the absence of context, it remains merely information and the dynamic process of knowledge creation is not activated (Hayek, 1945). As concerns the context-specific nature of knowledge creation, Nonaka *et al.* (2000: 8–9) introduce the Confucian concept of "Ba", where "*Ba* does not mean 'physical space,' but it is '*a specific time and space*'" (emphasis added). In "Ba" the context itself evolves through "self-transcendence to create knowledge."

According to the KCP$_2$ paradigm, firms can achieve rents through innovation and this is the product of the knowledge obtained through a collective process (Felin and Hesterly, 2007). KCP$_2$ has theoretical roots of various kinds: (a) sociological theories of situated human action; (b) social construction of reality (Berger and Luckmann, 1966); and (c) the influence of Japanese culture in the relationship between man and nature, and mind and body ("the oneness of humanity and nature"; Nonaka and Takeuchi, 1995: ch. 2).

These multiple influences help us understand how KCP$_2$ is not simply a speciation of the original RCP paradigm or of the RCP$_2$ paradigm. Nonetheless, the KCP$_2$ paradigm is able to exert influence on the integrated RCP paradigm, because it involves the need to promote "co-presence, that is the conjoint use, of knowledge creation, absorption, and integration" (Verona and Ravasi, 2003).

The importance of learning skills and increased environmental turbulence has fostered the evolution of the initial RCP and KCP frameworks towards more dynamic approaches (e.g. KCP_2). However, the focus here is not on the ownership of a stock of knowledge, but on the ability to create new knowledge and innovate repeatedly (Teece *et al.*, 1997; Kogut and Zander, 1992).

While KCP_1 is connected to mainstream economic analysis since it evaluates the economic analysis in the context of knowledge markets that are sufficiently efficient (in equilibrium), in the KCP_2 paradigm, economic action takes place in knowledge markets that are cyclically unbalanced (in disequilibrium). Firms with their creative behaviors deal with forces and factors underlying the development of the economic system.

Accordingly, the KCP_1 paradigm posits that sustainable competitive advantage comes from the knowledge and the ability to use knowledge to generate rents from efficiency. Hence, the reason why firm exist is to continually create knowledge (Teece *et al.*, 1997; Kogut and Zander, 1992). Conversely, in the KCP_2 view the firm is represented as a *planning* and *cognitive system* epitomized by organizational efforts to develop new knowledge, new competences and distinctive capabilities (Kogut and Zander, 1992; Teece *et al.*, 1997; Nonaka *et al.*, 2000; Nonaka and Toyama, 2002). Among these capabilities, *synthesizing capabilities* assume relevance. "The firm capability of synthesizing is the ability to manage forces in contradiction to each other, such as competition and cooperation, integration and disintegration, creativity and efficiency" (Nonaka and Toyama, 2002). The word "synthesize" can describe the "dialectic combination of thesis and antithesis" to generate a knowledge creation process.

Therefore, according to Nonaka and Toyama synthesizing capability "is not either/or but both/and: it is an action to transcend the existing self, which in essence is the interdependence, interpretation and unity of opposites" (2002: 999). The process of knowledge creation may be interpreted as a process of synthesizing opposites thereby leading to superior competitive advantages. Consequently, the KCP paradigm (in both its variations KCP_1 and KCP_2) clearly show how the firm is actually able to create new knowledge and capabilities in order to achieve competitive advantage.

In the following section, I will delve into the origin and structure of the fourth paradigm of strategic management, or the evolutionary paradigm.

D. Evolutionary paradigm

Concurrent to the emergence of KCP_2, it is possible to behold the formation of another relevant paradigm in strategic management: the evolutionary paradigm. Since it is rooted in the economic evolutionary perspective (Nelson and Winter, 1982, 2002), as well as in the behavioral approach that refers to the "Carnegie School" (March and Simon, 1958; Cyert and March, 1963; Gavetti, Levinthal, and Ocasio, 2007), I have chosen to term it as the evolutionary paradigm.

For its dynamic and process-oriented nature, the evolutionary paradigm has progressively enucleated in the strategy field so as to assume a specific identity. As regards firm growth processes, this paradigm is tied to the development of relevant concepts such as competence, learning, and routine (Nelson and Winter, 2002). Rather than in the industry position or in the firm's resources, capabilities, and knowledge, the evolutionary view locates the source of competitive advantage in routines, innovation, and learning processes (Baum and Singh, 1994; Barnett and Burgelman, 1996).

A forerunner of this view is Armen Alchian (1950) who, in his proto-evolutionary work, titled "Uncertainty, evolution and economic theory," proposed an economic system characterized by pervasive uncertainty arising from imperfect predictability and environmental complexity. The center of attention for Alchian is the firm. According to Alchian, the principle of profit maximization makes sense only if it is considered as the best result (*ex post*) that the firm can achieve in its competitive environment. Alchian posits that "uncertainty fuels variation" and "innovation" is the source of evolutionary variation: therefore, firm survival depends on profits, but profit occurs not as a consequence of deliberate choice, but as a result of *lucky* decisions or successful adaptation.

A complementary founding contribution of the evolutionary perspective is recognized in Nelson and Winter (1982). Nelson and Winter suggest that natural selection improves the development of new routines, while the old routines are abandoned. Hence, the firm is required to adapt in order to survive. The four key points of Nelson and Winter are: (a) organizational routines; (b) satisfying behavior; (c) concept of search; and (d) industry selection and selective equilibrium. Routines characterize and differentiate firms. First, activity routinization is the most important form of organizational conservation: consequently, routines take the function of organizational memory that evolves over time. Second, the particular routine may be considered as a form of truce or agreement as concerns intra-organizational conflict and motivational problems. The firm is an organization that knows how to produce. This knowledge is the result of its past experience and is represented by routines that are the skills underlying firm capabilities.

As concerns the biologically-grounded triad variation-selection-retention (VSR), the evolutionary paradigm find in VSR its core set (Sober, 2003). In particular, variation concerns the variations in the range of strategies the firm may pursue via search processes. Selection relates to the ways with which selective processes impact on and are influenced by the rhythm and direction of strategic change. Retention underscores the firm's possibility to appropriate and exploit knowledge in all its forms (e.g. competences, best practice, team or group interaction, community of practices, and so on), that is produced by the firm, or by the firms' environment, or co-produced with the firm's partners (Baum and Singh, 1994; Baum and McKelvey, 1999).

As concerns the key evolutionary features, with the aim of being systematic but not comprehensive, I refer to the points that follow:

(1) multiple analytical levels of evolution;
(2) coevolutionary perspective;
(3) managerial attention on the consequences generated by evolution;
(4) evolutionary conceptualization of organizational capabilities.

Multilevel analysis encompasses the inspection of multiple selection levels as well as the scrutiny of multiple processes of learning and accumulation. Multiple selection implies that some behavior and activity performed by a single selection unit (individuals, teams, firms, firm aggregates) may contribute to reduce the individual fitness of the selected level, thereby concurrently increasing the whole system fitness. In more detail, individuals in organizations or organizations in firm populations may be able to carry out behaviors that, if observed by themselves, undoubtedly reduce their *fitness*, or its longevity, or its performance, or its effectiveness as individual units. Nonetheless, at the same time and in the same process, their action enhances the level of fitness of the whole system (Murmann *et al.*, 2003).

Symmetrically, multiple routine learning processes and of accumulation (of resources and competences), occurring at different analytical levels (economic system, industry, firm aggregates, firm, business unit, team, individual), portray contradictory effects on the more inclusive level taken into account. This issue of evolutionary approach, on the one hand, regards the crucial relationship 'whole-part' typical of systems theory (Baum, 1999; Campbell, 1994), on the other casts some doubt on what is/are the most appropriate selection unit/s, and therefore on the opportunity to consider multiple selection units at the same time.

As regards coevolution, in strategy and organization studies the term 'coevolution' has been frequently utilized in a vague fashion and occasionally in differing fashion. Inevitably, this approximation has attracted critiques on the evolutionary perspective as a whole; critiques that at times have eventually unveiled as excessive as superfluous. Some authors have supported an extended interpretation of coevolution. According with this explanation, in coevolution "all evolves with all." In such a hyper-tautological angle, the coevolutionary process will never be able to supply a parsimonious explanation by keeping on hanging about a tautology that is methodologically regressive.

Given that coevolutionary issues have received certain attention in strategy and organizational studies (Baum and Singh, 1994; Levinthal and Myatt, 1994; Baum and McKelvey, 1999; Lewin and Volberda, 1999; Lewin *et al.*, 1999), I convey a terminological specification. Rather than two things that develop and evolve in parallel, with the term coevolution I wish to pinpoint two or more things that evolve *in connection* among them. In the biological world, it happens not that every species coevolves anarchically with every other existing species, but that coevolution occurs between two specific species: for instance a specific plant with particular insect or predator with its prey. Similarly, an industry coevolves not with all the other industries, but with a limited number of other industries, technologies and social institutions. Two populations coevolve if and only if both have a significant causal effect on the ability of the other to persist. Any given coevolutionary strategic process requires a crucial mechanism of *mutual causality* or *bidirectional causality* that ties closely the two parties involved in the relationship (Lewin and Volberda, 1999: 527; Murmann, 2003: 22–23).[4] Coevolutionary dynamics implies two fundamental effects: (i) acts at multiple analytical levels (i.e. microcoevolution and macrocoevolution); (ii) implies self-reinforcing and recursive processes of *feedforward*. These over time turn epidemically and exponentially small initial differences in huge final differences. McKelvey supports that: "coevolutionary effects take place at multiple levels within the firm (microcoevolution) as well as between firms and their niche (macrocoevolution)" (1997: 360).

According to cumulative causation, coevolutionary interaction generally leads to *collective* and *cumulative learning* processes, where the actors involved learn from each other, adapt to changing circumstances, develop and evolve specific heuristics and organizational routines, and accumulate memory of past circumstances. Circular causation results in *path dependent* behaviors that evolve over time, while feedforward suggest significant room for managerial action and discretion.

As concerns managerial focus on the consequences engendered by evolution, differently from other approaches on human action, the evolutionary paradigm centers its attention on *consequences*, not only intentions. In order to explain the evolution of industrial and organizational structures, it is grounded not only on agents' intentions, but rather on the consequences of agents' actions. When actions generate positive outcomes in presence of prevalent selection criteria (although results are not intentional), they are selected favorably by the environment and hence persist. Conversely, when they generate negative results, the same actions will be selected negatively (they will be emarginated and isolated) and thus tend to dissolve. The majority of firms operate on the basis of a simple principle: "if a given routine functions, we utilize it incrementally all the times further more; if it does not function, we get rid of it" (March, 1999). Therefore, in evolutionary terms, actions and routines within organizations are selected for the *perceived benefits* they originate. If it turns impossible to determine the systemic outcome of a single routine, given that single routines are intensely interdependent with other routines, the ones to be selected positively will be the collections of routines. Taking a step forward, when a firm fails because its overall routines are not adequately efficient vis-à-vis the routines of the rival firms, a specific routine will cease to exist together with all the other organizational routines. Straightforwardly, also in this instance we deal with two analytical levels: individual routine and the firm as a whole (Murmann, 2003).

Finally, as regards the evolutionary interpretation of organizational capabilities, they are intended as second-order routines that in turn allow the firm to access a strategic decision portfolio aimed to produce significant results.[5]

The one at hand has turned into one of the frontier territories with which the evolutionary paradigm is currently dealing in strategic management. In this debate, many contributors and, among them the most known of the field, in the last fifteen years have relentlessly intervened so that to contribute to the development of the evolutionary theory of the firm.

For it is more open and permeable, compared to the SCP, RCP, and KCP paradigms previously discussed, the evolutionary paradigm is a paradigm with much less deterministic flavor. Actually, the organic rationality epitomizing it is much weaker and encompassing than the stronger type of rationality underlying the former three paradigms. For this reason, as seen the evolutionary paradigm has coevolutionary potential that, from the methodological and epistemological viewpoint, can accommodate different research traditions in strategic management. Accordingly, it plays the role of a powerful integrative and cross-fertilizing approach since it pushes for conceptual and epistemic evolution and evolutionary enhancement (Nelson and Winter, 2002). This condition may be observed in Figure 2.9a and 2.9b where, in a straightforward set theory graphical representation, I have depicted the coevolutionary path of, respectively, RCP and KCP1/2 paradigms and of SCP, RCP, KCP1/2, and evolutionary paradigms.

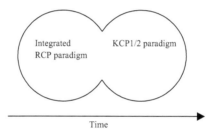

FIGURE 2.9A   Coevolution of RCP and KCP paradigms

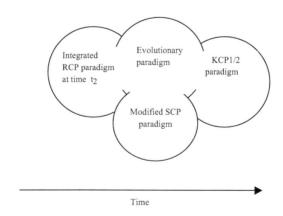

FIGURE 2.9B   Coevolution of SCP, RCP, KCP1/2, and evolutionary paradigms

Discussion and conclusion

Thanks to the contribution of evolutionary epistemology, I have been able to trace the sketch of succession and interaction of the key paradigms of strategic management. First, I underscore that it turned out impossible to identify a single paradigm in strategy. This condition occurs since the field has acquired the status of a theoretically wealthy milieu that proposes four paradigms with idiosyncratic sources of competitive advantage. Second, I support that, for it implies additional costs of communication and less effective coordination in the division scientific work, in Kuhnian terms paradigm plurality warrant a minimal condition of inefficiency of strategic management studies.

In this section, as follows the argument earlier put forth I shall juxtapose the four paradigms of strategic management (SCP, RCP, KCP, and evolutionary), thereby highlighting commonalities and differences. Then, I shall elaborate an outline of the crux argument in this chapter: the elucidation of the evolution of the dominant paradigms in strategic management as a history of incomplete dominances. The concluding section will feature a set of five arguments sketching the contours of current paradigm debate in strategic management and advances an epistemic call for action to management researchers for that interparadigm fertilization that can pave the way for the next wave of development of the strategy field.

Commonalities and differences among the paradigms of strategic management

As concerns SCP, RCP and KCP paradigms, I posit that the three relevant paradigms share a *common causal structure* that essentially consists of a similar conceptual triangulation. For all three paradigms, triangulation exhibits that performance are the ultimate output; while initially all the paradigms are related to a specific connotation of content (respectively, structure, resource and knowledge), whilst at the center is positioned a function related to a process (respectively, conduct, competences and capabilities).

The commonalities among them concern: (a) the three paradigms are essentially grounded in *neoclassical economics* and can be evaluated as a reinterpretation of these studies in the strategy perspective; (b) they emphasize the *sustainability* of competitive advantage and the production (protection) of long-lasting competitive rents; (c) they credit greater attention (even if in the original phase) to *strategy content and formulation*, rather than to strategy implementation; (d) from a methodological viewpoint, they present a *tautological* approach because structure, resources, and knowledge are not only the main sources of competitive advantage, but also the *loci* on which managers put their efforts to maintain competitive advantage. Therefore, structure, resources, and knowledge are the sources and the outcome of firm strategy.

The emphasis on performance of each paradigm does not come as a surprise, because strategic management was born to investigate the drivers of firm performance, and strategy studies have traditionally aimed to analyze both the *historical-retrospective* and the *enhancement-effect* of firm performance.

In the three strategy paradigms at hand, different explanations of the sources of competitive advantage are supplied: relating to exogenous context and the positioning of the firm (the SCP paradigm); the possession or access to resources and competences that are rare, unique, and not easily imitable (the RCP paradigm); the ability of the firm to create (and protect) knowledge and meta-capabilities of synthesizing (the KCP paradigm). The integration between the exogenous and endogenous characteristics of the firm, considered as features that, far from being in contradiction, are essentially complementary, has been repeatedly advocated by various scholars (Barney, 1995; Dierickx and Cool, 1989; Porter, 1991), and it is shown in Table 2.2.

Therefore, only by developing an appropriate understanding of the sources of competitive advantage from both perspectives can we achieve a more balanced vision of the evolution and status of the strategic theory of competitive advantage (see Table 2.3).

TABLE 2.2 Paradigms and sources of competitive advantage in strategic management

Paradigm	Source of competitive advantage
SCP paradigm	Industry position
RCP paradigm	Resources and capabilities allocation
KCP1/2 paradigm	Knowledge possession or generation
Evolutionary paradigm	Routine, innovation, and learning processes

TABLE 2.3 Key features of paradigms in strategic management

Paradigm	Configuration	Competitive advantage	Market	Rents
SCP	Static	Industry position	Products	Chamberlinian
RCP$_{(integrated)}$	Static dynamic	Resource heterogeneity	Factors	Ricardian Schumpeterian
KCP$_1$	Static	Knowledge protection, application, and integration	Knowledge	Ricardian
KCP$_2$	Dynamic	Knowledge creation	Knowledge	Nonakian
Evolutionary	Process dynamic	Routine, learning, and innovation	Selective force of capabilities and knowledge	Innovation Appropriation Schumpeterian

Source: Mocciaro Li Destri and Dagnino, 2005, with adaptations

The evolution of the dominant paradigms in strategic management as a history of incomplete dominances

In this chapter, I contended that the history of strategic management paradigms is since its onset a history of imperfect dominances. Actually, strategic management paradigms are located in the so-called strategic evolutionary space (see Figure 2.10). The strategic evolutionary space is the conceptual area in which evolutionary sequences and interactions between and among strategy paradigms take place. Whenever a strategy scholar uses a particular theory that is part of a paradigm, he/she acts to replicate and/or modify a portion of the strategic evolutionary space. A researcher, even without intentionality, can modify the strategic evolutionary space in a way that, over time, may reveal of relevance and significance. When they occur by means of interparadigm and intertheoretical relations, the variations and mutations that the strategic evolutionary space receives by means of scholarly intervention are usually intentional.

This condition occurs for two main reasons: first, each strategy paradigm is a partial, incomplete and imperfect paradigm. None of the four is usually able to offer by itself a complete explanation of the firm's hitches and problems. Second, none of the four paradigms has managed to have an uncontested dominance in the strategic evolutionary space, thereby leaving room to dissonant voices and possible cross-fertilizations, usually coming from outside the *pro tempore* dominant perspective. This is nothing else but the most apparent symptom of the conceptual polymorphism and epistemic effervescence of strategic management as a field of study. Probably for its multidisciplinary origin, ruling out the condition of the SCP paradigm in a good part of the 1980s, the field has in fact never hosted a single dominant paradigm.

Conclusion

This chapter has investigated the paradigm foundations of strategic management as a field of study. As I have stressed heretofore, the strategy field does not present a sole common ground unanimously accepted and universally shared. It is instead articulated in a dynamic composite kaleidoscope, rich of ideas and themes and open to discussion and debate. This condition occurs because, since its birth, the field has shown to be multidisciplinary and multidimensional. Multidisciplinary because, to establish itself, the field had to gather together scholars coming from different basic disciplines: economics, history, sociology, and engineering. Multidimensional because it encompasses various levels of analysis: the firm and the industry at the beginning, then strategic groups, interfirm alliances and, more recently, interorganizational relations and networks, platforms and ecosystems. In addition, we ought to consider the relations between managerial and governance levels.

On this ground, I am able to gather a set of five strictly intertwined arguments as follows:

(A) 1980s

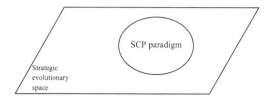

(B) 1990s

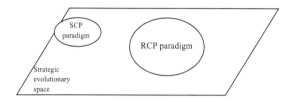

(C) Late 1990s and 2000s

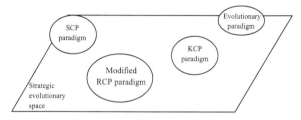

FIGURE 2.10 Paradigm sequence in the strategic evolutionary space

(1) The strategy field, far from being a monolith, is a multiplex universe, articulated and populated by a melting pot of planets, stars, and constellations. These are theories, perspectives, and approaches. Consequently, it is far from being condensed in a single paradigm.

(2) The strategic universe is articulated in a plurality of paradigms, and more precisely in four specific paradigms (i.e., SCP, RCP, KCP, and evolutionary), that have different histories, advancements, and evolutionary success (macroevolution).

(3) The four paradigms have followed evolutionary paths that, at least in some periods, were highly idiosyncratic. The paradigms present specific internal and external developments; the latter in the interaction among different paradigms can be at times divergent and at times convergent. Paradigm developments can be chronologically parallel, but neither are they constant or regular (microevolution).

(4) The four paradigms' evolutionary paths and their interrelations can be conveniently detected by means of the biologic-evolutionary lens, extended and integrated by a socio-cultural proclivity (metaevolution).

(5) The sketch of multiparadigm evolutionary history advanced in this chapter is nothing else but the original outcome of the simultaneous refinement of strategy instruments, the intensification in strategy theories and the use of the interpretive lens provided by evolutionary epistemology.

On this ground, I can therefore support that the next wave of development of the field of strategy may stem out not only by researchers digging within the existing paradigms, but also by means of the intense scholarly conversation and conceptual trade between and among different paradigms and, therefore, almost inevitably among interpretations of strategy seemingly at odds. In addition, a range of perspectives in the social sciences, as well as in the natural sciences, may conveniently complement this condition to trigger an outburst of fertile cross-fertilizations of the strategy field in the foreseeable future.

Notes

1   Evolutionary theory, from the time in which it was proposed by Darwin in 1859, has never ceased to trigger sustained debate among its supporters (the evolutionists) and opponents (the anti-Darwinian creationists). Nowadays, it is accepted by the vast majority of scholars and researchers in the natural sciences and represents a fundamental reference point for all biological disciplines. Nonetheless, interpretations are numerous and the discussion around evolutionary issues is always vibrant.

2   The underlying assumptions are those of the marginalist school of economics: the industry's structural factors are seen as exogenous constraints; structural changes only occur due to exogenous factors in the industry. In the industry, firms are supposed to be all identical in terms of cost function and demand curve, the firm's conduct is non-active, and there exists an average industry profitability to which firm performance tends to adjust.

3   The word "resource" is rooted in the French term *resourse*, that means "a source, a spring." The original etymology is Latin from the Indo-European root *reg* that means "moving in a straight line," from where the Latin verb *rigere*. In the French language, "soure" means "source" that, with the Latin prefix "*re*" (= "again"), becomes *re-source* that means "rise again." The etymological analysis of the word resource displays the intrinsic change dynamics that resources can initiate. The work of Edith Penrose (1959) is considered the theoretical avant-garde of the RCP paradigm. Penrose identifies the classes of elements that can be considered as "productive resources" and proposes a distinction between "productive resources" and "factors of production." RCP scholars have enriched the original set considered by Penrose.

4   Kauffman (1993) uses the idea of coupled fitness landscapes to express this conception of coevolution. In coevolution à la Kaufmann, one partner deforms the fitness

landscape of the second partner and vice versa. As a result, a coevolutionary relationship between entities can increase the average fitness of both populations, decrease the average fitness of both, or have negative or positive impact on the average fitness of one but not the other. Whether a coevolutionary process is beneficial or harmful for the parties involved depends on the particular causal relationship that links the parties; therefore, this relationship needs to be specified in the empirical analysis.

5   Sid Winter (2000) defines firm (operational) capabilities as "a high level routine that, together with its implementing input flows, confers upon an organization's management a set of decision options for producing significant outputs of a particular type" (983). More recently, Helfat and Winter (2011) define organizational capability as "the capacity to perform a particular activity in a reliable and at least minimally satisfactory manner" (1244).

References

Alchian, A. A. (1950). Uncertainty, evolution and economic theory. *Journal of Political Economy*, 58: 211–222.

Amit, R. and Schoemaker, P. J. H. (1993). Strategic assets and organizational rent. *Strategic Management Journal*, 14: 33–46.

Andrews, K. R. (1971). *The Concept of Corporate Strategy*, Homewood, IL: Irwin.

Ansoff, H. I. (1965). *Corporate Strategy*. New York: McGraw Hill.

Ansoff, H. I. (1987). The emerging paradigm of strategic behavior. *Strategic Management Journal*, Nov.–Dec., 8(6): 501–515.

Augier, M. and Teece, D. J. (2013). *The Palgrave Encyclopedia of Strategic Management*. New York: Palgrave-MacMillan.

Baden-Fuller, C. and Stopford, J. (1994). *Rejuvenating the Mature Business*, Cambridge, MA: Harvard Business School Press.

Bain, J. S. (1956). *Barriers to New Competition*, Cambridge, MA: Harvard University Press,

Bain, J. S. (1968). *Industrial Organization* 2nd edn, New York: Wiley.

Barnett, W. P. and Burgelmann R. A. (1996). Evolutionary perspectives on strategy. *Strategic Management Journal*, Summer Special Issue 17: 5–19.

Barney, J. B. (1986). Strategic factor markets: Expectations, luck, and business strategy. *Management Science*, 32 (10): 1231–1241.

Barney, J. B. (1991). Firm resources and sustained competitive advantage. *Journal of Management*, 17(1): 99–120.

Barney, J. B. (1995). Looking inside for competitive advantage. *Academy of Management Executive*, 9(4): 49–62.

Barney, J. B. and Zajac, E. (1994). Competitive organizational behavior: Toward an organizationally-based theory of competitive advantage. *Strategic Management Journal*, Winter Special Issue 15: 5–9.

Barry, D. and Helmes, M. (1997). Strategy retold: Toward a narrative view of strategic discourse. *Academy of Management Review*, 22(2): 429–452.

Baum, J. A. C. (1999). Whole-part coevolutionary competition in organizations. In Baum, J. A. C. and McKelvey, B. (eds), *Variations in Organization Science: In Honor of Donald T. Campbell*, Thousand Oaks, CA: Sage, 11–137.

Baum, J. A. C. and McKelvey B. (1999). Donald T. Campbell's evolving influence on organization science. In Baum, J. A. C. and McKelvey, B. (eds), *Variations in Organization Science: In Honor of Donald T. Campbell*, Thousand Oaks, CA: Sage, 1–15.

Baum, J. A. C. and Singh J. V. (eds) (1994). *Evolutionary Dynamics of Organizations*, New York: Oxford University Press.

Baumol, W. J., Panzar, J. C., and Willig, R. D. (1988). *Contestable Markets and the Theory of Industry Structure*, New York: Harcourt Brace.

Berger, P. L. and Luckmann, T. (1966). *The Social Construction of Reality: A Treatise in the Sociology of Knowledge*, Garden City, NY: Anchor Books Doubleday.

Besanko, D., Dranove, D., and Shanley, M. (2000). *Economics of Strategy* 2nd edn, New York: Wiley.

Boyd, R. and Richerson, P. J. (1985). *Culture and the Evolutionary Process*, Chicago: University of Chicago Press.

Campbell, D. T. (1974). Evolutionary epistemology. In Schlipp, P. A. (ed.), *The Philosophy of Karl Popper*, Vol.14 I and II, La Salle, IL: Open Court.

Campbell, D. T. (1994). How individual and face-to-face group selection undermine firm selection in organizational evolution. In Baum, J. A. C. and Singh J. V. (eds), *Evolutionary Dynamics of Organizations*, New York: Oxford University Press, 23–38.

Ceruti, M. (1985). La Hybris dell'Onniscienza e la Sfida della Complessità [The hybris of omniscience and the challenge of complexity]. In Bocchi, G. and Ceruti, M. (eds). *La sfida della complessità* [*The Challenge of Complexity*]. Milan: Feltrinelli, 18–43.

Chamberlin, E. H. (1933/1948). *The Theory of Monopolistic Competition*, Cambridge, MA: Harvard University Press.

Cyert, R. M. and March, J. G. (1963). *A Behavioral Theory of the Firm*, Englewood Cliffs, NJ: Prentice-Hall.

D'Aveni, R. A. (1994). *Hypercompetition: Managing the Dynamics of Strategic Maneuvering*, New York: Free Press.

D'Aveni R. A., Dagnino, G. B., and Smith, K. G. (2010). The age of temporary advantage. *Strategic Management Journal*, 31: 1371–1385.

Dagnino, G. B. (2005). *I paradigmi dominanti negli studi di strategia d'impresa*, Torino: Giappichelli.

Dagnino, G. B. (ed.) (2012). *Elgar Handbook of Research on Competitive Strategy*. Cheltenham: Edward Elgar

Dierickx, I. and Cool, K. (1989). Asset stock accumulation and sustainability of competitive advantage. *Management Science*, 35(12): 1504–1511.

Drucker, P. (1993). *Post-Capitalist Society*. London: Butterworth-Heinemann.

Durham, W. H. (1991). *Coevolution: Genes, Culture, and Human Diversità*. Stanford: Stanford University Press.

Faulkner, D. O. and Campbell, A. (eds) (2003). *The Oxford Handbook of Strategy*. New York: Oxford University Press.

Felin, T. and Hesterly, W. S. (2007). The knowledge-based view, nested heterogeneity, and new value creation: Philosophical considerations on the locus of knowledge. *Academy Management. Review*, 32 (1): 195–218.

Gavetti, G., Levinthal, D. A., and Ocasio, W. (2007). Neo-Carnegie: The school's past, present, and reconstructing for the future. *Organization Science*, 18(3), 523–536.

Grant, R. M. (1996). Toward a knowledge-based theory of the firm. *Strategic Management Journal*, Winter Special Issue 17: 109–122.

Grant, R. M. (2005). *Contemporary Strategy Analysis: Concepts, Techniques, Applications* 5th edn, Oxford: Blackwell.

Hamel, G. and Heene, A. (1994). *Competence-Based Competition*, Chichester: John Wiley.

Hay, D. A. and Morris, D. J. (1979). *Industrial Economics: Theory and Evidence*, Oxford: Oxford University Press.

Hayek, F. A. (1945). The use of knowledge in society. *American Economic Review*, 35(4): 519–530.

Helfat, C. E. and Winter, S. G. (2011). Untangling dynamic and operational capabilities:

Strategy for the (n)ever-changing world, *Strategic Management Journal* 32: 1243–1250.

Hitt, M. A., Freeman R. E., and Harrison J. S. (eds) (2001a). *The Blackwell Handbook of Strategic Management*. Malden, MA: Blackwell.

Hitt, M. A., Ireland, R. D., and Hoskisson, R. E. (2001b). *Strategic Management: Competitiveness and Globalization* 4th edn, Cincinnati: South Western College.

Hofer, C. W. and Schendel D. E. (1978). *Strategy Formulation: Analytical Concepts*, St. Paul, MN: West Publishing.

Hoskisson, R. E., Hitt, M. A., Wan, W. P, and Yiu, D. (1999). Theory and research in strategic management: Swings of a pendulum. *Journal of Management*, 25: 417–456.

Hull, D. L. (1988). *Science as a Process: An Evolutionary Account of the Social and Conceptual Development of Science*. Chicago: University of Chicago Press.

Hull, D. L. (2001). In search of epistemological warrant. In Hayes, C. and Hull, D. L. (eds), *Selection Theory and Social Construction: The Evolutionary Naturalistic Epistemology of Donald T. Campbell*, Albany: State University of New York Press, 155–167.

Jaquemin, A. P. and de Jong, H. W. (1977). *European Industrial Organization*, London: McMillan.

Kaufmann, S. A. (1993). *The Origin of Order: Self Organization and Selection in Evolution*. New York: Oxford University Press.

Kogut, B. and Zander, U. (1992). Knowledge of the firm, combinative capabilities, and the replication of technology. *Organization Science*, 3(3): 383–397.

Kuhn, T. S. (1970). *The Structure of Scientific Revolutions*. Chicago: University of Chicago Press.

Langlois, R. N. (2003). Strategy as economics versus economics as strategy. *Managerial and Decision Economics*, 34: 283–290.

Laudan, L. (1978). *Progress and Its Problems*. Berkeley, CA: University of California Press.

Levinthal, D. and Myatt, J. (1994). Co-evolution of capabilities and industry: The evolution of mutual fund processing. *Strategic Management Journal*, Winter Special Issue 15: 45–62.

Lewin, A. Y. and Volberda, H. W. (1999). Prolegomena on coevolution: A framework for research on strategy and new organizational forms. *Organization Science*, 10(5): 519–534.

Lewin, A. Y., Long, C. P., and Carroll, T. N. (1999). The coevolution of new organizational forms. *Organization Science*, 10(5): 535–550.

Lippman, S. A. and Rumelt, R. P. (1982). Uncertain imitability: An analysis of interfirm differences in efficiency under competition. *Bell Journal of Economics*, 13(2): 418–438.

March, J. G. (1999). *The Pursuit of Organizational Intelligence*, Walden, MA: Blackwell Business.

McKelvey, B. (1997). Quasi-natural organization science. *Organization Science*, 8(4): 352–380.

March, J. G. and Simon, H. A (1958). *Organizations*, New York: Wiley and Sons.

Mason, E. S. (1939). Price and production policies of large-scale enterprises. *American Economic Review*, 29 (March): 61–74.

Mason, E. S. (1949). The current status of monopoly problem in the United States. *Harvard Law Review*, 62: 1265–1285.

McGrath, R. G., MacMillan, I. C., and Venkatraman, S. (1995). Defining and developing competence: A strategic process paradigm. *Strategic Management Journal*, 16(4): 251–275.

Mintzberg, H. (1994). *The Rise and Fall of Strategic Planning*. New York: The Free Press.

Mocciaro Li Destri, A. and Dagnino, G. B. (2005). The development of the resource-based firm between value appropriation and value creation. *Advances in Strategic Management*, 22: 153–188

Morin, E. (1977). *La méthode. I. La nature de la nature*. Paris: Editions du Seuil.

Murmann, J. P. (2003). *Knowledge and Competitive Advantage. The Coevolution of Firms Technology and National Institutions in the Synthetic Dye Industry, 1850–1914*, Cambridge: Cambridge University Press.

Murmann, J. P., Aldrich, H., Levinthal, D., and Winter, S. (2003). Evolutionary thought in management and organization theory at the beginning of the new millennium. A symposium on the state of the art and opportunities for future research. *Journal of Management Inquiry*, 12(1): 1–19.

Nelson, R. R. and Winter, S. G. (1982). *An Evolutionary Theory of Economic Change*, Cambridge, MA: Belknap Press.

Nelson, R. R. and Winter, S. G. (2002). Evolutionary theorizing in economics. *Journal of Economic Perspectives*, 16(2): 23–46.

Nonaka, I. (1994). A dynamic theory of organizational knowledge creation. *Organization Science*, 5(1):14–37.

Nonaka, I. and Takeuchi, H. (1995). *The Knowledge-Creating Company: How Japanese Companies Create the Dynamics of Innovation*, New York: Oxford University Press.

Nonaka, I., Toyama, R., and Nagata, A. (2000). A Firm as a knowledge-creating entity: A new perspective on the theory of the firm. *Industrial and Corporate Change*, 9(1): 1–20.

Nonaka I. and Toyama R. (2002). A firm as a dialectical being: towards a dynamic theory of a firm. *Industrial and Corporate Change*, 11(5): 995–1009.

Penrose, E. T. (1959). *The Theory of the Growth of the Firm*. London: Basil Blackwell.

Peteraf, M. A. (1993). The cornerstones of competitive advantage: A resource-based view. *Strategic Management Journal*, 14: 179–191.

Pettigrew, A., Thomas, H., and Whittington, R. (eds) (2002). *Handbook of Strategy and Management*. Thousand Oaks, CA: Sage.

Porter, M. E. (1980). *Competitive Strategy*, New York: The Free Press.

Porter, M. E. (1981). The contributions of industrial organizations to strategic management, *Academy of Management Review*, 6(4): 609–620.

Porter, M. E (1991). Towards a dynamic theory of strategy. *Strategic Management Journal*, 12(S2 Winter): 95–117.

Porter, M. (1996). What is Strategy? *Harvard Business Review*. Nov.-Dec.: 61–78.

Porter-Liebeskind, J. (1996). Knowledge, strategy and the theory of the firm, *Strategic Management Journal*, Wnter Special Issue 17: 93–107.

Prahalad, C. K. and Hamel, G. (1990). The core competence of the corporation. *Harvard Business Review*, 68: 79–91.

Prahalad, C. K. and Hamel, G. (1994). Strategy as a field of study: Why search for new paradigms?. *Strategic Management Journal*, Summer Special Issue 15: 5–16.

Reus, T. H., Ranft, A. L., Lamont, B. T., and Adams, G. L. (2009) An interpretive systems view of knowledge investments. *Academic Management Review*, 34 (3): 382–400.

Rothaermel, F. (2012). *Strategic Management: Concepts and Cases*, New York: McGraw-Hill.

Rumelt, R. P. (1991). How much does industry matter? *Strategic Management Journal*, 12(3): 167–185.

Rumelt, R. P., Schendel, D. E., and Teece, D. J. (eds) (1994). *Fundamental Issues in Strategy*. Cambridge, MA: Harvard University Press.

Saloner, G., Shepard, A., and Podolny, J. (2001). *Strategic Management*, Chichester: John Wiley.

Sanchez, R. and Heene, A. (2003). *The New Strategic Management: Organization, Competition, and Competence*, Chichester: John Wiley.

Schelling, T. C. (2006). *Micromotives and Macrobehavior*. New York: Norton & Company.

Scherer, E. M. and Ross, J. (1990). *Industrial Market Structure and Economic Performance* 3rd edn, Boston: Houghton-Mifflin.

Schmalensee, R. (1985). Do markets differ much? *Economic Review*, 75: 341-351.

Schumpeter, J. A. (1954). *History of Economic Analysis*. London: Allen & Unwin.

Sirmon, D. G., Hitt, M. A., and Ireland, R. D. (2007). Managing firm resources in dynamic environment to create value: Looking inside the black box. *Academy of Management*

Review, 32(1), 273–292.

Sober, E. (2000). *The Philosophy of Biology* 2nd edn, Boulder, CL: Westview Press.

Teece, D. J. (ed.) (1987). *The Competitive Challenge: Strategies for Industrial Innovation and Renewal*, Cambridge, MA: Ballinger Publishing.

Teece, D. J. (2007). Explicating dynamic capabilities: the nature and microfoundations of (sustainable) enterprise performance. *Strategic Management Journal*, 28(13): 1319–1350.

Teece, D. J., Pisano, G. and Shuen, A. (1997) Dynamic capabilities and strategic management. *Strategic Management Journal* 18(7): 509–533.

Thompson, A. A. and Strickland, A. J. (2001). *Strategic Management: Concepts and Cases* 12th edn, Boston: McGraw-Hill/Irwin.

Verona, G. and Ravasi, D. (2003). Unbundling dynamic capabilities: An exploratory study of continuous product innovation. *Industrial and Corporate Change*, 12(3): 577–606.

Young, G. (1995). Comment: The resource-based view of the firm and 'Austrian' economics. Integration to go beyond the s-c-p paradigm of industrial organization economics. *Journal of Management Inquiry*, 4: 333–340.

Winter, S. G. (2000). The satisficing principle in capability learning. *Strategic Management Journal*, 21(10–11): 981–996.

PART I

Testing and developing theory in strategic management

3

MULTILEVEL MODELS FOR STRATEGY RESEARCH

An idea whose time (still) has come

Thomas P. Moliterno and Robert E. Ployhart[1]

The field of strategic management deals with the major intended and emergent initiatives taken by general managers on behalf of owners, involving utilization of resources, to enhance the performance of firms in their external environments.

(Nag et al. 2007: 944)

Multilevel theories rest, most fundamentally, on the premise that individual, group, and organizational characteristics interact and combine to shape individual, group, and organizational outcomes.

(Klein and Kozlowski 2000: xvi)

Introduction

As an area of scholarly inquiry, strategic management is, ultimately, focused squarely on explaining the performance of firms. In their inductive study designed to elicit an implicit and explicit definition of "strategic management," Nag *et al.* conclude, as illustrated by their imputed definition above, that firm-level "performance" is the central criterion being explained by strategy scholars. The definition is also fascinating for what else it says about the consensus perspective on the domain of strategic management scholarship; namely, that it comprises actions taken by *managers*, using *resources*, to affect an *organization* that is embedded in a broader *environment*. In other words, strategic management is inherently concerned with the multilevel perspective summarized in the quote from Klein and Kozlowski. In this way, the strategic management literature is populated by industries that are (or are not) favorable for firm-level profitability (Porter 1980, 1985); resource bundles that drive firm-level competitive advantage (Barney 1991); and organizational capabilities that comprise people and resources (Amit and Schoemaker 1993). Yet these topics – and many more in the strategy literature – can all be considered through the lens of multilevel theory: organizational capabilities are bundles or aggregations of individual resources; resources and capabilities themselves affect organizational outcomes when they have certain characteristics; and industries are aggregations of firms with characteristics that affect the potential for profitability of any individual firm.

Yet, it is our sense that strategic management scholars have relegated multilevel methodology to the domain of 'micro' research. Indeed, it is true that much—if not all—of the methodological approaches we outline in this chapter have their origins in research that has examined multilevel systems that are anchored on individuals: either the effect of a collective (e.g. team, unit, or group) on the individual, or the relationship of the individual to the collective. To be sure, as long as strategy scholars stay "within level" – using, for example, variables measured at the firm level to predict firm-level outcomes – there is no need to borrow the multilevel toolkit from our micro-level brethren. However, once the strategy scholar's research question crosses levels – and an ever increasing body of work does – then multilevel issues, and their respective methodological approaches, apply. Fortunately, the multilevel theory and methodology that has been used by our colleagues working at the micro-level ports perfectly to the firm level: what matters is the fact that the research question is crossing levels in the organizational system: not which levels those are. We encourage strategic management scholars to consider when their research considers multilevel issues (and it doesn't always!) and leverage the unique perspective that multilevel theory provides when it does. Accordingly, in this chapter we outline a methodological strategy to develop models that fully engage multilevel theory. To this end, we propose that many core topics in strategic management are characterized by one or more multilevel theoretical perspectives (Klein and Kozlowski 2000), which ultimately can be examined with multilevel analytic statistics.

In this chapter, we illustrate how these multilevel perspectives are manifest in strategy research, and offer a review of the multilevel methodological tools best suited to examine them. As such, our objective is not to be exhaustive in either our review of multilevel issues in strategy or the many multilevel analytical statistics available to researchers. Rather, and in keeping with the objective of this volume, we seek to build on the work of previous commentators who have made the conceptual argument for multilevel research in strategy (e.g. Drnevich and Shanley 2005) by pointing to a specific methodological approach that strategy researchers might employ if they want to fully and meaningfully engage in multilevel model development.

One more time: why do we need multilevel models ... and what are they?

We are certainly not the first to observe the need for multilevel theory in strategic management research and to call for a greater application and integration of multilevel modeling. Indeed, there is a considerable literature in this regard. Rousseau (1985), Klein and Kozlowski (2000), and Hitt, Beamish, Jackson, and Mathieu (2007) are among the most well-known statements of the case for multilevel research on organizations at large, although earlier statements of the perspective can be found in Simon (1973), and Von Bertalanffy (1968). With respect to strategic management in particular, a recent volume of *Research in Multi-Level Issues* (Dansereau and Yammarino 2005) was devoted to strategy topics, with important 'debates' on the strategy-specific application of multilevel theory and analytical statistics. Scholars have also taken a multilevel theoretical approach to a number of specific theoretical and topical areas in strategic management: international management (Arregle *et al.* 2006; Dess *et al.* 1995); industry- and firm-level effects on performance (Short *et al.* 2006, Short *et al.* 2007); entrepreneurship (Shepherd 2011); strategic human capital (Ployhart and Moliterno 2011); governance (Dalton and Dalton 2011); resource-based theory (Peteraf 2005); upper echelons (Cannella and Holcomb 2005); and network analysis (Moliterno and Mahony 2011) have all been viewed through the lens of multilevel theory.

Considering this body of work, our view is that the question is not one of *whether* multilevel theory and analytical tools should be incorporated into the strategic management literature: they should be and rightly have been. Drnevich and Shanley (2005) offer an insightful perspective in this regard, arguing that the questions examined by strategy scholarship are complex and often studied in the context of large firms. This argument aligns conceptually with the growing interest in research on the "microfoundations" of strategic management constructs (Abell *et al.* 2008; Felin and Foss 2005; Felin and Hesterly 2007), which calls for explicit integration of individual-level heterogeneity into strategy theories on higher-level (i.e. "collective") strategy theories. Accordingly, we concur that the strategy literature is ready – and has long been ready – for a greater integration of multilevel methodology. The question, then, is one of *how* to undertake this endeavor. Given that so many strategic management theories and topics are primed for modeling multilevel questions, researchers working in these domains need clear and concise guidance on how multilevel methodology can be leveraged to explore these questions, how the analytical tools in the multilevel researcher's toolkit are used, and what questions cannot (yet) be fully examined with current multilevel analytical statistics.

Before we embark on providing that guidance, it seems prudent to reiterate in broad strokes the core concepts invoked by the multilevel theoretical perspective. Here again, there exists a rich literature that has explored and developed the intricacies of multilevel theory. As a conceptual approach, multilevel theory has its origins in general systems theory (Simon 1973; Von Bertalanffy 1968) and was developed by organizational scholars (House *et al.* 1995; Rousseau 1985) who posited that organizational phenomena at one level of analysis (e.g. the firm), might have antecedents and/or consequences at another level (e.g. TMT; industry). Conceptually, the core proposition of multilevel theory is quite simple: phenomena of all types are nested within a hierarchical system. Planets are nested within solar systems, which in turn are nested within galaxies. Atoms are nested within elements, which are in turn nested within compounds. In the social sciences, it is interesting to note that nesting occurs as well, across cultures, countries, and time. Thus students are nested within classes and schools, just as employees are nested within work units and organizations. Simply put, nature is hierarchical, and hierarchies are natural.

Nested hierarchical systems dominate organizational life. These structures may be formal (e.g. lines of authority within an organizational chart) or informal (networks of friends and acquaintances). The nature of the hierarchy in organizations is for all practical purposes a reasonable means to define levels. A level is simply a place within the system. For example, a faculty member in a management department lives within several levels: department, school or college, and university. The levels are defined by the way the organization formally has structured itself. Most organizational research has focused on a relatively small number of levels (see Hitt *et al.* 2007): group or team, department or work unit (e.g. store, branch), firm, industry group, industry, country, or culture.

Moving from the general premises of the multilevel perspective to the specific implications, we note that much of the contemporary thinking on multilevel theory was collected in Klein and Kozlowski (2000). Strategy researchers who want fully to leverage the multilevel perspective might well start with this canonical volume: a current and rigorous review of the theory's origins and recent developments can be found in Mathieu and Chen (2011). For our purposes, it's sufficient, but important, to summarize briefly some of the key concepts here. These concern first the distinction between levels of theory, measurement, and analysis, and second the nature of cross-level processes and relationships.

Central to multilevel theorizing and modeling are the distinctions between the levels of "theory," "measurement," and "analysis" (Hitt *et al.* 2007; Kozlowski and Klein 2000; Rousseau 1985). Specifically, the level of theory is the organizational level at which a particular construct or effect is predicted to exist, while the level of measurement is the organizational level where data are collected. To illustrate these ideas in a well-known strategic management context, consider the question of corporate governance. A core research question in this area of inquiry involves the composition of the board of directors and firm performance. Notwithstanding the observation that inquiries into this association are anything but unequivocal,[2] we observe here that the *theory* is at the firm level: researchers examine the association between a firm-level predictor (i.e. composition of the firm's board of directors) and a firm-level outcome (i.e. firm performance). However, *measurement* is at the individual level. For example, the long-standing predictor variable of interest in this literature is whether a director is an "insider" or "outsider," thus measuring an attribute of the individual directors (Dalton *et al.* 2007). Finally, *analysis* is at the firm level, because researchers examine board composition as a firm-level phenomenon and associate it empirically with firm-level performance. As suggested by Dalton and Dalton (2011), the fact that in this literature the levels of measurement and theory are different indicates that multilevel methods are indicated.

Recognizing organizational levels of theory, measurement, and analysis provides a point of entry into understanding the processes that link these different levels. Figure 3.1 illustrates two major types of cross-level models, albeit in a simplified and somewhat reduced manner. In this illustration we follow the common practice of referring to levels with a number, such that higher levels are indicated by a larger number (e.g. Level 2 is of a higher level in the organizational system than Level 1). In addition we use the term "phenomenon" in the most general sense of the term to refer to any construct or within-level association of theoretical interest. We do this only to illustrate how processes work across levels. In this way, we might consider firm-level resources, firm-level performance, and the firm-level association between resources and performance all firm-level "phenomena" for the purposes of Figure 3.1a. Likewise, in Figure 3.1b, we might consider individual-level job satisfaction, individual-level performance, and the individual-level association

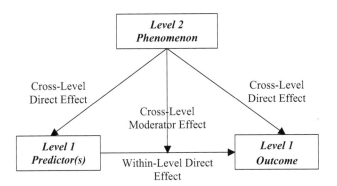

a. Top-down cross-level models

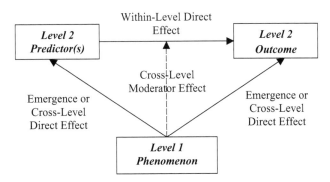

b. Bottom-up cross-level model

FIGURE 3.1 Examples of multilevel models

between job satisfaction and performance all individual-level "phenomena." Later, we will a put a finer point on these ideas, but for the present, our objective is only to illustrate these cross-level models in the most general terms.

The first of these are *top-down* cross-level models (see Figure 3.1a), where phenomena at a higher level of analysis (e.g. industry dynamics) influence the manifestation of a lower-level predictor (e.g. resource) or outcome (e.g. firm-level competitive advantage) construct. These types of cross-level models are sometimes called "contextual" models (Kozlowski and Klein 2000) because the higher-level phenomenon is oftentimes an environmental or background context that affects the lower level in the system. A familiar example might be the industry that provides a context within which all firms compete for market position (Porter 1985). Models of this sort are perhaps the most common in the multilevel literature, and have already begun to be leveraged by strategy scholars (e.g. Short *et al.* 2007). Top-down models are of two types: cross-level direct effects and cross-level interactions. The former describes a model where a higher-level phenomenon directly influences a lower level construct: for example, the effect of industry factors on firm-level profitability. The latter describes a process where a higher level phenomenon moderates the association between predictor(s) and an outcome at the lower level. The literature on dynamic capabilities (Eisenhardt and Martin 2000; Helfat *et al.* 2007) – where environmental factors affect the association between firm-level capabilities and performance – is illustrative of this type of model. Top-down processes, whether direct or moderator, are typically analyzed using hierarchical linear modeling (HLM).

Alternatively, organizational levels can be linked through *bottom-up* cross-level models that occur in the other direction: lower-level phenomena affect the higher level (see Figure 3.1b). The most common type of bottom-up model is known as "emergence" (Kozlowski and Klein 2000). Here we are concerned with how higher-level construct (e.g. organizational capabilities) are manifest as the combination of discrete lower-level phenomena (e.g. resources). The distinction regarding levels of theory and measurement are particularly relevant to understanding emergence. The emergent construct is theorized to exist at the higher level, but is measured at the lower level where the component elements reside. Consider the conceptual perspective of a firm-level capability as an aggregation of resources (Amit and Schoemaker 1993). The level of theory here is at the firm level: we are theoretically interested in capabilities as a firm-level construct. However, a capability comprises individual-level resources, and does not exist except as an aggregation of those resources. Accordingly, if we want to create an empirical measure of some characteristic of the firm-level capability, we must actually sample the individual-level component resources. Thus while the level of theory is the firm level, the level of measurement is the individual level. An example of this can be found in Ployhart and Moliterno (2011) where we described how human capital can be conceptualized as a firm-level resource, but one that is emergent through the aggregation of individual-level human resources. In this way, empirical examination of the theoretically interesting higher-level phenomenon necessarily involves measurement of the lower-level components. Scholars – particularly those working in the strategic management literature – are often theoretically interested in phenomena that exist at the firm level, but which have their component parts at lower levels of the organization: research on strategic groups (Fiegenbaum and Thomas 1990); diversification (Rumelt 1982); and top management team (TMT) demography (Hambrick and Mason 1984; Wiersema and Bantel 1992) are among the theoretical perspectives where emergence models could be specified.

There is a second way to conceptualize bottom-up models, but it is only starting to receive scholarly attention. This is a bottom-up model where the lower-level phenomenon has a direct or moderating effect on the higher level. For example, a single firm may create a new product that significantly alters an industry (e.g. Apple's launch of the iPod changed the nature of competition in digital music player industry). Within a firm, a whistleblower may share information that brings down an entire firm (e.g. Sherron Watkins and Enron), or a "star" employee might affect the performance or attitudes of the group with which they work (Azoulay *et al.* 2010; Lockwood and Kunda 1997). In these examples, an individual entity, whether a firm or an employee, has an effect at the higher level in the system. However, modeling bottom-up effects presents unique empirical challenges. We address these challenges later in this chapter since many strategic management theories and topics fall into the category of bottom-up effects.

The foregoing is certainly not an exhaustive review of the many complex multilevel topics. Thorough treatments of this material abound: readers should consult Klein and Kozlowski's (2000) edited volume, as well as the many seminal and recent articles that have addressed specific topics in this area (Hitt *et al.* 2007; Klein *et al.* 1994; Mathieu and Chen 2011; Rousseau 1985). Such a review is beyond the scope of this chapter, just as is an exhaustive catalogue of the many strategic management theories that might be prime for multilevel examination. Rather, it is our hope that the general principles and examples outlined here might serve as a primer for future researchers to consider whether the research question they are considering might benefit from a multilevel analysis. If they conclude it does, then the question becomes not one of "whether" but rather "how."

Toward a multilevel methodology for strategy research

To help answer the "how" question, in this section we outline a 6-step framework that strategy scholars might follow when designing multilevel studies. Our efforts in this regard are informed by, and draw upon, the framework by Ployhart and Schneider (2005), as well as the broader suggestions of Kozlowski and Klein (2000), Bliese (2000), Chan (1998), LeBreton and Senter (2008), and Chen, Mathieu, and Bliese (2004). Indeed, the fact that we are able to hew so close to this prior research is illustrative of the observation that since organizations are, in general, multilevel systems of relationships, the methodological approach leveraged to examine one particular multilevel phenomenon in that system (e.g. staffing) should be useful in exploring a multilevel phenomenon (e.g. the firm-level dynamic capabilities) existing at a different place in that system. We begin with some general propositions that underlie all multilevel systems.

General propositions

General systems theory has identified several key features of multilevel systems in organizations (Simon 1973; Von Bertalanffy 1968). It is important that we note them at the outset. Doing so will allow us to keep these ideas front and center when considering the methodological issues we discuss below. Moreover, it is important to appreciate that multilevel methodology has a long history, suggesting that at least some of the thorny issues have already had some resolution and do not need to be "rediscovered" (or "resolved") by strategy researchers.

First, levels capture span and scope. As one moves up the organizational hierarchy, the number of observations *below* that level increase, while the number of observations *at* the level decreases. For example, as one moves down the organizational hierarchy there is only one CEO, a relatively small number of executive team members, a larger group of middle managers, and correspondingly larger numbers of employees. Second, lower-level processes move more quickly than higher-level processes. Thus, all else equal, it takes longer for organizations to react than it does for individuals to react. Third, cross-level effects are asymmetrical in the rate at which they occur. That is, top-down effects happen more quickly, and usually more strongly, than bottom-up effects. For example, a firm may change to a performance-based HR system (e.g. pay-for-performance) that causes an immediate change in employee behavior. However, it will take a considerable amount of time for the effects of that system to be felt at the firm level.

Understanding these basic multilevel guiding principles helps researchers better develop and critique cross-level strategy research. For example, knowing that bottom-up effects occur slowly should lead to the recognition that the design of such studies needs to adopt a longitudinal perspective; possibly a lengthy one. On the other hand, researchers should not feel the need to hypothesize and test these guiding principles, as they have been established for nearly 50 years (Klein and Kozlowski 2000; Mathieu and Chen 2011; Rousseau 1985).

Step 1: Articulate the theory and specify relationships

The first step in leveraging multilevel methodology for strategy research is not analytical: it's theoretical. As we will see, this is generally true for the first several steps, and particularly so at the outset. A methodology is only as useful as the theory which it tests, and this is true in multilevel research as in any other area. Accordingly, Step 1 is concerned with articulating the nature of both the within- and cross-level associations in the model being proposed, as well as the theoretical mechanisms linking levels in the model. While the evolution of multilevel research in the micro-level disciplines of OB, HR, and psychology, has been motivated by scholarship on the methodology rather than the application of theory (see, for example, Chan 1998), scholars have long noted that the existence of organizational levels requires a theoretical approach: Rousseau (1985), and Klein, Dansereau, and Hall (1994) offer some of the clearest, most informative frameworks in this regard. Strategy scholars interested in taking a multilevel approach would do well to study these seminal contributions: robust multilevel methodology must start with a robust multilevel theory. In other words, leveraging multilevel methodology does not simply entail multilevel statistical analysis. Rather, the multilevel research should begin with understanding the within-level theoretical associations (most strategy scholars are expert at this), and then looking for causal mechanisms and effects that exist at other levels of the organizational system.

As described above, Figure 3.1 illustrates, in the most general way, two multilevel models. It would be wrong, however, to suggest that the theorizing indicated in this first step is simply an exercise of choosing between a top-down or bottom-up model: the story is much more complex than that. In Figure 3.2, we have essentially combined Figure 3.1a and 3.1b: taken together in this way, we observe that there is (literally!) a web of cross-level associations and processes that can, and should, be illuminated by a robust multilevel approach to any given strategy theory. Stated differently, any attempt to get at the microfoundations of strategy concepts (Abell *et al.* 2008; Felin and Foss 2005; Felin and Hesterly 2007) requires more than identifying one or more theoretical antecedent at a lower (i.e. individual) level in the organizational system. Rather, the search for microfoundations must – on a theory by theory basis – unpack the multidimensional nature of cross-level associations in the system. The corollary of this, of course, is that there will not be *one* multilevel model that applies to all theoretical domains in the strategic management literature. Rather, it falls to the researcher to make the specific theoretical connections that will leverage the multilevel approach to linking organizational levels.

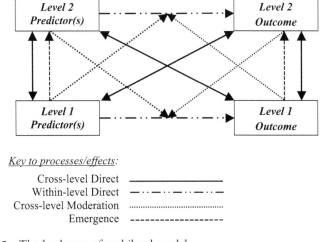

FIGURE 3.2 The landscape of multilevel models

Notions of level of theory are deeply embedded in this step. In strategic management research at least one construct in the focal conceptual model is usually theorized to exist at the firm level of analysis. At this point, there are many paths to a multilevel model. Perhaps a construct at a higher level of theory affects a firm-level construct directly (e.g. industry characteristics have an effect on firm performance; Rumelt 1982). Or perhaps a construct at a higher level of theory moderates a firm-level relationship (e.g. environmental dynamism affects the association between a firm's capabilities and competitive advantage; Eisenhardt and Martin 2000). Or perhaps a construct at a lower level of theory affects the firm-level construct (e.g. human resource bargaining power affects firm-level rent appropriation; Coff 1999). When the theory or research question wanders into such cross-level relationships, a number of theoretical issues arise that need to be addressed:

- What levels of theory do constructs in the model span?
- Why should we expect cross-level associations, and (importantly) when are cross-level associations not theoretically indicated (Kozlowski and Klein 2000)?
- What cross-level processes link those levels?

Consider, for example, strategic management's well-known strategic factor market theory (Barney 1986), which argues that firms can generate rents by strategically acquiring resources in the factor market at prices below the value those resources can create in the firm's product market. This is a single-level theory: firm-level resource acquisition leads to firm-level rent generation. Now, there are many ways to move from this starting point to a multilevel theory. Coff's (1999) argument that human resources are not like other resources, inasmuch as they can appropriate the value they create would suggest one approach to a multilevel extension to factor market theory. In a model of bottom-up cross-level moderation we might argue that the (Level 1) individuals in an organization may have sufficient bargaining power to moderate the (Level 2) firm-level association between human resource acquisition and rent appropriation. This model can be contrasted with Mackey and Barney's (2005) description of how the availability of managerial talent in the labor market affects the firm- and individual-level appropriation of rents created by strategic human capital (i.e. managerial) resources. Here the authors theorize that scarcity of talent in the (Level 3) labor market – which is top-down contextual phenomenon – has effects at both the (Level 2) firm and (Level 1) individual level.[3] In particular, they argue that a scarcity of talent in the labor market moderates the association between firm-level discretion (i.e. the size and risk of managerial decisions) and firm-level rent appropriation, as well as the association between individual-level investments in talent improvements and individual-level rent appropriation. In this way, the authors describe a model that has two top-down cross-level moderations.

These two exemplars illustrate different theoretical paths to a multilevel model from the single-level strategic factor market theory. But these are only two of the potential paths suggested by Figure 3.2. Thus, these studies – even when taken together – may hint at some multilevel extensions of strategic factor market theory, but they do not present a full multilevel perspective on that theory. Indeed, additional progress could be made on a multilevel strategic factor market theory by unpacking any number of the remaining associations and mechanisms represented in Figure 3.2. In this way scholars might examine how a firm's existing (Level 2) capabilities effect the rent generating value of (Level 1) resources acquired *de novo* in the factor market (Adegbesan 2009; Clougherty and Moliterno 2010; Maritan and Peteraf 2011): this is a top-down moderation model. Or researchers might examine how (Level 2) firm-level competitive advantage emerges from an aggregation of (Level 1) resource-level rent generation: this is an emergence model. Or researchers might examine how (Level 3) strategic factor market conditions effect the firm's (Level 2) resource decision-making (Moliterno and Wiersema 2007): this is a top-down direct effect model.

Our point here is that leveraging multilevel methodology for strategy research begins with taking a particular theoretical domain of strategy research, identifying the level of that theory, and then (minimally) moving up and down (Hackman 2003) the levels in the organizational system to better understand the within-level associations predicted by the extant theory. Of course, where this process leads, and how elaborate a multilevel model this approach yields, will be idiosyncratic to the respective theory being considered: it is well beyond the scope of this chapter to attempt to outline what this model might look like for even the most central strategic management theories. However, we point readers toward notable exemplars. First, Cannella and Holcomb (2005) offer an exceptionally thorough multilevel perspective on upper-echelons theory. Second, Short, Palmer, and Ketchen (2003) leverage multilevel concepts to offer an insightful integration of the resource-based and strategic groups theoretical perspectives. Both of these works offer a multilevel perspective on a strategy theory, and as such illustrate quite well the nature and depth of theorizing we advocate.

We are hopeful, then, that strategy scholars will integrate more explicitly the work of our micro-level colleagues who have described the construction of such multilevel theoretical models (Klein *et al.* 1994; Klein and Kozlowski 2000; Rousseau 1985). At the same time, we note that where the micro-level multilevel research has been focused predominantly on the methodology, the extant multilevel work in the strategy domain has been focused largely on making conceptual progress on such theoretical models. Like Coff (1999) and Mackey and Barney (2005), this work has endeavored to make the connections between levels and/or specify the theoretical mechanisms by which such connections occur. A thoughtful example of work on the mechanisms that connect levels in strategy research can be found in Drnevich and Shanley (2005), where the authors argue that the core constructs in strategic management – competitive advantage and value creation – are fundamentally multilevel in nature and suggest three mechanisms that link the levels embedded in these constructs: "transaction," "managerial role," and "atmosphere." Of course, the latter is largely a top-down cross-level contextual effect. Other examples of conceptual work on mechanisms that link these levels can be found in Eisenhardt *et al.* (2010) who consider the role of organizational leadership, and Teece's (2007) well-known "sensing"/"seizing"/ "transforming" framework. Inasmuch as fully integrating multilevel methodology into strategy research requires a robust justification for linking levels of theory, the extant strategy research on cross-level mechanisms suggests that a necessary piece of the puzzle is in place for scholars interested in answering the call to more fully integrate the methodological tools that have been specifically designed to develop multilevel models.

This is not to say that all theoretical questions in strategy research are, or need be, multilevel in nature. For example, the relationship between the structure of a firm's collaboration network and its innovation output (e.g. Ahuja 2000) is a perfectly acceptable, and interesting, area for strategy research. It is also one that can be theorized about within a single level of analysis (i.e. firm-level), and there is clearly well-established theory to inform such within-level relationships. However, we could also frame our interest in this phenomenon by looking at how the individual-level networks of the scientists who participate in firm-level collaborations effect firm-level innovation output (Moliterno and Mahony 2011). The former approach makes progress on understanding a within-level effect of particular theoretical interest to strategy scholars. The latter adds the multilevel perspective to that understanding.

Specifying multilevel models for strategy scholarship will necessarily require strategy researchers to work outside of their zone of theoretical comfort. For example, in our consideration of the origins of the strategically important firm-level human capital resource, Ployhart and Moliterno (2011) proposed that an "emergence enabling process" affected the nature of the emergent human capital resource. In this way, we employed a multilevel perspective to articulate the microfoundations (Felin and Hesterly 2007) of firm-level human capital. We drew on insights from the extensive I/O psychology literature (e.g. Schmidt and Hunter 1998) as well as the voluminous groups and teams literature (e.g. Kozlowski and Ilgen 2006). Accordingly, strategy researchers interested in testing or extending the ideas in Ployhart and Moliterno (2011) will be required to immerse themselves in these (perhaps) foreign literatures if they want to examine the constructs and mechanisms embedded in the original model. This is non-trivial since it requires strategy researchers, who are generally trained to theorize at the firm and industry level, to fully understand the nature of within-level theoretical associations at lower levels of analysis. Interdisciplinary research provides an efficient way to address this challenge. Indeed, we believe the interdisciplinary nature of our collaboration (one micro researcher and one macro researcher) played a vital role in our efforts at building the multilevel model described in Ployhart and Moliterno (2011).

Emergence

When the theoretical model being specified includes an emergence process, some additional theoretical work is indicated. In particular, when considering an emergence process, it falls to the researcher to articulate the theoretical justification for why it is appropriate for lower-level phenomena to coalesce into a higher level phenomenon. The firm-level focus of strategic management research frequently, and necessarily, invokes collective-level constructs (e.g. firm-level knowledge, experience, capabilities, etc.) and yet seldom specified is the exact process mechanism at work in the formation of these collective constructs. In particular, there are two distinct modes of emergence described in the multilevel literature: "composition" and "compilation" (Kozlowski and Klein 2000). The distinction between composition and compilation are important inasmuch as the two different theoretical processes require different measurement and empirical strategies. Accordingly, the theoretical specification of the mode of emergence is an important element of Step 1.

While determining the appropriate mode of emergence is a theoretical concern, it is perhaps easiest to describe the difference between composition and compilation in methodological terms. In emergent constructs characterized by composition, the homogeneity among some lower-level construct is an important determinant of the higher-level construct, whereas in compilation models variation in the lower-level construct is the important attribution when considering the higher- or collective-level construct. In both cases, the higher level construct is only partially isomorphic (i.e. theoretically and conceptually equivalent [Rousseau 1985]) with its lower-level origins. Conceptually, then, the distinction between composition and compilation models of emergence comes down to the degree to which the lower- and higher-level constructs are, respectively, based on similarity (homogeneity) or dissimilarity (heterogeneity) (Klein and Kozlowski 2000). Because composition models are based on homogeneity, the average level of the higher-level construct's lower-level components is an appropriate measure. Conversely, in compilation models, when constructs are based on heterogeneity or variability, some measure of variation is required.

Consider, first, innovation. If there is a performance return to a single innovation at the lower-level (e.g. the iPod), then we might well theorize that a performance benefit to being a very innovative firm (e.g. Apple). This might lead us to theorize a composition model of emergence for innovation, such that greater firm-level innovation – measured as, say, the average number of patents per year (Rothaermel and Hess 2007) – might be predicted to be associated with greater firm-level performance. Now consider knowledge. While greater levels of knowledge pay a performance dividend at the individual-level (Schmidt and Hunter 1998), variation in knowledge structures may be more beneficial for performance at the organizational level (March 1991). Of course, the conceptual arguments and empirical findings in both the innovation and knowledge literatures are more complicated than we characterize them to be here. Our argument is only that a multilevel model of organizational innovation or knowledge would necessarily need to consider how the observation of the innovation or knowledge construct at the firm-level emerges from the lower-level constructs it comprises. This is a necessary first step since, as we have noted (and will discuss more below), the theoretical distinction between composition and compilation models of the emergence process has measurement implications. This illustrates clearly the significance in the distinction between levels of theory and measurement: an emergence process demonstrates how a construct at a given level of theory might actually be measured at a lower level.

Two caveats are in order. First, composition and compilation anchor a continuum of emergence models: readers should consult Kozlowski and Klein (2000) for a thorough discussion of the many forms of emergence falling between pure-form composition and compilation; Bliese (2000) and Chan (1998) make important related arguments. Second, while most strategy research has articulated composition models, this is purely a function of the types of questions most strategy scholars focus upon, which generally operate at the firm level of theory but are measured at a lower level. Indeed, this proposition is fundamental to the interest in the microfoundations of strategy. Yet we believe both composition and compilation models have an important role in strategy research. Moreover, this might be true even within a single theoretical framework. For example, if we conceptualize firm-level capabilities as a combination of individual-level resources (Amit and Schoemaker 1993), we might theorize that a composition model is appropriate: higher quality resources, on average, should make for a higher quality capability. So when considering a firm's R&D capability, our hypothesis might be that if a research scientist's innovation productivity is a function of her career tenure, firms where the research scientists have, on average, longer career tenure should have a more productive R&D capability, *ceteris paribus*, than firms where the scientists have a shorter average career tenure. Alternatively, we might theorize a compilation model. Here we might predict that diversity in career tenure is valuable inasmuch as younger scientists infuse an R&D capability with fresh perspectives. This would lead us to predict that a firms where the research scientists have, on average, more diverse career tenure should have a more productive R&D capability, *ceteris paribus*, than firms where the scientist have less diverse career tenure.

The foregoing example highlights the important issue: specification of the mode of the emergence process is primarily a *theoretical* concern. When developing a model where a construct theorized to exist at a particular level of the organizational system comprises components that are measured at a lower level, it falls to the multilevel researcher to articulate the appropriate theory of emergence: why do the lower level data aggregate, and what is the theoretical mechanism which manifests that aggregation? Ultimately, it is the theoretical mechanisms that will inform the particular mode of emergence. For example, in Ployhart and Moliterno (2011) we focused our attention on describing the process that affects the emergence of a unit-level human capital resource from individual-level human resources. Of course, once that theoretical mechanism has been specified, the researcher can begin to consider what measure of aggregation is the appropriate: we discuss testing inferences of aggregation in Step 5.

Step 2: Specify levels of measurement

The specification of different levels in models of multilevel systems has important measurement implications. Accordingly, in Step 2 we turn our attention to measurement and the need to clearly identify the level at which the constructs in the multilevel model will be measured. We again comment first on general multilevel measurement issues, and then consider measurement of emergence in particular. The distinction between the level of theory and the level of measurement is both relevant and non-trivial, and it falls to the researcher to appropriately match the level of theory with the level of measurement (Klein *et al.* 1994; Rousseau 1985). When a phenomenon is theorized to exist at a particular level, but it is measured at a different level, the resulting mismatch between levels of theory and measurement make it hard, if not impossible, to draw meaningful inferences from any related empirical analysis. Klein *et al.* (1994: 206) provide a useful example of this in their commentary on Lawless and Price's (1992) theoretical model of technology champions.

For most research in general, and for strategy research in particular, the level of theory and the level of measurement are identical. For example, resource-based theory (Barney 1991; Peteraf 1993; Rumelt 1984; Wernerfelt 1984) theorizes that firm-level resources have an association with firm-level performance. Accordingly, both resources and performance have been measured at the firm level in this body of work (Newbert 2007). However, frequently the level of theory and level of measurement are different. For example Silverman (1999) measured the firm-level "technological resource applicability" with data collected at the level of the firm's individual patents. Perhaps the most obvious example levels of measurement and theory in the strategy literature comes from empirical work on upper echelon theory (Hambrick and Mason 1984). To illustrate this (and other points we'll want to make about measurement), we draw on Wiersema and Bantel's (1992) well-known research on firm-level diversification strategy. Consistent with the arguments found in the upper echelons literature, Wiersema and Bantel theorized that top management team's (TMT's) "cognitive base" would be associated with corporate change: this is a within-level (firm-level) association. However, the researchers measured the TMT's cognitive base with the individual-level demographic variables age, organizational tenure, executive tenure, educational level, and educational specialization. While the authors don't use multilevel language, this is clearly a process of emergence. Moreover, the researchers' discuss of how "homogeneity" and "heterogeneity" in the demographic variables shape the (emergent) firm-level construct (Wiersema and Bantel 1992: 95–96). Recalling our earlier comments, this is notable inasmuch as it a clearly articulated theory of whether the process of emergence is a composition or compilation model.

Emergence

Perhaps the place where level of measurement concerns is greatest is when specifying an emergence process in the multilevel model. There are a range of important measurement issues to consider when studying emergence. Empirically, emergence is operationalized via aggregation (Bliese 2000), which is the methodological basis for taking actual measurements at the lower level and combining these scores to create a valid measure of the higher-level phenomenon. Thus, whether considering a composition or compilation model, the emergence of higher-level phenomena from lower-level phenomena concludes with the creation of an aggregate value measuring some higher level variable of theoretical interest (e.g. TMT cognitive base in Wiersema and Bantel, 1992). This higher-level score is then used to influence or predict other outcomes or processes at the same or lower levels. For example, organizational climate emerges from individuals, but can then be used to predict firm performance (a within-level effect) or individual performance (a cross-level effect).

It is important to recognize that bottom-up effects usually work indirectly on higher-level outcomes, through emergence processes or by influencing the emergence of predictor constructs. More recent research is starting to consider how a lower-level phenomenon can influence a collective (e.g., Mollick 2012), either directly or by moderating a higher-level predictor-criterion relationship. However, such theory is just starting to appear, and to our knowledge there is currently no way to statistically model a lower-level phenomenon directly influencing a higher-construct (e.g. a front-line employee influencing the firm's performance): we comment more in this below when we discuss analytical statistics.

Finally, it is important to note that it is possible that different measurement strategies will be necessary for the core predictors and outcomes in a given multilevel model (Ployhart and Schneider 2005). Of course, and again, these methodological decisions will be driven by the theory underlying the model. Drawing on Wiersema and Bantel (1992) again, we note that both the core predictor and the firm-level outcome in the model ("strategic change") were emergent. Here the researchers conceptualized the firm-level strategic change as absolute percentage change in the firm's diversification strategy, which they measured using Jacquemin and Berry's (1979) entropy measure of diversification. Note that in this way they specified different theories of emergence for the predictor and outcome variables and accordingly employed different measurement strategies for each. Moreover, note that the firm-level predictor construct (cognitive base) was measured at the individual level, whereas the firm-level outcome variable (corporate change) was measured at the business unit level. Of course, a different multilevel model might theorize emergence (and thus use lower-level measurement) only for the predictors, while theorizing and measuring the outcome at the firm level (e.g. firm performance measured with stock market or accounting measures).

Step 3: Sample the appropriate number of units at each level of the model

The importance of the multilevel guiding principles mentioned earlier becomes apparent when thinking about sampling. In multilevel studies, the sample sizes will necessarily change across levels, such that higher levels will nearly always have fewer observations than lower levels (e.g. firms and employees nested within firms). Importantly, researchers need a sufficient number of higher- and lower-level observations to conduct a cross-level study: statistical power issues are always important in statistical analysis, and they are complicated in multilevel designs (Mathieu *et al.* 2012). Consider for example, the multilevel approach to studying strategic groups (Short *et al.* 2003). As described in Fiegenbaum and Thomas (1990) a single industry might comprise six or seven strategic groups, which in turn comprise the top 30 firms.[4] If we wanted, then, to examine the top-down cross-level effect of an attribute of this industry (Porter 1980; 1985) on the strategic groups nested within it, we would lack the statistical power to analyze such an effect since the higher-level (i.e. industry level) sample size is one.

To understand the appropriate sample size in multilevel studies, it is helpful to think about a simple heuristic suggested by Kreft and DeLeeuw (1998). These authors propose a '30-30" rule: optimal statistical power occurs when there are at least 30 higher-level observations and at least 30 lower-level observations nested within each higher-level observation. Thus, to fully examine the top-down effects of industries on competitive groups, a researcher would need to sample 30 industries, with 30 competitive groups nested in each (thus, 900 lower-level observations). A multilevel study of top-down industry-level effects on individual firms would also require 30 industries with 900 nested firms. Note that in these two examples, it doesn't matter (empirically) whether firms or strategic groups are the Level 1 observations: what matters is the sample size at the nested level. If there are fewer higher-level observations (e.g. fewer than 30 industries), then the researcher needs to increase the number of lower level observations (e.g. sample more than 900 firms); and vice versa.

Kreft and DeLeeuw's (1998) 30-30 rule is simply a heuristic to help researchers understand statistical power in multilevel studies. However, it is important to note that issues of power in such studies are complicated: Mathieu *et al.* (2012) offer a detailed discussion. The important point for strategy researchers who are interested in multilevel methodology is that the power requirements of these approaches necessitate sample frames that are considerably large, and perhaps larger than often used by strategy researchers. Nonetheless, it is vital to have a sufficient number of observations at both higher and lower levels if one has any hope of finding statistically significant cross-level effects.

Step 4: Use appropriate measures

Having developed the theory, the level of measurement, and the appropriate sampling frame, the multilevel researcher then needs to construct appropriate measures at the level of measurement. The suggestion here is as basic as those found in any measurement or research design course. First, measures are only as good as the theories upon which they are based. Vague or imprecise theories contribute to vague or imprecise measures. Second, one does not actually care about measures, but rather the scores that are provided by the measures. For example, researchers may use patent-level data as a measure of firm-level technological applicability (Silverman 1999), but the patent-level data are imperfect indicators of attributes of the firm-level technological capabilities, which is the construct of real interest. Third, construct validity refers to whether the scores from a measure are consistent with their intended purpose. For example, individual-level traits may be useful for predicting a TMT's shared mental models (Hambrick and Mason 1984), but not organizational culture. Finally, it is necessary that the measures show with sufficient reliability that it is possible to make valid inferences about their meaning.

These points need to be considered within multilevel contexts, which can be challenging because there are now other sources of variance that influence the measures and hence their corresponding scores. For example, strong contextual effects may introduce range restriction (restricted variance) on a set of scores within an organization, but offer great variability across organizations. Hence, the evaluation of measures, scores, construct validity, and reliability, must be done in light of multilevel theory (see Dyer *et al.* 2005; LeBreton and Senter 2008; Ludke *et al.* 2011; Zyphur *et al.* 2008).

Step 5: Test inferences of aggregation

Step 5 is concerned specifically with testing emergence processes. Consider first *composition* models of emergence which, as noted above, are based on similarity or homogeneity. Hence, estimates of agreement are necessary to statistically evaluate where there is sufficient similarity. There are three main indices which we briefly summarize here (see LeBreton and Senter [2008] and Cohen and Doveh [2005] for a detailed treatments of these approaches).

First, the intraclass correlation coefficient (ICC)1 is an estimate of how much variance is attributable to within and between unit effects. The ICC1 ranges from 0 to 1, with higher numbers indicating greater variance due to higher-level effects. For example, an ICC1 of 0.25 for firm performance suggests that 25 percent of the variance in firm performance is due to higher level phenomena. Most ICC1 estimates will be less than 0.30, and outside of the laboratory, substantially less. Generally speaking, one tests the statistical significance of the ICC1, and if it is greater than zero given chance levels, it is taken as statistical evidence for aggregation. Bliese (2000) offers a very readable introduction to the ICC1, and Cohen and Doveh (2005) describe both the formal statistical models underlying ICC and the inferences that can be drawn from this estimate.

Second, the ICC2 is an estimate of the reliability of the unit's mean score (e.g. the firm level climate score). ICC2 estimates are treated like reliability in a more traditional sense. ICC2 estimates range from 0 to 1, with higher numbers indicating higher reliability. ICC2 estimates are heavily affected by sample size: units with five members will have lower ICC2 estimates than units with 50 members, *ceteris paribus*. For analyses that occur within a level, where the data are based on aggregation, it becomes vital to have reasonably high ICC2 estimates. Again, Bliese (2000) provides a simple introduction into the ICC2.

Finally, r_{wg} is an estimate of agreement that compares an observed distribution to a hypothesized distribution (usually a null distribution). If there is homogeneity greater than chance, the observed distribution will differ from the one that is based on zero agreement (James 1982; James *et al.* 1984). In this manner it is possible to compare an observed distribution to different plausible alternative distributions based on different assumptions about agreement. Usually, all three indices are reported because they provide different pieces of information (LeBreton and Senter 2008). ICC1 estimates and r_{wg} help determine whether there is sufficient between-unit variability and agreement to aggregate lower level scores to the higher level, while ICC2 estimates help determine whether the reliability of the higher-level scores allows for meaningful statistical inferences.

When theorizing a *compilation* model of emergence, where the higher-level constructs are based on dissimilarity or heterogeneity, the situation is somewhat more straight forward: there is no need to demonstrate similarity because compilation models are inherently about variability. In this way, TMT diversity cannot exist at the individual level, it is only a property of the higher-level group. However, there are different types of compilation models that may exist such as Blau's (1960) diversity index (see Harrison and Klein [2007] for a variety of indices for demographic diversity). It is vital that the theory underlying the compilation form of emergence clearly specify the type of variability of interest. In all cases, the indices are based on dispersion.

Step 6: Use appropriate analytical statistics

Note that we only now come to data analysis! As the foregoing illustrates, multilevel methodology is about much more than multilevel statistical analysis – in fact, statistical analyses are usually the easiest part. While we think that the strategy literature will make considerable progress on developing multilevel models by following the five foregoing steps, empirical researchers will ultimately need to test their multilevel conceptual models empirically. The previous section summarizes the core analytical tools (i.e. the aggregate indices) that are usually the focus of statistical analysis of bottom-up models. In contrast, top-down effects are usually modeled using different statistical procedures. Accordingly, in this section we briefly comment on hierarchical linear models (HLM).

HLM is used to model top-down effects (cross-level direct and moderation effects). Excellent overviews of HLM can be found in Hofmann (1997), Aguinis *et al.* (2013), and Raudenbush and Bryk (2002). The key statistical consequence of nesting that is inherent in multilevel systems is non-independence. Within hierarchical systems, lower-level observations are not entirely independent, and this non-independence produces some degree of similarity among the individual observations. When such non-independence is present, it shrinks standard errors and increases Type I error rates. HLM estimates and incorporates this non-independence directly into the analysis, so that cross-level effects are correctly estimated and tested. Conceptually, HLM is just a merging of regression and ANOVA; it is regression at lower levels with between-group differences (ANOVA) in the estimates.

Simply put, HLM models lower- and higher-level effects simultaneously. To illustrate, let us consider a multilevel model that examines a key proposition in the dynamic capabilities literature: namely, the effect of industry dynamism on the firm-level association between capabilities and performance (Eisenhardt and Martin 2000). Let Level 1 and 2 refer to the lower- (i.e., firm-) and higher- (industry-) level effects, respectively. HLM, then, models:

$$\text{Level 1:} Y_{ij} = B_{0j} + B_{1j} \text{(capabilities}_{ij}) + e_{ij}$$
$$\text{Level 2:} B_{0j} = g_{00} + g_{01} \text{(industry}_j) + u_{0j}$$
$$B_{1j} = g_{10} + g_{11} \text{(industry}_j) + u_{1j}$$

Just like in a typical regression, Y is the outcome of interest at Level 1 (e.g. some measure of "technological" or "evolutionary fitness" as described by Helfat *et al.* 2007), B_o is the intercept or estimated score on Y when capabilities are zero, B_1 is the slope or relationship between firm-level capabilities and the performance outcome Y. If there is non-independence, then the residuals (e) will not meet the assumptions of the regression model. Therefore, HLM can relax these assumptions by modeling the Level 2 variability via the estimates u. Variability can be modeled in the intercept, such that the estimated mean score when the Level 1 predictor is zero (B_o) is variable (U_o) across Level 2 observations. Variability can also be modeled in the slope, such that the estimated slope B_1 is variable (U_1) across Level 2 observations. Thus, the intercepts and/or slopes at Level 1 may differ across observations at Level 2.

To the extent such Level 2 variability exits, it is possible to explain it. For example, this model can test the hypothesis that differences in industries causes the variation in firm-level intercepts and slopes, such that some industries produce higher measures of some firm-level performance variable Y and some industries moderate the relationship between firm-level capabilities and performance Y. Thus, the Level 2 questions have a predictor (industry) as part of the model. The model $B_{0j} = g_{00} + g_{01} \text{(industry}_j) + u_{0j}$ tests the direct-effect relationship shown in Figure 3.1a, while the model $B_{1j} = g_{10} + g_{11} \text{(industry}_j) + u_{1j}$ tests the cross-level moderator effect shown in Figure 3.1a. Thus, the HLM model tests all of the arrows illustrated in Figure 3.1a. While a full discussion of HLM is outside the scope of this chapter, the foregoing example simply demonstrates how top-down effects are modeled empirically. We reiterate that we feel the "heavy lifting" in multilevel methodology is in the theoretical set-up of the models.

Finally, it is important to note, equally briefly, that to our knowledge, there are no commonly-used statistical methodologies that can be employed to model bottom-up direct effects. Rather, it is most common for bottom-up effects to be represented in terms of emergence, and then the higher-level emergent construct linked to higher-level outcomes (i.e. via a within-level effect). We have already discussed analytical tools for testing emergence processes that can be used in this manner. To be sure, scholars require a robust statistical approach to model bottom-up direct effects if multilevel models are to be fully integrated into the strategy literature. This is particularly the case if scholarship hopes to make progress on understanding the microfoundations of strategy constructs (Abell *et al.* 2008; Felin and Foss 2005; Felin and Hesterly 2007), which we understand as largely an inquiry into bottom-up models. So while additional analytical tools are needed, we are encouraged by promising new approaches to modeling bottom-up effects: see Croon and van Veldhoven (2007) and Mollick (2012) for two different approaches. However, these models appear to be less cross-level, and more single-level, in their ultimate application. That is, these models would appear to be less useful in explaining the direct effect of a lower-level construct on one at a higher-level than they do in helping us parameterize a higher-level construct (e.g. by deconstructing it into its lower level components) which can then be associated with another higher-level (i.e. within-level construct). We expect to see considerably more methodological attention to analytical statistics for modeling cross-level effects in the near future, and are encouraging of those efforts.

Conclusion and a look ahead

The time is indeed right for strategy scholars to take (another?) look at leveraging multilevel methodology. We suspect that one reason that there has been limited adoption of multilevel methodology in the strategy literature is owing to the misperception that multilevel issues are limited to the more "micro" areas of management scholarship. While it is true that multilevel management research is more dominant in micro HR and OB, multilevel theory and methods are based upon broader systems theory (Simon 1973; Von Bertalanffy 1968), and as we have illustrated in this chapter, are well-suited to the organizational systems of interest to strategy scholars.

We suspect that recent conceptual arguments regarding the microfoundations of strategy constructs (Abell *et al.* 2008; Felin and Foss 2005; Felin and Hesterly 2007) will encourage scholars to take a renewed look at multilevel methodology. At various points throughout this chapter we have noted that the core argument surrounding microfoundations – as we understand it – seems distinctly positioned to leverage the power of multilevel methodology. To date, inquiry into the microfoundations of strategy has been the subject of more theorizing than empirical testing. Theory is obviously vital for understanding, but ultimately empirical research is needed to evaluate the veracity of these theories. We suspect that the difficulty for microfoundations research in making the transition to empirical testing comes from the methodological challenges associated with questions about multilevel phenomena: as we've noted, most strategy scholars are not expert in multilevel methodology. Yet, by definition the "microfoundations project" (Abell *et al.* 2008: 489) spans multiple levels of analysis. Thus, addressing these multilevel issues is the *sine qua non* for the appropriate modeling and testing of microfoundations questions.

Interestingly, in one of the original calls for greater inquiry into microfoundations, Felin and Foss (2005) appear somewhat less optimistic than we are about the prospects of a greater integration of multilevel theory. In particular, they raise four concerns: the borrowing of psychological theories and applying them to higher level; viewing analysis at all levels as somehow complementary and equally valid; the presence of an upward infinite regress associated with levels of theory; and how lower-level constructs transform into higher-level ones. We agree that these are all potential problems ... but they all occur due to a misapplication of multilevel methodology. Aligning with comments we made in describing our 6-step framework, we suggest that these concerns arise due to, respectively, cross-level fallacies (Rousseau 1985) owing to assumptions of isomorphism (Kozlowski and Klein 2000); inadequate theorizing concerning the mechanisms and processes embedded in the multilevel model; carelessness in specifying levels of theory, measurement, and analysis; and poorly specified models of emergence.

In short, we wholehearted agree with Felin and Foss' observation that "arguing that individuals are heterogeneous does not imply that the collective level is non-existent or unimportant. Rather, it suggests the importance of *explicitly linking the individual and the collective levels*" (2005: 443 emphasis added). It is this linkage that multilevel methodology is uniquely positioned to achieve. Our hope is that this chapter helps interested scholars make that connection.

More generally, we feel that strategy research is at the threshold of making great progress on developing multilevel models that will extend and enrich the existing literature. To paraphrase Kozlowski and Klein (2000: 11) we believe many strategy scholars are interested in not only "thinking macro" but also "thinking micro." Indeed, it is an established part of the strategy canon that the firm as embedded in a broader industry and environmental context ... that middle managers affect firm-level decision-making ... that discrete resources are combined to create capabilities that yield competitive advantage ... etc. These are all fundamentally multilevel propositions. And so the time is (still) right for strategy scholars to leverage the very robust multilevel methodology that has been developed over the past 50 years on a separate, but parallel scholarly track. We look forward to the next generation of strategy research that illuminates how the firm is affected by both the context and foundations of the hierarchical organizational system in which it is embedded.

Notes

1 We thank Rory Eckardt for his helpful insights and feedback.
2 Interestingly, Dalton and Dalton (2011) suggest that this fact may be owing to a lack of multilevel studies in the literature.

3   Figures 3.1 and 3.2 present only two levels of analysis, purely for expositional simplicity. Of course, there are multiple levels that can, and do, occur in any organizational system. In Mackey and Barney (2005) the authors describe three levels, which we indicate by adding a higher-level Level 3: naturally, the numbers labeling levels are irrelevant, but convention dictates that the lowest level is always denoted as Level 1.

4   As noted in Fiegenbaum and Thomas (1990) there were actually some 5000 firms in the industry they studied (insurance). However, the authors focused only on the top 30, and used this subsample to elicit the number of strategic groups in the industry.

References

Abell, P., Felin, T., and Foss, N. (2008) "Building micro-foundations for the routines, capabilities, and performance links," *Managerial and Decision Economics*, 29: 489–502.

Adegbesan, J. A. (2009) "On the origins of competitive advantage: Strategic factor markets and heterogeneous resource complementarity," *Academy of Management Review*, 34: 463–475.

Aguinis, H., Gottfredson, R. K., and Culpepper, S. A. (2013) "Best practice recommendations for estimating cross-level interaction effects using multilevel modeling," *Journal of Management*, 39: 1490–1528.

Ahuja, G. (2000) "Collaboration networks, structural holes, and innovation: A longitudinal study," *Administrative Science Quarterly*, 45: 425–455.

Amit, R. and Schoemaker, P. J. H. (1993) "Strategic assets and organizational rent," *Strategic Management Journal*, 14: 33–46.

Arregle, J.-L., Hébert, L., and Beamish, P. W. (2006) "Mode of international entry: The advantages of multilevel models," *Management International Review*, 46: 597–618.

Azoulay, P., Graff Zivin, J. S. and Wang, J. (2010) "Superstar extinction," *Quarterly Journal of Economics*, 25: 549–589.

Barney, J. B. (1986) "Strategic factor markets: Expectations, luck, and business strategy," *Management Science*, 32: 1231–1241.

Barney, J. B. (1991) "Firm resources and sustained competitive advantage," *Journal of Management*, 17: 99–120.

Blau, P. M. (1960) "Patters of deviation in workgroups," *Sociometry*, 23: 245–261.

Bliese, P. D. (2000) "Within-group agreement, non-independence, and reliability: Implications for data aggregation and analysis," in K. J. Klein and S. W. J. Kozlowski (eds) *Multilevel Theory, Research, and Methods in Organizations, Foundations, Extensions, and New Directions*, San Francisco: Jossey-Bass Publishers, 349–381.

Cannella, A. A. and Holcomb, T. R. (2005) "A multi-level analysis of the upper-echelons model," in F. Dansereau and F. J. Yammarino (eds) *Multi-Level Issues in Strategy and Methods: Research in Multi-level Issues*, Boston: Elsevier (JAI Press), 197–237.

Chan, D. (1998) "Functional relations among constructs in the same conent domain at different levels of analysis: A typology of composition models," *Journal of Applied Psychology*, 83: 234–246.

Chen, G., Mathieu, J. E., and Bliese, P. D. (2004) "A framework for conducting multilevel construct validation," in F. Dansereau and F. J. Yammarino (eds) *Multi-level Issues in Organizational Behavior and Processes: Research in Multi-level Issues*, Oxford: Elsevier Science, 273–303.

Clougherty, J. A. and Moliterno, T. P. (2010) "Empirically eliciting complementarities in capabilities: Integrating quasi-experimental and panel data methodologies," *Strategic Organization*, 8: 107–131.

Coff, R. W. (1999) "When competitive advantage doesn't lead to performance: The resource-based view and stakeholder bargaining power," *Organization Science,* 10: 119–133.

Cohen, A. and Doveh, E. (2005) "Significance tests for differences between dependent intraclass correlation coefficients (ICCs)," in F. Dansereau and F. J. Yammarino (eds) *Multi-Level Issues in Strategy and Methods: Research in Multi-level Issues,* Boston: Elsevier (JAI Press), 375–420.

Croon, M. A. and van Veldhoven, M. J. P. M. (2007) "Predicting group-level outcome variables from variables measured at the individual level: A latent variable multilevel model," *Psychological Methods,* 12: 45–57.

Dalton, D. R. and Dalton, C. M. (2011) "Integration of micro and macro studies in governance research: CEO duality, board composition, and financial performance," *Journal of Management,* 37: 404–411.

Dalton, D. R., Hitt, M. A., Certo, S. T. and Dalton, C. M. (2007) "The fundamental agency problem and its mitigation," *The Academy of Management Annals,* 1: 1–64.

Dansereau, F. and Yammarino, F. J. (eds) (2005) *Multi-level issues in Strategy and Methods:Research in Multi-level Issues,* Boston: Elsevier (JAI Press).

Dess, G. G., Gupta, A. K., Hennart, J.-F., and Hill, C. W. L. (1995) "Conducting and integrating strategy research at the international, corporate, and business levels: Issues and directions," *Journal of Management,* 21: 357–393.

Drnevich, P. L. and Shanley, M. (2005) "Multi-level issues for strategic management research: Implications for creating value and competitive advantage," in F. Dansereau and F. J. Yammarino (eds) *Multi-Level Issues in Strategy and Methods: Research in Multi-level Issues,* Boston: Elsevier (JAI Press), 116–162.

Dyer, N. G., Hanges, P. J., and Hall, R. J. (2005) "Applying multilevel confirmatory factor analysis techniques to the study of leadership," *Leadership Quarterly,* 16: 149–167.

Eisenhardt, K. M. and Martin, J. A. (2000) "Dynamic capabilities: what are they?," *Strategic Management Journal,* 21: 1105–1121.

Eisenhardt, K. M., Furr, N. R. and Bingham, C. B. (2010) "Microfoundations of performance: Balancing efficiency and flexibility in dynamic environments," *Organization Science,* 21: 1263–1273.

Felin, T. and Foss, N. J. (2005) "Strategic organization: A field in search of micro-foundations," *Strategic Organization,* 3: 441–455.

Felin, T. and Hesterly, W. S. (2007) "The knowledge-based view, nested heterogeneity, and new value creation: Philosophical considerations on the locus of knowledge," *Academy of Management Review,* 35: 195–218.

Fiegenbaum, A. and Thomas, H. (1990) "Strategic groups and performance: The US insurance industry, 1970–84," *Strategic Management Journal,* 11: 197–215.

Hackman, J. R. (2003) "Learning more by crossing levels: Evidence from airplanes, hospitals, and orchestras," *Journal of Organizational Behavior,* 24: 905–922.

Hambrick, D. C. and Mason, P. A. (1984) "Upper echelons: The organization as a reflection of its top managers," *Academy of Management Review,* 9: 193–206.

Harrison, D. A. and Klein, K. J. (2007) "What"s the difference? Diversity constructs as separation, variety, or disparity in organizations," *Academy of Management Review,* 32: 1199–1228.

Helfat, C. E., Finkelstein, S., Mitchell, W., Peteraf, M. A., Singh, H., Teece, D. J., and Winter, S. G. (2007) *Dynamic Capabilities: Understanding Strategic Change in Organizations,* Malden, MA: Blackwell Publishing.

Hitt, M. A., Beamish, P. W., Jackson, S. E., and Mathieu, J. E. (2007) "Building theoretical and empirical bridges across levels: Multilevel research in management," *Academy of Management Journal,* 50: 1385–1399.

Hofmann, D. A. (1997) "An overview of the logic and rationale of hierarchical linear models," *Journal of Management*, 23: 723–744.

House, R., Rousseau, D. M. and Thomas-Hunt, M. (1995) "The meso paradigm: A framework for the integration of micro and macro organizational behavior," in L. L. Cummings and B. M. Staw (eds) *Research in Organizational Behavior*, Greenwich, CT: JAI Press, 71–114.

Jacquemin, A. P. and Berry, C. H. (1979) "Entropy measure of diversification and corporate growth," *Journal of Industrial Economics*, 27: 359–369.

James, L. R. (1982) "Aggregation in estimates of perceptual agreement," *Journal of Applied Psychology*, 67: 219–229.

James, L. R., Demaree, R. G., and Wolf, G. (1984) "Estimating within-group interrater reliability with and without response bias," *Journal of Applied Psychology*, 69: 85–98.

Klein, K. J., Dansereau, F., and Hall, R., J. (1994) "Levels issues in theory development, data collection, and analysis," *Academy of Management Review*, 19: 195–229.

Klein, K. J. and Kozlowski, S. W. J. (eds) (2000) *Multilevel Theory, Research, and Methods in Organizations*, San Francisco: Jossey-Bass Publishers.

Kozlowski, S. W. J. and Ilgen, D. R. (2006) "Enhancing the effectiveness of work groups and teams," *Psychological Sciences in the Public Interest*, 7: 77–124.

Kozlowski, S. W. J. and Klein, K. J. (2000) "A multilevel approach to theory and research in organizations: Contextual, temporal, and emergent processes," in K. J. Klein and S. W. J. Kozlowski (eds) *Multilevel Theory, Research, and Methods in Organizations*, San Francisco: Jossey-Bass Publishers, 3–90.

Kreft, I. and De Leeuw, J. (1998) *Introduction to Multilevel Modeling*: London: Sage.

Lawless, M. W. and Price, L. L. (1992) "An agency perspective on new technology champions," *Organization Science*, 3: 342–355.

LeBreton, J. M. and Senter, J. L. (2008) "Answers to 20 questions about interrater reliability and interrater agreement," *Organizational Research Methods*, 11: 815–852.

Lockwood, P. and Kunda, Z. (1997) "Superstars and me: Predicting the impact of role models on the self," *Journal of Personality and Social Psychology*, 73: 91–109.

Ludke, O., Marsh, H. W., Robitzsch, A., and Trautwein, U. (2011) "A 2 x 2 taxonomy of multilevel latent contextual models: Accuracy-bias trade-offs in full and partial error correction models," *Psychological Methods*, 16: 444–467.

Mackey, A. and Barney, J. B. (2005) "Developing multi-level theory in strategic management: The case of managerial talent and competitive advantage," in F. Dansereau and F. J. Yammarino (eds) *Multi-Level Issues in Strategy and Methods: Research in Multi-level Issues*, Boston: Elsevier (JAI Press), 163–175.

March, J. G. (1991) "Exploration and exploitation in organizational learning," *Organization Science*, 2: 71–87.

Maritan, C. A. and Peteraf, M. A. (2011) "Building a bridge between resource acquisition and resource accumulation," *Journal of Management*, 37: 1374–1389.

Mathieu, J. E. and Chen, G. (2011) "The etiology of the multilevel paradigm in management reserach," *Journal of Management*, 37: 610–641.

Mathieu, J. E., Aguinis, H., Culpepper, S. A. and Chen, G. (2012) "Understanding and estimating the power to detect cross-level interaction effects in multilevel modeling," *Journal of Applied Psychology*, 97: 951–966.

Moliterno, T. P. and Mahony, D. M. (2011) "Network theory of organization: A multilevel approach," *Journal of Management*, 37: 443–467.

Moliterno, T. P. and Wiersema, M. F. (2007) "Firm performance, rent appropriation, and the strategic resource divestment capability," *Strategic Management Journal*, 28: 1065–1087.

Mollick, E. (2012) "People and process, suits and innovators: The role of individuals in firm performacne," *Strategic Management Journal*, 33: 1001–1015.

Nag, R., Hambrick, D. C. and Chen, M.-J. (2007) "What is strategic management, really? Inductive derivation of a consensus definition of the field," *Strategic Management Journal*, 28: 935–955.

Newbert, S. (2007) "Empirical research on the resource-based view of the firm: An assessment and suggestions for future research," *Strategic Management Journal*, 28: 121–146.

Peteraf, M. A. (1993) "The cornerstones of competitive advantage: A resource-based view," *Strategic Management Journal*, 14: 179–191.

Peteraf, M. A. (2005) "A resource-based lens on value creation, competitive advantage, and multi-level issues in strategic management research," in F. Dansereau and F. J. Yammarino (eds) *Multi-Level Issues in Strategy and Methods: Research in Multi-level Issues*, Boston: Elsevier (JAI Press), 177–188.

Ployhart, R. E. and Moliterno, T. P. (2011) "Emergence of the human capital resource: A multilevel model," *Academy of Management Review*, 36: 127–150.

Ployhart, R. E. and Schneider, B. (2005) "Multilevel selection and prediction: Theories, methods, and models," in A. Evers, N. Anderson, and O. Voskuijl (eds) *The Blackwell Handbook of Personnel Selection*, Malden, MA: Blackwell Publishing Limited, 495–516.

Porter, M. E. (1980) *Competitive Strategy*, New York: The Free Press.

Porter, M. E. (1985) *Competitive Advantage*, New York: The Free Press.

Raudenbush, S. W. and Bryk, A. S. (2002) *Hierarchical Linear Models: Applications and Data Analysis Methods*, Thousand Oaks, CA: SAGE Publications.

Rothaermel, F. T. and Hess, A. M. (2007) "Building dynamic capabilities: Innovation driven by individual-, firm-, and network-level effects," *Organization Science*, 18: 898–921.

Rousseau, D. M. (1985) "Issues of level in organizational research: Multi-level and cross-level perspectives," in L. L. Cummings and B. M. Staw (eds) *Research in Organizational Behavior*, Greenwich, CT: JAI Press, Inc., 1–37.

Rumelt, R. P. (1982) "Diversification strategy and profitability," *Strategic Management Journal*, 3: 359–369.

Rumelt, R. P. (1984) "Towards a strategic theory of the firm," in R. B. Lamb (ed.) *Competitive Strategic Management*, Englewood Cliffs, NJ: Prentice-Hall, 556–570.

Schmidt, F. L. and Hunter, J. E. (1998) "The validity and utility of selection methods in personnel psychology: Practical and theoretical implication of 85 years of research findings," *Psychological Bulletin*, 124: 262–274.

Shepherd, D. A. (2011) "Multilevel entrepreneurship research: Opportunities for studying entrepreneurial decision making," *Journal of Management*, 37: 412–420.

Short, J. C., Ketchen, D. J., Bennett, N., and du Toit, M. (2006) "An Examination of firm, industry, and time effects on performance using random coefficients modeling," *Organizational Research Methods*, 9: 259–284.

Short, J. C., Ketchen, D. J., Palmer, T. B., and Hult, G. T. M. (2007) "Firm, strategic group, and industry influences on performance," *Strategic Management Journal*, 28: 147–167.

Short, J. C., Palmer, T. B., and Ketchen, D. J. (2003) "Multi-level influences on firm performance: Insights from the resource-based view and strategic groups research," in F. Dansereau and F. J. Yammarino (eds) *Multi-Level Issues in Organizational Behavior and Strategy: Research in Multi-level Issues*, Boston: Elsevier (JAI Press), 155–187.

Silverman, B. S. (1999) "Technological resources and the direction of corporate diversification: Toward an integration of the resource-based view and transaction cost economics," *Management Science*, 45: 1109–1124.

Simon, H. A. (1973) "The organization of complex systems," in H. H. Pattee (ed.) *Hierarchy Theory*, New York: Braziller, 1–27.

Teece, D. J. (2007) "Explicating dynamic capabilities: The nature and microfoundations of (sustainable) enterprise performance," *Strategic Management Journal*, 28: 1319–1350.

Von Bertalanffy, L. (1968) *General Systems Theory*, New York: Braziller.

Wernerfelt, B. (1984) "A resource-based view of the firm," *Strategic Management Journal*, 5: 171–180.

Wiersema, M. F. and Bantel, K. A. (1992) "Top management team demography and corporate strategic change," *Academy of Management Journal*, 35: 91–121.

Zyphur, M. J., Kaplan, S. A. and Christian, M. S. (2008) "Assumptions of cross-level measurement and structural invariance in the analysis of multilevel data: Problems and solutions," *Group Dynamics: Theory, Research, and Practice*, 12: 127–140.

4

CONTEXTUALIZED EXPLANATION IN STRATEGY RESEARCH

Harry Sminia

The methodology of contextualized explanation is ideal for answering "how" questions in strategy research. The majority of strategy research addresses "why" questions. It produces results that indicate the extent to which variables correlate with each other. Questions that start with "how" probe the arrows that link the boxes. What is it that actually happens that makes that one variable causally linked with another variable?

Explaining the way in which effects are generated involves probing the process by which an outcome is realized. In the case of strategy research, the question of why a firm performs the way it does, changes into how performance is generated. The question why a firm has competitive advantage changes into how competitive advantage is created and maintained. It is not about which merger, acquisition, or strategic alliance variables explain their failure or success. It is about the course of events that make up a merger, an acquisition, or a strategic alliance, and what their contributions are towards the outcome. In short, it is about explaining how strategy is realized.

Contextualized explanation therefore moves away from a variance approach and embraces a process approach (Mohr, 1982; Pettigrew, 1990; Poole *et al.*, 2000; Sminia, 2009; Van de Ven and Poole, 1995; Van de Ven and Sminia, 2012). The process approach does not theorize about social reality by formulating hypotheses about the relationship between variables. Instead it sees social reality as a process consisting of activities and investigates how event sequences or process courses lead to outcomes (Abbott, 1990; Langley, 1999).

Contextualized explanation is a case study methodology by which theory can be developed and tested (Tsang, 2013). It aims for causal explanation while acknowledging the context in which the process takes place (Welch *et al.*, 2011). It requires the research to track the way in which a process plays out over time and leads to a specific outcome. However, this methodology has been dubbed "an emerging alternative" (ibid.: 747). It has not crystalized out yet to the extent that the proverbial handbook has been written which describes the methods and procedures of how contextualized explanation should be done.

This chapter is an attempt to do so. It draws on the experiences of the author and empirical and methodological work by others, which has adopted various elements of contextualized explanation. The argument starts with elaborating the kind of explanations that this methodology has on offer. It probes the multiple causes that feature in the course of a process and explicates the essentially limited scope of any explanation that is being provided. From then on, the methodology itself is explained, starting with how a research project can be set up, to continue with what data to collect and how these data should be analyzed. The chapter ends with a few final thoughts on the (practical) usefulness of contextualized explanation and how it can link up with variance approaches.

What to explain and what to explain it with?

Contextualized explanation as a methodology is rooted in critical realism (Tsang and Kwan, 1999; Miller and Tsang, 2010; Tsang, 2013; Tsoukas, 1989; Welch et al., 2011). The ontology is realist but the epistemology is subjectivist (Johnson et al., 2006). It is based on the premise that there is a reality out there, existing independently of human perception. Yet it recognizes that any knowledge is mediated by human interaction and interpretation. In effect, the combination of interaction and interpretation continuously recreates a collectively constructed social reality. It is this social constructed reality that people experience in their day-to-day activities. This social constructed reality is unique to a particular time and place. Therefore, the basic stance of any explanation is contextualist (Pepper, 1942; Pettigrew, 1990). This does not mean that social reality has an ephemeral existence. There can be considerable continuity and coverage with regard to many aspects of social reality. That is why it takes on this independent existence beyond individual human perception.

This means that social reality essentially is processual, as it is continuously recreated and reenacted. Human individuals are taken to possess a reflective practical consciousness that allows them to evaluate situations and to decide on their activities (Giddens, 1984). A process is a sequence of events (Langley, 1999; Pettigrew, 1987; Van de Ven and Poole, 1995). Therefore, any explanation of how things have been realized is due to a specific course of events the process has taken. To understand how a course of events is generated, a distinction is made between the "real domain," the "actual domain," and the "empirical domain" (Tsoukas, 1989).

The "real domain" is where generative mechanisms exist. A generative mechanism refers to the "ways of acting of things" (Bhaskar, 2008: 14). They are at the heart of anything that happens. However, their presence does not mean that they are operating. Their effects are contingent on the specific circumstances that surround them. A generative mechanism may be dormant or counteracted by another generative mechanism (Tsoukas, 1989). However, generative mechanisms are unobservable. Their operation can only be gauged by referring to the "actual domain."

Van de Ven and Poole (1995) distinguish between four basic generative mechanisms or process motors that drive social process. A process driven by a life-cycle motor goes through successive phases on the basis of a logic that governs its progression. A process driven by a teleological motor moves towards a predetermined end state while dealing with various requirements and constraints. The dialectical motor is based on contradiction and conflict that has to be endured or resolved. The evolutionary motor creates a process of variation, selection, and retention among a population of entities in a restricted environment.

The "actual domain" is where the process as a sequence of events can be investigated. There is a continuum here. Process courses can vary between very stable recurrent interaction patterns that are produced time and time again and unique event sequences that play out only once in the history of mankind.

At the recurrent interaction pattern end of the scale, the event sequence can take on the form of a social mechanism. This is in line with Gross' (2009) view of "social mechanisms as composed of chains or aggregations of actors confronting problem situations and mobilizing more or less habitual responses" (368). It is through these habitualized interaction patterns that are made up of day-to-day activities among various individuals, that effects like firm performance or competitive advantage can be generated. Sminia's (2011) study of collusion in the Dutch construction industry is an example of this kind of explanation. This study found that the dialectic generative mechanism as a basic cause for institutional change was prevented from operating as a consequence of social mechanisms that created recurrent interaction patterns, by which the inherent contradictions were repaired and concealed, resulting in institutional continuity. This study in effect demonstrates how social reality can be both processual and stable.

At the unique sequence end of the scale, an outcome is the consequence of a specific chain of events. These event chains can be quite elaborate affairs with various tributaries coming together to generate an outcome, as the intricate case studies of strategic change by, for instance, Burgelman (1983) or Pettigrew (1985) show. These studies come close to an extensive historical investigation of one firm. However, in their analysis they do build on a generative mechanism: evolution in the case of Burgelman and contradiction in the case of Pettigrew. And they draw theoretical conclusions. Burgelman (1983) developed a model of internal corporate venturing. Pettigrew (1985) characterized the strategic change process as politics as the management of meaning. What these and similar intensive case studies have shown is the contingent nature of the explanation.

The "empirical domain" refers to the incidents that can be observed and about which data can be collected. In the context of a research project, these are the raw data. Incidents have to be attributed with meaning to be lifted out of the empirical domain and become part of the actual domain. This is what turns an incident into an event (Abbott, 1990; Van de Ven and Poole, 1990; Poole *et al.*, 2000). Implications are attributed in terms of causes and consequences.

Causality

With regard to the causality that can be found in individual incidents, drawing on Aristotle, there is choice between material cause, formal cause, efficient cause, and final cause (Van de Ven, 2007). Material cause refers to the ingredients that need to be in place for the activities that make up the incident to happen. For instance, Giddens (1986) argues that for social interaction to take place, agents need to be able to draw on the rules and resources that constitute a social structure. Other theoretical insights have come up with similar requirements and these are often turned into variables for the purpose of variance approach studies in strategy research. Material cause makes the availability or lack of essential ingredients that need to be in place a reason for something to happen or not happen.

It is not only the circumstances that have to be right for things to be able to happen. There are also individuals and agents who have to actually do something and there is often variability in the way in which things can be done. Formal, final, and efficient causes are reasons associated with the actor or agent as to whether and what activity takes place. Formal cause refers to the way in which the activities that make up an incident have been enacted. There normally are requirements with regard to the way in which activities should be done to make them effective. Efficient cause refers to the fact that the activities that make up the incident actually have taken place. Final cause refers to the motivations and purposes for which the activities that make up the incident have been enacted. To pull it all together, incidents turn into events if the raw data reveal material, formal, efficient, or final cause.

Additionally, an incident becomes an event if the raw data indicates an effect on subsequent events. This can be either an intended or unintended consequence (Giddens, 1984). An intended consequence is the case if the effect on subsequent events is in line with the final cause of an earlier event. All other effects are effectively unintended but effectual enough to infuse an incident with impact. This effect from one event to another one can take on two forms. There can be an input-output relationship and there can be a feedback relationship between events (Sminia, 2011). In either case, this effect can indicate continuity or change. An input-output relationship exists when one event has to make use of something that is produced by a preceding event. There are many occasions where the ingredients for (material cause), the way in which (formal cause), or the reason why (final cause) activities take place depend on what has happened previously. A change of input will result in a change in activities, or may stop the activities taking place altogether (efficient cause). The feedback relationship incorporates the practical consciousness of the agents who are involved in the activities that make up an event. By interpreting what has happened previously and comparing it with what was intended (final cause), participants in an event can decide to act differently next time if they are not happy with the result, or stick to what they have done previously if they are.

Explanation

So what can be explained by contextualized explanation? This methodology is able to explain an outcome state at a specific moment in space and time. This outcome state can refer to one or more levels of aggregation, from, for instance, the mindset of an individual strategist, to firm performance, or to the state of the environment. This outcome state basically is the final event of a sequence that has led up to it. Contextualized explanation can also explain whether continuity or change has been realized by comparing an earlier (starting) event with the outcome event, or by examining the variety and regularity by which events occur over the course of time. It does mean that an outcome state is just one moment in time in a continuous process, although – in the case of continuity in the process – this state of affairs can extend over quite a long period.

What is there to explain it with? What is it that an outcome is a consequence of? In its most basic form, an explanation is found in the course of events, which preceded the outcome event. More specifically, the explanation can be further specified in terms of the material, formal, final, and efficient causes that generated each event in the event sequence, and with these causes affected by previous events; creating a causal chain. This tends to result in an elaborate and detailed narrative, which sometimes is summed up in a simple statement. Chandler's (1962) extensive case studies of the emergence of the M-form were summed up by "structure follows strategy." Pettigrew's (1985) elaborate case study of strategic change at ICI created the insight that the management process is a matter of "politics of meaning."

It could be that a specific key event in the sequence can be identified, which by itself can be earmarked as a turning point or tipping point (Gladwell, 2000) without which the subsequent event sequence and outcome would not have happened. Nevertheless, further questions can always be asked about the event sequence that preceded this key event and what it was about the causal chain that contributed to this key event to become so pivotal. For instance, the Challenger disaster was such a turning point for NASA. But there was a specific course of events that led to the disaster to happen in the first place (Vaughan, 1990).

The "unique event sequence" is one end of the scale. At the other end of the scale, there is the social mechanism explanation. Outcomes can be explained in terms of the degree to which event sequences form recurrent patterns, and more specifically in the reasons for this social mechanism to stay in place and continue to operate. The investigation into collusion in the Dutch construction industry (Sminia, 2011) is an example here. Everybody in the industry continued to act in a specific way because these activities maintained the circumstances that prompted everybody involved to act in the same way over and over again. Event sequences generated by a social mechanism tend to keep a causal chain intact, which acts as a vicious or virtuous circle, or a self-denying or self-confirming prophecy.

This continuum between unique event sequence and social mechanism is found at the level of "actual domain." By definition, any contextualized explanation is limited in time and space, although the time and the sphere to which especially the social mechanism applies can be quite long and substantial. Underlying the actual domain is the "real domain," where the generative mechanisms exist. An additional layer of explanation refers to the generative mechanisms of life cycle, teleology, dialectics, or evolution, which can all operate and drive a process on. However, whether they do is determined by the sequence of events as it takes shape at the actual level. The process course itself can be driven by but can also prevent any of these generative mechanisms to drive the process.

Contextualized explanation is a multi-causal, multi-layered and an essentially contingent affair (Miller and Tsang, 2010; Welch *et al.*, 2011). There very rarely is a single cause – if ever – that explains an outcome. What is expected is a configuration of causes associated with events, which over a period of time combine into a particular conjunction of circumstances. It reflects the multi-faceted nature of social reality (Poole and Van de Ven, 1989). But this configuration is not a random occurrence. Ultimately the attributes of events in terms of causes and consequences, and the chronological and spatial order, in which they appear at the actual level of social reality, are responsible for how an outcome is realized. In short, it is the course of events, which determines how social reality takes shape.

How to set up a research project?

Research questions can be derived from existing variance-based strategy theory. Any presumed or empirically tested relationship between a set of variables warrants the "how" question. How is the relationship between two or more variables realized? What process is responsible for this relationship to apparently exist? There are numerous calls in the strategy literature to query to process by which things are realized (e.g. Foss, 1998; Maritan and Peteraf, 2011; Pettigrew, 1992; Porter, 1991; Shanley and Peteraf, 2006; Sminia and de Rond, 2012).

In fact, the "how" question can take on the form of at least four different and more specific questions that intend to query the process by which an outcome is realized (Van de Ven and Sminia, 2012). There is the question of "How did we get there?", putting the focus on the past. The "What is occurring?" question asks about what is happening right now. The "Where are we going?" question asks about a possible outcome in the future. And finally the "What should we do?" question wonders about the possibilities for interventions in the process to reach a preferred outcome. Although they differ with regard to their temporal orientation, they all require an understanding of how the process works.

A good justification for asking the "how" question and employing contextualized explanation is the appearance of an anomaly (Miller and Tsang, 2010; Van de Ven, 2007, Welch *et al.*, 2011). This can be an actual anomaly, an unexplained phenomenon or outcome that defies current theoretical insights. For instance, in Sminia (2003), the failure of a new sports TV channel was investigated because existing theory could not account for this to have happened. A theoretical anomaly, an inconsistency within a theory or among rival theories, can also act as a justification. This was the case in Sminia (2011). Institutional continuity as the normal state of affairs was questioned because contradiction as a reason for institutional change had been put forward as so endemic to institutions that continuity should be seen as an exceptional state.

Drawing on incomplete theory and doing empirical research to come up with an explanation means that the overall orientation of the research project is abductive (sometimes also referred to as retroductive) (Langley and Tsoukas, 2010; Klag and Langley, 2013; Van de Ven, 2007; Welch *et al.*, 2011). There is going to be a constant comparison between existing theory and data to eventually arrive at a new theoretical insight that answers the "how" question and dissolves the anomaly. However, this does not preclude that there are possibilities to test existing theory (Miller and Tsang, 2010; Tsang, 2013).

What data to collect?

Empirical work for contextualized explanations involves the collection of raw incident data. This, however, is not without its problems. There is a temptation to just go in and record everything that happens. This will lead to data asphyxiation (Pettigrew, 1990). Moreover, it will not be possible to record everything anyway and the researcher is very likely to end up with data that do not refer to the research question. It pays therefore to think in advance what activities need to be recorded. However, because of the processual nature of contextualized explanation, the data obviously should be longitudinal.

An incident as an instance of activity to be recorded and analyzed is a somewhat troublesome notion. What is it that makes such an instance an incident? As Langley observed, an incident can "include a bad year, a merger, a decision, a meeting, a conversation, or a handshake" (1999: 693). At one extreme end, an incident can be one individual or agent doing one particular thing, with incident data collected as fine grained as recording all the instances when somebody does something. The process then is conceived as the actions and reactions of all these individual participants. At the other end, incidents can be as coarse as a firm disposing and acquiring one subsidiary after another, with the process conceived as firms contracting and expanding in this way. This is referred to as granularity. It is just one of the many issues that should be considered when collecting incident data.

With contextualized explanation requiring abduction as the overall research orientation, data collection should be informed by the (incomplete) theoretical insights on which the project is based. It also is required to collect data beyond what the (incomplete) theory would indicate because creating an opportunity for the empirical domain to inform the actual domain is very much part of the inquiry. It is relatively easy to collect incident data on the basis of pre-conceived theoretical insights because the theory will tell what to look for. It is more difficult to decide what data to collect beyond that.

Collecting incidents

Van de Ven's (2007: 218) definition of an incident as a qualitative datum is of use for making decisions about what data to collect. In turn, he describes a qualitative datum as:

(1) a bracketed string of words capturing the basic elements of information;
(2) about a discrete incident or occurrence (the unit of analysis);
(3) that happened on a specific date;
(4) which is entered as a unique record (or case);
(5) is subsequently coded and classified as an indicator of a theoretical event.

The "string of words" refers to the incident data usually being recorded as a text. Moreover, the acid test that the researcher has captured an incident is that it can be described and labeled by using a verb (Pepper, 1942; Poole *et al.*, 2000). This is perhaps the most defining feature of contextualized explanation. The recognition that we are dealing with a process compels the researcher to collect truly processual data. Processual data means that the datum refers to activity. This implies that the incident label, as well as the "string of words," has to have verbs at its core.

"Bracketed" refers to some decision rule about what is relevant to be recorded and what it is going to be recorded as. Examples of recorded incidents can be a moment that something has changed (Van de Ven *et al.*, 1989), an episode of strategic activity (Hendry and Seidl, 2003), an interaction sequence in a meeting (Sminia, 2005), or an enacted practice (Sminia, 2011). This is where existing theory is useful as providing a first indication about what makes an instance of activity an incident. The "basic elements of information" would refer not only to the activities that make up the incident but also to the various cause and consequence attributes that will turn the incident into an event when that data analysis takes place. Again, what can be considered a priori is to be derived from the initial theoretical insights that inform the research project.

The "discrete incident or occurrence" refers to the importance to have the data collection informed with an initial idea of what will constitute an incident. This will also serve as the unit of analysis. This is to a large extent the decision about the appropriate level of granularity. Again, initial theoretical insights can act as a first guide, as can the definition of the process itself that is under investigation. Metaphorically speaking, processes and the incidents that make them up can be looked upon as Russian dolls. When an incident is looked at more closely, it can be analyzed as a process by itself and found to consist of a range of sub-incidents that make up the larger incident. These sub-incidents can be opened up as well, revealing another sphere of sub-incidents and so on. The sphere about which data needs to be collected should at least be one level below the process that is under investigation, but it can go deeper if the need arises.

For instance, in Sminia (2005), to investigate a process of strategy formation, incident data were collected of the various meetings that took place among the top management group members. Within that, sub-incidents were found to occur that referred to the various items on the agendas of these meetings. These sub-incidents could be decomposed further into sub-sub-incidents, as various individual participants in these discussions interacted by putting forward their opinions and observations on each agenda item. These sub-sub-incidents eventually were recorded and analyzed. It led to a conclusion that strategy formation is layered. At a superficial level, agenda items themselves were discussed. However, many deliberations – no matter how mundane the agenda item – also, albeit covertly, discussed the overall strategic direction of the firm as a whole because any stance taken on an agenda item contained a message about where the firm was supposed to go. All of these seemingly insignificant agenda items acted as a forum to debate strategy.

This example illustrates the going back and forth between theory and data, as is to be expected with abduction, while refining the data collection. To start with, the researcher has to define the process under investigation and to start with collecting data about the first constituting layer of sub-processes that make up the larger process and take it from there. This also re-affirms, as many process researchers have indicated (e.g. Pettigrew, 1990; Van de Ven *et al.*, 1989), that data collection often requires more than one go to fill in blanks and gaps when initial analysis shows them to exist. This also allows the researcher to probe into areas that initially were not considered and collect data beyond what the existing but incomplete theoretical insights indicated. At some point, a level of saturation sets in and the data collection can stop (Corbin and Strauss, 1990).

Data collection that is not initially inspired by theoretical considerations is an important part of contextualized explanation. Yet if theoretical insights cannot inform the researcher what data to collect, what can? The problem with this, as was indicated earlier, is that there is a limit to what can be recorded. A considerable part of what is going on and what has been going on will not be reflected in the data. It leaves any contextualized explanation open to criticism with regard to not having captured the incidents that could have mattered.

This inherent subjectivity does not necessarily need to be a weakness of the methodology. By involving the participants in the process that is being investigated in making decisions about what the salient incidents are, there is an inbuilt check on capturing those incidents that are the most relevant. This localized appreciation of the process is the subjectivity you want. Contextualized explanation is about taking the course of events as the ultimate explanation of an outcome. By capturing the incidents that the participants themselves are saying are the most relevant for what has been going on, the chances of getting it "right" for a particular course of events will only increase.

Adding information about an incident with regard to the "specific date" – and place where the incident took place as well – is required because of the contextual nature of the inquiry and the explanation. It also brings home that data collection has to be longitudinal to incorporate the time dimension into the research project. However, data collection can be real-time, retrospective, or both. Each one comes with advantages and disadvantages (Glick *et al.*, 1990; Golden, 1992; Pettigrew,

1990; Poole *et al.*, 2000; Van de Ven *et al.*, 1989). Every data source has its biases but also offers opportunities to capture something special and revealing for a particular moment in time.

It is advisable to use multiple data sources, not only to be able to collect as many relevant incidents as possible but also to find out as much about individual incidents as you can (Pettigrew, 1990; Poole *et al.*, 2000). Contextualized explanation relies on qualitative conformation (Pepper, 1942). That does not require for the data to say the same thing about the same incident. Multiple interpretations of what has happened can be very much part of the analysis. Data sources normally consist of observations, interviews, and archival (written) documentation. Examples of more specific data collection methods that have been employed are (participant) observation, interviews, periodic questionnaires, archival records, and self-reporting diaries.

Finally, the requirements of an incident being "entered as a unique record" and to be "subsequently coded and classified" again indicate the close relationship between data collection and analysis. As was said above, they have to inform each other as part of the abduction that needs to take place. The key to good contextualized explanation is internal validity (Pettigrew, 1990; Poole *et al.*, 2000; Stevenson and Greenberg, 1998). This is safeguarded with clear and comprehensive data collection and data analysis procedures combined with multiple sources corroborating each other.

How to analyze?

The purpose of the analysis is to find the multi-causal, multi-layered, and essentially contingent explanation of the outcome that needs to be explained, but also to strip it down to its bare essence. This explanation has to answer the "how" question that informed the research project. It hopefully will have relevance beyond the immediate case(s) from which data has been collected.

The analytical activities that need to take place involve coding the raw incident data and linking the incidents up to draft an overall process account from which an answer to the research question can be abstracted. Both the initial coding and the drafting of the process account are retroductive activities. Going back and forward between empirical observations and theoretical ideas is continuous here. To facilitate abduction, the coding can start as soon as the first incident data has been collected.

Coding

The raw incident data have to be coded to turn them into events that can become part of the overall process account. By doing that, the researcher moves out of the more concrete empirical domain and enters the more abstract actual domain.

The initial coding scheme can be derived from the theoretical insights that were used to justify the "how" question in the first place. These theoretical insights can

TABLE 4.1 Causal coding

Efficient cause	What activities make up the incident? Who is involved? What type of incident?
Formal cause	What different ways are there for the incident to happen? Which one of them happened?
Final cause	What reason/motivation is there for the incident to occur?
Material cause	What ingredients need to be in place for the incident to happen?

provide a first indication of the various kinds and types of incidents that can be expected to take place. Codes can be attached accordingly.

More specifically, re-appreciating the initial theoretical insights in terms of the various ways in which causality can work will yield a number of initial incident codes (see Table 4.1). Every observed incident consists of one or more activities that have taken place. Efficient cause codes can be derived from the various activities that are expected to take place as part of the phenomenon that is being investigated. One obvious way to code an incident is whether and what activities have taken place or not. There even is the possibility to allow for the coding of incidents that (theoretically) should have taken place but which have not. Final cause codes can be derived from the reasons why agents chose to embark upon particular activities (or why not) to create the incident. Formal cause codes can be derived from the various ways in which the activities can be done. Finally, material cause codes can be derived from the ingredients that need to be in place for the activities and therefore the incident to happen at all. Furthermore, incidents can be evaluated in terms of their results or outcomes, and coded accordingly. Finally and in accordance with the contextualized nature of the explanation, incidents have to be coded in terms of time when and place where they happened (see Table 4.2).

Additional codes have to be added that refer to the way in which incidents are linked together. This requires another coding category that does not refer to individual incidents and their attributes but to links between (types of) incidents. Based on the consequences that incidents can have, one link that can be expected to exist is an input/output relationship, where an outcome of one incident feeds into a subsequent incident. The other link that can be coded refers to the feedback relationship. Agents evaluate the effect of an incident that they have participated in by reflecting on the incidents that follow on from it. Whatever they observe can

TABLE 4.2 Contextual coding

Time	When did the incident take place?
Place	Where did the incident take place?

inform how they will participate in an incident the next time it needs to be accomplished.

Coding the links between incidents becomes more informative when the input/output relationships and the feedback relationships can be specified in terms of whether and in what way they affect the incident attributes. Table 4.3 provides an overview of the various ways in which these effects can be gauged. This requires a careful examination of how incidents are linked up.

Additionally, the incident data can be scrutinized for evidence of the generative mechanisms or process motors that might be operating (see Table 4.4). Although the actual operation of the process motors as generative mechanisms is not observable, elements that indicate their presence are discernable. When incidents can be grouped together in successive phases, indications are the life cycle motor is operating. Finding evidence in the incident data of a predetermined state alongside requirements and impediments of reaching it, points at a teleological motor. The dialectical motor may be operating when contradiction and conflict is evident in the data. When incidents can be associated with variation, selection, and retention, the evolutionary motor may be operating. These process motors are not mutually exclusive and the data may reveal that more than one is at work. Coding for process motors also helps in laying foundations for the process account later.

TABLE 4.3 Relational coding

	Input/output relationship	Feedback relationship
Efficient cause	Has an outcome of an incident affected whether activities that are part of a subsequent incident have taken place?	Has an evaluation of an effect by a participant in an incident led to different activities being undertaken the next time such an incident takes place?
Formal cause	Has an outcome of an incident affected the way in which activities that are part of a subsequent incident have taken place?	Has an evaluation of an effect by a participant in an incident led to changes in the way in which activities are done the next time such an incident takes place?
Final cause	Has an outcome of an incident affected the reasons why activities that are part of a subsequent incident should take place?	Has an evaluation of an effect by a participant in an incident led to changes in reasons why activities are done the next time such an incident takes place?
Material cause	Has an outcome of an incident affected the ingredients necessary for the activities that are part of a subsequent incident?	Has an evaluation of an effect by a participant in an incident affected the ingredients necessary for the activities that are part of a subsequent incident?

TABLE 4.4 Process motor coding

Life cycle motor	Can incidents be divided up across sequential phases?
Teleological motor	Do incidents feature as requirement or impediment to reaching a predetermined end state?
Dialectical motor	Do incidents feature contradiction and/or are part of the initiation and settlement of a conflict?
Evolutionary motor	Can incidents be associated with moments of variation, selection, and retention?

This is only the initial coding scheme. What is bound to happen is that incidents and activities that were not anticipated are apparent in the data. This will also be the case for the various attributes of an incident and the way they link up. The coding scheme will develop accordingly. This coding and re-coding will have to happen until the incident data, the process account, and the explanation emerging from it can be validated against each other (Strauss and Corbin, 1990).

Drafting a process account

Once the coding has started, it becomes possible to look at the events that result from this and the way they relate to each other to start drafting a process account. This account eventually will lead to an answer to the "how" question that informed the research project.

The first thing to do is to put the events in chronological order and to locate them in space. From this, a story can be developed about what happened when and where and what events affected and were affected by other events. Langley (1999) refers to this as the narrative strategy for making sense of process data. The result is a detailed story of how the process progresses almost from event to event. By scrutinizing the various event attributes and whether, where, and when the relationships between them change these attributes, the process will get into focus. Such a detailed description of the course of events will reveal the multi-causal, multi-layered, and contingent nature of the explanation.

What also will become apparent is where the process under investigation sits on the continuum between recurrent interaction pattern and unique chain of events. A process that is supposed to explain a stable relationship between variables can be expected to reside towards the recurrent interaction pattern end of the scale. Narratives that explain actual anomalies can end up at the unique chain of events end. One easy trap that many process researchers fall into, is to just leave it at this stage and tell the story of what happened when and present that as the answer. The chronology of when things happened, of course, is important and can be insightful by itself. However, the challenge is to provide an explanation that at least has the potential to be relevant beyond the case(s) that have been studied.

One way to do this is to adopt an alternate template strategy (Langley, 1999). This is especially appropriate when alternative theoretical insights exist with regard to the process under study. Such a strategy tests the relative merit of alternative explanations by seeing how much of the process can be made to fit pre-conceived process courses. For instance, there are now at least five alternative theoretical approaches by which a process of strategy formation can be understood, varying between rationalism, logical or political incrementalism, or cognitive or symbolic interpretativism (Johnson, 1987). Obviously, the coding schemes that are employed have to be derived from the different theoretical approaches. Allison's (1971) study of the Cuban missile crisis is a classic example of the alternative template strategy.

When existing theory is lacking, a more grounded theory strategy can be adopted (Langley, 1999). This would mean that the analysis has to try to move away from the concreteness of the narrative to provide a more abstract account that utilizes a limited theoretical vocabulary that is developed as part of the analysis. The story, as it were, needs to be retold in more abstract terms. Barley's (1986; 1990) account of the structuring of technology on the basis of his observations of the introduction of CT scanners in a hospital is an example here.

Alternatively, or in conjunction with a grounded theory strategy, a visual mapping strategy can be employed (Langley, 1999). Instead of re-telling the story with more abstract terminology, a visual map or process flowchart can be constructed, which contains the essential actions and elements of the process under investigation. Mintzberg *et al.* (1976) is an early demonstration of how this works. Unstructured strategic decision-making is presented as a basic flow diagram consisting of various routines and interrupts, in which actual decision processes can be mapped out depending on the interrupts that occur and the number of times the process goes down a specific loop of routines.

A temporal bracketing strategy (Langley, 1999) has to be adopted when the process under investigation is found to consist of sub-processes that mutually affect each other. The bracketing strategy provides an analytical means to tease out this mutual causality by examining each link separately. This, of course, requires the researcher to decompose (i.e. bracket) one process into various sub-processes. A way to meaningfully distinguish between the various building blocks that make up the larger process is to look for pockets of continuity or stability in activity and find demarcations where this stops and starts. These demarcations can be both temporal and spatial. This is where the imagery of processes, events, and incidents as Russian dolls can be useful. The temporal and spatial bracketing of distinguishing sub-processes within processes is like opening up a doll to investigate the smaller doll(s) inside.

These various strategies to get to grips with the incident data and to go beyond the detailed narrative or story of what happened when are all in aid of getting to the "bare essence" of the process. In the case of a recurrent interaction pattern, it is the identification of this pattern and the reasons why it is recurrent that should appear as a consequence of the analysis. What is expected here is some form of a social mechanism (Gross, 2009; Sminia, 2011) that can be offered as an explanation.

This is what you can expect when the "how" question refers to the correlations between a set of variables.

In the case of a unique sequence of events that explains a very particular outcome that might never happen again, the narrative can be very insightful by itself. However, statements like "structure follows strategy (Chandler, 1962) or "politics of meaning" (Pettigrew, 1985) that depict the bare essence of a storyline can be offered as a summary explanation.

The move that turns a collection of events into a process account that explains an outcome requires an act of interpretation from the researcher. Inevitably, there is a moment of creativity there, or what Klag and Langley (2013) have dubbed the "conceptual leap." However, it is here where the process motors can be of tremendous help. They provide a backbone to any storyline and also a first depiction of how the dynamic in the process is brought about. Therefore it can be expected that part of any contextualized explanation is an indication whether the process essentially is one of sequential phases, of reaching a predetermined state, of dealing with contradiction, of natural selection, or of some combination of these four process motors.

Will there be something to contribute to the strategy literature?

There is a widespread expectation that the contribution of a research project depends on the generality of its findings. This is in sharp contrast with the basic idea of contextualized explanation. Contextual means that many phenomena are taken to only occur as a consequence of factors coming together in a specific way. It also means that a phenomenon can be a one off, or it can happen more often but still be confined to a certain period in time, to a limited geographical space, or a specific social setting. Many things in strategic management are the consequence of a process during which specific circumstances conspire to generate a particular outcome.

This particularly applies to the issues that practicing strategists have to contend with. They have to make sense of situations as they occur. Those situations that are acutely strategic are the ones for which an explanation is not "ready-to-hand" and it is not immediately clear how the situation is to be understood (Chia and MacKay, 2007). These situations require a "conscious coping" that not only explains "what has happened?", "what is going on?," or "where is this going?", but moreover, "what should we do?" (Van de Ven and Sminia, 2012). These are situations that are very specific to that firm at that moment in time, but also came into being as a consequence of a particular course of events. For instance, the resource-based view recognizes the particularities of process and context in that a resource base is unique to a firm as a consequence of a process of resource accumulation (Dierickx and Cool, 1989). Uniqueness is one of the defining components of sustainable competitive advantage (Barney, 1991; Peteraf, 1993). More recently in the realm of international business, contextuality has been recognized as a major component of the field (Michailova, 2011; Welch et al., 2011).

It is up to strategy research to provide the means by which strategists can practice strategy. There is a paradox here. If strategy theories and the tools that are derived from them have to fulfill this criterion of generalizability, then it would make them less useful for those situations that are really strategic. Generalizable theory would only contribute to the stock of "ready-to-hand" explanations while strategy theory has to be suitable for situations that are completely new and ill-understood. Is "theory" possible that has enough versatility to be useful for very specific strategy situations, yet has to have enough universality to be widely usable? Adopting a critical realist stance, and within that aiming for contextualized explanation, offers a way of dealing with this conundrum. The criterion of general-izability is downplayed. The emphasis is put upon internal validity and upon providing insight in the particularities of the processes by which strategy is realized.

The key question for making a contribution to the strategy literature is whether a contextualized explanation has relevance beyond the case(s) that have been investigated. The answer can be yes. Relevance can be found with regard to the generative mechanisms or process motors operating at the real level of social reality, the social mechanisms and the unique event sequences at the actual level of social reality, and the methodology of contextualized explanation itself for practicing strategists at the empirical level of social reality. These contributions can be made in terms of developing and refining theory but also in testing theory and replicating earlier findings (Tsang and Kwan, 1999; Tsang, 2013).

The actual operations of the four process motors that have been put forward as generative mechanisms at the real level of social reality are unobservable and therefore untestable. However, their presence is discernable by looking for particular evidence when coding incident data. Their usefulness is further strengthened when they serve to provide an explanatory backbone to a process account. By following the logic of replication (Tsang and Kwan, 1999; Yin, 2014), any additional contextualized explanation that makes use of them amplifies their relevance for answering "how" questions (e.g. de Rond, 2003).

Social mechanisms at the actual level of social reality – by definition – are limited in time and space. However, the extent of time and space to which they apply can be quite considerable. Especially when a social mechanism addresses the "how" of observed correlations in a set of variables, the generalizability of these correlations indicates the scope to which the social mechanism might apply. Finding out about the social mechanisms that underpin observed regularities among variables adds a much-needed level of understanding to the dominant variance approach in strategy research (Gross, 2009; Miller and Tsang, 2010). In that sense, theory is developed and refined.

When the extent of time and space to which a social mechanism applies becomes more limited, the possibilities for generalization diminish. Eventually, the contextualized explanation becomes a unique chain of events, specific to a particular outcome. Yet there still are possibilities for extending the relevance beyond the case in question. This relevance is then found more in terms of contrast and comparison (Pettigrew and Whipp, 1991). Furthermore, the particular arrangement of ingredients and course of events may be unique; there still could be more general characteristics in terms of the contributing ingredients and events that transcend the case(s) that have been investigated. For instance, generally speaking the process of competing in an industry takes place in terms of value and costs (Porter, 1980). What constitutes value at a certain point in time in a particular industry and therefore what determines the performance of a firm is contextual to that time and place. Earlier in the chapter, the examples of "structure follows strategy" (Chandler, 1962) and "politics of meaning" (Pettigrew, 1985) were mentioned.

These examples also illustrate the relevance of contextualized explanation itself, especially in practical terms. Strategy practitioners practice their strategic management in the empirical domain of social reality. Contextualized explanation allows them to make sense of what is happening in aid of their "conscious coping". What they can do is use existing theoretical insights and apply them to the specific situation that they need to understand. Contrast and comparison, making use of theoretical terminology describing common ingredients and events and finding out in what specific way they are arranged, and the occurrence and identification of social mechanisms that they have to contend with, are all lines of inquiry that strategists can utilize to develop and maintain firm performance. Yet, contextualized explanation is based on the premise that explanations about social reality are limited in time and space.

Final thoughts

Contextualized explanation is an "emerging alternative" in strategy research (Welch *et al.*, 2011: 747). Reflecting the multi-facetted social reality of strategic management (Poole and van de Ven, 1989), it provides a multi-causal, multi-layered, and essentially contingent explanation (Miller and Tsang, 2010; Welch *et al.*, 2012). Yet, it is the course of the process that provides the ultimate understanding of the realization of strategy. It deals with "how" questions by investigating the process by which things come about but also continue to be (Van de Ven and Sminia, 2012). This chapter is a first attempt to systematically describe how contextualized explanation should be done. Although it was presented in successive steps of how a research project should be set up, how to collect incident data, and how to analyze the data by coding and drafting a process account, the actual research process is much more circular. Each of these research activities have to inform each other, as is to be expected when the research essentially is abductive.

Contextualized explanation departs from the dominant variance approach in strategy research and embraces a process approach. The social constructed reality that it assumes is there to be investigated is essentially processual. It is a reality that consists of activity. It is by way of activity that things come into being and continue to exist. This is reflected in defining the basic qualitative datum that can be collected as an "incident" that in its basic form is a recording of activities. There is, however, a certain compatibility with variance research. The observed regularities between variables can serve as a prompt for asking the question "how" this regularity can exist. The other way round, contextualized explanations, especially in the form of social mechanisms, provide a much-needed underpinning for understanding observed regularities between variables (Miller and Tsang, 2011). Langley's (2009) quantification strategy and synthetic strategy for making sense of process data are two ways in which process research can inform variance research. Finally there is the claim that contextualized explanation offers a means for the "conscious coping" that strategy practitioners have to do when problems become really strategic (Chia and Mackay, 2007).

References

Abbott, A. (1990), A primer on sequence methods. *Organization Science*, vol.1, no.4, 375–392.

Allison, G. T. (1971), *Essence of Decision: Explaining the Cuban Missile Crisis*. Boston, MA: Little Brown.

Barley, S. R. (1986), Technology as an occasion for structuring: Evidence from observations of CT scanners and the social order of radiology departments. *Administrative Science Quarterly*, vol.31, 78–108.

Barley, S. R. (1990), Images of imagining: Notes on doing longitudinal fieldwork. *Organization Science*, vol.1, no.3, 220–247.

Barney, J. B. (1991), Firm resources and sustained competitive advantage. *Journal of Management*, vol.17, 99–120.

Bhaskar R. (2008), *A Realist Theory of Science*, 2nd edn. London: Verso.

Burgelman, R. A. (1983), A process model of internal corporate venturing in the diversified major firm. *Administrative Science Quarterly*, vol.28, 223–244.

Chandler, Jr., A. D. (1962), *Strategy and Structure*. Cambridge, MA: MIT Press.

Chia, R. and B. MacKay (2007), Post-processual challenges for the emerging strategy-as-practice perspective: Discovering strategy in the logic of practice. *Human Relations*, vol.60, no.1, 217–242.

Corbin, J. and A. Strauss (1990), Grounded theory research: Procedures, canons, and evaluative criteria. *Qualitative Sociology*, vol.13, no.1, 3–21.

De Rond, M. (2003*), Strategic Alliances as Social Facts*. Cambridge: Cambridge University Press.

Dierickx, I. and K. Cool (1989), Asset stock accumulation and sustainability of competitive advantage. *Management Science*, vol.35, no.12, 1504–1511.

Foss, N. J. (1998), The resource-based perspective: An assessment and diagnosis of problems. *Scandinavian Journal of Management*, vol.14, no.3, 133–149.

Giddens, A. (1984), *The Constitution of Society: Outline of a Theory of Structuration*. Cambridge: Polity Press.

Gladwell, M. (2000), *The Tipping Point: How Little Things Can Make a Big Difference*. London: Little Brown.

Glick, W. H., G. P. Huber, C. C. Miller, D. H. Doty, and K. M. Sutcliffe (1990), Studying changes in organizational design and effectiveness: Retrospective event histories and periodic assessments. *Organization Science*, vol.1, no.3, 293–312.

Golden, B. R. (1992), The past is the past — or is it? The use of retrospective accounts as indicators of past strategy. *Academy of Management Journal*, vol. 35, no.4, 848–860.

Gross, N. (2009), A pragmatist theory of social mechanisms. *American Sociological Review*, vol.74, no.3, 358–379.

Hendry, J. and D. Seidl (2003), The structure and significance of strategic episodes: Social systems theory and the routine practices of strategic change. *Journal of Management Studies*, vol.40, no.1, 175–196.

Johnson, G. (1987), *Strategic Change and the Management Process*. Oxford: Basil Blackwell.

Johnson, P., A. Buehring, C. Cassell, and G. Symon (2006), Evaluating qualitative management research: Towards a contingent criteriology. *International Journal of Management Reviews*, vol.8, no.3, 131–156.

Klag, M. and A. Langley (2013), Approaching the conceptual leap in qualitative research. *International Journal of Management Reviews*, vol.15, no.2, 149–166.

Langley, A. (1999), Strategies for theorizing from process data. *Academy of Management Review*, vol.24, no.4, 691–710.

Langley, A. and H. Tsoukas (2010), Introducing "perspectives on process organization studies." In: T. Hernes and S. Maitliss (eds), *Process, Sensemaking, and Organizing*. Oxford: Oxford University Press, 1–25.

Maritan, C. A. and M. A. Peteraf (2011), Building a bridge between resource acquisition and resource accumulation. *Journal of Management*, vol.37, no.5, 1374–1389.

Michailova, S. (2011), Contextualizing in international business research: Why do we need more of it and how can we be better at it? *Scandinavian Journal of Management*, vol.27, 129–139.

Miller, K. D. and E. W. Tsang (2010), Testing management theories: Critical realist philosophy and research methods. *Strategic Management Journal*, vol.32, 139–158.

Mintzberg, H., D. Raisinghani, and A. Théorêt (1976), The structure of "unstructured" decision processes. *Administrative Science Quarterly*, vol.21, 246–275.

Mohr, L. B. (1982), *Explaining Organizational Behavior: The Limits and Possibilities of Theory and Research*. San Francisco: Jossey-Bass.

Pepper, S. C. (1942), *World Hypothesis*. Berkeley, CA: University of California Press.

Peteraf, M. A. (1993), The cornerstones of competitive advantage: A resource-based view. *Strategic Management Journal*, vol.14, 179–191.

Pettigrew, A. M. (1985), *The Awakening Giant: Continuity and Change in ICI*. Oxford: Basil Blackwell.

Pettigrew, A. M. (1987), Context and action in the transformation of the firm. *Journal of Management Studies*, vol.24, no.6, 649–670.

Pettigrew, A. M. (1990), Longitudinal field research on change: Theory and practice. *Organizations Science*, vol.1, no.3, 267–292.

Pettigrew, A. M. (1992), The character and significance of strategy process research. *Strategic Management Journal*, vol.13, 5–16.

Pettigrew, A. M. and R. Whipp (1991), *Managing Change for Competitive Success*. Oxford: Basil Blackwell.

Poole, M. S. and A. H. Van de Ven (1989), Using paradox to build management and organization theories. *Academy of Management Review*, vol.14, no.4, 562–578.

Poole, M. S., A. H. Van de Ven, K. Dooley, and M.E. Holmes (2000), *Organizational Change and Innovation Processes: Theory and Methods for Research*. New York: Oxford University Press.

Porter, M. E. (1980), *Competitive Strategy: Techniques for Analyzing Industries and Competitors*. New York: Free Press.

Porter, M. E. (1991), Towards a dynamic theory of strategy. *Strategic Management Journal*, vol.12, winter issue, 95–117.

Shanley, M. and M. Peteraf (2006), The centrality of process. *International Journal of Strategic Change Management*, vol., no.1/2, 4–19.

Sminia, H. (2003), The failure of the Sport7 TV-channel: Controversies in a business network. *Journal of Management Studies*, vol.40, no.7, 1621–1649.

Sminia, H. (2005), Strategy formation as layered discussion. *Scandinavian Journal of Management*, vol.21, no.3, 267–291.

Sminia, H. (2009), Process research in strategy formation: Theory, methodology, and relevance. *International Journal of Management Reviews*, vol.11, no.1, 97–125.

Sminia, H. (2011), Institutional continuity and the Dutch construction industry fiddle. *Organization Studies*, vol.32, no.11, 1559–1586.

Sminia, H. and M. de Rond (2012), Context and action in the transformation of strategy scholarship. *Journal of Management Studies*, vol.49, no.7, 1329–1349.

Stevenson, W. B. and D. N. Greenberg (1998), The formal analysis of narratives of organizational change. *Journal of Management*, vol.24, no.6, 741–762.

Strauss, A. L., J. Corbin (1990), *Basics of Qualitative Research: Grounded Theory Procedures and Techniques*. Newbury Park, CA: Sage.

Tsang, E. W. K. (2013), Case study methodology: Causal explanation, contextualization, and theorizing. *Journal of International Management*, vol.19, 195–202.

Tsang, E. W. K. and K. M. Kwan (1999) Replication and theory development in organizational science: A critical realist perspective. *Academy of Management Review*, vol.24, no.4, 759–780.

Tsoukas, H. (1989), The validity of idiographic research explanations. *Academy of Management Review*, vol.14, no. 4, 551–561.

Vaughan, D. (1990), Autonomy, interdependence, and social control: NASA and the space shuttle Challenger. *Administrative Science Quarterly*, vol.35, no.2, 225–257.

Van de Ven, A. M. (2007), *Engaged Scholarship: A Guide for Organizational and Social Research*. Oxford: Oxford University Press.

Van de Ven, A. H., H. L. Angle and M. S. Poole (eds) (1989), *Research on the Management of Innovation*. New York: Harper and Row.

Van de Ven, A. H. and M. S. Poole (1995), Explaining development and change in organizations. *Academy of Management Review*, vol.20, no.3, 510–540.

Van de Ven, A. H. and H. Sminia (2012), Aligning process questions, perspectives and explanations. In: M. Schultz, S. Maguire, A. Langley and H. Tsoukas (eds), *Constructing Identity In and Around Organizations*. Oxford: Oxford University Press, 306–319.

Welch, C., R. Piekkari, E. Plakoyiannaki, and E. Paavilainen-Mäntymäki (2011), Theorising from case studies: Towards a pluralist future for international business research. *Journal of International Business Studies*, vol.42, 740–762.

Yin, R. K. (2014), *Case Study Research: Design and Methods*, 5th edn. Thousand Oaks, CA: Sage.

5

STRUCTURAL EQUATIONS MODELING

Theory and applications in strategic management

Gaetano "Nino" Miceli and Claudio Barbaranelli

Introduction

Structural equation modelling (SEM) is a fundamental analytical tool for any behavioral researcher (Bagozzi and Yi 2012; Iacobucci 2009). SEM represents a natural extension of factor analysis and regression analysis and is therefore used to investigate relationships between observed variables (i.e. quantities that can be measured directly) and latent variables (i.e. concepts that cannot be measured directly), as well as causal relationships between latent variables. Thanks to its flexibility, SEM may be applied to a wide range of research problems, from construct measurement and the assessment of psychometric properties to theory testing and path analysis (Byrne 1998).

Indeed, the whole SEM framework includes the *measurement model*, which allows the researcher to specify the relationships between observed variables and latent variables; and the *structural model*, which permits the researcher to specify the relationships between latent variables (Bollen 1989). Importantly, it is possible to estimate either the whole SEM framework or, by applying appropriate restrictions, only specific sub-models. In detail, a researcher has the opportunity:

- to estimate only the measurement model, that is, applying confirmatory factor analysis (CFA);
- to estimate only the structural model limiting the analysis to observed variables, that is, applying path analysis with observed variables;
- to estimate simultaneously the measurement model and the structural model, that is, a full structural equation model to test causal relationships among latent variables measured by observed variables.

Before discussing the framework in detail, we introduce some general features of SEM philosophy and theory.

The philosophy underlying SEM can be effectively discussed by introducing preliminarily some of its mechanisms. On the one hand, the input data of any SEM consists of the *observed variance-covariance matrix* computed on the observed variables. On the other hand, and based on a set of covariance algebra rules, the model specified by the researcher is expressed as a function of parameters in the shape of the *implied variance-covariance matrix*. The construction of the implied variance-covariance matrix depends crucially on model specification, which refers to the researcher's decisions about which parameters should be estimated (e.g. *free* parameters), set to certain values (e.g. zero), or constrained to functions of other parameters (e.g. equality constraints). Therefore, the implied variance-covariance matrix is generated on the basis of the model (i.e. the theory) to be tested. While we refer the reader to the fourth section (p. 113) for a discussion of how the implied variance-covariance matrix can be constructed, it is important to immediately clarify that SEM estimation is based on comparing the observed variance-covariance matrix and the implied variance-covariance matrix − in other words, *reality* (i.e. the data) and *theory* (i.e. the researcher's model). The more similar the two matrices, the better the model fit, and, therefore, the possibility to accept the proposed theory as correct. The higher the difference between the two matrices, the lower the model fit, and, therefore, the tenability of the proposed theory. In this respect, SEM is considered a *confirmative tool*, that is, it can be applied to test a pre-existing theory and to verify whether it fits the data.

For estimating a SEM, it is then crucial to *identify* the model, that is, to take care of a set of conditions ensuring that there is enough input information to estimate the unknown parameters in measurement and structural equations. Technically (see pp. 115–116 for more detail), it is required that the model has non-negative degrees of freedom. If this is true, there exist different potential sets of parameters satisfying the model equations and it is possible to select the one achieving an optimal criterion (i.e. minimizing the distance between the observed variance-covariance matrix and the implied variance-covariance matrix). Although SEM was originally developed as a purely confirmative technique, its powerful diagnostics (i.e. modification indices, residuals) allow, and are often used, to re-specify a model lacking in fit. Clearly, such practice may be criticized to the extent to which model re-specification to improve fit capitalizes on data and not on theory. Based on this introductory section, Figure 5.1 presents a schematic general sequence of SEM.

SEM is a tremendously useful tool as it overcomes several limitations of regression analysis. First, SEM allows to estimate simultaneously several regression equations and therefore permits to specify models with multiple dependent variables. As an example, consider a classic mediation model in which X influences M, and M influences Y; the simultaneous fitting of these two paths via SEM is not only more parsimonious than in a regression framework (which would require the estimation of two separate models), but it is also able to produce more precise, less biased, and more efficient estimates. Thus, while regression analysis is a limited information model/technique, SEM is a full information model/technique, since it considers simultaneously all the relations among variables that a researcher is

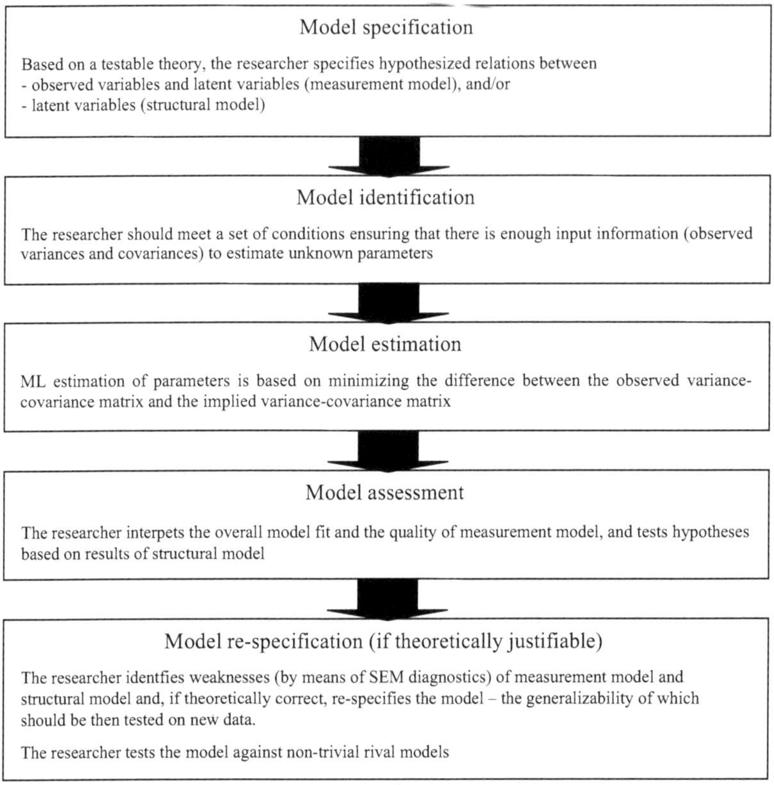

Model specification
Based on a testable theory, the researcher specifies hypothesized relations between - observed variables and latent variables (measurement model), and/or - latent variables (structural model)

Model identification
The researcher should meet a set of conditions ensuring that there is enough input information (observed variances and covariances) to estimate unknown parameters

Model estimation
ML estimation of parameters is based on minimizing the difference between the observed variance-covariance matrix and the implied variance-covariance matrix

Model assessment
The researcher interpets the overall model fit and the quality of measurement model, and tests hypotheses based on results of structural model

Model re-specification (if theoretically justifiable)
The researcher identfies weaknesses (by means of SEM diagnostics) of measurement model and structural model and, if theoretically correct, re-specifies the model – the generalizability of which should be then tested on new data. The researcher tests the model against non-trivial rival models

FIGURE 5.1 A common sequence in SEM

interested to test (Iacobucci 2009). Second, upon certain conditions, SEM enables the researcher to estimate *non-recursive models*, in which, for instance, X influences Y, and Y influences X (reciprocal causation); or X influences Y, Y influences Z, which in turn influences X (feedback effect). Such models cannot be accommodated using regression analysis, but can be estimated via SEM by imposing some needed restrictions on the model (Kline 2010). Finally, and again contrarily to regression analysis, SEM deals with measurement error by separating error variance from constructs' substantial variability. While in regression analysis both measurement error and error attributable to models' lack of fit fall into an overall residual quantity, within the SEM framework the researcher can model (and isolate) these two types of errors. This property is particularly relevant because, by isolating measurement error from constructs' scores used in path analysis, SEM reduces the deleterious effects of *unreliability* (Bollen 1989). Indeed, unreliability of measures related to independent variables produces biased parameter estimates (most of the times reducing the influences of independent variables on dependent variables), whereas unreliability related to the dependent variable reduces the variance explained by the model, that is, the R^2. This means that, particularly when unreliability of measures is likely to be substantial, using SEM instead of regression analysis produces unbiased parameter estimates and increases the probability to capture statistically significant effects. Also, the opportunity to discriminate different sources of errors consents more precise diagnostics for improving the model fit (when allowed by theory-driven reasons), as it is possible to assess whether the lack of fit is due to either measurement error or to model misspecification (Iacobucci 2009).

Disadvantages of using SEM are often over-emphasized by researchers that are not comfortable with modeling and model programming. While software packages have increasingly become more user-friendly, thus reducing operational costs and the user learning curve, it is undeniable that SEM requires a reasonable sample size, stringent distributional assumptions on data, and some knowledge about statistics and (preferably) matrix algebra. About sample size, assuming there are no major problems with data (e.g. missing or non-normal data), a minimum sample size of 200 is often recommended for any SEM. However, there is evidence that the optimal sample size may depend on the desired power and the model complexity (MacCallum, Browne, and Sugawara 1996), with larger sample sizes that are needed when more power is desired and more complex models are estimated. If the measures are highly reliable, the effects are expected to be strong, and the model not overly complex, smaller samples may be reasonable (Bearden, Sharma, and Teel 1982). In these cases SEM can perform well even with small samples (50 to 100) (Iacobucci 2010); still, it is preferable to meet a 10-to-1 (or at least 5-to-1) observations-to-parameters ratio (Bentler and Chou 1987). If deciding the sample size is a particularly crucial decision, it is possible to compute the N required for a specific model and the desired level of power, as well as an estimate of power for a given sample size (MacCallum, Browne, and Cai 2006).

Most of the time, SEM estimation is based on *maximum likelihood* (ML), which assumes that the observed variables jointly follow the *multivariate normal distribution*. Such an assumption is often violated in real-world data, causing inflated misfit indices and standard errors (Bollen 1989). The violation of this crucial assumption is one of the arguments used by SEM critics and followers of rival techniques (e.g. regression, partial least squares). However, there is enough evidence showing that ML is robust to non-severe violations of the assumption of multivariate normal distribution (e.g. Hu, Bentler, and Kano 1992). Also, robust ML estimators are widely available to get unbiased estimates of standard errors and fit indices (Satorra and Bentler 1988). Finally, new weighted least squares robust estimators (WLS), which do not require any distributional assumption, have been recently developed. These WLS estimators allow to obtain unbiased parameter estimates, standard errors and fit indices even in the presence of severe non-normality and moderate sample size (Flora and Curran 2004). Arguably, for those willing to learn SEM theory, disadvantages are largely overcome by advantages offered by SEM.

A final forewarning concerns SEM and causality. Assessing causal relationships is of crucial importance and, at the same time, highly controversial. To establish causal relationships, philosophers of science adopt the criteria of Hume and Mill, requiring: (1) concomitant variation (i.e., if X causes Y, then X and Y should be correlated); (2) temporal precedence of the independent variable over the dependent variable; and (3) elimination of rival explanations of the causal effect. Accordingly, experimentation is considered the best research approach to establish causality thanks to manipulation of independent variables, subsequent measurement of the dependent variable, and control of external sources of variation through randomized assignment of participants to experimental and control conditions.

SEM is often applied on non-experimental data and therefore many researchers argue that results of SEM cannot be used to claim causal effects. The problem does not concern only SEM but all techniques applied on non-experimental data (e.g. regression analysis). As discussed by Iacobucci (2009), while SEM has often been related to causal modelling, "many statisticians are conservative regarding the use of the term 'causal' (or even 'affects' or 'impacts'), preferring instead to conclude, 'X helps predict Y'" (674). Although these concerns are well-grounded, it is also important to point out that the combination of a strong theory and SEM is probably the best recipe a researcher – working on non-experimental data – may adopt to make her/his causal claims more convincing. Indeed, SEM allows confronting a theory-driven model (proposing certain causal effects) with data, and also with potential rival models (proposing different causal effects). Even in the absence of experimental data, a model that fits the data better than competing causal representations and that has strong theoretical arguments is likely to be correct, including its causal claims. As Pearl has recently pointed out:

> One can legitimately be in a possession of a parameter that stands for a causal effect and still be unable, using statistical means alone, to determine the magnitude of that parameter given non-experimental data. As a matter of fact, we know that, no such statistical means exists; that is, causal effects in observational studies can only be substantiated from a combination of data and untested, theoretical assumptions; not from the data alone. Thus, if reliance on theoretical assumptions disqualifies SEM's parameters from having an interpretation as causal effects, no method whatsoever can endow any parameter with such interpretation, and causal vocabulary should be purged from scientific discourse – an unthinkable restriction.
>
> *(Pearl 2012: 68)*

That is, SEM is not a *panacea* to assess causality, but if applied correctly to test a strong theory it may certainly help a lot.

In this chapter, we illustrate SEM from both theoretical and applicative perspectives. Specifically, we describe the measurement model and the structural model, illustrate the estimation procedure, and address relevant criteria and indices to assess SEM. Also, we review and discuss the application of SEM in the strategic management literature. Finally, we briefly present some advanced topics.

The measurement model

The measurement model consists of a set of linear relationships linking observed variables and latent variables. Estimating only the measurement model is equivalent to apply *confirmatory factor analysis* (CFA). This part of the model is crucial to achieve the goal of measuring theoretical constructs (i.e. latent variables) that cannot be directly measured. Indeed, estimating CFA is considered an unavoidable step to assess reliability and construct validity of measures of latent constructs (Anderson and Gerbing 1988; Churchill 1979).

Before introducing the measurement model, it is important to discuss the *variables* that can be analyzed within the SEM framework.[1] As already mentioned, based on the possibility to register manifestations of the phenomenon under study, one can distinguish *observed* (directly measurable) and *latent* (not directly measurable) variables. Moreover, and anticipating the discussion of causal relationships specified in a theoretical model (i.e. the structural model), it is possible to identify *exogenous* variables, which act only as independent variables, and the variances of which are determined outside the scope of the hypothesized model; and *endogenous* variables, which act in at least one equation of the model as dependent variable, and the variances of which are partially determined within the scope of the hypothesized model. Crossing these two classifications, it is possible to identity four types of variables:

- *latent exogenous variables,* which are represented by the Greek letter ξ (ksi);
- *observed exogenous variables*, which are represented by the letter x, and are measures of latent exogenous variables;
- *latent endogenous variables,* which are represented by the Greek letter η (eta);
- *observed endogenous variables*, which are represented by the letter y, and are measures of latent endogenous variables.

The four types of variables are not necessarily present in any SEM model. Actually, when we apply confirmatory factor analysis there are no hypothesized causal relationships among latent variables, that is, all the involved latent variables are exogenous variables (or independent variables). In such a model, there is no need to specify η or y variables.[2] Later (p. 111), we will discuss other instances in which the researcher may be interested only in sub-models of the whole SEM framework and, therefore, in specific types of variables.

Coming back to the discussion of the measurement model, it consists, in the whole SEM framework, of a set of equations expressing the relationships between:

- observed exogenous variables and latent exogenous variables;
- observed endogenous variables and latent endogenous variables.

The measurement model aims at specifying the observed variables as linear functions of latent variables and measurement errors. Following the tradition of *reflective measurement* (Edwards and Bagozzi 2000), in the measurement model the variance of each observed variable is modelled as the sum of two parts: the variance shared with other observed variables (expressed by the hypothesized latent variable) and the variance due to uncontrolled sources, that is, the measurement error.

The relationships between observed and latent variables are typically expressed, in compact matrix forms, as follows:

$$x = \Lambda_x \xi + \delta \qquad (5.1)$$

$$y = \Lambda_y \eta + \varepsilon \qquad (5.2)$$

in which x is the vector containing the k observed exogenous variables; Λ_x (lambda-x) is the matrix containing the parameters expressing the relationships between observed exogenous variables and latent exogenous variables; ξ is the vector containing the l latent exogenous variables; δ (delta) is the vector containing the k measurement errors acting on the x's; y is the vector containing the m observed endogenous variables; Λ_y (lambda-y) is the matrix containing the parameters expressing the relationships between observed endogenous variables and latent endogenous variables; η is the vector containing the n latent endogenous variables; ε (epsilon) is the vector containing the m measurement errors acting on the y's. Equations (5.1) and (5.2) are short forms for the following matrix expressions:

$$\begin{pmatrix} x_1 \\ x_2 \\ \cdots \\ x_k \end{pmatrix} = \begin{pmatrix} \lambda^x_{11} & \lambda^x_{12} & \cdots & \cdots & \lambda^x_{1l} \\ \lambda^x_{21} & \lambda^x_{22} & \cdots & \cdots & \cdots \\ \cdots & \cdots & \cdots & \cdots & \cdots \\ \lambda^x_{k1} & \cdots & \cdots & \cdots & \lambda^x_{kl} \end{pmatrix} \begin{pmatrix} \xi_1 \\ \xi_2 \\ \cdots \\ \xi_l \end{pmatrix} + \begin{pmatrix} \delta_1 \\ \delta_2 \\ \cdots \\ \delta_k \end{pmatrix} \qquad (5.3)$$

$$\begin{pmatrix} y_1 \\ y_2 \\ \cdots \\ y_m \end{pmatrix} = \begin{pmatrix} \lambda^y_{11} & \lambda^y_{12} & \cdots & \cdots & \lambda^y_{1n} \\ \lambda^y_{21} & \lambda^y_{22} & \cdots & \cdots & \cdots \\ \cdots & \cdots & \cdots & \cdots & \cdots \\ \lambda^y_{m1} & \cdots & \cdots & \cdots & \lambda^y_{mn} \end{pmatrix} \begin{pmatrix} \eta_1 \\ \eta_2 \\ \cdots \\ \eta_n \end{pmatrix} + \begin{pmatrix} \varepsilon_1 \\ \varepsilon_2 \\ \cdots \\ \varepsilon_m \end{pmatrix} \qquad (5.4)$$

Notice that equations (5.1) and (5.2) do not consider intercepts. As a matter of fact, in most SEM models, intercepts are not modeled and therefore implicitly set to zero, thus treating variables as mean-centered. This approach is normally used in standard single-sample analysis. However, in single-group analysis concerning longitudinal data or growth-curve models (e.g. McArdle and Anderson 1990; Aber and McArdle 1991), as well as in multi-group analysis (e.g. Steenkamp and Baumgartner 1998), the researcher usually needs to model also the mean part of the model and therefore to specify intercepts.

The expressions reported in equations (5.1)–(5.4) can be easily re-written into a set of linear equations. Let's consider the following example, in which a researcher wants to specify a measurement model of three constructs related to Business-to-Business relationships: Partner's dependability (DEP – ξ_1), cooperation (COOP – ξ_2), and long-term orientation in business relationships (LTO – ξ_3). Each construct is measured by means of four observed variables (DEP: x_1, x_2, x_3, and x_4; COOP: x_5, x_6, x_7, and x_8; and LTO: x_9, x_{10}, x_{11}, and x_{12}), which could be seven–point Likert scales expressing facets of the related constructs. Then, assuming that the researcher is interested in estimating a CFA, the measurement model can be expressed in terms of the following sets of equations:

$$
\begin{aligned}
x_1 &= \lambda_{11}^x \xi_1 + \delta_1 & x_5 &= \lambda_{52}^x \xi_2 + \delta_5 & x_9 &= \lambda_{93}^x \xi_3 + \delta_9 & (5.5)\\
x_2 &= \lambda_{21}^x \xi_1 + \delta_2 & x_6 &= \lambda_{62}^x \xi_2 + \delta_6 & x_{10} &= \lambda_{103}^x \xi_3 + \delta_{10}\\
x_3 &= \lambda_{31}^x \xi_1 + \delta_3 & x_7 &= \lambda_{72}^x \xi_2 + \delta_7 & x_{11} &= \lambda_{113}^x \xi_3 + \delta_{11}\\
x_4 &= \lambda_{41}^x \xi_1 + \delta_4 & x_8 &= \lambda_{82}^x \xi_2 + \delta_8 & x_{12} &= \lambda_{123}^x \xi_3 + \delta_{12}
\end{aligned}
$$

It is immediately evident that, while the Λ_x matrix shown in equation (5.3) would potentially include 12×3 parameters, the specified model considers only 12 "free" lambda-x parameters. The other 24 lambda-x parameters are set to zero in accordance to the measurement theory proposed by the researcher, who suggests that x_1, x_2, x_3, and x_4 are related to DEP, but not to COOP and LTO; that x_5, x_6, x_7, and x_8 are related to COOP but not to DEP and LTO; and that x_9, x_{10}, x_{11}, and x_{12} are related to LTO but not to DEP and COOP. Differently, in an exploratory factor analysis, the Λ_x matrix would be fully estimated. Parameters contained in the lambda matrices, indeed, are interpreted as *factor loadings*.

Notice that this model, representing an example of CFA, does not concern equations (5.2) or (5.4). As we have not hypothesized (so far) causal relationships among the investigated constructs, dependability, cooperation, and long-term orientation all act in the model as independent variables. Therefore, we just need to specify equations (5.1) or (5.3). If we would hypothesize any causal relationships between the investigated constructs (i.e. introducing also the structural model), then those acting *only* as independent variable would still be treated as exogenous latent variables, but those acting *even in a single equation* as dependent variable would then be treated as endogenous latent variables. In this case, we would need to specify *also* equations (5.2) or (5.4).

Equations (5.5) make evident an important formal rule in SEM. Parameters expressing causal relationships have subscripts in which the number of the dependent variable precedes the number of the independent variable. As an example, the lambda-x parameter expressing the relation between x_3 (dependent variable) and ξ_1 (independent variable) is λ_{31}^x.

The measurement model also includes the Φ (phi) matrix, that is, the variance-covariance matrix among exogenous latent variables:

$$\Phi = \begin{pmatrix} \phi_{11} & & & \\ \phi_{21} & \phi_{22} & & \\ \dots & \dots & \dots & \\ \phi_{l1} & \dots & \dots & \phi_{ll} \end{pmatrix} \tag{5.6}$$

Elements on the diagonal of the Φ matrix are variances of exogenous latent variables whereas elements below the diagonal are covariances between exogenous latent variables. Notice that when considering standardized variables, a variance-covariance matrix becomes a correlation matrix. This applies to the Φ matrix, which allows the researcher either to estimate or to set to zero correlations among exogenous latent variables. Parameters expressing covariances, as ϕs below the diagonal, have subscripts in which the order of the numbers related to specific exogenous latent variables is arbitrarily chosen, though it is common to use the lower triangle of the Φ matrix and therefore to postpone the lowest number to the highest number in the pair of variables. Parameters expressing variances, as ϕs on the diagonal, have subscripts with the number of the related exogenous latent variable repeated twice. For instance, ϕ_{31} is the covariance between ξ_3 and ξ_1; ϕ_{11} is the variance of ξ_1.

As a matter of fact, the Φ matrix is set as: (a) *symmetrical*, when the researcher hypothesizes that at least two exogenous latent variables are correlated with each other (then the relative covariances are estimated), a decision comparable to an *oblique rotation* in exploratory factor analysis; or (b) *diagonal*, when the researcher hypothesizes that exogenous latent variables are uncorrelated with each other (all the covariances are set to zero), a decision comparable to an *orthogonal rotation* in exploratory factor analysis.

The measurement model expressed in analytical form in equations (5.5) can be represented graphically in a *path diagram*. Assuming that DEP, COOP, and LTO are correlated with each other, the path diagram of the discussed model is represented in Figure 5.2.

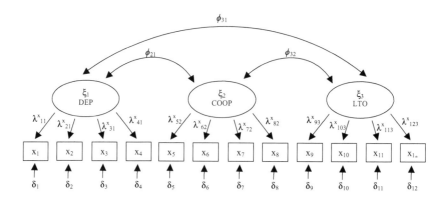

FIGURE 5.2 Path diagram for a CFA

SEM path diagrams follow a set of formal rules (Bollen 1989), which posit that latent variables should be represented into circles or ellipses and observed variables should be represented in squares. Errors and parameters are reported with no boxes, single-headed arrows represent relationships between independent and dependent variables as expressed in linear equations, while curved double-headed arrows represent covariances.

Path diagrams, as well as Equations (5.1)–(5.5), do not fully show how errors are modelled in SEM. In fact, errors are unobserved parts of linear equations and are assumed to conform to usual OLS-like assumptions (zero mean, constant variance, independence from independent variables). Beyond relying on assumptions, in SEM one can model variances and covariances concerning errors and therefore control for such quantities.

This is a most relevant feature, because it consents, in equations (5.5), to distinguish the variance of x's (dependent variables) in the sum of explained variance (the R^2 for each equation, due to the contribution of ξ's) and unexplained variance, the latter being indeed the error variance. Therefore, we need to introduce two further matrices, containing variances and covariances of measurement errors δ and ε:

$$\Theta^\delta = \begin{pmatrix} \theta^\delta_{11} & & & \\ \theta^\delta_{21} & \theta^\delta_{22} & & \\ ... & ... & ... & \\ \theta^\delta_{k1} & ... & ... & \theta^\delta_{kk} \end{pmatrix} \tag{5.7}$$

$$\Theta^\varepsilon = \begin{pmatrix} \theta^\varepsilon_{11} & & & \\ \theta^\varepsilon_{21} & \theta^\varepsilon_{22} & & \\ ... & ... & ... & \\ \theta^\varepsilon_{m1} & ... & ... & \theta^\varepsilon_{mm} \end{pmatrix} \tag{5.8}$$

Elements on the diagonal of the Θ^δ (theta-delta) and Θ^ε (theta-epsilon) matrices are variances of measurement errors δ and ε, respectively. Elements below the diagonal in these two matrices are error covariances. Again, notice that the CFA model under discussion concerns only Equation (5.1) or (5.3), and therefore takes into account the Θ^δ matrix but not the Θ^ε matrix (but see Note 2). If we would hypothesize any causal relationships between the investigated constructs (i.e. introducing also the structural model), then we would need to specify *also* Equation (5.2) or (5.4) and therefore model *also* the Θ^ε matrix.

The Θ^δ and Θ^ε matrices can be set as symmetrical; however, it is common and advisable to specify them as diagonal and therefore estimating only the error variances, thus setting error covariances to zero. Estimating covariances between errors, though often beneficial for the model fit, is strongly criticized as it equals to admit some weaknesses in the proposed measurement model (i.e. there exists something linking the observed variables that it was not modeled). It is possible to identify specific contingencies in which estimating error covariances may be justifiable – e.g. to accommodate for reverse-scored items (e.g. Marsh 1996), to control for repeated measures of the same construct (e.g. Bollen and Curran 2006), or when estimating the *correlated uniqueness model* in the so-called multi-trait-multi-method analysis (e.g. Bagozzi and Yi 1990; Podsakoff, MacKenzie, Lee, and Podsakoff 2003). The SEM literature converges in warning researchers to resist temptations to estimate error covariances that would certainly improve the model fit but definitely reduce the theory tenability (MacCallum, Roznowski, and Necowitz 1993).

To sum up, we have so far introduced four types of variables (ξ, η, x, and y), two parameter matrices (Λ^x and Λ^y), one variance-covariance matrix between exogenous latent variables (Φ), and two variance-covariance matrices between measurement errors (Θ^δ and Θ^ε).

The structural model

The structural model deals with causal relationships among latent variables. Therefore, the structural model is specified when the researcher is interested, beyond measurement modeling, to specify effects from exogenous latent variables to endogenous latent variables, or even between endogenous latent variables. As for the measurement model, the structural model can be expressed in compact matrix form:

$$\eta = B\eta + \Gamma\xi + \zeta \tag{5.9}$$

in which **B** (beta) is the matrix containing the parameters expressing the relationships between latent endogenous variables; η is the vector containing the n latent endogenous variables; Γ (gamma) is the matrix containing the parameters expressing the relationships between latent exogenous variables and latent endogenous variables; ξ is the vector containing the l latent exogenous variables; ζ (zeta) is the vector containing the n structural errors acting on the η's. Notice that equation (5.9) does not consider intercepts, and is a short form for the following matrix expression:

$$
\begin{pmatrix} \eta_1 \\ \eta_2 \\ \dots \\ \eta_n \end{pmatrix} = \begin{pmatrix} 0 & \beta_{12} & \dots & \beta_{1n} \\ \beta_{21} & 0 & & \dots \\ \dots & \dots & 0 & \dots \\ \beta_{n1} & \dots & \dots & 0 \end{pmatrix} \begin{pmatrix} \eta_1 \\ \eta_2 \\ \dots \\ \eta_n \end{pmatrix} + \begin{pmatrix} \gamma_{11} & \gamma_{12} & \dots & \dots & \gamma_{1l} \\ \gamma_{21} & \gamma_{22} & \dots & \dots & \dots \\ \dots & \dots & \dots & \dots & \dots \\ \gamma_{n1} & \dots & \dots & \dots & \gamma_{nl} \end{pmatrix} \begin{pmatrix} \xi_1 \\ \xi_2 \\ \dots \\ \xi_l \end{pmatrix} + \begin{pmatrix} \zeta_1 \\ \zeta_2 \\ \dots \\ \zeta_n \end{pmatrix} \tag{5.10}
$$

If the researcher is interested in estimating only the structural model, thus limiting the analysis to observed variables and applying path analysis on observed variables, Equations (5.9) and (5.10) should be adapted accordingly. When one estimates relations among observed variables (but not latent variables) the y-variables are set equal to the η variables (the corresponding λ^y parameter is implicitly set to one, and the measurement error variance θ^ε is set to zero), and the x-variables are set equal to the ξ variables (the corresponding λ^x parameter is implicitly set to one, and the measurement error variance θ^δ is set to zero). Therefore, we introduce equations (5.9bis) and (5.10bis) that represent a structural model with observed variables in compact and extended forms:

$$y = By + \Gamma x + \zeta \tag{5.9bis}$$

$$
\begin{pmatrix} y_1 \\ y_2 \\ \dots \\ y_m \end{pmatrix} = \begin{pmatrix} 0 & \beta_{12} & \dots & \beta_{1m} \\ \beta_{21} & 0 & & \dots \\ \dots & & \dots & 0 \\ \beta_{m1} & \dots & & 0 \end{pmatrix} \begin{pmatrix} y_1 \\ y_2 \\ \dots \\ y_m \end{pmatrix} + \begin{pmatrix} \gamma_{11} & \gamma_{12} & \dots & \dots & \gamma_{1k} \\ \gamma_{21} & \gamma_{22} & \dots & \dots & \dots \\ \dots & \dots & \dots & \dots & \dots \\ \gamma_{m1} & \dots & \dots & \dots & \gamma_{mk} \end{pmatrix} \begin{pmatrix} x_1 \\ x_2 \\ \dots \\ x_k \end{pmatrix} + \begin{pmatrix} \zeta_1 \\ \zeta_2 \\ \dots \\ \zeta_m \end{pmatrix} \tag{5.10bis}
$$

We will continue the discussion of the structural model, however, focusing on Equations (5.9) and (5.10). Before presenting an example, it is worthwhile to add some comments. First, as discussed for the measurement model, the B matrix and the Γ matrix potentially contain a certain number of parameters depending on the numbers of endogenous and exogenous latent variables. However, in most cases, the researcher builds upon her/his theory and is interested in estimating only some specific parameters and setting the others to zero. Second, the B matrix, which contains parameters expressing the effects of latent endogenous variables on other latent endogenous variables, has intuitively zero-effects on the diagonal (it is not possible to model the effect of a variable on itself). Third, the structural errors contained in the ζ vector, though statistically similar to measurement errors δ and ε, are interpreted in a slightly different mode. While δ's and ε's express the misfit of the measurement model, ζ's represent the part of unexplained variance in the dependent variables η's.

To discuss a simple instance of structural model, let us come back to the dependability-cooperation-long-term orientation example. We assume that our theory suggests that DEP positively affects COOP and LTO. Also, we hypothesize that COOP positively influences LTO. In contrast to the CFA model, in which all the latent variables were exogenous (they do not act as dependent variables), in this structural model we need to label any latent variable acting as dependent variable (in at least one equation) as an endogenous latent variable (η), and any latent variable acting only as independent variable as an exogenous latent variable (ξ). In our model, accordingly, LTO (η_1) and COOP (η_2) are endogenous latent variables and DEP (ξ_1) is an exogenous latent variable. Assuming that the three constructs are measured by the same four observed variable each, we also need to update our measurement model, as well as our labelling of observed variables. Indeed, observed variables related to endogenous latent variables LTO (η_1) and COOP (η_2) should become endogenous observed variables (y_1-y_4 and y_5-y_8, respectively); measures of DEP (ξ_1) can be labelled again as x_1-x_4. Accordingly, the measurement model can be updated and expressed in terms of the following sets of equations:

$$x_1 = \lambda^x_{11}\xi_1 + \delta_1 \qquad y_1 = \lambda^y_{11}\eta_1 + \varepsilon_1 \qquad y_5 = \lambda^y_{52}\eta_2 + \varepsilon_5 \qquad (5.11)$$
$$x_2 = \lambda^x_{21}\xi_1 + \delta_2 \qquad y_2 = \lambda^y_{21}\eta_1 + \varepsilon_2 \qquad y_6 = \lambda^y_{62}\eta_2 + \varepsilon_6$$
$$x_3 = \lambda^x_{31}\xi_1 + \delta_3 \qquad y_3 = \lambda^y_{31}\eta_1 + \varepsilon_3 \qquad y_7 = \lambda^y_{72}\eta_2 + \varepsilon_7$$
$$x_4 = \lambda^x_{41}\xi_1 + \delta_4 \qquad y_4 = \lambda^y_{41}\eta_1 + \varepsilon_4 \qquad y_8 = \lambda^y_{82}\eta_2 + \varepsilon_8$$

The structural model includes as many equations as those derivable from the theory (i.e. the hypotheses) under discussion. In our example, the structural equations are:

$$\eta_1 = \beta_{12}\eta_2 + \gamma_{11}\xi_1 + \zeta_1$$
$$\eta_2 = \gamma_{21}\xi_1 + \zeta_2 \qquad (5.12)$$

that is, as stated in the hypotheses, LTO (η_1) is determined by COOP (η_2) and DEP (ξ_1), and COOP (η_2) is determined by DEP (ξ_1). The full structural equation model discussed in our example can be represented in the path diagram shown in Figure 5.3.

As discussed with reference to measurement errors δ and ε, we need to introduce a specific matrix containing variances and covariances concerning structural errors ζ's, which represent the parts of unexplained variance in the dependent variables η's. Considering a standardized solution (in which variables are standardized, that is, they have mean equal to zero and variance equal to one), the sum of the R^2 of, say, the equation of LTO (η_1) and the variance of ζ_1 will be 1.

The variance-covariance matrix of structural errors ζ's is called Ψ (psi).

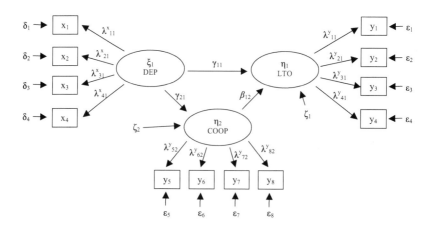

FIGURE 5.3 Path diagram for a full SEM

$$(5.13)$$

$$\Psi = \begin{pmatrix} \psi_{11} & & & \\ \psi_{21} & \psi_{22} & & \\ \dots & \dots & \dots & \\ \psi_{n1} & \dots & \dots & \psi_{nn} \end{pmatrix}$$

Elements on the diagonal of the Ψ matrix are variances of structural errors ζ, whereas elements below the diagonal are covariances between the same errors. The Ψ matrix can be set as diagonal when the researcher is interested in estimating only structural error variances. Alternatively, the Ψ matrix can be set as symmetrical when the researcher is interested in estimating both variances and either all or specific covariances between structural errors. The latter approach is commonly adopted when the researcher wants to control correlations between two or more endogenous latent variables about which no causal effect (i.e. β) is specified. Therefore, it is important to point out that, differently from that discussed with reference to the measurement model, estimating covariances among structural errors can be absolutely reasonable, particularly in models with multiple dependent variables the variances and covariances of which could be explained by some omitted independent variable. To control for such a potential source of misfit, the researcher may allow structural errors to covary with each other (Kline 2010).

To sum up, we have further introduced two parameter matrices (Γ and B), and one variance-covariance matrix between structural errors (Ψ). In total, we have discussed the eight matrices that can be specified in single-sample SEM. Table 5.1 shows the basic models that can be estimated using the SEM framework and the eight parameter matrices.

As already mentioned, by focusing only on the measurement model (ignoring causal relations among constructs), the researcher basically applies CFA and has to estimate only three matrices of parameters. Alternatively, it is possible to estimate only the structural model (setting the measurement model to zero), which consists of a set of regression equations, usually with multiple dependent variables, that are estimated simultaneously. In this case, the researcher should specify at most four matrices. Estimating both the measurement model and the structural model

TABLE 5.1 Basic models estimable within the SEM framework

Type of analysis	Measurement model	Structural model	Matrices to be specified
CFA	Specified	Unspecified (set to zero)	Λ^x, Φ, Θ^δ (or Λ^y, Ψ, Θ^ε in "all-y" models)
Path analysis with observed variables	Unspecified (set to zero)	Specified	Γ, B, Ψ, Φ
Full SEM	Specified	Specified	Λ^x, Λ^y, Θ^δ, Θ^ε, Φ, Γ, B, Ψ

corresponds to applying path analysis with latent variables, thus specifying a *full* SEM. Of course, Table 5.1 does not cover all the possible models that can be specified within the SEM framework. Instances of more advanced applications will be briefly discussed later (see pp. 128–132). In most cases, however, the researcher can specify more sophisticated models relying on the same eight matrices that have been introduced so far.

Estimation of SEM

The estimation objective in SEM consists in identifying numeric values for the model parameters that are able to approximate as accurately as possible the data. The most applied estimation method used to solve the analytical problem is *maximum likelihood* (ML), although other estimators have been proposed to overcome some of the (rigid) ML assumptions.

The logic underlying ML estimation is reasonably straightforward. As anticipated, SEM estimation is based on the comparison of the *observed variance-covariance matrix* and the *implied variance-covariance matrix*; the former (Σ) concerns the observed variables, whereas the latter ($\Sigma(\theta)$) is function of the model parameters. Accordingly, Σ is easily computed based on observed data. Let's consider a very simple CFA model concerning three observed variables, x_1, x_2, and x_3, which measure one latent variable (the presented logic can be extended to more complicated models). The observed variance-covariance matrix, which can be computed from the raw data, is:

$$\Sigma = \begin{pmatrix} \text{var}(x_1) & & \\ \text{cov}(x_2, x_1) & \text{var}(x_2) & \\ \text{cov}(x_3, x_1) & \text{cov}(x_3, x_2) & \text{var}(x_3) \end{pmatrix} \tag{5.14}$$

The true challenge is to understand how $\Sigma(\theta)$ can be expressed as a function of the model parameters. To do so, we need to use some basic rules of covariance algebra and a set of assumptions. Specifically, we will use the following covariance algebra rules:

$$
\begin{aligned}
&\text{cov}(x_1, x_1) = \text{var}(x_1) \\
&\text{cov}(a, x_1) = 0 \\
&\text{cov}(ax_1, x_2) = a\,\text{cov}(x_1, x_2) \\
&\text{cov}(x_1 + x_2, x_3 + x_4) = \text{cov}(x_1, x_3) + \text{cov}(x_1, x_4) + \text{cov}(x_2, x_3) + \text{cov}(x_2, x_4) \\
&\text{var}(x_1 + x_2) = \text{var}(x_1) + \text{var}(x_2) + 2\,\text{cov}(x_1, x_2) \\
&\text{var}(ax_1 + bx_2) = a^2\,\text{var}(x_1) + b^2\,\text{var}(x_2) + 2ab\,\text{cov}(x_1, x_2)
\end{aligned}
\tag{5.15}
$$

Also, we have to adopt a set of assumptions, which state that errors in linear equations are independent from independent variables; errors are stochastic quantities that are mutually independent from each other; observations are independent from each other. Finally, ML assumes that the observed variables jointly follow the *multivariate normal distribution*.[3]

While Σ is expressed in general form in (5.14), we now need to express $\Sigma(\theta)$ as a function of the model parameters. Let's assume that we want to estimate our basic CFA model. The model can be expressed as follows:

$$x_1 = \lambda_{11}^x \xi_1 + \delta_1$$
$$x_2 = \lambda_{21}^x \xi_1 + \delta_2 \qquad\qquad (5.16)$$
$$x_3 = \lambda_{31}^x \xi_1 + \delta_3$$

Figure 5.4 shows the graphical specification of this basic model.

By substituting these three model equations in (5.14) and applying the covariance algebra rules presented in (5.15), together with ML assumptions, we get:

$$\Sigma(\theta) = \begin{pmatrix} \mathrm{var}(x_1) = \lambda_{11}^{x^2} \mathrm{var}(\xi_1) + \mathrm{var}(\delta_1) & & \\ \mathrm{cov}(x_2,x_1) = \lambda_{21}^x \lambda_{11}^x \mathrm{var}(\xi_1) + \mathrm{cov}(\delta_2,\delta_1) & \mathrm{var}(x_2) = \lambda_{21}^{x^2} \mathrm{var}(\xi_1) + \mathrm{var}(\delta_2) & \\ \mathrm{cov}(x_3,x_1) = \lambda_{31}^x \lambda_{11}^x \mathrm{var}(\xi_1) + \mathrm{cov}(\delta_3,\delta_1) & \mathrm{cov}(x_3,x_2) = \lambda_{31}^x \lambda_{21}^x \mathrm{var}(\xi_1) + \mathrm{cov}(\delta_3,\delta_2) & \mathrm{var}(x_3) = \lambda_{31}^{x^2} \mathrm{var}(\xi_1) + \mathrm{var}(\delta_3) \end{pmatrix} \qquad (5.17)$$

Considering that in many instances covariances between measurement errors are fixed to zero, and substituting some of the algebraic elements with SEM parameters, we obtain a nice and intuitive form of $\Sigma(\theta)$, completely expressed as a function of the model parameters:

$$\Sigma(\theta) = \begin{pmatrix} \lambda_{11}^{x^2}\phi_{11} + \theta_{11}^\delta & & \\ \lambda_{21}^x \lambda_{11}^x \phi_{11} & \lambda_{21}^{x^2}\phi_{11} + \theta_{22}^\delta & \\ \lambda_{31}^x \lambda_{11}^x \phi_{11} & \lambda_{31}^x \lambda_{21}^x \phi_{11} & \lambda_{31}^{x^2}\phi_{11} + \theta_{33}^\delta \end{pmatrix} \qquad (5.18)$$

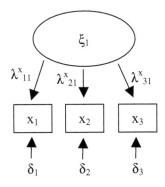

FIGURE 5.4 Path diagram for a basic CFA model

In many SEM textbooks (e.g., Bollen 1989) Equation (5.18) is expressed in matrix notation as follows:

$$\Sigma(\theta) = \Lambda\Phi\Lambda' + \Theta^\delta \tag{5.19}$$

Indeed, and considering this simple example, it is straightforward to get (5.18) from (5.19) using matrix algebra:

$$\Sigma(\theta) = \Lambda\Phi\Lambda' + \Theta^\delta = \begin{bmatrix} \lambda_{11}^x \\ \lambda_{21}^x \\ \lambda_{31}^x \end{bmatrix} \times \begin{bmatrix} \phi_{11} \end{bmatrix} \times \begin{bmatrix} \lambda_{11}^x & \lambda_{21}^x & \lambda_{31}^x \end{bmatrix} + \begin{bmatrix} \theta_{11}^\delta & & \\ 0 & \theta_{22}^\delta & \\ 0 & 0 & \theta_{33}^\delta \end{bmatrix} = \begin{pmatrix} \lambda_{11}^{x^2}\phi_{11} + \theta_{11}^\delta & & \\ \lambda_{21}^x\lambda_{11}^x\phi_{11} & \lambda_{21}^{x^2}\phi_{11} + \theta_{22}^\delta & \\ \lambda_{31}^x\lambda_{11}^x\phi_{11} & \lambda_{31}^x\lambda_{21}^x\phi_{11} & \lambda_{31}^{x^2}\phi_{11} + \theta_{33}^\delta \end{pmatrix} \tag{5.20}$$

From Equation (5.18) it is evident that variances of observed variables can be expressed as summations of two parts: the one shared with other observed variables (described by the squared factor loading) and the one related to measurement error. Clearly, a similar approach can be applied to the structural model and express $\Sigma(\theta)$ as a function of the structural parameters.

ML performs a certain number of iterations by means of which the algorithm tries to find those parameter values that minimize the difference between Σ (i.e., data) and $\Sigma(\theta)$ (i.e., the model). In more detail, the ML function – that should be minimized – is:

$$F_{ML} = \ln(\det(\Sigma(\theta))) + tr(\Sigma \times \Sigma(\theta)^{-1}) - \ln(\det(\Sigma)) - (p + q) \tag{5.21}$$

where p is the number of x-variables and q is the number of y-variables in the model. Substantially, Equation (5.21) suggests that F_{ML} depends on the discrepancy between Σ and $\Sigma(\theta)$. Under the assumption of multivariate normality of observed variables, $(N - 1) \times F_{ML}$ follows a chi-square distribution with degrees of freedom equal to

$$df_{F_{ML}} = (1/2(p + q)(p + q + 1)) - t \tag{5.22}$$

where $(1/2 (p + q)(p + q + 1))$ is equal to the number of non-redundant elements in the observed variance-covariance matrix, and t is the number of free parameters. Therefore $(N - 1) \times F_{ML}$ is called the *model chi-square* and represents a measure of *badness of fit*. The more similar Σ and $\Sigma(\theta)$, the lower the model chi-square, and, therefore, the higher the possibility to accept the proposed model as correct. The higher the difference between Σ and $\Sigma(\theta)$, the higher the model chi-square, and, therefore, the lower the tenability of the proposed model.

The matrix $(\Sigma - \Sigma(\theta))$ contains the so-called *residuals*. These quantities, which should be reasonably low, are used to compute specific fit indices (see later, pp. 118–119). Under the assumption of multivariate normality, ML parameter estimates are unbiased, consistent, and efficient, and follow a normal distribution. The latter property allows us to conduct a t-test on each parameter, by dividing the parameter estimate by its standard error. ML parameter estimates are reported by software packages also in standardized transformations, which permits an easier interpretation and simplify the computation of some relevant indices (see later, pp. 121–122).

SEM estimation requires meeting some *identification conditions* (Bollen 1989). An identified model is a model the parameters of which are all identified: an identified parameter is a parameter for which it exists only one numerical optimal solution. Generally speaking, all of the equations in the model need to be identified, that is, there should be enough input information (i.e. non-redundant elements in the observed variance-covariance matrix) compared to the unknown parameters that need to be estimated. In other words, each piece of the model should have non-negative degrees of freedom.

A first requirement to achieve model identification is to define the unit of measurement for each latent variable. The latter, being unobservable, do not have a known unit of measurement and are therefore unidentified. To overcome such a problem, the researcher can alternatively:

(a) set, for each latent variable, an observed variable that defines the unit of measurement – for each latent variable, one lambda parameter is set to one;
(b) standardize exogenous latent variables (ξ), setting their variances (ϕ_{jj}) to one;
(c) rely on automatic procedures allowed by some SEM software packages (e.g. Lisrel), which standardize latent variables if neither option (a) nor option (b) are used.

Adopting option (a), the researcher equals the unit of measurement of, say, x_1 and ξ_1 by imposing $\lambda^x_{11} = 1$, and therefore $x_1 = \xi_1 + \delta_1$. Adopting option (b) or (c), latent variables would be standardized ($\phi_{jj} = 1$), thus assuming the standard deviation as unit of measurement.

Several authors have tried to synthesize a set of general identification conditions. Table 5.2 shows identification conditions for the measurement model and the structural model proposed by Bollen (1989).

With reference to the measurement model, and assuming that each latent variable is identified, an important necessary condition concerns the need for positive degrees of freedom, that is, the number of non-redundant elements in the observed variance-covariance matrix ($\frac{1}{2} p(p+1)$) should be larger than the number of free parameters. The measurement model is identified if it assumes uncorrelated errors (Θ^δ diagonal) and each observed variable load onto only one latent variable (a non-zero element per row in the Λ_x matrix). Additionally, each latent variable should be related to three or more observed variables. Alternatively, each latent variable may be related to two or more observed variables if at least one correlation per latent variable is different from zero.

For what concerns the structural model, the general requirement that the number of non-redundant elements in the observed variance-covariance matrix ($\frac{1}{2} \times (p+q)(p+q+1)$) should be larger than the number of free parameters is still a necessary condition. Any structural model in which no relation between

TABLE 5.2 Identification conditions

Model	Rule	Condition	Necessary condition?	Sufficient condition?
Measurement model	t-rule	$t \leq \frac{1}{2} p(p+1)$ p = # of x-variables, t = # of free parameters	Yes	No
	Identified unit of measurement	Each construct should have a clear unit of measurement, by either setting one lambda parameter to one per each construct or standardizing the construct	Yes	No
	Three-indicator rule	Three or more indicators per latent variable A non-zero element per row in the Λx matrix Θ^δ diagonal	No	Yes
	Two-indicator rule	Two or more indicators per latent variable A non-zero element per row in the Λx matrix Θ^δ diagonal $\phi_{ij} \neq 0$ for at least one i,j couple per each latent variable, with $i \neq j$	No	Yes
Structural model	t-rule	$t \leq \frac{1}{2} (p+q)(p+q+1)$ p = # of x-variables, q = # of y-variables, t = # of free parameters	Yes	No
	Null B rule	$B = 0$	No	Yes
	Recursive rule	B triangular, Ψ diagonal	No	Yes
	Order condition	Restrictions in $C \geq n-1$ (matrix C is $[(I-B) \mid -\Gamma]$) with Ψ symmetric and free, n = # of η	Yes	No
	Rank condition	Matrix C rank = $n-1$ (matrix C is $[(I-B) \mid -\Gamma]$) with Ψ symmetric and free, n = # of η	Yes	No

Source: adapted from Bollen 1989

endogenous latent variables is specified (B = 0) is identified. In presence of free beta-parameters, the structural model is identified if it is a *recursive model*, that is, no reciprocal or feedback effects among endogenous latent variables are specified, and with uncorrelated structural errors (Ψ is diagonal). In this case, the B matrix is *triangular*, that is, the researcher estimates either above-the-diagonal or below-the diagonal beta-parameters. If the researcher is interested in estimating a *non-recursive model*, in which reciprocal and/or feedback effects among endogenous latent variables are specified, she/he has to further comply with the order and rank conditions. These two conditions are particularly tricky and imply the creation of an auxiliary matrix called *C*. Such matrix is computed subtracting the specified B matrix from an identity matrix (I) with the same dimension, and then adjoining to the right the specified Γ matrix multiplied by minus one. To achieve model identification, the number of restrictions (e.g. zeros) in each row of the C matrix should be equal or larger than the number of endogenous latent variables minus one. Also, the rank of the C matrix should be equal to the number of endogenous latent variables minus one.

Assessing SEM

SEM assessment firstly concerns the overall fit of the proposed model to the data. As discussed above (p. 114), it is possible to compute a measure of model *badness of fit* as $(N - 1) \times F_{ML}$. Generally speaking, the larger this quantity the worse model fit. Actually, we know that $(N - 1) \times F_{ML}$ follows a chi-square distribution with degrees of freedom equal to $df_{FML} = (1/2\ (p + q)(p + q + 1)) - t$ and therefore we can immediately test the null hypothesis that Σ and $\Sigma(\theta)$ are equal to each other. A first information that any researcher should produce when estimating a SEM is the model chi-square, including the degrees of freedom and the p-value associated to the comparison of the model chi-square and the corresponding critical chi-square. Following this approach, a good model should show a *non-significant* chi-square, which would allow to conclude in favor of the hypothesis of equality between Σ and $\Sigma(\theta)$, or, in other words, between data and theory. The model chi-square, however, is very sensitive to sample size (N) and to the violation of the assumption of multivariate normality. As a consequence, the model chi-square tends to be inflated even for good models when sample size is large and/or in presence of even light violations of the assumption of multivariate normality.

To overcome such a problem, the SEM literature has proposed several, alternative fit indices that can be used to reject or to accept (i.e. to not falsify) a model. A first class of fit indices includes the so-called *absolute fit indices*, which are based on elaborations on the model chi-square or residuals. Table 5.3 presents the most used absolute fit indices, their formulas, common cut-offs, and some specific notes.

The chi-square/degrees of freedom ratio is a quite popular index. Kline (2010) proposes that a ratio lower than 3 indicates a good model. The researcher should be aware that values lower than 1 may indicate an overly good model and raise doubts

TABLE 5.3 Absolute fit indices

Absolute fit index	Formula	Cut-offs	Notes
Chi-square/ df ratio	χ^2 / df	$\chi^2 / df < 3$ (Kline 2010)	Ratio lower than 1 may indicate over parameterized models
Goodness of fit index	$GFI = 1 - \dfrac{tr\left(\left(\Sigma(\theta)^{-1}\,\Sigma - I\right)^2\right)}{tr\left(\left(\Sigma(\theta)^{-1}\,\Sigma\right)^2\right)}$	GFI > .90 AGFI > .90 (Jöreskog and Sörbom 1993)	Not much used, they tend to increase as the sample size increases; not recommended by Hu and Bentler (1999)
Adjusted goodness of fit index	$AGFI = 1 - \left[\dfrac{(p+q)(p+q+1)}{2t}\right](1 - GFI)$		
Standardized root of mean residual	$SRMR = \sqrt{\displaystyle\sum_{i=1}^{p+q}\sum_{j=1}^{p+q} \dfrac{\left((\sigma_{ij} - \hat{\sigma}_{ij})/(\sigma_{ij}\,\hat{\sigma}_{ij})\right)^2}{(p+q)(p+q+1)}}$	SRMR < .05 (Byrne 1998) SRMR < .09 (Hu and Bentler 1999)	Less sensitive to sample size, it decreases with "cleaner" measurement models
Root of mean squared error of approximation	$RMSEA = \sqrt{\dfrac{(\chi^2 - df)}{df(N-1)}}$	RMSEA < .08 (Browne and Cudeck 1993); RMSEA < .06 (Hu and Bentler 1999)	It tends to be inflated in small samples and to support parsimonious models; The distribution is known (test of close fit, H_0: RMSEA < .05)

about the model parsimony. GFI and AGFI were proposed by Karl Jöreskog and Dag Sörbom, who are considered SEM's dads. Both indices fall between zero and one, with values larger than .90 indicating good models. Compared to GFI, AGFI penalizes non-parsimonious models, that is, models estimating too many parameters. Though historically relevant, these two indices are nowadays less used because of their sensitivity to sample size and poor performance in simulation studies (Hu and Bentler 1999; Sharma, Mukherjee, Kumar, and Dillon 2005). In the last decades, the most commonly used absolute fit indices have been SRMR and RMSEA. Both indices fall between zero and one (though this is not always true for RMSEA), with lower values indicating better models. SRMR is the standardized square root of the average residual, that is, the difference scores computed comparing Σ and $\Sigma(\theta)$. Byrne (1998) proposed a .05 cut-off for SRMR; however, Hu and Bentler (1999) reported that values close to .09 are deemed acceptable. RMSEA is the square root of the average error of approximation accepted in considering the model a close (not exact) representation of data. Browne and Cudeck (1993) suggested that values lower than or equal to 0.05 indicate a close fit, whereas values not larger than .08 imply a reasonable fit. Based on their extensive simulation study, Hu and Bentler (1999) conclude that RMSEA should be used in combination with SRMR and be lower than .06. A disadvantage of RMSEA concerns its sensitivity to sample size (small samples inflate RMSEA), whereas an advantage regards its known distribution; therefore, it is available an inferential test of close fit, which tests the null hypotheses that RMSEA is lower than .05.

A second class of fit indices concerns the so-called *incremental fit indices*, which are based on comparing the model chi-square (χ^2_m) and a baseline model chi-square (χ^2_b). It is worthwhile pointing out that, while absolute fit indices should be invariant when estimating the same model with different software packages, the latter may yield different values for incremental fit indices because of the specific baseline model used in computations. A commonly used baseline model considers the estimation of variances only, thus setting all covariances among observed variables to zero. Table 5.4 presents the most used incremental fit indices, their formulas, common cut-offs, and some specific notes.

NFI is a goodness of fit index proposed by Bentler and Bonnet (1980) and compares the baseline model chi-square and the estimated model chi-square. Simulation studies show that NFI underestimates fit in small samples (e.g. Marsh, Balla, and McDonald 1988) and, for this reason, was soon abandoned in favor of alternative incremental fit indices. TLI, though may fall outside the 0–1 range, appears less sensitive to sample size but only when the measurement model shows factor loadings larger than .50 (Sharma *et al.* 2005). Nowadays, the most used fit index is probably CFI (Bentler 1990). While Bentler (1990) and Hu and Bentler (1999) demonstrated that CFI works well in identifying good models, Fan, Thompson, and Wang (1999) and Iacobucci (2010) have showed that with more than a hundred observations CFI is insensitive to sample size. For NFI, TLI, and CFI a .95 cut-off is required to accept a model as a good representation of reality. There is a general consensus that the researcher should avoid assessing a model focusing on a single fit index; rather, it is important to consider multiple indices, as some of them are differently sensitive to sample size, model complexity/parsimony, and the quality of measurement model.

With reference to model fit assessment, another relevant topic concerns alternative model comparison, which is particularly crucial when the researcher is interested to propose causal claims. It is possible to identify two general classes of model comparisons.

TABLE 5.4 Incremental fit indices

Absolute fit index	Formula	Cut-offs	Notes
Normed fit index	$NFI = \dfrac{\chi^2_b - \chi^2_m}{\chi^2_b}$	NFI > .95 TLI > .95 CFI > .95 (Hu and Bentler 1999)	It underestimates fit in small samples; not recommended by Hu and Bentler (1999)
Tucker-Lewis fit index	$TLI = \dfrac{\chi^2_b / df_b - \chi^2_m / df_m}{(\chi^2_b / df_b) - 1}$		AKA Non Normed Fit Index (NNFI), it may fall outside the 0–1 range; less sensitive to sample size with large factor loadings
Comparative fit index	$CFI = 1 - \dfrac{\max((\chi^2_m - df_m)0)}{\max((\chi^2_m - df_m)(\chi^2_b - df_b)0)}$		Robust to sample size; nowadays it is probably the most used fit index (Iacobucci 2010)

Nested model comparison: when it is possible to specify Model A applying k restrictions to Model B, Model A is said to be *nested* into Model B. In other words, and considering the same set of observed variables, Model A requires the estimation of t parameters, while Model B requires the estimation of $t + k$ parameters. Because Model A uses k parameters less than Model B, Model A will always have a worse fit to the data than Model B ($\chi^2_A > \chi^2_B$). At the same time Model A is *more parsimonious* than Model B (parsimony is a generally appreciated property for any model) and therefore will have higher degrees of freedom ($df_A > df_B$). It is possible to compare nested Models A and B by means of a *delta chi square test*, $\Delta\chi^2 = \chi^2_A - \chi^2_B$, which is distributed with $df_A - df_B$ degrees of freedom (equal to the k restrictions). If $\Delta\chi^2$ is significant, the k restrictions reduce significantly the model fit when passing from Model B to Model A; therefore Model B has a better performance than Model A and should be selected as a better alternative. If $\Delta\chi^2$ is not significant, the k restrictions do not reduce significantly the model fit when passing from Model B to Model A; therefore Model A has a similar performance compared to Model B, but Model A is more parsimonious (it requires less estimated parameters) and should be selected as a better alternative. Nested model comparison is commonly conducted when the researcher is interested in assessing the validity of adding new parameters (i.e. new relations) to the model, but also when she/he wants to test the tenability of constraints on parameters (e.g. $\beta_{21} = \beta_{31}$), which imply restrictions and therefore less parameters to be estimated.

Non-nested model comparison: when Models A and B are non-nested into each other, particularly when they have the same number of degrees of freedom, it is not possible to apply a delta chi square test. This is a common situation when the researcher wishes to compare alternative nomological nets, that is, rival represen-tations of causal relationships among constructs. This form of comparison is particularly relevant to enforce causal interpretation of SEM results. For instance, if the researcher proposes the model A ➔ B ➔ C, beyond proposing theoretical arguments in favor of such specific nomological net, may demonstrate by means of non-nested model comparison that her/his model fits the data better than, say, model B ➔ A ➔ C. Non-nested model can be compared by means of *information criteria*, which are based on algebraic elaborations of the model log-likelihood function. The most popular information criteria are *Akaike Information Criteria* (AIC) and *Consistent Akaike Information Criteria* (CAIC).[4] Both criteria are used only in a comparative sense (AIC and CAIC of a single model have not much meaning), with lower values indicating better models. CAIC tends to be preferable because it considers both parsimony and sample size. In the SEM literature there is a certain consensus that the researcher should compare her/his proposed model with some nontrivial rival models, derived from the substantive literature, to demonstrate the superiority of the hypothesized nomological representation (Iacobucci 2010).

Besides the overall assessment of model fit, the researcher should evaluate the quality of the measurement model, and, eventually, the face validity of the structural model. The measurement model (or CFA) is estimated to assess some fundamental psychometric properties of measures: *reliability*, *convergent validity*, and *discriminant validity*. While a thorough discussion of these psychometric properties is beyond the scope of this chapter (the interested reader may refer to Bagozzi 1980; DeVellis 1991; Edwards and Bagozzi 2000), it is worthwhile to remind that reliability is the property of a measurement scale of representing *systematically* (temporal stability) and *consistently* (internal consistency) the construct of interest; convergent validity is the property of indicators of the same measurement scale of *converging* onto the same latent construct; and discriminant validity is the property of indicators of the same measurement scale of being *well discriminated* from indicators of *other* latent constructs. CFA is unanimously considered the most powerful tool to assess psychometric properties. In particular, the opportunity to distinguish common variance and measurement error in observed variables' variances offer the chance to assess correctly reliability and validity.

A fundamental pre-condition to assess the quality of the measurement model is that all of the factor loadings (lambda parameters) are significantly and substantially different from zero. Indeed, one would prefer (standardized) lambda parameters to be significant and larger than .50. To assess the *internal consistency* dimension of reliability (mind that assessing temporal consistency requires longitudinal data), Fornell and Larcker (1981) suggest computing, for each construct, the *composite reliability index* (ρ_c):

$$\rho_c = \frac{\left(\sum_i \lambda_i\right)^2 \text{var}\,\xi}{\left[\left(\sum_i \lambda_i\right)^2 \text{var}\,\xi + \sum_i \theta_{ii}\right]} \qquad (5.23)$$

A similar formula can be applied to a specific observed variable i:

$$\rho_i = \frac{\lambda_i^2 \text{var}\,\xi}{\lambda_i^2 \text{var}\,\xi + \theta_{ii}} \qquad (5.24)$$

In both formulas, standardized estimates are often used; therefore the latent variable variance equals one and can be ignored. For each construct, ρ_c should be larger than .70, while, for each observed variable, ρ_i should be preferably larger than .50, though Bagozzi and Yi argue that "cut-off values for indicator and composite reliability might be taken with some leeway in mind" (2012: 17).

To achieve convergent validity, it is required, beyond significant and substantial factor loadings, to obtain, for each construct, *average variance extracted* (AVE) larger than .50 (Fornell and Larcker 1981). AVE is computed as follows:

$$AVE = \frac{\left(\sum_i \lambda_i^2\right)\text{var}\,\xi}{\left[\left(\sum_i \lambda_i^2\right)\text{var}\,\xi + \sum_i \theta_{ii}\right]} \qquad (5.25)$$

Looking at Equations (5.16), (5.17), and (5.18), it is possible to notice that a construct AVE can be interpreted as that construct average R^2. Indeed, it is possible to compute a R^2 for each observed variables (x_1, x_2, and x_3) measuring ξ_1. We also know that the variance of, say, x_1 can be re-written as $\text{var}(x_1) = \lambda_{11}^{x2} \phi_{11} + \theta_{11}^{\delta}$. Var($x_1$) can be therefore decomposed in a common part, $\lambda_{11}^{x2} \phi_{11}$, that is, the explained variance or R^2 of x_1, plus the error variance θ_{11}^{δ}. Using standardized estimates (which considers standardized variables), $\text{var}(x_1) = 1$ and $\text{var}(\xi_1) = \phi_{11} = 1$, and therefore $\lambda_{11}^{x2} + \theta_{11}^{\delta} = 1$. Summing up the R^2s of each observed variable measuring a specific latent variable, one may obtain the numerator of AVE, whereas the sum of the variances of those observed variables is the denominator of AVE.

AVE is also used to assess discriminant validity. To demonstrate that constructs are sufficiently discriminated from each other, it is required that for each pair of constructs their squared correlation is lower that the two AVEs (Fornell and Larcker 1981). Another common practice to assess discriminant validity is based on delta chi square tests by comparing the estimated measurement model with rival models imposing, per each pair of constructs, a correlation equal to one (e.g. Bagozzi and Yi 2012). Discriminant validity is achieved if models imposing such constraints deteriorate significantly the model fit.

The assessment of the structural model makes sense only after having demonstrated the measurement model reliability and validity. The researcher estimates a structural model to test specific predictions on the relationships among constructs. Accordingly, it is important to check the face validity of the proposed hypotheses by focusing on statistical significance, sign, and intensity of structural parameters (β and/or γ). It is also important to verify that R^2 of structural equations show reasonable values, thus demonstrating that the proposed determinants are able to predict a significant part of dependent variables' variances.

A final topic concerning SEM assessment regards misfit diagnostics. In particular, *standardized residuals* and *modification indices* are two sets of powerful tools that may help the researcher to identify the sources of model misfit. As previously mentioned, standardized residuals are the standardized elements of matrix ($\Sigma - \Sigma(\theta)$). Values larger than $|2.58|$ (or, more flexibly, larger than $|3|$) suggest that the estimated model is not able to replicate specific elements in Σ. Modification indices, instead, are basically univariate delta chi square tests that are computed on each fixed parameter (i.e. a parameter that was not freely estimated). Therefore, a modification index concerning, say, the fixed parameter β_{21}, indicates the improvement in model fit (i.e. the decrease in the model chi square) that could be achieved by estimating that fixed parameter. Some software packages (e.g. EQS) also compute *Lagrange Multipliers*, which are basically univariate and multivariate modification indices.

It is evident that standardized residuals and modification indices are extremely interesting tools to detect model weaknesses. It is also clear that these diagnostics could guide model re-specification, by suggesting parameters to be estimated to improve model fit. Post-hoc re-specification, however, is a deplorable practice if the researcher is not able to offer theoretical arguments supporting model change. Model re-specification that only capitalizes on data (and not on theory) would raise serious doubts about the model generalization and replicability (MacCallum, Roznowski, and Necowitz 1993). In sum, one should always look at standardized residuals and modification indices to assess SEM, but also be extremely cautious in using these diagnostics as mere fit-improving tools.

Applications of SEM in the strategic management literature

In this section, we first discuss the general use of SEM in the strategic management literature. Second, we review, with more depth, a specific application of SEM that was published in the *Strategic Management Journal* and examine the reported results.

The use of SEM in the strategic management literature has grown dramatically since the seminal application of Fahr, Hoffman, and Hegarty (1984). In their review of the 1984–2002 publications on ten top strategic management journals, Shook *et al.* (2004) included 92 published articles applying SEM. In this study, the authors emphasize good and bad practices in SEM applications and recommend a checklist of issues that should be discussed in any SEM study.

The relative majority (37 percent) of the articles reviewed by Shook *et al.* were published in the *Strategic Management Journal* (SMJ). Accordingly, we decide to further focus on the use of SEM in the strategic management literature by narrowing down our search to the articles published in the SMJ between 2003 and 2013. Using specific keywords related to confirmatory factor analysis and structural equation modeling, we found 84 articles that report some form of SEM application.[5] Compared to 1984–2002, we certainly notice a striking increase of SEM studies, although in the 2003–2013 period there is not a clear linear trend. In the eleven years, we found a minimum of five and a maximum of 12 SEM applications, with peaks in 2007 (12 studies) and 2013 (11 studies). This evidence suggests that SEM is nowadays a widely used technique in the strategic management literature, and specifically within the SMJ. The reviewed SEM applications concern a variety of topics – including vertical partnerships, customer orientation, human capital, alliances, disruptiveness of innovation, outsourcing, diversification, CEO self-evaluation – and contexts. Seventy-six studies report data from a single country, with the USA (34 cases) and China (15 cases) appearing more frequently; in eight cases SEM was applied to datasets from multiple countries.

With reference to specific SEM sub-models, we found that in two cases (Govindarajan and Kopalle 2006; Murillo-Luna, Garcés-Ayerbe, and Rivera-Torres 2008) the authors estimated only the measurement model (i.e. CFA) for achieving goals purely related to construct definition and measurement. In other cases, a CFA was followed by the application of specific techniques aimed at testing hypotheses. In 29 articles (e.g. Li, Poppo, and Zhou 2008; Zatzick, Moliterno, and Fang 2012), the authors used OLS regressions after a CFA, often because OLS regressions were deemed more flexible than SEM to estimate interaction effects. In 20 articles (e.g. Baum and Wally 2003; Tanriverdi and Venkatraman 2005), a full SEM was estimated to test hypotheses – thus following the well-known two-step approach proposed by Anderson and Gerbing (1988). Interestingly, in one instance (Song, Droge, Hanvanich, and Calantone 2005) the authors demonstrate that the full SEM estimation yielded unbiased results contrarily to those obtained with OLS regression. Additionally, in ten articles (e.g. Homburg and Bucerius 2006; Morgan, Vorhies, and Mason 2009) a CFA was followed by *both* OLS regressions and SEM, the latter often representing a robustness tool to reinforce evidence provided by the former. In fewer instances (e.g. Parmigiani 2007; Weigelt and Sarkar 2012), a CFA was applied before other types of techniques, including choice models (e.g. multinomial logit, binary probit), hierarchical linear models, seemingly unrelated regressions, or Poisson regressions.

Despite Shook *et al.'s* recommendations (2004), almost 60 percent of the articles we reviewed do not report the software used to estimate SEM. Considering the articles reporting such information, Lisrel is the most used software (18 cases), followed by AMOS (9 cases), EQS and Mplus (3 cases each). In one article both Lisrel and Mplus were used (Bou and Satorra 2007). It is interesting to notice that, contrary to other fields in which SEM applications basically refer only to survey data, the reviewed SMJ articles are often based on a mix of primary and secondary data. This feature certainly enhances the quality and rigor of the research design, reducing concerns about common method bias and spurious effects.

Beyond this brief review, we discuss in more detail a selected SEM application, that is, the 2008 SMJ article "Comparing the resource-based and relational views: Knowledge transfer and spillover in vertical alliances," written by Luiz F. Mesquita, Jaideep Anand, and Thomas H. Brush. In this article, the authors propose a conceptual model to compare the effectiveness of elements related to either the resource-based view (RBV – e.g. Barney 1991) or the relational view (RV – e.g. Dyer and Singh 1998). Focusing on the context of buyer-supplier alliances, the authors identify a variable related to the RBV, supplier knowledge acquisition effort (SKAE); and three variables expressing the RV, joint buyer-supplier knowledge acquisition efforts (JBSKAE), supplier dyad-specific assets and capabilities (SDSAC), and buyer-supplier relational governance mechanisms (BSRGM). Analogously, the authors distinguish two dimensions of supplier performance: supplier re-deployable performance and supplier relational performance. While the former is related to the RBV, the latter is consistent with the RV. Therefore, the authors develop a set of hypotheses predicting differential effects of SKAE (which should influence to a greater extent supplier re-deployable performance than supplier relational performance), JBSKAE, SDSAC, and BSRGM (which should influence to a greater extent supplier relational performance than supplier re-deployable performance) on the two dimensions of supplier performance. Additionally, the authors hypothesize that JBSKAE positively influences SDSAC, which in turn positively influences BSRGM. Figure 5.5 shows the proposed conceptual model, which includes the effects of control variables (supplier size, importance of the customer, and competitive pressure) on the two dimensions of supplier performance.

To test the research hypotheses, Mesquita, Anand, and Brush (2008) estimated several structural equation models on data concerning 253 US suppliers of equipment manufacturers, producing goods that involve machining, stamping, cutting, and similar materials. For each supplier company, the most knowledgeable manager about the relationships with buyers and knowledge management answered the questionnaire. The items used to measure the constructs are reported in the appendix of the article.

The authors applied the well-known two-step approach to SEM (Anderson and Gerbing 1988). First, they estimated the measurement model and assessed the validity of measures. Despite a significant chi square ($\chi^2_{(176)}$ = 233.95, p < .01), the most used indices suggest a good fit of the model to the data (CFI = .98, NNFI =.95, RMSEA = .03).

The authors claim convergent validity because all of the estimated factor loadings (i.e., lambda-x parameters) are significantly different from zero (all t > 4.61). To assess discriminant validity, the authors compared the measurement model with rival models in which the correlation between two constructs (at a time) was set to one. In all cases, the delta chi square test turned out to be significant, suggesting that constraining each factor correlation to one deteriorates the fit to such an extent that the authors should conclude in favor of the unconstrained model (i.e. correlations are different from one), and therefore of

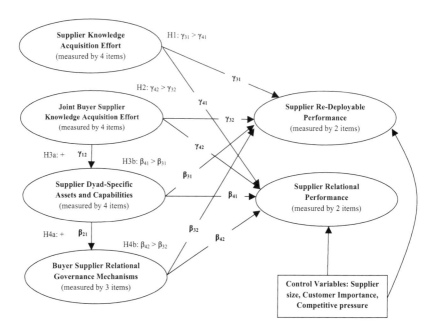

FIGURE 5.5   Conceptual model and hypotheses

Source: Mesquita, Anand, and Brush 2008

discriminant validity. Although the discussion of the measurement model results is correct, the authors could have reported composite reliability and AVE for each construct to enrich the assessment of convergent and discriminant validity.

Second, the authors estimated a full structural equation model to test the hypothesized effects. With reference to H1, the authors found that SKAE positively influences supplier re-deployable performance ($\gamma_{31} = .18, p < .01$), but not supplier relational performance ($\gamma_{41} = -.04$, *ns*). To formally test H1, the authors compare the estimated SEM with a constrained model in which these two effects were equal to each other. A delta chi square test ($\Delta\chi^2_{(1)} = 18.97, p < .01$) showed that this equality constraint is not tenable and therefore it is possible to conclude, in support of H1, that SKAE influences to a greater extent supplier re-deployable performance than supplier relational performance.

With reference to H2, the authors found that the effect of JBSKAE on supplier re-deployable performance is not significant ($\gamma_{32} = .03$, *ns*), whereas the effect of JBSKAE on supplier relational performance is positive and significant ($\gamma_{42} = .11$, $p < .05$). When the authors compared the estimated SEM with a constrained model in which these two effects were equal to each other, they found a non-significant difference ($\Delta\chi^2_{(1)} = 1.58$, *ns*). Therefore, it cannot be excluded that the two parameters are equal to each other, and this evidence forced the authors to reject H2.

In support of H3a, the authors found a positive and significant effect of JBSKAE on SDSAC ($\gamma_{12} = .19$, $p < .01$). Although it was not explicitly stated in H3a, the authors compared this parameter with the one expressing the effect of SKAE on SDSAC, which proved to be non-significant ($\gamma_{11} = -.00$, ns). A delta chi square test indeed showed that the two effects are significantly different from each other ($\Delta\chi^2_{(1)} = 14.23$, $p < .01$).

With reference to H3b, the authors found that SDSAC does not influence supplier re-deployable performance ($\beta_{31} = -.02$, ns), However, SDSAC does influence supplier relational performance ($\beta_{41} = .26$, $p < .01$). In support of H3b, a delta chi square test ($\Delta\chi^2_{(1)} = 22.26$, $p < .01$) showed that indeed the effect of SDSAC on supplier relational performance is stronger than that on supplier re-deployable performance.

The authors found support for H4a, as the effect of SDSAC on BSRGM is positive and significant ($\beta_{21} = .18$, $p < .01$). Additionally, the authors found that the effect of BSRGM on supplier re-deployable performance is not significant ($\beta_{32} = -.03$, ns), However, BSRGM positively influences supplier relational performance ($\beta_{42} = .21$, $p < .01$). In support of H4b, a delta chi square test ($\Delta\chi^2_{(1)} = 15.96$, $p < .01$) showed that indeed the effect of BSRGM on supplier relational performance is stronger than that on supplier re-deployable performance. The authors also discuss the effects of control variables on the two dimensions of performance. Arguably, this section could have been shortened considering the roles of control variables of supplier size, importance of the customer, and competitive pressure. Alternatively, the authors should have proposed formal hypotheses on these effects and not just generic predictions.

As additional analyses, the authors compared the proposed model with what they call "the best model," obtained by trimming off non-significant parameters. Not surprisingly, they found that the fit of the proposed model is not statistically different from the fit of the best model. More interestingly, the authors contrasted the proposed model with several *non-recursive* models involving, for each estimated effect, the opposite effect, thus estimating reciprocal relations. In all cases, the authors found that the proposed effect remained consistent with the hypotheses, while the opposite effects proved to be either non-significant or marginally significant. Finally, the authors tested an alternative model of the moderating roles of SDSAC and BSRGM on the effects of JBSKAE on supplier relational performance. To specify such a model, the authors used a procedure proposed by Ping (1995) to include multiplicative terms in a SEM (see later for a brief discussion on the treatment of moderating variables in SEM, p. 130). To compare the proposed model (which instead implies a *mediating* role of SDSAC and BSRGM on the effects of JBSKAE on supplier relational performance) and the alternative model, the authors correctly used information criteria (e.g. AIC, BIC). All the information criteria suggest that the alternative model performs much worse than the proposed model, which was then accepted as an adequate representation of reality.

The authors should be praised for their additional analyses, which certainly reinforce their claims and indeed offer sufficient support to the proposed hypotheses. Considering that the authors propose a model involving mediation of SDSAC and BSRGM on the effects of JBSKAE on supplier relational performance, it could have been possible to further explore and to distinguish the *indirect* effects and the *direct* effects of JBSKAE on supplier relational performance. Indeed, SEM software packages, to different extents, allow the researcher to estimate mediated effects and to split total effects into indirect and direct effects.

Advanced models

This chapter deals with basic SEM. The flexibility of the SEM framework, however, allows the researcher to estimate several different models and to account for specific characteristics of data, relations, and theory to be tested. In this section, we briefly introduce some advanced SEM models and provide selected references.

Higher-order factors

Latent constructs modelled within the SEM framework represent the common variance among some observed variables. Accordingly, the (first-order) latent factor is supposed to exist at a higher level of abstraction compared to observed variables. Similarly, it is possible to conceptualize *higher-order factors* as the shared variance among first-order latent constructs. Modeling a higher-order factor is often a very elegant solution when the researcher assumes that first-order (correlated) factors are sub-dimensions of an even more abstract construct (Rindskopf and Rose 1988). To identify SEM featuring second-order factors, the common rules reported in Table 5.2 apply. Also, it is needed to specify at least three first-order factors. Analytically, a model with a second-order factor and three first-order factors has exactly the same fit and degrees of freedom of a model with three correlated first-order factors (and no higher-order factor). With four or more first-order factors the higher-order factor model will always perform worse than the correlated factors model, because the former has more degrees of freedom. However, modeling a higher-order factor can be more consistent with conceptualizations of multidimensional constructs, and indeed represents a correct and formal solution widely adopted in the strategic management literature (e.g. Tippins and Sohi 2003).

Formative measures

SEM follows the tradition of *reflective measurement*, in which indicators (i.e. observed variables) are reflections or manifestations of a latent construct (Edwards and Bagozzi 2000). In a reflective measurement model, the latent construct represents the variance shared by its indicators. Also, the latent construct influences all of the indicators, that is, a variation in the latent construct is supposed to produce variations in all of the indicators. In *formative measurement*, instead, the construct is formed by the aggregation of indicators, which are composite elements that exist at the same level of abstraction of the construct (Bollen and Lennox 1991). The formative or aggregate construct is influenced by its indicators, that is, a variation in any formative indicator produces a variation in the aggregate construct. Despite the fact that SEM is analytically consistent with reflective measurement, it is possible to include formative constructs in a SEM as a single-item latent construct, using a composite score (i.e. a mean score of formative items) as an observed variable. A more elegant solution is the so-called MIMIC model (Diamantopoulos and Winklhofer 2001), in which the aggregate construct receives effects from its formative indicators and has also a certain number of reflective indicators. Actually, reflective indicators are needed to ensure identification, which could be alternatively achieved by specifying effects of the aggregate construct on at least two other latent constructs. Generally speaking, to identify a formative construct it is needed to specify at least two effects stemming from the formative construct towards either reflective indicators or other latent constructs. Recently, the debate on reflective vs. formative measurement has gained new interest from several researchers and further developments are expected (Cadogan and Lee 2013; Rigdon 2014). For instance, a recent contribution (Treiblmaier, Bentler, and Mair 2011) proposes a very promising two-step approach that allows the identification of formatively measured constructs and their inclusion as independent or dependent latent variables in a full SEM without altering their meaning. Also, and integrating the discussion on higher-order constructs and reflective vs. formative measurement, it is possible to conceptualize different forms of multidimensional constructs that can be either latent or formative in nature, and be related to either latent or formative first-order constructs. The SEM literature provides several nice discussions of these opportunities to specify multidimensional constructs (Jarvis *et al.* 2003; Edwards and Bagozzi 2000).

Multi-group SEM

Our discussion of SEM has so far concerned single-sample analysis. SEM, however, can be applied simultaneously on multiple, independent groups in what is commonly called *multi-group SEM*. Estimating SEM in multiple groups allows the researcher to investigate several research problems. Arguably, the most relevant applications of multi-group SEM are: (a) the assessment of *measurement invariance*, concerning the comparison of the same measurement model in different groups to verify its tenability across, say, genders, industries, countries; indeed, there are different extents to which a measurement model can (or cannot) be invariant across groups, and multi-group SEM offers a flexible and powerful framework to assess the existence of weak vs. strong forms of invariance; and (b) the comparison of effects or means across groups, which concerns *the analysis of the moderating role* of a categorical variable forming groups in a specified SEM; in this respect, multi-group SEM represents an alternative technique to moderated regression and ANOVA in the analysis of interaction effects. Meredith (1993) and Steenkamp and

Baumgartner (1998) provide excellent reviews on multi-group SEM, while Simonin's (1999) article on knowledge transfer in strategic alliances represents a nice example of multi-group SEM application in the strategic management literature.

Mediation and moderation

The opportunity to estimate simultaneously multiple regression equations makes SEM an ideal framework to test mediation models, in which an independent variable X influences a mediating variable Me, which in turn influences a dependent variable Y. Although the "causal steps" approach to test mediation (Judd and Kenny 1981; Baron and Kenny 1986) has been largely applied in all social sciences and proved resistant to several criticss (Iacobucci, Saldanha, and Deng 2007; MacKinnon 2008), SEM is gradually being recognized as the most powerful technique – particularly if integrated with bootstrap or asymmetric inferential tests of indirect effects (Preacher and Hayes 2008; MacKinnon 2008) – to assess mediated effects. Simultaneous estimation, handling of multiple mediators, modelling of measurement and structural errors, and the opportunity to control for correlations among multiple mediators are all distinctive features that should favor the application of SEM instead of regression analysis in mediation testing.

Moderated effects – the influence of an independent variable X on a dependent variable Y depends on a moderating variable Mo – can be modeled in the SEM framework differently depending on the nature of the moderating variable. As already mentioned, if the moderating variable is categorical (i.e. it forms groups), moderated effects can be effectively analyzed through multi-group analysis. If the moderating variable is numerical it is needed to introduce a multiplicative term (the independent variable multiplied by the moderating variable) in the structural model. The introduction of the multiplicative term automatically violates the assumption of multivariate normality of distributions, therefore requiring the researcher to apply robust estimators (Satorra and Bentler 1988). The multiplicative term between latent constructs can be modeled following different approaches (Cortina, Chen, and Dunlap 2001; Ping 1996), which require a stronger statistical background to correctly specify SEM for analyzing moderating effects. Accordingly, it is not uncommon in the strategic management literature to find papers in which the researcher applies CFA to assess measures reliability and validity and then regression analysis on constructs' means or factor scores as a more flexible framework to test for moderating effects (Shervani, Frazier, and Challagalla 2007; Elenkov, Judge, and Wright 2005).

Longitudinal analysis

Although it is common to apply SEM on cross-sectional data, the SEM framework has been extended to accommodate for time-series and longitudinal analyses. On the one hand, it is possible to study the evolution along time of a specific variable by estimating stability coefficients and random components (Rosel and Plewis 2008). Such models can handle either an observed variable (autoregressive or *Simplex* model) or a latent variable (reliable Simplex). On the other hand, the researcher can combine multiple autoregressive models and include the estimation of cross-lagged effects. A most interesting development of SEM application to longitudinal data concerns *latent growth curve models* (McArdle and Anderson 1990; Aber and McArdle 1991; Bollen and Curran 2006). In such models, repeated measures along time are used to estimate a latent trajectory of the variable of interest. SEM is applied to model the mean level and the change of the variable of interest along time. Additionally, random error components are used to model inter-individual changes, therefore offering further information about group- and individual-related changes in the variable of interest. Latent growth models allow the researcher to test empirically for linear and non-linear pattern of change, and can be even integrated with latent class models to cluster individual variability (Muthén 2001). Despite the potential of longitudinal data analysis with SEM, the strategic management literature does not offer many instances of autoregressive or latent growth models applications (a notable exception is Bou and Satorra 2007): there is certainly room for contributions to divulgate and to develop SEM applications to longitudinal data.

Multilevel models

One of the assumption of SEM concerns independence of observations. However, such an assumption is often violated in research concerning employees nested in work-teams, customers nested in communities, or, in more general terms, individual observations nested in groups. In these cases, the dataset has a *hierarchical* or *multilevel structure* (Hox 2002) and appropriate models should be applied to handle variability at all the levels of observations (i.e. individuals and groups) and to account for the inherent heteroskedasticity of the dataset. While the application of multilevel regression analysis is increasingly common in the strategic management literature (e.g. Short, Ketchen, Palmer, and Hult 2007; Nielsen and Nielsen 2013), multilevel SEM (du Toit and du Toit 2008) represents an up-to-date, sophisticated technique that has the potential to become a standard approach in research involving hierarchical data.

Models with non-metric variables

SEM has been developed using covariance algebra rules, which assume metric variables. The increasing need to handle categorical data in several social sciences has stimulated the extension of the SEM framework to account for non-metric variables. On the one hand, Jöreskog and Sörbom (1993) have proposed the computation of polychoric (for ordinal variables) or tetrachoric (for binary variables) correlations – instead of Pearson correlations – as data input for standard SEM. On the other hand, Muthén (1983) has developed, and implemented in the

Mplus software package, a flexible approach to handle categorical data within the SEM framework by means of a robust, weighted least squares estimator. In the strategic management literature, Steensma and Lyles (2000) applied such an estimator to analyze determinants of international joint-ventures survival, which was indeed modeled as a dichotomous dependent variable.

Notes

1   Our discussion of SEM variables follows the traditional JKW approach – labelled as such in honour of the seminal contributions of Joreskog (1971), Keesling (1972) and Wiley (1973) – that was later implemented in the LISREL software. It is worthwhile to mention that other SEM approaches have been proposed (see Bagozzi and Yi [2012] for an insightful comparison of alternative modelling approaches to SEM) and implemented in different software packages (e.g. EQS, Mplus).
2   In this section we follow a didactic approach and present the basic models that can be estimated in the SEM framework. However, though it may be confusing to the naïve reader, it is important to acknowledge that it is possible to estimate "all-y" (or "all-eta") variables CFA. Actually, it is not uncommon to find review papers using all-y models (e.g. Cortina, Chen, and Dunlap 2001).
3   As anticipated, such an assumption is often violated in real-world data. Appropriate tests (e.g. Mardia test) are available in many SEM software to assess the tenability of the multivariate normality assumption. In case of severe violations of this assumption, the researcher should adopt robust ML estimators (e.g. Satorra-Bentler 1988) or different algorithms (e.g. WLS) to ensure unbiased fit measures and parameter estimates, as well as correct inferential conclusions.
4   AIC is equal to $\chi^2_{NTWLS} + 2t$, where χ^2_{NTWLS} is the Normal Theory Weighted Least Squares Chi-Square and t is the number of free parameters. CAIC is equal to $\chi^2_{NTWLS} + (1+\ln(N)) \times t$, where N is the sample size.
5   Following Shook et $al.$ (2004), as well as recent contributions clarifying their inappropriateness in most cases (Iacobucci 2010; Reinartz, Haenlein, and Henseler 2009; Rönkkö and Evermann 2013), we did not consider in our search Partial Least Squares (PLS) applications. In spite of this decision, we found seven articles in which the authors claim to have applied PLS as a more preferable (or somewhat equivalent) analytical approach than SEM. A comparison between SEM and PLS is beyond the scope of this chapter and we refer the reader to Rönkkö and Evermann (2013) for a thorough discussion of the superiority of SEM over PLS in basically any research.

References

Aber, M. S. and McArdle, J. J. (1991) "Latent growth curve approaches to modeling the development of competence," in M. Chandler and M. Chapman (eds) *Criteria for Competence: Controversies in the Conceptualization and Assessment of Children's Abilities*, Hillsdale, NJ: Lawrence Erlbaum Associates, 231–58.

Anderson, J. C. and Gerbing, D. W. (1988) "Structural equation modeling in practice: A review and recommended two-step approach," *Psychological Bulletin*, 103 (3): 411–23.

Bagozzi, R. P. (1980) *Causal Models in Marketing*, New York: Wiley.

Bagozzi, R. P. and Yi, Y. (1990) "Assessing method variance in multitrait-multimethod matrices: The case of self-reported affect and perceptions at work," *Journal of Applied Psychology*, 75 (5): 547–60.

Bagozzi, R. P. and Yi, Y. (2012) "Specification, evaluation, and interpretation of structural equation models," *Journal of the Academy of Marketing Science*, 40 (1): 8–34.

Barney, J. (1991) "Firm resources and sustained competitive advantage," *Journal of Management*, 17 (1): 99–110.

Baron, R. M. and Kenny, D. A. (1986) "The moderator-mediator variable distinction in social psychological research: Conceptual, strategic, and statistical considerations," *Journal of Personality and Social Psychology*, 51 (6): 1173–82.

Baum, J. R. and Wally, S. (2003) "Strategic decision speed and firm performance," *Strategic Management Journal*, 24 (11): 1107–29.

Bearden, W. O., Sharma, S., and Teel, J. E. (1982) "Sample size effects on chi square and other statistics used in evaluating causal models," *Journal of Marketing Research*, 19 (4): 425–30.

Bentler, P. M. (1990) "Comparative fit indexes in structural models," *Psychological Bulletin*, 107: 238–46.

Bentler, P. M. and Bonnet, D. G. (1980) "Significance tests and goodness of fit in the analysis of covariance structures," *Psychological Bulletin*, 88 (3): 588–606.

Bentler, P. M. and Chou, C.P. (1987) "Practical issues in structural modeling," *Sociological Methods & Research*, 16 (1): 78–117.

Bollen, K. A. (1989) *Structural Equations with Latent Variables*, New York: Wiley.

Bollen, K. A. and Curran, P. J. (2006) *Latent Curve Models: A Structural Equation Approach*, Hoboken, NJ: Wiley.

Bollen, K. A. and Lennox, R. (1991) "Conventional wisdom on measurement: A structural equation perspective," *Psychological Bulletin*, 110 (2): 305–14.

Bou, J. C. and Satorra, A. (2007) "The persistence of abnormal returns at industry and firm levels: Evidence from Spain," *Strategic Management Journal*, 28 (7): 707–22.

Browne, M. W. and Cudeck, R. (1993) "Alternative ways of assessing model fit," in K. A. Bollen and J. S. Long (eds) *Testing Structural Equation Models*, Beverly Hills: Sage, 136–62.

Byrne, B. M. (1998) *Structural Equation Modeling with Lisrel, Prelis, and Simplis: Basic Concepts, Applications, and Programming*, Mahwah, NJ: Lawrence Erlbaum.

Cadogan, J. W. and Lee, N. (2013) "Improper use of endogenous formative variables," *Journal of Business Research*, 66 (2): 233–41.

Churchill, G. A., Jr. (1979) "A paradigm for developing better measures of marketing constructs," *Journal of Marketing Research*, 16 (February): 64–73.

Cortina, J. M., Chen, G., and Dunlap, W. P. (2001) "Testing interaction effects in LISREL: Examination and illustration of available procedures," *Organizational Research Methods*, 4 (4): 324–62.

DeVellis, R. F. (1991) *Scale Development: Theories and Applications*, Newbury Park, CA: Sage.

Diamantopoulos, A. and Winklhofer, H. M. (2001) "Index construction with formative indicators: An alternative to scale development," *Journal of Marketing Research*, 38 (May): 269–77.

du Toit, S. H. C. and du Toit, M. (2008) "Multilevel structural equation modeling," in J. De Leeuw and E. Meijer (eds) *Handbook of Multilevel Analysis*, New York: Springer, 435–78.

Dyer, J. H. and Singh, H. (1998) "The relational view: Cooperative strategy and sources of interorganizational competitive advantage," *Academy of Management Review*, 23 (4): 660–79.

Edwards, J. R. and Bagozzi, R. P. (2000) "On the nature and direction of relationships between constructs and measures," *Psychological Methods*, 5 (2): 155–74.

Elenkov, D. S., Judge, W., and Wright, P. (2005) "Strategic leadership and executive innovation influence: An international multi-cluster comparative study," *Strategic Management Journal*, 26 (7): 665–82.

Fahr, J.-L., Hoffman, R. C., and Hegarty, H. (1984) "Assessing environmental scanning at the subunit level: A multitrait-multimethod analysis," *Decision Sciences*, 15 (2): 197–220.

Fan, X., Thompson, B., and Wang, L. (1999) "Effects of sample size, estimation methods, and model specification on structural equation modeling fit indexes," *Structural Equation Modeling*, 6 (1): 56–83.

Flora, D. B. and Curran, P. J. (2004) "An empirical evaluation of alternative methods of estimation for confirmatory factor analysis with ordinal data," *Psychological Methods*, 9 (4): 466–91.

Fornell, C. and Larcker, D. F. (1981) "Evaluating structural equation models with unobservable variables and measurement error," *Journal of Marketing Research*, 18 (1): 39–50.

Govindarajan, V. and Kopalle, P. K. (2006) "Disruptiveness of innovations: Measurement and an assessment of reliability and validity," *Strategic Management Journal*, 27 (2): 189–99.

Homburg, C. and Bucerius, M. (2006) "Is speed of integration really a success factor of mergers and acquisitions? An analysis of the role of internal and external relatedness," *Strategic Management Journal*, 27 (4): 347–67.

Hox, J. (2002) *Multilevel Analysis: Techniques and Applications*, Mahwah, NJ: Erlbaum.

Hu, L. and Bentler, P. M. (1999) "Cutoff criteria for fit indexes in covariance structure analysis: Conventional criteria versus new alternatives," *Structural Equation Modeling*, 6 (1): 1–55.

Hu, L., Bentler, P.M., and Kano, Y. (1992) "Can test statistics in covariance structure analysis be trusted?," *Psychological Bulletin*, 112 (2): 351–62.

Iacobucci, D. (2009) "Everything you always wanted to know about SEM (structural equations modeling) but were afraid to ask," *Journal of Consumer Psychology*, 19 (4): 673–80.

Iacobucci, D. (2010) "Structural equations modeling: Fit Indices, sample size, and advanced topics," *Journal of Consumer Psychology*, 20 (1): 90–8.

Iacobucci, D., Saldanha, N., and Deng, X. (2007) "A meditation on mediation: Evidence that structural equations models perform better than regressions," *Journal of Consumer Psychology*, 17 (2): 139–53.

Jarvis, C. B., MacKenzie, S. B., Podsakoff, P. M., Mick, D. G., and Bearden, W.O. (2003) "A critical review of construct indicators and measurement model misspecification in marketing and consumer research," *Journal of Consumer Research*, 30 (2): 199–218.

Jöreskog, K. G. (1971) "Simultaneous factor analysis in several populations," *Psychometrika*, 36 (4): 409–26.

Jöreskog, K. G. and Sörbom, D. (1993) *LISREL 8: Structural equation modeling with the SIMPLIS command language*, Chicago: Scientific Software International.

Judd, C. M. and Kenny, D. A. (1981) "Process analysis: Estimating mediation in treatment evaluations," *Evaluation Review*, 5 (5): 602–19.

Keesling, W. (1972), "Maximum likelihood approaches to causal analysis," Ph.D. Dissertation, Department of Education, University of Chicago.

Kline, R. B. (2010) *Principles and Practice of Structural Equation Modeling*, 3rd edn, New York: Guildford.

Li, J. J., Poppo, L., and Zhou, K. Z. (2008) "Do managerial ties in China always produce value? Competition, uncertainty, and domestic vs. foreign firms," *Strategic Management Journal*, 29 (4): 383–400.

MacCallum, R. C., Browne, M. W., and Cai, L. (2006) "Testing differences between nested covariance structure models: Power analysis and null hypotheses," *Psychological Methods*, 11 (1): 19–35.

MacCallum, R. C., Browne, M. W., and Sugawara, H. M. (1996) "Power analysis and determination of sample size for covariance structure modeling," *Psychological Methods*, 1 (2): 130–49.

MacCallum, R. C., Roznowski, M., and Necowitz, L.B. (1993) "Model modifications in covariance structure analysis: The problem of capitalization on chance," *Psychological Bulletin*, 111 (May): 490–504.

MacKinnon, D. P. (2008) *Introduction to Statistical Mediation Analysis*, Mahwah, NJ: Erlbaum.

Marsh, H. W. (1996) "Positive and negative global self-esteem: A substantively meaningful distinction or artifactors?," *Journal of Personality and Social Psychology*, 70 (4): 810–9.

Marsh, H. W., Balla, J. R., and McDonald, R. P. (1988) "Goodness-of-fit indexes in confirmatory factor analysis: The effect of sample size," *Psychological Bulletin*, 103 (3): 391–410.

McArdle, J. J. and Anderson, E. (1990) "Latent variable growth models for research on aging," in J. E. Birren and K. W. Schaie (eds), *Handbook of the Psychology of Aging*, 3rd edn, San Diego: Academic Press, 21–44.

Meredith, W. (1993) "Measurement invariance, factor analysis and factorial invariance," *Psychometrika*, 58 (4): 525–43.

Mesquita, L. F., Anand, J., and Brush, T. H. (2008) "Comparing the resource-based and relational views: Knowledge transfer and spillover in vertical alliances," *Strategic Management Journal*, 29 (9): 913–41.

Morgan, N. A., Vorhies, D. W., and Mason, C. H. (2009) "Market orientation, marketing capabilities, and firm performance," *Strategic Management Journal*, 30 (8): 909–20.

Murillo-Luna, J. L., Garcés-Ayerbe, C., and Rivera-Torres, P. (2008) "Why do patterns of environmental response differ? A stakeholders' pressure approach," *Strategic Management Journal*, 29 (11): 1225–40.

Muthén, B. O. (1983) "Latent variable structural equation modeling with categorical data," *Journal of Econometrics*, 22 (1): 43–65.

Muthén, B. O. (2001) "Second-generation structural equation modeling with a combination of categorical and continuous latent variables: New opportunities for latent class/latent growth modeling," in L. M. Collins and A. G. Sayer (eds) *New Methods for the Analysis of Change*, Washington, DC: American Psychological Association, 291–322.

Nielsen, B. B. and Nielsen, S. (2013) "Top management team nationality diversity and firm performance: A multilevel study," *Strategic Management Journal*, 34 (3): 373–82.

Parmigiani, A. (2007) "Why do firms both make and buy? An investigation of concurrent sourcing," *Strategic Management Journal*, 28 (3): 285–311.

Pearl, J. (2012) "The causal foundations of structural equation modeling," in R. H. Hoyle (ed.) *Handbook of Structural Equation Modeling*, New York: Guildford Press, 68–90.

Ping, R. A. J. (1995) "A parsimonious estimating technique for interaction and quadratic latent variables," *Journal of Marketing Research*, 32 (3): 336–47.

Ping, R. A. J. (1996) "Estimating latent variable interactions and quadratics: The state of this art," *Journal of Management*, 22 (1): 163-83.

Podsakoff, P. M., MacKenzie, S. B., Lee, J. Y., and Podsakoff, N. P. (2003) "Common method biases in behavioral research: A critical review of the literature and recommended remedies," *Journal of Applied Psychology*, 88 (5): 879–903.

Preacher, K. J. and Hayes, A. F. (2008) "Asymptotic and resampling strategies for assessing and comparing indirect effects in multiple mediator models," *Behavior Research Methods*, 40 (3): 879–91.

Reinartz, W., Haenlein, M., and Henseler, J. (2009) "An empirical comparison of the efficacy of covariance-based and variance-based SEM," *International Journal of Research in Marketing*, 26 (4): 332–44.

Rigdon, E. E. (2014) "Comment on 'Improper use of endogenous formative variables'," *Journal of Business Research*, 67 (1): 2800–2802.

Rindskopf, D. and Rose, T. (1988) "Some theory and applications of confirmatory second-order factor analysis," *Multivariate Behavioral Research*, 23 (1): 51.

Rönkkö, M. and Evermann, J. (2013) "A critical examination of common beliefs about partial least squares path modeling," *Organizational Research Methods*, 16 (3): 425–48.

Rosel, J. and Plewis, I. (2008) "Longitudinal data analysis with structural equations," *Methodology: European Journal of Research Methods for the Behavioral and Social Sciences*, 4 (1): 37–50.

Satorra, A. and Bentler, P. (1988) "Scaling corrections for chi-square statistics in covariance structure analysis," *Proceedings of the Business and Economic Statistics Section of the American Statistical Association*, Alexandria, VA: American Statistical Association, 308–13

Sharma, S., Mukherjee, S., Kumar, A., and Dillon, W. R. (2005) "A simulation study to investigate the use of cutoff values for assessing model fit in covariance structure models," *Journal of Business Research*, 58 (7): 935–43.

Shervani, T. A., Frazier, G., and Challagalla, G. (2007) "The moderating influence of firm market power on the transaction cost economics model: An empirical test in a forward channel integration context," *Strategic Management Journal*, 28 (6): 635–52.

Shook, C. L., Ketchen, D. J., Jr., Hult, G. T., and Kacmar, K. M. (2004) "An Assessment of the use of structural equation modeling in strategic management research," *Strategic Management Journal*, 25 397–404.

Short, J. C., Ketchen, D. J., Jr., Palmer, T. B., and Hult, G. T. (2007) "Firm, strategic group, and industry influences on performance," *Strategic Management Journal*, 28 (2): 147–67.

Simonin, B. L. (1999) "Ambiguity and the process of knowledge transfer in strategic alliances," *Strategic Management Journal*, 20 (7): 595–623.

Song, M., Droge, C., Hanvanich, S., and Calantone, R. (2005) "Marketing and technology resource complementarity: An analysis of their interaction effect in two environmental contexts," *Strategic Management Journal*, 26 (3): 259–76.

Steenkamp, J. B. E. M. and Baumgartner, H. (1998) "Assessing measurement invariance in cross-national consumer research," *Journal of Consumer Research*, 25 (1): 78–90.

Steensma, H. K. and Lyles, M. A. (2000) "Explaining IJV survival in a transitional economy through social exchange and knowledge-based perspectives," *Strategic Management Journal*, 21 (8): 831–51.

Tanriverdi, H. and Venkatraman, N. (2005) "Knowledge relatedness and the performance of multibusiness firms," *Strategic Management Journal*, 26 (2): 97–119.

Tippins, M. J. and Sohi, R. S. (2003) "IT competency and firm performance: Is organizational learning a missing link?," *Strategic Management Journal*, 24 (8): 745–61.

Treiblmaier, H., Bentler, P. M., and Mair, P. (2011) "Formative constructs implemented via common factors," *Structural Equation Modeling*, 18 (1): 1–17.

Weigelt, C. and Sarkar, M. B. (2012) "Performance implications of outsourcing for technological innovations: Managing the efficiency and adaptability trade-off," *Strategic Management Journal*, 33 (2): 189–216.

Wiley, D. E. (1973) "The Identification Problem For Structural Equation Models With Unmeasured Variables," in A. S. Goldberger and O. D. Duncan (eds) *Structural Equation Models in the Social Sciences*, New York: Academic Press, 69–83.

Zatzick, C. D., Moliterno, T. P., and Fang, T. (2012) "Strategic (mis)fit: The implementation of TQM in manufacturing organizations," *Strategic Management Journal*, 33 (11): 1321–30.

6

TEMPLATES AND TURNS IN QUALITATIVE STUDIES OF STRATEGY AND MANAGEMENT

Ann Langley and Chahrazad Abdallah[1]

This chapter discusses a range of ways in which qualitative methods may be used to study and theorize about strategy processes, that is, to examine the how questions of strategic management that deal with phenomena such as decision making, learning, strategizing, planning, innovating, and changing (Van de Ven, 1992). Qualitative data have particular strengths for understanding processes because of their capacity to capture temporally evolving phenomena in rich detail, something that is hard to do with methodologies based on quantitative surveys or archival databases that are coarse-grained and tend to "skim the surface of processes rather than plunging into them directly" (Langley, 1999: 705).

Our focus will thus be on the study of strategy processes taken as an empirical phenomenon drawing on qualitative data that examines these processes over time, that is, using what has been called "process data" (Langley, 1999). Process data tend to incorporate a mix of *in vivo* observations (meetings, conversations, events, shadowing, etc.), memories and interpretations (real time or retrospective interviews, focus groups, questionnaires, diaries, etc.) and artifacts (minutes, plans, reports, archival records, etc.). However, the key challenge of doing qualitative research on organizational processes lies not so much in collecting these data but in making sense of them to generate a valuable theoretical contribution. The data tend to be complex, messy, eclectic, and with varying degrees of temporal embeddedness. In a previous paper, the first author proposed seven strategies for addressing this challenge include composing case narratives, quantification of incidents, using alternate theoretical templates, grounded theorizing, visual mapping, temporal decomposition, and case comparisons (Langley, 1999).

In this chapter, while building on previous work, we take a somewhat different perspective on the mobilization of qualitative data to analyze strategy processes. First, the chapter recognizes that qualitative methods are associated with a range of different epistemological assumptions and that these may have important implications for the way in which data are interpreted as well as for the theoretical products generated by the analysis. Second, the chapter also recognizes that part of the challenge of doing qualitative research lies in writing it up to communicate its insights in a credible way. Thus while describing methods, we also draw attention to effective forms of writing. Third, we focus the chapter around two rather well-established "templates" for doing qualitative studies of strategy processes and contrast these with two more recent "turns" that offer promising routes to novel insight as well as having particular ontological and epistemological affinities with qualitative research methods.

We begin by describing the two "templates" that have each given rise to a body of work where it seems that the norms of presentation and methodological process have become to a degree standardized and institutionalized among a set of scholars. These templates are far from exhaustive of approaches for qualitative research on strategy processes. However, we believe that they are particularly instructive. Then we consider the implications of two nascent "turns" (the practice turn and the discursive turn) in qualitative analysis of strategy processes that we argue merit greater attention.

Two templates

One of the common complaints (but for some of us, the rather attractive qualities) about qualitative research is that unlike quantitative studies, the rules, formats, and norms for doing, writing, and publishing it are not uniform or well-established. It is not for nothing that Michael Pratt titled a recent editorial in *Academy of Management Journal* about writing qualitative research for the journal "For the lack of a boilerplate" (Pratt, 2009). We do however see the emergence of at least two templates for qualitative studies that have achieved some penetration in the North American management journals, that are each based on different epistemological assumptions, and that are sometimes being used as yardsticks by others. In honor of their originators, we label these the Eisenhardt method and the Gioia method. Both of these have given rise to some highly influential contributions to strategy process research.

As mentioned earlier, in describing these approaches, we not only focus on the logical structure of the method itself but also on the rhetorical structure that is used to support it in published articles. These two dimensions seem to us to be inextricably linked and indeed contribute to constituting the template. Since Golden-Biddle and Locke (2006, 1993) drew our attention to the way in which skillful writers of qualitative research convince their readers, there is increasing realization that writing and rhetoric matter. Thus, the two approaches each have their own internal logics and rhetorical power that we describe below and summarize in Table 6.1. Note that our accounts of these approaches are based for the most part on a close reading of published papers by key authors, but include also ideas gleaned from conference presentations and in the second case from personal communication.[2]

TABLE 6.1 Two templates for qualitative studies of strategy and management

	The "Eisenhardt Method"	The "Gioia Method"
Key methodological reference	Eisenhardt (1989a)	None, but see Gioia (2004) for personal reflections on research philosophy
Exemplar empirical articles	Eisenhardt (1989b), Brown and Eisenhardt (1997), Martin and Eisenhardt (2010)	Gioia and Chittipeddi (1991), Corley and Gioia (2004), Gioia *et al.* (2010)
Central methodological inspirations	Yin (2009) on case study research, but see also Miles and Huberman (1994)	Glaser and Strauss (1967); Strauss and Corbin (1990) on grounded theory
Epistemological foundations and purposes	*Post-positivist assumptions* • Purpose: developing theory in the form of testable propositions • Search for facts (e.g. emphasis on court-room style interviewing) • Product: nomothetic theory	*Interpretive assumptions* • Purpose: capturing and modeling of informant meanings • Search for informants' understandings of organizational events. • Product: process model/ novel concept
Logic of the method	*Design to maximize credible novelty* • Multiple cases (4–10) chosen to be sharply distinct on one key dimension (e.g., performance) while similar on others • Interview data with diverse informants • Identify elements that distinguish high and low performing cases building on cross-case comparison • Validity and reliability from multiple researchers, triangulation of data	*Design for revelation, richness and trustworthiness* • Single case chosen for its revelatory potential and richness of data • Real-time interviews and observation • Build "data structure" by progressive abstraction starting with informant first-order codes and building to second-order themes and aggregate dimensions • Trustworthiness from insider-outsider roles, member checks, triangulation
Rhetoric of the writing	*Establishing novelty*: Contrasting findings with previous research; *Providing evidence*: Data presentation in two steps: (a) data tables; (b) narrative examples of high and low cases *Offering explanation*: Ask why for every proposition. Reasons offered building on data and literature; *Integrating contribution*: Link separate propositions together to build theory	*Establishing the gap*: Show how this study fills a major gap *Distilling the essence*: Present the data structure emphasizing second-order themes and overarching dimensions *Elaborating the story*: Elaborate the model in two ways; (a) present the narrative; (b) additional quotes in tables *Reaffirm contribution*: Return to opening gap to show novel insight.

TABLE 6.1 continued

	The "Eisenhardt Method"	The "Gioia Method"
Examples of other authors using similar approaches	Zott and Huy (2007), Gilbert (2005), Maitlis (2005)	Maguire and Phillips (2008), Anand, Gardner, and Morris (2007), Anand et al. (2007), Rindova et al. (2011)

The Eisenhardt template: Credibly novel nomothetic theory from case comparisons

Kathleen Eisenhardt's (1989a) article on "Building theories from case study research" is now a classic methodological reference both within the field of management and beyond (Ravenswood, 2011), with over 11,000 citations on Google scholar at time of writing (2011). Even more impressive perhaps, Eisenhardt and her colleagues have published a continuous stream of exemplars of the approach that while innovating in their substantive topic foci, replicate both the logic of the method and the rhetoric underpinning its first empirical applications (Eisenhardt and Bourgeois, 1988; Eisenhardt, 1989b). For example, papers co-authored by Eisenhardt or her students and collaborators have examined factors associated with fast decision making (Eisenhardt, 1989b), successful approaches to continuous innovation (Brown and Eisenhardt, 1997), charter changes in multi-divisional businesses (Galunic, 2001; Galunic and Eisenhardt, 1996), how entrepreneurs successfully shape organizational boundaries and markets in their favor (Santos and Eisenhardt, 2009), networking strategies associated with successful industry positioning (Ozcan and Eisenhardt, 2009), the role of seller perspectives and trust in acquisitions (Graebner and Eisenhardt, 2004; Graebner, 2004, 2009), patterns of planning and improvisation in successful internationalization (Bingham, 2009), the origins of success in cross-business collaboration (Martin and Eisenhardt, 2010), and the strategies used by entrepreneurs to build relationships with venture capitalists (Hallen and Eisenhardt, 2009).

In another sign of the influence of this approach, in the late 1990s, the first author received a review on a submission to a journal in which the reviewer used Eisenhardt's (1989a) eight-step method as a framework to guide the review. Every one of the eight steps was analyzed in detail and the submission was matched up against its standards. For better or worse, the method had already acquired something of the character of a template.

Epistemological foundations and purposes: Toward testable propositions

Eisenhardt establishes her method as positivist in orientation, aimed at "the development of testable hypotheses and theory which are generalizable across settings" (1989a: 546). The method is oriented toward induction, that is, generating sets of formal propositions from case study evidence, and is presented as suitable for situations where little is known about a phenomenon or where current perspectives are conflicting or confusing, and where case study evidence can therefore be seen to contribute novel insight. At the same time, the method draws inspiration from Yin's (2009 [1984]) discussion of case study research, emphasizing a logic of replication in which different cases are considered (much like different experiments) as occasions for verifying and elaborating theoretical relationships developed from previous cases. Overall, after reading many of the articles produced with this approach, its power seems to lie in its ability to generate findings that are claimed as novel, even "surprising," and yet at the same time to render these findings highly credible, something that appears paradoxical at first sight. The need for both defamiliarization and plausibility in qualitative research is probably universal and has been noted before (e.g. Golden-Biddle and Locke, 1993). However, it seems to be a particularly strong leitmotiv underlying this particular approach, and both the logic of the method and the rhetoric of the writing in empirical articles seem designed to achieve it.

Logic of the method: Designing to maximize the chances of credible novelty

The replication logic proposed by Eisenhardt requires a substantial number of comparative units of analysis or cases (Eisenhardt [1989a] suggests from four to ten) because the objective is to abstract from these cases common constructs that can then be used to describe and compare generic process components across all the cases (usually in terms of categorical or ordinal scales), and ultimately to relate these to outcome constructs representing some kind of performance. Although the specifics of individual cases contribute importantly to the nature of the constructs induced from the data, it is their common dimensions across cases and not their idiosyncratic features that are emphasized. Thus, the processes examined using this approach are taken as wholes synthesized into a limited number of descriptive dimensions (constructs), rather than being elaborated idiographically.

However, to make this logic work, and to optimize the chances of credible but novel insight, the cases cannot be and are not chosen arbitrarily. Key elements of design include choosing and gaining access to promising phenomena where new knowledge is likely to emerge, setting up comparisons to maximize differences on one dimension while controlling for differences on others, and ensuring coverage of perspectives within each case.

Planning for novel insight of course begins with the research questions and empirical phenomena studied. Thus, Eisenhardt and her colleagues have studied phenomena that have often been subject to quantitative research previously (e.g. acquisitions, alliances, new technology ventures), but where prior process-oriented research has been limited, and particularly so in the dynamic fast-paced techno-logical settings they have favored. Additionally, recent studies demonstrate an impressive level of access to complex situations that few have been able to obtain previously, enhancing the probability of novel findings. For example, Ozcan and Eisenhardt (2009) accessed six new entrants to the wireless video-gaming industry (of which two turned out to be the top players) conducting three waves of interviews with multiple organization members over time as well as interviews with their main partner firms as they constructed their alliance portfolios. One might speculate that the potential for such good access to novel situations might be enhanced by previous successful research that has had practical impact (as evidenced in this case by several *Harvard Business Review* articles).

While controlling for secondary sources of variation (such as size, industry, etc.), cases are also carefully selected to represent what Pettigrew (1990) labeled "polar types," thus emphasizing comparisons between extremes so that, for example, the distinguishing features of high-performing and low-performing cases have the strongest possible chance of emerging clearly. As Eisenhardt and Graebner explain, "Although such an approach can surprise reviewers because the resulting theory is so consistently supported by the empirical evidence, this sampling leads to very clear pattern recognition of the central constructs, relationships, and logic of the focal phenomenon" (2007: 27). Sometimes, the authors have collected data on more cases than they actually used in the analysis to preserve the sharpness of the contrast (e.g. Brown and Eisenhardt, 1997). One might ask what is missing from our understanding by removing consideration of average run-of-the-mill firms. However, the sharpness in contrast is clearly helpful in enhancing the clarity of insights.

The credibility of those insights is further enhanced by sampling multiple perspectives within each case. For example, Graebner (2004, 2009) interviewed both buyers and sellers in her study of acquisitions, Martin and Eisenhardt (2010) interviewed managers at corporate and business unit levels in their study of cross-divisional collaboration. While interviews tend to be the main source of information with all their inherent limitations, strong emphasis is also placed on collecting several kinds of data (e.g. quantitative scales embedded in interview protocols to triangulate responses; archival sources), as well as on obtaining factual accounts through techniques such as "courtroom style questioning" (mentioned in the methods sections of most published articles). Finally, tandem interviewing, electronic recording, and rapid transcription are cited as further means of enhancing validity and reliability.

A good research question, a strong design and excellent data are clearly helpful for developing novel and credible insight, but it is in the analysis that this all comes together. Eisenhardt and her colleagues describe data analysis as essentially a two-stage process, beginning first with the construction of complete within-case narratives and followed by iterative processes of case comparison that continues until a set of constructs that might explain similarities and differences in outcomes begins to emerge (Eisenhardt, 1989a). The fashioning of these constructs is a creative moment of the method because it involves bringing together pieces of case evidence to refine emerging measures of constructs by tabulating data, as well as elaborating understanding of how and why emerging relationships might make sense. Clearly without being there, it is hard to experience the process of analysis itself. However, its products can be appreciated more easily, which brings us to the rhetorical dimension of the template.

Rhetoric of the writing: Establishing novelty, providing evidence, and offering explanation

In addition to a methodological approach that maximizes the chances of offering a novel but credible contribution, Eisenhardt and her colleagues have perfected a distinct mode of writing case study articles that establishes this value. We will use Eisenhardt's (1989b) article on the speed of organizational decision making and a more recent study by Martin and Eisenhardt (2010) to illustrate the approach. The most interesting rhetorical feature concerns how each individual finding or proposition is argued in three key moves.

The first move involves establishing novelty. Here, for each finding, a contrast is explicitly drawn between what previous literature and theory would lead one to expect and the current finding. For example, Eisenhardt (1989b) uses expressions such as, "The data from this research indicate a different view" (549), and "In contrast" (555, 559, 562). Martin and Eisenhardt (2010) use expressions such as "unexpectedly" (271) and "However we observed the opposite" (283). The sharply constructed contrast serves to introduce an unexpected or novel finding but also sets up a tension that then has to be resolved – if this is so surprising, can we believe it?

The resolution begins with the second move involving the presentation of the evidence. In most of this stream of work, this occurs in two steps. The first step involves presenting an overall semi-quantitative portrait of the evidence supporting the proposed relationship in a table in which cases are ordered vertically from more to less high performing. The columns of the table draw together evidence from various sources. For example, Martin and Eisenhardt (2010) argued that engaging in deliberate learning activities contributes to successful cross-divisional collaboration and tabulated evidence on this that included both counts of the number of activities engaged in and two or three quotes from different sources in each firm. As is typical, their chapter includes one table for each proposition (five in this case; with from four to seven columns) plus an additional table documenting evidence of performance (including multiple columns for different quantitative assessments as well as quotes). Some writers might stop the presentation of the data here, since the tabulations generally provide unambiguous support for the propositions and extracts from the data on all the cases.[3] However, the authors generally elaborate on the findings by offering more qualitative narrative examples of typically two high-performing and two low-performing units that add depth to the information provided in tables.

Eisenhardt and colleagues then always engage in an important final move before closing the presentation of their propositions. This is to ask themselves why the observed relationships might hold, that is, offering not just evidence but explanation. Usually two or three reasons are offered for each proposition. To present these, the authors draw on both the data themselves and on prior theory and research in an attempt to deepen understanding, and thus further enhance the credibility of the relationships discovered. This may also be an occasion to reconcile the findings of the research with prior literature (see, e.g. Eisenhardt, 1989b). The importance of offering explanation is sometimes forgotten in qualitative research, but it is particularly important, because it is here that a mere observed empirical regularity is transformed into the beginnings of a *theoretical* contribution.

Extending this theme, a theory-building multiple case study will offer a strong contribution to knowledge if its atomistic propositions can further be integrated into a coherent theoretical story that reaches beyond the individual components. This final step is also important and can be quite challenging because the need for novelty and credibility must also be maintained. For example, after presenting a series of propositions about factors that seemed associated with successful continuous innovation, it is at this stage that Brown and Eisenhardt (1997) began to draw on complexity theory as a metaphor to tie their findings together, noting that a persistent theme in their work was the simultaneous need for structure but also for flexibility.

Assessing the template: Limitations and variations

Overall, the "Eisenhardt method" has emerged as a very successful approach to strategy process research as shown by the multiple publications of the author and her collaborators. Although its logical and rhetorical structure have not been quite so sharply replicated by other authors, many have drawn inspiration from it while adapting it to their distinctive research problems and contexts and mobilizing other sources of methodological inspiration. For example, Zott and Huy (2007) used a comparative case method with similar features to examine how more or less successful entrepreneurial startups used symbolic management approaches, including a focus on extreme cases to sharpen insights. In a prize-winning paper, Gilbert (2005) used a similar method to explore patterns of inertia and modes of overcoming them in the newspaper industry. Others have used multiple case study methods that although not necessarily directly inspired by Eisenhardt's work share methodological and rhetorical elements. For example, Maitlis (2005) used multiple cases to generate a model of different forms of leader and stakeholder sensemaking and their relationships with outcomes using extensive tabulated data to add credibility to the relationships she identified.

The template has however its boundary conditions and limitations. First, while empirical processes are analyzed and interesting new process "constructs" emerge from these studies, the approach often tends to lead to "variance" rather than "process" theorizations, that is, the emphasis in most applications is on explaining variation in outcomes rather than on understanding patterns of evolution over time (Mohr, 1982; Langley, 1999, 2009). Variance models have their own value but they compress time, limit attention to temporal ordering, and assume that there is such a thing as a final outcome, something that can be questionable in many cases. For example, firm performance evolves over time – it is not fixed once and for all. Performance "outcomes" are just way-stations in ongoing processes. Indeed, they might sometimes better be seen as inputs to ongoing processes since evaluations and interpretations of performance can have important effects on subsequent actions (Langley, 2007).

There is however actually no inherent reason why multiple case analyses cannot be used to develop process models and elements of ordering do appear in a few studies (e.g. Bingham, 2009; Galunic and Eisenhardt, 1996). Yet, when this is the objective, the logic is different from the dominant pattern described above. Rather than seeking explanations for differences between cases, a process theoretical analysis requires looking for regularities in temporal patterns across cases. One study that does this rather well using multiple cases is Ambos and Birkinshaw's (2010) article on the developmental patterns and transitions of new science-based ventures. This study indeed demonstrates how the outcomes of one phase of development become stimuli for change for the next. Nevertheless, the retrospective interview methodology used in multiple case studies often limits the depth of evolutionary process detail that can be captured in these studies.

A second issue concerns the degree to which the findings emerging from such studies are indeed as theoretically novel and surprising as often claimed. However interesting the studies are, the subsequent capacity of the authors to explain their results drawing on other literature suggests that the rhetoric of surprise might sometimes be overemphasized. Several authors have mitigated such claims while still legitimating their research efforts and methods by referring to them as "theory elaboration" rather than "theory development" (Lee, Mitchell, and Sablynski, 1999). In most cases, this would seem to be a more realistic and yet valuable research enterprise, because it involves explicitly building on previous work while developing it in new directions.

Finally, as we noted at the beginning of this section, the Eisenhardt multiple case method is positivist in orientation (or more precisely, what Guba and Lincoln [1994] would label post-positivist). It attempts to access "factual" data about what happened in a sample of relevant processes, and it aims to develop generalizable nomothetic causal laws about objectively observable phenomena in the real world. There are other ways of conceiving the research enterprise with qualitative research, one of which we shall consider in the next section.

The Gioia method: Interpretive modeling of informant understandings over time

Ever since Kathleen Eisenhardt published her first papers using the distinctive comparative case method described above, the approach has been both a source of admiration and emulation for many, yet a source of some discomfort to certain other qualitative researchers who have seen in it a distortion of the principles of the traditional interpretive case method that emphasizes depth of understanding of unique situations (Dyer and Wilkins, 1991; Ahrens and Dent, 1998). Yet, cross-case comparative studies and single case analyses have very different objectives and make different kinds of theoretical contributions, valued for different reasons (Langley, 1999).

One group of scholars who appear to have perfected an approach for both doing and successfully publishing single in-depth interpretive case studies is Dennis Gioia and his colleagues and students. Their qualitative work has a distinctive flavor that has given rise to numerous empirical studies, beginning with a series on strategic sense-making and sensegiving in the 1990s (Gioia and Chittipeddi, 1991; Gioia, Thomas, Clark, and Chittipeddi, 1994; Gioia and Thomas, 1996) and following up with another impressive series of articles on organizational identity change in different settings with or by colleagues and students (e.g. Corley and Gioia, 2004; Corley, 2004; Nag, Corley, and Gioia, 2007; Clark, Gioia, Ketchen, and Thomas, 2010; Gioia, Price, Hamilton, and Thomas, 2010). The article by Corley and Gioia (2004) dealing with identity ambiguity during a spinoff (based on Kevin Corley's Ph.D. thesis) received the ASQ Scholarly Contribution Award for the most significant paper published five years earlier and has been frequently cited not only as a strong contribution to organizational identity theory but also as a methodological exemplar by other authors (e.g. Pratt, 2009; Rindova, Dalpiaz, and Ravasi, 2011; Maguire and Phillips, 2008). From our personal observations, it is frequently mentioned by reviewers. There is evidence that we have here the elements of another emergent template.

Epistemological foundations and purposes: Toward interpretive understanding

Unlike Kathleen Eisenhardt, Dennis Gioia has never published a paper explicitly describing step-by-step his methodology. However, in a reflexive piece about his career as an organizational scholar, he noted:

> In my research life, I am a grounded theorist. I pick people's brains for a living, trying to figure out how they make sense of their organizational experience. I then write descriptive, analytical narratives that try to capture what I think they know. Those narratives are usually written around salient themes that represent their experience to other interested readers.
>
> *(Gioia, 2004: 101)*

This quotation neatly sums up the interpretive philosophy driving the approach described here. The data Gioia and his colleagues are interested in concern how people understand the changes they are both instigating and dealing with, and how those meanings evolve. The key methodological references the authors build on are the original grounded theorists (Glaser and Strauss, 1967; Strauss and Corbin, 1990). The theoretical products they generate are narratives that attempt at the same time to provide closeness to so-called "first order" participant perspectives, and yet to add the authors' "second-order" interpretations of these perspectives distilled into a set of interrelated overarching categories or themes that resonate with both participants and readers, and yet communicate new insight. Of course, as in the previous case, there remains a certain tension between novelty and plausibility. We now briefly summarize the logic of the method and the rhetoric of the writing that contribute to achieve both.

The logic of the method: Designing for revelation, richness, and trustworthiness

When studying one case at a time in the hope of offering distinctive insights, it would seem important to choose the right site. Yin (2009) suggests that three different logics can be used to select sites for holistic case studies: choose "critical" cases for the "test" of a particular theory, choose "extreme" cases where something exceptional seems to be occurring, or choose "revelatory" cases that offer high potential for developing new insight into an understudied phenomenon. Gioia and colleagues' recent contributions seem to have been designed to build successively on a developing body of cognitively oriented theories of sensemaking and identity change, each study adding new identity-critical situations in a kind of sequential revelatory case logic. For example, while Corley and Gioia (2004) examined the dynamics of identity change during a spinoff, Nag et al. (2007) looked at identity change in the context of the addition of new forms of knowledge, Clark et al. (2010) focused on evolving identity dynamics during a merger, and Gioia et al.'s (2010) study investigated the emergence of identity in a new organization. The timing of these studies has been such that although others have worked in the area organizational identity, each individual study was able to lay claim to a novel context and related set of insights and the whole series of studies takes on a programmatic character.

Beyond the technical criterion of selecting cases for their revelatory potential, in-depth ethnographic studies of change require organizations that provide good access to ensure data richness. Thus, Gioia and colleagues have not hesitated to study organizations close to home: "No organization is more salient or more important to me than my own organization, so that helps to explain why I sometimes study my own university" (Gioia, 2004: 102). For several articles, Gioia and colleagues have also developed a rather innovative insider-outsider perspective that truly optimizes access to richness, in which one member of the research team has been an active participant in the events studied (e.g. Gioia et al., 1994, 2010; Gioia and Chittipeddi, 1991). The authors argue that the combination of insider and outsider perspectives both enriches the research and can contribute to its trustworthiness as long as precautions are taken to ensure confidentiality and independence (Gioia et al., 2010). In terms of data collection more generally, the researchers have made extensive use of interviews, often carried out in multiple rounds and at multiple levels and positions, but also of observational data (Clark et al., 2010; Gioia and Chittipeddi, 1991; Corley and Gioia, 2004).

Following Strauss and Corbin (1990), the methods sections of these articles generally describe a highly disciplined coding and analysis process whose central artifact, a hierarchical "data structure" is presented as a key output of the research, usually in the form of a horizontal tree-shaped figure (see, e.g. Corley and Gioia, 2004: 184). To arrive at this, the authors first develop *in vivo* codes through "open coding" of data extracts using the words of participants, and then group these into "first order" (participant-based) concepts through "constant comparison" (Strauss and Corbin, 1990) between different extracts. Linkages between first-order concepts are then sought through "axial coding" leading to so-called second-order themes situated at a higher level of abstraction. Through further comparisons of the data, the researchers generally arrive at a limited number of "aggregate dimensions" or "core categories" that serve to summarize the elements of an emerging theoretical model. For example, the ideas of "sensemaking" and "sensegiving" emerged as the key explanatory concepts from the study of the initiation of strategic change in a university (Gioia and Chittipeddi, 1991); the notion of "identity ambiguity" along with its triggers and consequences emerged as central in the study of identity change following a corporate spinoff (Corley and Gioia, 2004). Each of these concepts is linked to others and underpinned by the first-order and second-order themes that successively and in tree-like fashion gave rise to it. All this takes place iteratively, with constant moving back and forth between codes and data, and with emerging ideas leading to additional data collection to fill out the framework as the research progresses. Instead of terms like validity and reliability, the authors use Lincoln and Guba's (1985) set of criteria for naturalistic inquiry to assess the quality of their research method. In particular, their claims for the "trustworthiness" of their data are supported by the involvement of multiple researchers and by member-checking (i.e. gaining feedback from insiders on emerging interpretations).

Again, the simple description of the design and procedures does not do justice to the uncertainties involved in generating these outputs. Finding the twist that will pull all the ideas together is of course necessarily a creative act. As Suddaby (2006) has noted, grounded theory is not easy, although when examining its products, it sometimes looks easy, since at least in the case of these researchers, the emerging models tend to be neatly parsimonious despite the mass of data that generated them. This brings us to the question of rhetoric.

Rhetoric of the writing: Establishing the gap, "distilling the essence," elaborating the story

> My awareness of my cognitive limitations helps me empathize with the poor reader trying to understand the point(s) I am trying to make in a given article. For that reason, I work hard at trying to distil findings to their essences and to communicate them in simple compelling ways. Although I once disdained it, I have developed a great appreciation for "sound-bite" research reporting … A well-constructed sound-bite has a certain memorability about it-what I like to call a "cognitive stickiness" that allows readers to remember the most important points you are trying to make.
>
> *(Gioia, 2004)*

The rhetorical structure of the articles by Gioia and colleagues that we have reviewed here is perhaps not as uniform as that described above for Eisenhardt and colleagues' work. However, there are some very instructive commonalities that are worthy of note. First, the positioning of the contribution is more often in the nature of establishing a gap in understanding of important processes than of establishing a contradiction with previous research as we saw above.

However, perhaps the most striking and powerful rhetorical pattern lies in the presentation of the findings. This begins with the overall "data structure" diagram we described in the previous section. For example, Corley and Gioia's (2004) data structure diagram has 24 "first-order" concepts grouped into 9 "second-order themes," which are in turn grouped again into three "aggregate dimensions" that form the core of the theoretical contribution. Gioia *et al.*'s (2010) study of the creation of a new identity in a university department has 16 "first-order categories" grouped into 8 "second-order themes." In both these papers and others, another figure that shows how the second-order themes are related with each other over time is also provided. These figures, accompanied by a short verbal description, provide an upfront distillation of the paper's central message (see Gioia's remarks at the beginning of this section).

All that remains then is to elaborate on each of the main themes. This is done in two ways that together provide compelling support for the emerging model. First each of the themes is elaborated as part of a narrative account in the body of the paper, with multiple references to specific incidents and quotations from informants or documents. Second, additional quotations for each theme are displayed in a large accompanying table (with very little overlap in content with the textual narrative). This data presentation strategy, very obvious in the Corley and Gioia (2004) article and followed through in subsequent writings, builds strong credibility around the findings. In an *Academy of Management Journal* editorial, Pratt (2009) noted the value of this approach, suggesting that writers might keep their most striking "power quotes" (Gioia's sound-bites?) for the narrative, but place additional "proof quotes" in tables to solidify their arguments. Finally, after the presentation of the findings, the authors return to a description of the overall model, and elaborate on the contribution of the paper, often though not always in a series of propositions.

Assessing the template: Limitations and variations

Again, the "Gioia method" has been very successful on its own terms in generating knowledge about strategic and identity change in various situations. Several of its elements have also been taken up by others, especially but not only by researchers in the area of organizational identity. Specifically, the authors' approach to summarizing the derivation of their emergent grounded conceptual framework in the form of a data structure diagram has become increasingly common. For example, Maguire and Phillips (2008) used this device in a study of identity change at Citigroup, Anand *et al.* (2007) used it for a study of the development of new practices in consulting firms, and Rindova *et al.* (2011) used it in their study of Alessi's incorporation of new cultural resources into their strategy.

This template has limitations too. One potential limitation that seems, however, not to have hindered these researchers concerns the challenge of convincing readers about the transferability and relevance of the findings given the propensity to study single cases. In interpretive research, it is argued that it is the depth of contextual detail in a case study that provides the understanding necessary for a reader to judge whether the theoretical elements might apply to their own situation. Also, one might expect that cases (of for example mergers) might have certain generic qualities that could make some types of findings relevant almost anywhere. And yet, working with a single idiographic case considered holistically is, in our own experience, often more challenging than working with some form of comparative design where similarities and differences more naturally stimulate theorization (Langley, 1999). With a single case, it is easy to fall into the trap of having nothing but a boring sequential narrative to tell, with no insightful plot or any hope of catching readers' minds and imaginations with the "cognitive stickiness" that Gioia (2004) was referring to. The ability to generate theoretical insights that have obvious value beyond the specific context of their development is a crucial skill for this type of research.

Finally, although the Gioia method does lead to process models of how people make sense over time, these models sometimes seem to describe phenomena at rather a high level of aggregation (as described in the second-order themes) so that a complete understanding of how and why things occur in the everyday from one moment to the next is to a degree glossed over. This may be partly a consequence of the grounded theory methodology where the coding and categorizing process may generate a certain decontextualization; to achieve generality, the chaining and interplay of particular events may sometimes become lost in this process. In addition, despite their interpretive roots, these studies usually produce singular narratives where differences in perspective are subsumed as "tensions" but are not elaborated in depth (Buchanan and Dawson, 2007). As we shall see in the next section, there may be other ways of approaching strategy processes that get closer to everyday strategic practices and the way in which they are reproduced and adapted and that take into account multiple perspectives.

Two turns

The two approaches to qualitative analysis of strategy process phenomena described above are not of course the only ones. However, we chose to present them because they are not only powerful and useful but also representative of the most common sets of epistemological assumptions, methodological toolkits, and rhetorical frames supporting qualitative research in this field. In the second part of this chapter, we move toward some more recent and less traditional approaches to qualitative studies in strategy and management. These approaches are broader and less codified than the templates described above, so our mode of presentation will be somewhat different. However, they are currently generating a great deal of interest. Each has different epistemological assumptions, suggests different methodologies, and may involve different styles of writing. We begin by focusing on the "practice turn" and then move on to the "discursive turn" drawing on selected methodological texts and empirical exemplars in each case (for a summary of this discussion, see Table 6.2).

TABLE 6.2 Two "turns" in qualitative research on strategy and management

	"Strategy as practice"	*"Strategy as discourse"*
Empirical focus	*The "doing" of strategy:* Activities of strategy practitioners and regularities emerging from or underlying them	*Language and strategy:* How discourses are shaped and shape understandings of strategy and organizational direction
Foundational references	Whittington (2006, 2007), Jarzabkowski (2004), Johnson *et al.* (2007), Rasche and Chia (2009), Feldman and Orlikowski (forthcoming)	Phillips *et al.* (2008), Vaara (2010), Phillips and Hardy (2002), Vaara and Tienari (2004)
Epistemological foundations and key theoretical elements	*Practices as constitutive of social world; diverse theoretical roots but some key common elements:* • Knowledge as embedded in practices • Socio-material nature of practice • Recursivity of practices	*Social world created and maintained through discourse; Key elements:* • Hermeneutic: focus on meaning • Critical: revealing politics and power • Interdiscursive: focus on interplay among discourses at multiple levels
Empirical exemplars	Rouleau (2005), Kaplan (2011), Jarzabkowski (2008)	Heracleous and Barrett (2001), Vaara and Monin (2010)
Methodological and rhetorical elements	• Ethnographic observation to detect elements of practice (e.g., implicit knowledge; sociomateriality) not usually consciously perceived • Need for in-depth longitudinal studies to capture recursivity of practices • Writing around detailed vignettes to reveal underlying dynamics • Use of temporal bracketing to structure recursive analysis	• Detailed analyses of content of texts (e.g., themes, structure, etc.) • Need for ethnographic or process data on context (writers, readers, intentions, events, practices surrounding text) • Longitudinal data to capture temporality • Writing including both detailed analysis of text and as well as data on how texts are used in context

The practice turn: Studying strategy as a social practice

Epistemological foundations and empirical exemplars

The practice turn in strategy research, or the "strategy as practice" perspective (Whittington, 2006; Jarzabkowski, 2005; Johnson, Langley, Melin, and Whittington, 2007) has developed considerable momentum in recent years building on an interest in practice-based studies that has spread from philosophy and sociology (Schatzki, Knorr Cetina, and Von Savigny, 2001; Reckwitz, 2002; Giddens, 1984; Bourdieu, 1977) into various subfields of organization theory and management including strategy (Feldman and Orlikowski, 2011; Miettinen, Samra-Fredericks, and Yanow, 2009; Corradi, Gherardi, and Verzelloni, 2010). Specifically, scholars of strategy as practice argue that rather than being seen as something that organizations have, strategy should be viewed as "something people do" (Whittington, 2006; Jarzabkowski, Balogun, and Seidl, 2007). Practice thinking thus begins with an empirical focus on activity, and in this case with the concrete micro-level activities that strategy practitioners, broadly defined, engage in, and with the regularities constituted and reproduced by these activities.

For some, practice thinking ends where it begins: the "doing of strategy" is an interesting empirical phenomenon that can be and indeed has been studied in a variety of different ways using methods that are often not all that different from those we described earlier. Indeed, the studies of Eisenhardt (1989b) on fast decision making and Gioia and Chittipeddi (1991) on sensemaking and sensegiving in strategic change can be seen as studies of strategy as practice in that sense (Johnson et al., 2007). This empirically driven notion of practice has renewed interest in the human and practical elements of strategy making, giving rise to some innovative and interesting studies (e.g. Johnson, Prashantham, Floyd, and Bourque's [2010] multiple case studies of success and failure in strategy workshops drawing on ritual theory; Maitlis and Lawrence's [2003] single case study of strategy failure; Balogun and Johnson's [2004] interpretive study of the role of middle-manager sensemaking in strategic change using diaries and focus groups).

However, the notion of strategy as practice can become deeper and more distinctive if the notion of practice is taken to refer not just to an empirical interest in the doing of strategy but to include a commitment to theories of social practice, and eventually to a practice-based ontology in which "practices are understood to be the primary building blocks of social reality" (Feldman and Orlikowski, 2011: 3; Schatzki et al., 2001). This point has been argued in different ways by both proponents (Whittington, 2007; Rasche and Chia, 2009) and critics (Chia and MacKay, 2007; Carter, Clegg, and Kornberger, 2008; Corradi et al., 2010) of the strategy as practice perspective. However, what exactly this means is obscured by the fact that, as Miettinen et al. note, "social practice theory is not a unified theory, but rather a collection of authors and approaches interested in studying or theorizing practice, each of whom has his or her own distinctive vocabulary" (2009: 1312; see also Corradi et al., 2010). Nevertheless, some common features of practice theorizing can be identified (Miettinen *et al.*, 2009; Rasche and Chia, 2009; Feldman and Orlikowski, 2011) and we will draw on three of these to illustrate the implications for empirical research, using exemplars for each.

First, practice theorizing emphasizes the way in which knowledge is embedded in and regenerated through practical activity (Cook and Brown, 1999; Gherardi, 2006). Thus when individuals engage in practices, they draw on unconscious tacit understandings of how to "go on" in specific situations that have been learned over time and that are enacted collectively (Rasche and Chia, 2009). From this perspective, the knowledge of how strategy or indeed any practical activity is accomplished may not be easily available only from asking questions in interviews, the dominant methodology in qualitative studies of strategy and management. Rather, it is implicit in what people do in specific situations. To appreciate and to a degree capture this form of knowledge requires close ethnographic observation, and sensitivity not just to surface activity but to the skills and competencies that underlie it (Rasche and Chia, 2009). Rouleau's (2005) study of everyday sensemaking and sensegiving practices illustrates this focus. Specifically, through a fine-grained analysis of incidents and conversations observed among middle managers and clients in a clothing firm, Rouleau (2005) shows how enacting a new strategy in the everyday involves adjusting stories to the people addressed ("translating the new orientation"), drawing on broad cultural repertoires associated with gender and ethnic origin ("overcoding the strategy"), mobilizing space, the body and displayed emotions to channel attention ("disciplining the client") and framing legitimate reasons for strategic change ("justifying the change"). All these micro-practices and their embedded skills appear to be enacted subtly, smoothly, and naturally with little readily apparent conscious reflection.

A second common tenet of practice theory is that material objects ranging from sophisticated technologies to the everyday tools of living are deeply intertwined in everyday practices, mediating how and what is accomplished (Latour, 2005). Practices are thus often qualified as "socio-material" to encompass the notion of the inseparability of human and nonhuman agency (Feldman and Orlikowski, 2011). This too has implications for research, again suggesting a need for fine-grained attention to how material elements intervene within the context of practice. An interesting recent ethnographic study by Kaplan (2011) reveals how PowerPoint technology is deeply implicated in the ways in which strategic decisions are constructed. Through the fine analysis of strategy-making negoti-ations, Kaplan shows how the materiality, mutability, modularity, and digitality of PowerPoint slides contributes to enabling both collaboration among people holding different perspectives (through information sharing and idea generation), but also to what she calls "cartography" – the political effort to pin down and "draw boundaries around the scope of the strategy" (21) by selective inclusion of information and actors manifested materially in the slides themselves and in the way in which they are diffused and presented.

Finally, a third important notion in practice theory is the idea that practices are recursive (Feldman and Orlikowski, 2011; Jarzabkowski, 2004). Ongoing activity leads to the stabilization and reification of social orders or social structures that become resources for subsequent activity. For example, in Giddens' (1984) theory of structuration, social structures constituted through practice include power dependencies ("structures of domination"), shared meanings or interpretive schemes ("structures of signification"), and norms ("structures of legitimation"). Ongoing activities are constrained and enabled by these social structures, but they are simultaneously the means by which they are produced and reproduced over time. The mutually constitutive nature of structure and agency implicit in these theories of practice can be hard to pin down in empirical research and detailed ethnographic observation again seems desirable. In addition however, the ability to capture the recursive nature of practices requires fairly long time frames. For example, in a seven-year study of university strategy making, Jarzabkowski (2008) used a structuration theory framework to examine how strategizing iteratively involved ad hoc decisions about specific strategies (interactive strategizing), the enactment of embedded routines and structures that generated decisions while reproducing those routines (procedural strategizing), and activity that creating new routines and structures that would serve to embed later decisions (integrative strategizing).

Doing and writing research from the practice turn

As we have suggested above, studying strategy from the perspective of the practice turn often requires deeper and closer contact with the doing of strategy than is often seen in other approaches. Thus, ethnography has been a favored research method because it enables researchers to capture what participants themselves are unable to articulate, at least not as well (Rouleau, 2005; Rasche and Chia, 2009) and to physically see how material objects, the body, space, and time are mobilized within practices (Rouleau, 2005; Kaplan, 2011). For example, strategy as practice scholars have begun to use video ethnography and photographs to capture systematically what is happening beyond the merely verbal component of strategic practices (Molloy and Whittington, 2005; Liu and Maitlis, 2010). In addition, longitudinal observations over long time periods are required to capture the recursive nature of practices as in Jarzabkowski's (2008) seven-year study.

Clearly however, such work generates immense databases of disparate kinds of information, and the researcher is faced with another complex task in communicating it in the context of journal articles. Without suggesting that these are the only ways of analyzing and communicating insight about practice, we observe two interesting ways in which authors reveal their findings that are somewhat different from those described earlier. The first is particularly evident in the Rouleau (2005) and Kaplan (2011) articles and involves the detailed elaboration and unfurling of highly specific but powerfully illustrative vignettes. For example, Rouleau's (2005) ethnographic study took place over six months with four days per week of presence on the site. However, she uses six small vignettes (three routines and three conversations) to build her in-depth analysis of the practices. She draws an interesting analogy between her own approach and that of the natural scientist when she says, "Just as using a microscope helps understanding of the whole through its tiny parts, routines and conversations offer an interesting insight to examine strategic change" (1419). As each of the microscopic samples reveals similar underlying phenomena whose workings are finely traced out, cumulative understanding becomes increasingly layered and credible. Similarly, Kaplan undertook an 18-month ethnography. However, her analysis draws intensively on two sequences of PowerPoint-based negotiations with detailed illustrations and a complex table in which modifications over time are illustrated. The explicit showing of how the practices she is describing are manifested in every element of these concrete sequences adds to the credibility of her theoretical insights.

A second analytical and rhetorical device that has been useful in practice-based studies draws on Barley's (1986: 82) sawtooth representation of the recursive nature of actions and institutions (or structures) where the realm of action and institution are shown as horizontal parallel lines that interact (see also Barley and Tolbert, 1997). In this representation, institutions are shown as directly influencing the practices carried out in the action realm. Each iteration of a practice implies its recursive reproduction or adaptation. Over time, ad hoc adaptations progressively cumulate and eventually result in sharper shifts in the institutional frame itself. This classic sawtooth model is used by Jarzabkowski (2008) in her study of strategizing in universities, by Howard-Grenville (2007) in her study of shifts in issue-selling practices in a chip-making company, and by Rerup and Feldman (2011) in their study of evolution in interpretive schemes in a research unit. The framework provides a heuristic for breaking down analysis into successive temporal brackets (Langley, 1999: 703) to explicitly examine how iterative actions taken during one period lead over time to changes in the context that will affect action in subsequent periods.

Assessing the turn: Limitations and variations

The practice turn offers potential to understand the doing of strategy and management rather differently, throwing light on its implicit, sociomaterial and recursive nature, something that is largely absent in the two templates we presented earlier. The practice turn also has a natural affinity for qualitative and ethnographic research methods because of its empirical focus on the situated and particular. As Feldman and Orlikowski (2011) note, however, this does not mean that practice theorizing has no generality. Rather, strong practice-based studies like those mentioned above generate new concepts and understandings that have much broader relevance. In a striking example of this potential, Feldman's ethnographic study of practices in a university housing department generated broadly applicable theories of the performative and ostensive aspects of routines (Feldman, 2000) as well as the development of the notion of "resourcing" (Feldman, 2004). Both these ideas have many interesting applications far beyond the original context of their production, and more particularly in the area of strategy.

The key limitation of the practice turn in strategy may be that as some critics have suggested (Chia and MacKay, 2007; Carter *et al.*, 2008), it is not quite yet a "turn" in the epistemological sense. "Strategy as practice" is more in the nature of an "umbrella" concept (Corradi *et al.*, 2010) that enables the grouping together of a community of people interested in similar empirical phenomena and drawing on a loose collection of theoretical lenses that have something to do with practice. So far, this seems to be leading to a renewal and enrichment of qualitative methodology in strategy and management, a positive trend it seems to us. As the perspective develops through its own empirical research practice, its theoretical reach will no doubt recursively shift and hopefully deepen. The emphasis on practice has also in many ways fed into the second turn we examine here.

The discursive turn: Studying strategy as discourse

Epistemological foundations and empirical exemplars

As the result of a more general "linguistic turn" in organization studies (Alvesson and Karreman, 2000), and building on the progression of socio-constructivist epistemologies inspired by Berger and Luckmann (1967), discursive approaches have become increasingly prevalent in organization and management research (Phillips, Sewell, and Jaynes, 2008; Vaara, 2010). In particular, a wide variety of linguistic approaches to strategy have been proposed varying from critical discourse analysis (CDA) (Phillips *et al.*, 2008) to narrative analysis (Barry and Elmes, 1997) to conversation analysis (Samra-Fredericks, 2003). In this section, we will focus more particularly on exemplars of discursive approaches used to study multilevel strategy processes over time.

One of the most widely shared definitions of discourse was offered by Parker (1992) for whom discourse does not refer simply to text, but is a set of texts and of the practices related to their production, dissemination, and reception. Texts can take on different forms: written, spoken, images, symbols, and other artifacts (Grant, Keenoy, and Oswick, 1998). Discourse analysis involves examining how discourses shape understandings of social reality, and how they are in turn shaped through discursive practices including the production, distribution, transformation, movement, and interpretation of texts. It aims to understand how social phenomena are produced or constructed and maintained through time (Phillips and Hardy, 2002). Thus, there are clear links between this approach and the practice-based approach described in the previous section. Paralleling the traditional themes of strategy research, discourse studies in strategy "all share an interest in exploring how organizations, industries and their environment are created and maintained through discourse" (Phillips *et al.*, 2008: 770).

As in the case of practice studies, there is no strong coherence among discursive approaches, but three main concerns are featured in this type of research that we identify as hermeneutic, critical and interdiscursive. The hermeneutic dimension is related to the need to understand how certain meanings are discursively constructed and interpreted and how they evolve over time (Heracleous and Barrett, 2001). Discourse studies also share a critical concern that calls for a multidimensional or intertextual analysis of discourse to bridge micro, meso, and meta levels of analysis and to critically examine the shaping of various organizational processes (Phillips et al., 2008; Vaara, 2010). Finally, while some discourse analyses tend to be static focusing on specific documents or narratives, as noted by Vaara (2010), the greatest potential of discursive approaches for strategy comes from analyses of the interplay of discourses over time and across multiple levels, what he labels "interdiscursivity." This could involve for example looking at how macro-level discourses about the nature of strategy are taken up in specific organizations (Mantere and Vaara, 2008), how multiple discourses interact and conflict (Heracleous and Barrett, 2001), or how dominant discourses come to emerge or are contested over time (Ezzamel and Willmott, 2008). Discursive approaches can therefore offer a new way of introducing complexity into the study of strategic processes by examining their nonlinearity, their linguistic nature, and the various forms of their internal dynamics (Vaara, 2010).

The two exemplars of discourse studies we chose to present in this chapter represent two very different ways of studying strategy processes from a discursive standpoint. The first by Heracleous and Barrett (2001) uses discourse analysis with a primarily hermeneutic concern. It examines organizational change from a discursive perspective through an exploration of the implementation process of a risk-placing support system in the London Insurance Market over a five-year period. The article, one of the first of its nature to be published in the *Academy of Management Journal*, makes a strong case for a structurationist conceptualization of discourse as made up of both deep meaning structures and surface communicative actions and defends this conceptualization as a means of reconciling the social dualisms of structure and action (Giddens, 1984). Again the linkage with the previous perspective is clear, although the emphasis here is clearly on communicative actions and their underlying meaning, rather than on practices.

The article is a longitudinal (five-year) investigation of how a change process (the implementation of a new IT system) is shaped by the discourses of different stakeholders over time. It is both an inquiry into the nature of the discourse employed by various stakeholders and an inquiry into its role in shaping the change process. Interestingly, a combined discourse analysis method, termed "Rhetorical-Hermeneutic" by the authors, was used and constitutes an original way of bridging multiple levels of analysis: the deep discursive structure level, the surface communicative action level and the contextual level through interpretive schemes that are used as modalities that mediate between the two discursive levels. This methodological bridging apparatus generated a systematic processual analysis that tracks shifts and transformations in the change process over time. The study shows how the deep structures of discourse act as stable patterns that shape action in various ways for different stakeholders through contextual elements of interpretation. Its approach is "interdiscursive" in that it examines the struggles among alternate meanings inherent in stakeholder's communicative actions.

The second article by Vaara and Monin (2010) is a study of a process of discursive legitimation in a post-merger situation using a multimethod critical approach. The paper also shows the recursivity of discourse and action in that the discursive legitimation process unfolds by simultaneously shaping and being shaped by organizational action. The interesting aspect of the process as described in the paper is how a key discursive "device" of justification, termed "theranostics" (a combination of the two strategic resources of the merging entities, respectively "therapy" and "diagnostics") was taken up and echoed in media discourse, creating enthusiasm around this concept not only in the business press but by ricochet within the firm itself as its members came increasingly to believe it, and indeed attempted to enact it despite its origin as a useful "story" developed to legitimate a merger that had been promulgated for other reasons. The study illustrates the potentially performative nature of discourse (producing that of which it speaks) and its role in the merger outcome. It shows the process of transformation of theranostics from a discursive resource of legitimation into a source of unrealistic expectations, as the ideas underlying it ultimately proved to be illusory.

In their article, Vaara and Monin (2010) interestingly also echo themes like sensemaking, sensegiving, or sensehiding often examined by others through the "Gioia method," but they analyse them using a discursive approach that is based on a multidimensional conception of discourse as made up of texts but also of a set of material actions that transform or are transformed by it.

Doing and writing research from the discursive turn

Aside from the two examples of published research from a discursive perspective described above, it is important to note that a large number of studies have been using this perspective in recent management research. In their recent review of and call for applying CDA to strategy research, Phillips et al. (2008) show the increase in the number of published papers including CDA since 1995, reaching around 140 in 2005. Although a wide range of methodologies can be found under the discourse analysis umbrella, three main elements structure the discursive approach methodologically in relation to studying processes: the multiple forms of text(s), the crucial role of context, and the temporality of discourse.

First, the textual dimension of discourse analysis is of course fundamental since it is mainly through texts in their various forms that any discursive work can be done. The juxtaposition of written, spoken and other symbolic textual devices characterizes the aim of discursive approaches to accentuate in more depth the internal circumvolutions of process and its interdiscursive nature. The studies we describe each contain specific ways of systematically analyzing the content of texts, for example, looking at "ethymeme components" or rhetorical structures in the texts for Heracleous and Barrett (2001) and looking at legitimation strategies inherent in the texts for Vaara and Monin (2010). Other kinds of textual analysis methods such as conversation analysis or narrative analysis would be possible. However, it is not only the text as a micro analytical device that is of interest here but texts as multiple forms of discursive manifestations embodied in their practices of production, dissemination, and consumption that are at the heart of this relatively new methodological approach.

It is important to note here the differences in the way textual data (interviews, documents, and other materials) are treated in this perspective as compared with the approaches we presented in the first half of this chapter. The Eisenhardt method involves analyzing such data to establish facts while the Gioia method would treat the same data as interpretations. In the discursive approach, texts are discourses that are analyzed not only for what they say but for what they *do*: for example, the meanings they construct, reproduce, contest or maintain, the effects they have and the precise means by which these effects are achieved (Vaara, 2010). These effects may include the propagation of managerial concepts (e.g."theranostics"; strategy itself), the transformation of institutional fields (Suddaby and Greenwood, 2005) or the reproduction of power relations (Knights and Morgan, 1991; Ezzamel and Willmott, 2008), with critical researchers being particularly concerned with revealing the latter.

Second, in almost all the studies that use a discursive approach to understand organizational processes, the notion of context is presented as the stepping stone upon which a strong analysis should be built. No "thick description" is possible without it and no sense of unfolding or of temporality can be conveyed if context is not addressed. For example, in Heracleous and Barrett's study (2001), context is taken into account through the collection of ethnographic data that is used in conjunction with the textual data in the analysis of the change process. In a constant hermeneutic interplay between texts and discourses defined as "constituted of the totality of single texts" (762), the analysis illustrates the importance of their "texts-in-context" approach (interviews, written texts, ethnographic data) to understand the temporal unfolding of the process. Similarly, in recent research by Vaara and his colleagues, (e.g. Vaara, Kleymann, and Seristo, 2004; Vaara and Monin, 2010; Mantere and Vaara, 2008), context is always given a preponderant role in explaining the dynamics of the processes under examination. Elements of context are drawn from data collected during lengthy contact with the studied organizations and are included in the narrative constructions around the unfolding of the examined processes. Generally, context gives the necessary depth and grounding to studies that move from the meso to the micro levels of analysis.

Finally, temporality is one of the main issues in studying processes and it seems that recent discursive approaches with their multidimensional and multilevel methodological choices are tackling the temporality issue in an interestingly relevant manner. Echoing the methodological opening-up to multiple dimensions, the conceptualization of temporality is broader here than in the more traditional process research studies. The temporality revealed in these studies is not simply a linear progression through time but a dynamic interdiscursive process that evolves in sinuous, nonlinear ways. For example, in the Heracleous and Barrett (2001) study, temporality is crucial and is shown through the description of the evolution of both levels of discourse and their mutual structuring broken down into distinct phases of evolution. In their description of the legitimation process of a merger, Vaara and Monin's (2010) conception of temporality is anchored within the particular interpretive context of individuals in the two merging organizations. Temporality becomes a relative notion that might have to be taken into account in a different way in different contexts and for different organizational actors.

Assessing the turn: Limitations and variations

Like its main proponents (Phillips *et al.*, 2008; Vaara, 2010), we believe that the discursive turn offers potential to open up research on strategy processes, through a more performative conception of discourse, to a multidimensional examination of organizational processes. In its critical manifestation, the discursive turn also draws attention to the ways in which realities that favor certain groups over others are socially constructed but also to how those relations might be thought of differently (Ezzamel and Willmott, 2008; Mantere and Vaara, 2008).

Nevertheless, we see several ways in which discursive studies might be developed and improved. First, some of the earlier difficulties associated with publishing discourse-based studies in major journals were perhaps associated with the relatively opaque nature of some of their analyses. Recent work including the studies by Heracleous and Barrett (2001) (see also Heracleous, 2006), by Vaara and colleagues (see also Vaara and Tienari, 2004; Mantere and Vaara, 2008) and by Phillips and Hardy (2002) have begun to render the methods more accessible, providing more methodological detail and worked examples to build confidence in and understanding of findings that this type of analysis can generate.

Second, greater emphasis could be placed on the pragmatic aspects of discourse studies in strategy research to enable them to reach a wider audience. An understanding of the way in which discursive practices contribute to defining the realities organizations live with ought to have serious practical implications, but these have not necessarily been strongly emphasized. As with any academic enterprise, there is a risk of becoming too self-referential (Luhmann, 1995), and this arises particularly with approaches that build on their own specialized methodological language. Put differently, the knowledge generated by the more traditional templates has perhaps in the past been a little easier to consume.

Conclusions

This chapter has considered four different ways in which qualitative research can contribute to developing valuable knowledge about strategy processes. By describing two somewhat institutionalized approaches to conceptualizing qualitative research and of writing qualitative articles (the two "templates"), we illustrate some ways in which positivist and interpretive conceptions of reality and knowledge development have been successfully mobilized to generate insight. We have also shown how these approaches achieve their persuasive effects by examining not only the logic behind the methods used, but also by revealing the related rhetorical moves underlying their presentation and argumentation.

Second, we attempted to move beyond the positivist and interpretive frames reflected in the two more traditional templates to consider alternative ways in which qualitative data might be used to throw light on strategic management processes. Drawing on a number of illustrative exemplars, we showed the potential for the practice and discursive turns in strategy research to offer important and original ways of seeing these processes. From these perspectives, qualitative data is not simply something that can be valuable in the "early stages" of research as is often assumed in the positivist paradigm, but something that is inherent to the ability to uncover certain types of knowledge about organizational phenomena, for example, knowledge that is embedded in strategic practices or that is itself constructed through language. We hope that the ideas presented in this chapter will encourage researchers interested in using qualitative research methods to examine the approaches presented here for themselves, perhaps by delving into some of the exemplars we identified. We also hope that through their own reading and research, they might discover, articulate and/or invent others. There is, fortunately, still ample room for innovation and creativity in the area of qualitative research on strategy and management.

Notes

1 Ann Langley, Chahrazad Abdallah, (2011), "Templates and Turns in Qualitative Studies of Strategy and Management," in Donald B. Bergh, David J. Ketchen (eds) *Building Methodological Bridges (Research Methodology in Strategy and Management, Volume 6)*, Emerald Group Publishing, pp. 201–235.
2 We thank Dennis Gioia for an instructive telephone conversation about his approach to qualitative research.
3 Note that while Eisenhardt (1989a) indicated that the data do not have to perfectly fit the proposed model, in most published papers, it is hard to observe any lack of fit in the tabulated evidence that almost always exhibits perfect correlation.

References

Ahrens, T. and Dent, J. F. (1998). Accounting and organizations. *Journal of Management Accounting Research*, 10(1), 1–39.

Alvesson, M. and Karreman, D. (2000). Varieties of discourse: On the study of organizations through discourse analysis. *Human Relations*, 53(9), 1125–1149.

Ambos, T. C. and Birkinshaw, J. (2010). How do ventures evolve? An inductive study of archetype change in science-based ventures. *Organization Science*, 21(6), 1125–1140.

Anand, N., Gardner, H., and Morris, T. (2007). Knowledge-based innovation: Emergence and embedding of new practice areas in management consulting firms. *Academy of Management Journal*, 50(2), 406–428.

Balogun, J. and Johnson, G. (2004). Organizational restructuring and middle manager sensemaking. *Academy of Management Journal*, 47(4), 523–549.

Barley, S. R. (1986). Technology as an occasion for structuring: Evidence from observations of CT scanners and the social order of radiology departments. *Administrative Science Quarterly*, 31, 78–108.

Barley, S. R. and Tolbert, P. S. (1997). Institutionalization and structuration: Studying the links between action and institution. *Organization Studies*, 18(1), 93–117.

Barry, D. and Elmes, M. (1997). Strategy retold: Toward a narrative view of strategic discourse. *Academy of Management Review*, 2, 429–452.

Berger, P. L. and Luckmann, T. (1967). *The Social Construction of Reality*. New York: Doubleday Anchor.

Bingham, C. B. (2009). Oscillating improvisation: How entrepreneurial firms create success in foreign market entries over time. *Strategic Entrepreneurship Journal*, 3, 321–345.

Bourdieu, P. (1977). *Outline of a Theory of Practice*. Cambridge: Cambridge University Press.

Brown, S. L. and Eisenhardt, K. M. (1997). The art of continuous change: Linking complexity theory and time-paced evolution in relentlessly shifting organizations. *Administrative Science Quarterly*, 42(1), 1–34.

Buchanan, D. and Dawson, P. (2007). Discourse and audience: Organizational change as a multi-story process. *Journal of Management Studies*, 44(5), 669–686.

Carter, C., Clegg, S. R., and Kornberger, M. (2008). Strategy as practice? *Strategic Organization*, 6(1), 83–99.

Chia, R. and MacKay, B. (2007). Post-processual challenges for the emerging strategy-as-practice perspective: Discovering strategy in the logic of practice. *Human Relations*, 60(1), 217–242.

Clark, S. M., Gioia, D. A., Ketchen, D. J., and Thomas, J. B. (2010). Transitional identity as a facilitator of organizational identity change in a merger. *Administrative Science Quarterly*, 55, 397–438.

Cook, S. D. N. and Brown, J. S. (1999). Bridging epistemologies: The generative dance between organizational knowledge and organizational knowing. *Organization Science*, 10(4), 381–400.

Corley, K. G. (2004). Defined by our strategy or our culture? Hierarchical differences in perceptions of organizational identity and change. *Human Relations*, 57(9), 1145–1177.

Corley, K. G. and Gioia, D. A. (2004). Identity ambiguity and change in the wake of a corporate spin-off. *Administrative Science Quarterly*, 49(2), 173–208.

Corradi, G., Gherardi, S., and Verzelloni, L. (2010). Through the practice lens: Where is the bandwagon of practice studies heading? *Management Learning*, 41(3), 265–283.

Dyer, W. G. and Wilkins, A. L. (1991). Better stories, not better constructs, to generate better theory: A rejoinder to Eisenhardt. *Academy of Management Review*, 16(3), 613–619.

Eisenhardt, K. M. (1989a). Building theories from case study research. *Academy of Management Review*, 14(4), 532–550.

Eisenhardt, K. M. (1989b). Making fast strategic decisions in high velocity environments. *Academy of Management Journal*, 32(4), 543–576.

Eisenhardt, K. M. and Bourgeois, L. J. (1988). Politics of strategic decision making in high velocity environments: Toward a midrange theory. *Academy of Management Journal*, 31(4), 737–770.

Eisenhardt, K. M. and Graebner, M. E. (2007). Theory building from cases: Opportunities and challenges. *Academy of Management Journal*, 50(1), 25–32.

Ezzamel, M. and Willmott, H. (2008). Strategy as discourse in a global retailer: A supplement to rationalist and interpretive accounts. *Organization Studies*, 29, 191–217.

Feldman, M. S. (2000). Organizational routines as a source of continuous change. *Organization Science*, 11(6), 611–629.

Feldman, M. S. (2004). Resources in emerging structures and processes of change. *Organization Science*, 15(3), 295–309.

Feldman, M. S., and Orlikowski, W. (2011). Theorizing practice and practicing theory. *Organization Science*, 22: 1240–1253.

Galunic, D. C. (2001). Architectural innovation and modular corporate forms. *Academy of Management Journal*, 44(6), 1229–1249.

Galunic, D. C. and Eisenhardt, K. M. (1996). The evolution of intracorporate domains: Divisional charter losses in high-technology multidivisional corporations. *Organization Science*, 7(3), 255–282.

Giddens, A. (1984). *The Constitution of Society*. Berkeley, CA: University of California Press.

Gilbert, C. G. (2005). Unbundling the structure of inertia: Resources versus routine rigidity. *Academy of Management Journal*, 48(5), 741–763.

Gioia, D. A. (2004). A renaissance self: Prompting personal and professional revitalization. In: R. E. Stablein and P. J. Frost (eds), *Renewing Research Practice* (97–114). Stanford, CA: Stanford University Press.

Gioia, D. A. and Chittipeddi, K. (1991). Sensemaking and sensegiving in strategic change initiation. *Strategic Management Journal*, 12, 433–448.

Gioia, D. A., Price, K. N., Hamilton, A. L., and Thomas, J. B. (2010). Forging an identity: An insider-outsider study of processes involved in the formation of organizational identity. *Administrative Science Quarterly*, 55(1), 1–46.

Gioia, D. A. and Thomas, J. B. (1996). Identity, image and issue interpretation: Sense making during strategic change in academia. *Administrative Science Quarterly*, 41(3), 370–403.

Gioia, D. A., Thomas, J. B., Clark, S. M., and Chittipeddi, K. (1994). Symbolism and strategic change in academia: The dynamics of sensemaking and influence. *Organization Science*, 5(3), 363–383.

Gherardi, S. (2006). *Organizational Knowledge: The Texture of Workplace Learning*. Oxford: Blackwell Publications.

Glaser, B. G. and Strauss, A. L. (1967). *The Discovery of Grounded Theory*. Chicago: Aldine.

Golden-Biddle, K. and Locke, K. (1993). Appealing work: An investigation of how ethnographic texts convince. *Organization Science*, 4(4), 595–616.

Golden-Biddle, K. and Locke, K. (2006). *Composing Qualitative Research*. Thousand Oaks, CA: Sage Publications.

Graebner, M. E. (2004). Momentum and serendipity: How acquired leaders create value in the integration of technology firms. *Strategic Management Journal*, 25, 751–777.

Graebner, M. E. (2009). Caveat venditor: Trust asymmetries in acquisitions of entrepreneurial firms. *Academy of Management Journal*, 52(3), 435–472.

Graebner, M. E. and Eisenhardt, K. M. (2004). The seller's side of the story: Acquisition as courtship and governance as syndicate in entrepreneurial firms. *Administrative Science Quarterly*, 49, 366–403.

Grant, D., Keenoy, T., and Oswick, C. (1998). *Discourse and Organization*. London: Sage Publications.

Guba, E. and Lincoln, Y. S. (1994). Competing paradigms in qualitative research. In: N. K. Denzin and Y. S. Lincoln (eds), *Handbook of Qualitative Research* (105–117). Thousand Oaks, CA: Sage Publications.

Hallen, B. L. and Eisenhardt, K. M. (2009). Catalyzing strategies: How entrepreneurs accelerate inter-organizational relationship formation to secure professional investments. *Social Science Research Network*. Available at: http://ssrn.com/abstract¼1372328.

Heracleous, L. (2006). *Discourse, Interpretation, Organization*. Cambridge: Cambridge University Press.

Heracleous, L. and Barrett, M. (2001). Organizational change as discourse: Communicative actions and deep structures in the context of information technology implementation. *Academy of Management Journal*, 44, 755–778.

Howard-Grenville, J. A. (2007). Developing issue-selling effectiveness over time: Issue selling as resourcing. *Organization Science*, 16(6), 618–636.

Jarzabkowski, P. (2004). Strategy as practice: Recursiveness, adaptation, and practices-in-use. *Organization Studies*, 35(4), 529–560.

Jarzabkowski, P. (2005). *Strategy as Practice: An Activity-Based Approach*. London: Sage Publications.

Jarzabkowski, P. (2008). Shaping strategy as a structuration process. *Academy of Management Journal*, 51(4), 621–650.

Jarzabkowski, P., Balogun, J., and Seidl, D. (2007). Strategizing: The challenges of a practice perspective. *Human Relations*, 60(1), 5–27.

Johnson, G., Langley, A., Melin, L., and Whittington, R. (2007). *Strategy as Practice*. Cambridge: Cambridge University Press.

Johnson, G., Prashantham, S., Floyd, S. W., and Bourque, N. (2010). The ritualization of strategy workshops. *Organization Studies*, 31(12), 1589–1618.

Kaplan, S. (2011). Strategy and PowerPoint: An inquiry into the epistemic culture and machinery of strategy making. *Organization Science*, 22(2), 320–346.

Knights, D., and Morgan, G. (1991). Corporate strategy, organizations, and subjectivity: A critique. *Organization Studies*, 12, 251–273.

Langley, A. (1999). Strategies for theorizing from process data. *Academy of Management Review*, 24(4), 691–710.

Langley, A. (2007). Process thinking in strategic organization. *Strategic Organization*, 5(35), 271–282.

Langley, A. (2009). Studying processes in and around organizations. In: D. Buchanan and A. Bryman (eds), *Sage Handbook of Organizational Research Methods* (409–429). London: Sage Publications.

Latour, B. (2005). *Reassembling the Social*. Oxford: Oxford University Press.

Lee, T. W., Mitchell, T. R., and Sablynski, C. J. (1999). Qualitative research in organizational and vocational psychology, 1979–1999. *Journal of Vocational Behavior*, 55, 161–187.

Lincoln, Y. S. and Guba, E. (1985). *Naturalistic Enquiry*. Beverly Hills, CA: Sage Publications.

Liu, F. and Maitlis, S. (2010). Changing plans: Emotional dynamics in the construction of a strategic plan. Workshop on talk, text, tools in the practice of strategy, Montreal, August 5, 2010.

Luhmann, N. (1995). *Social Systems*. Stanford, CA: Stanford University Press.

Maguire, S. and Phillips, N. (2008). "Citibankers" at Citigroup: A study of the loss of institutional trust after a merger. *Journal of Management Studies*, 45(2), 372–401.

Maitlis, S. (2005). The social processes of organizational sensemaking. *Academy of Management Journal*, 48(1), 21–49.

Maitlis, S. and Lawrence, T. (2003). Orchestral manoeuvres in the dark: Understanding failures in organizational strategizing. *Journal of Management Studies*, 40(1), 109–140.

Mantere, S. and Vaara, E. (2008). On the problem of participation in strategy: A critical discursive perspective. *Organization Science*, 19, 341–358.

Martin, J. A. and Eisenhardt, K. M. (2010). Rewiring: Cross-business-unit collaborations in multi-business organizations. *Academy of Management Journal*, 53(2), 265–301.

Miettinen, R., Samra-Fredericks, D., and Yanow, D. (2009). Re-turn to practice: An introductory essay. *Organization Studies*, 30(12), 1309–1327.

Miles, M. B. and Huberman, A. M. (1994). *Qualitative Data Analysis*. Thousand Oaks, CA: Sage Publications.

Mohr, L. B. (1982). *Explaining Organizational Behavior: The Limits and Possibilities of Theory and Research*. San Francisco, CA: Jossey-Bass.

Molloy, E. and Whittington, R. (2005). Practices of organising inside and outside the processes of change. *Advances in Strategic Management*, 22, 497–521.

Nag, R., Corley, K. G., and Gioia, D. A. (2007). The intersection of organizational identity, knowledge and practice: Attempting strategic change by knowledge grafting. *Academy of Management Journal*, 50(4), 821–847.

Ozcan, P. and Eisenhardt, K. M. (2009). Origin of alliance portfolios: Entrepreneurs, network strategies and performance. *Academy of Management Journal*, 52(2), 246–279.

Parker, I. (1992). *Discourse Dynamics: Critical Analysis for Social and Individual Psychology*. London: Routledge.

Pettigrew, A. M. (1990). Longitudinal field research on change: Theory and practice. *Organization Science*, 1(3), 267–292.

Phillips, N. and Hardy, C. (2002). *Discourse Analysis: Investigating Processes of Social Construction*. Thousand Oaks, CA: Sage Publications.

Phillips, N., Sewell, G., and Jaynes, S. (2008). Applying critical discourse analysis in strategic management research. *Organizational Research Methods*, 11(4), 770–789.

Pratt, M. G. (2009). For the lack of a boilerplate: Tips on writing up (and reviewing) qualitative research. *Academy of Management Journal*, 52(5), 856–862.

Rasche, A., and Chia, R. (2009). Researching strategy practices: A genealogical social theory perspective. *Organization Studies*, 30(7), 713–734.

Ravenswood, K. (2011). Eisenhardt's impact on theory in case study research. *Journal of Business Research*, 64(7), 680–686.

Reckwitz, A. (2002). Toward a theory of social practices: A development in cultural theorizing. *European Journal of Social Theory*, 5(2), 243–263.

Rerup, C. and Feldman, M. (2011). Routines as a source of change in organizational schema: The role of trial-and-error learning. *Academy of Management Journal*, 54(3), forthcoming.

Rindova, V., Dalpiaz, E., and Ravasi, R. (2011). A cultural quest: A study of organizational use of new cultural resources in strategy formation. *Organization Science*, 22(2), 413–431.

Rouleau, L. (2005). Micro-practices of strategic sensemaking and sensegiving: How middle managers interpret and sell change every day. *Journal of Management Studies*, 42(7), 1413–1441.

Samra-Fredericks, D. (2003). Strategizing as lived experience and strategists' everyday efforts to shape strategic direction. *Journal of Management Studies*, 40(1), 141–174.

Santos, F. M. and Eisenhardt, K. M. (2009). Constructing markets and shaping boundaries: Entrepreneurial power in nascent fields. *Academy of Management Journal*, 52(4), 643–671.

Schatzki, T. R., Knorr Cetina, K., and Von Savigny, E. (2001). *The Practice Turn in Social Theory*. London: Routledge.

Strauss, A. and Corbin, J. (1990). *Basics of Qualitative Research*. Newbury Park, CA: Sage Publications.

Suddaby, R. (2006). What grounded theory is not. *Academy of Management Journal*, 49(4), 633–642.

Suddaby, R. and Greenwood, R. (2005). Rhetorical strategies of legitimacy. *Administrative Science Quarterly*, 50, 35–67.

Vaara, E. (2010). Taking the linguistic turn seriously: Strategy as a multifaceted and interdiscursive phenomenon. *Advances in Strategic Management*, 27, 29–50.

Vaara, E., Kleymann, B., and Seristo, H. (2004). Strategies as discursive constructions: The case of airline alliances. Journal of Management Studies, 41(1), 1–35.

Vaara, E. and Monin, P. (2010). A recursive perspective on discursive legitimation and organizational action in mergers and acquisitions. *Organization Science*, 21(1), 3–22.

Vaara, E. and Tienari, J. (2004). Critical discourse analysis as a methodology for international business studies. In: R. Piekkari (ed.), *Handbook of Qualitative Research Methods for International Business* (342–362). Cheltenham: Edward Elgar.

Van de Ven, A. H. (1992). Suggestions for studying strategy process: A research note. *Strategic Management Journal*, 13 (Summer special issue), 169–188.

Whittington, R. (2006). Completing the practice turn in strategy research. *Organization Studies*, 28, 613–634.

Whittington, R. (2007). Strategy practice and strategy process: Family differences and the sociological eye. *Organization Studies*, 28(10), 1575–1586.

Yin, R. K. (2009 [1984]). *Case Study Research*. Thousand Oaks, CA: Sage Publications.

Zott, C., and Huy, Q. N. (2007). How entrepreneurs use symbolic management to acquire resources. *Administrative Science Quarterly*, 52, 70–105.

PART II

Analyzing texts and talks in strategic management

7

IN SEARCH OF STRATEGY MEANINGS

Semiotics and its applications

Maria Cristina Cinici

Semiotics is in principle the discipline studying everything which can be used in order to lie. If something cannot be used to tell a lie, conversely it cannot be used to tell the truth: it cannot in fact be used "to tell" at all.

(Eco, 1976)

The word "good" has many meanings. For example, if a man were to shoot his grandmother at a range of five hundred yards, I should call him a good shot, but not necessarily a good man.

(Chesterton, 1912)

Introduction

"Oh, it's just semantics," ordinary folks are inclined to say when there are disputes over words' meanings, such as whether some word is connectable to a given concept or whether using a particular word might be advisable to connotate a given circumstance. The implicit assumption behind such dismissive response is that which forms convey which meanings is essentially arbitrary and thus not matter to worry about.

Fortunately, this was not the reaction of those academics and practitioners that have taken into account the cognitive, social, and historical dimensions of linguistically mediated communication in Strategic Management (hereinafter SM). Their explicit assumption has been rooted in the consideration that the exponential growth of SM has seriously exposed the field to the risk of incorporating ambiguous constructs that have undermined its collective identity and distinctiveness (Nag *et al.*, 2007). As a result, on the one side, the editors of the most important journals have called for meaningful conversations based on clear constructs (Suddaby, 2010). On the other side, on the ground of a consensus definition of SM as discipline (Nag *et al.*, 2007), researchers have questioned themselves as regards the meanings and connotations of specific constructs. In order to do that, scholars employed an array of research methods ranging from discourse analysis to reveal how actors shape the meaning of whole market and industries (Khaire and Wadhwani, 2010), to co-word analysis and phenomenography to examine the evolution of the strategy concept (Ronda-Pupo and Guerras-Martins, 2012; Mainardes and Raposo, 2014), survey analysis to investigate cultural diversity in dealing with threats and opportunities (Barr and Glynn, 2004), and thematic analysis to test the reification of absorptive capacity (Lane *et al.*, 2006) and dynamic capabilities (Giudici and Reinmoller, 2012) – just to mention a few.

In line with these received calls and endeavors, I introduce *structural semiotics* as specific research method to thoroughly analyze texts, understand the unspoken rules or codes that underpin the meanings words both generate and covey, and eventually determine how scholars make sense of SM constructs. Broadly speaking, semiotics is the study of how humans create meaning and how meaning is understood by the people to whom meaning is being communicated (Eco, 1976). Its origins lie in the academic study of how signs and symbols (visual and linguistic) create meaning. I argue that in the ecosocial system in which SM researchers typically are involved (made of social processes and figurative practices), semiotics can contribute to express and make explicit constructs in a way that is clear, precise, and non-ambiguous, so that they can be shared. Researchers, but also participants of their ecosocial system, should have a common understanding. In other words, they should speak the same language, but also reach the same meaning of the SM concepts. Constructs made meaningful and explicit can be (a) criticized, (b) related to other constructs, (c) operationally defined, and (d) tested (i.e. they are measurable). Accordingly, the more we understand about how words work ad constructs acquire meanings, the more SM researchers will engage in a fruitful interaction with their communities.

In spite of the above potential benefits its use might bring to SM research and its wide use in related discipline such as in information systems (Liebeau and Backhouse, 1990; Liu, 2000) and marketing (Floch, 2001; Mick *et al.*, 2004), semiotics has been overlooked by strategy scholars. As a matter of fact, semiotics has found some space in organizational behavior research where Barley (1983) employed it to demonstrate that identical codes structure a funeral director's understanding of his various tasks. By means of semiotics Fiol examined letters to shareholders to analyze corporate language use (1989) and the meaning of the concept of "power" (1991) while Brannen formalized the process through which Walt Disney's assets take on new meanings in different cultural contexts. More recently, Cinici and Dunbar (2012) proposed semiotics as a tool to detect how firms frame their competitive strategy in annual reports.

Whereas semiotics has been applied in few instances to management studies, there are several critical ways in which it can add to SM research. Its ability to provide into our understanding essential insights on how meanings are generated and conveyed makes this research method proper for understanding any form of textual communication in SM (e.g., among scholars, between academia and practitioners, and between firms and shareholders). For the advancement of SM theory uncovering the meaning of constructs is essential to both senior and young research scholars striving not only for top-tier publications so as to find their place in the academic sun, but also for making their researches even more appealing to firms and practitioners.

The chapter is structured as follows. The second section portrays the historical evolution of semiotics and highlights its main branches. The third section clarifies the reasons why semiotics is different from other textual analysis. The fourth section focuses on semiotic analysis of texts and illustrate how it can be conducted by the means of a semiotic square. The fifth section gives a practical example of semiotic analysis by comparing the meaning of the word "strategy" in the written texts of two of the founders of SM field, namely Alfred Chandler and Kenneth Andrews. The sixth section accounts for criticisms and strengths of the semiotic analysis adoption in SM. An appendix with the glossary of the key semiotic terms closes the chapter.

What is semiotics really? An overview of its definition(s), history and branches

Definition of semiotics

The etymology of *semiotics* is related to the Greek words "sema" (σημα: signal), "semeion" (σημειον: sign), and "semeiotikos" (σημειοτικοσ: interpreter of sign).[1] Since the sign is in general something that represents something else, as medieval philosophers said "*aliquid stat pro aliquot*," semiotic could be seen as the science that studies the phenomena of signification and communication. The signification is the relation that determines the linkage between something that is present and something that isn't, which determines a process of communication. Semiotics studies both linguistics and non-linguistics sign systems. It considers all signs as polysemic, which means that every sign generates a multiple significations within the mind of whom has to analyze it, creating an association among different things.

There have been so many definitions of semiotics that currently it is a field of study involving many different theoretical stances and methodological tools (see Table 7.1). One of the broadest definitions is that of Umberto Eco, who states that "semiotics is concerned with everything that can be taken as a sign" (Eco, 1976: 7). Semiotics involves the study not only of what we refer to as "signs" in every text (i.e. words), but of anything which "stands for" something else. In a semiotic sense, signs take not only the form of words, but also of images, sounds, gestures and objects. Whilst for the linguist Saussure, "semiology" was "a science which studies the role of signs as part of social life," for the philosopher Charles S. Peirce "semiotic" was the "formal doctrine of signs" which was closely related to logic (Peirce, 1931: 58). For him, "a sign is something which stands to somebody for something in some respect or capacity" (Peirce, 1931: 58).

Contemporary semioticians study signs not in isolation but as part of semiotic

TABLE 7.1 Definitions of semiotics

Author	Definition
Saussure (1916)	Semiology is a science which studies the role of signs as part of social life.
Peirce (1934)	Semiotic is the "formal doctrine of signs" which is closely related to Logic. A sign is something which stands to somebody for something in some respect or capacity.
Morris (1938)	Semiotics embraces semantics, along with the other traditional branches of linguistics. *Semantics*: the relationship of signs to what they stand for; *syntactics* (or syntax): the formal or structural relations between signs; *pragmatics*: the relation of signs to interpreters.
Barthes (1964)	Semiology aims to take in any system of signs, whatever their substance and limits; images, gestures, musical sounds, objects, and the complex associations of all of these, which form the content of ritual, convention or public entertainment: these constitute, if not languages, at least systems of signification.
Eco (1976)	Semiotics is concerned with everything that can be taken as a sign.
Sturrock (1986)	Whereas semantics focuses on what words mean, semiotics is concerned with how signs mean.

sign systems (such as a medium or genre). In this vein, John Sturrock argues that whereas semantics focuses on what words mean, semiotics is concerned with how signs mean (Sturrock 1986: 22). For Charles Morris (deriving this threefold classification from Peirce), semiotics can be divided into (Morris 1938: 6–7):

- *semantics*: the relationship of signs to what they stand for;
- *syntactics* (or syntax): the formal or structural relations between signs;
- *pragmatics*: the relation of signs to interpreters.

History and branches of semiotics

The history of semiotics cannot be reduced to research which has been placed under the heading of semiotics.[2] There is much older tradition of implicitly semiotic studies concerned with the nature of signs and communication.[3] A pioneering exploration of the role of signs in the real world was carried out by Plato and Aristotle. While in Plato's view the study of words reveals the true nature of things since the realm of ideas is independent of its representation in the form of words, for Aristotle the difference in the structure of sign systems is only a matter of the expression-plane, not of the content-plane as a name is a spoken sound significant by convention when it becomes a symbol.

Actually in its oldest usage, semiotics referred to a branch of medicine.[4] In English, the term was first used by the British writer and scholar Henry Stubbes in 1670 to denote the branch of medicine concerning the study of signs or symptoms. Twenty years later, in 1690, John Locke used the term in his work *An Essay Concerning Human Understanding* and treated semiotics together with physics and ethics as one of the three main branches of human knowledge.

Semiotics only began to crystallize as a full-blown recognized field of investigation in the course of twentieth century as branch of philosophy and Chander S. Peirce started to be conventionally accepted as one of its founders. According to Peirce, signs consist of three interrelated parts (triad relation model): (a) the *representamen*, which is the form which the sign takes, for example, a written word; (b) an *interpretant*, which is the understanding that we have of the sign; and (c) an *object*, which is something beyond the sign, for example, the object to which the written word attaches. The process, deriving from the interaction between representamen (sign proper), interpretant (interpretation or response with the observer/communicator), and object (to which the sign refers), is called *infinite semiosis*. The elements are dependent from each other and can be understood only if considered in relation among them.

Signs might be of three orders. The *iconic sign* is the one that looks like its object, it reminds of its object, it communicates by resemblance. It is the case of visual images, such as maps, photographs, diagrams, and so on. The *indexical sign* is the one that is in inherent relationship with its object. The sign and the object are directly linked because of casualty, existentiality or contiguity. They are in a logical connection. This is the case of smoke, thunder, footprints, flavors. The *symbolic sign* is not connected or resembled to its object. Signs and objects are in an arbitrary relation, purely based on conventions, rules or agreement among users, such as word or numbers. So the only way to understand these kinds of signs is learning the conventions and rules attached to them.

Contemporaneously with Peirce, and apparently independently both of him and of Locke, the Swiss linguist Ferdinand de Saussure was also suggesting that language is a system of codes or a social phenomenon. In particular, he distinguished between *langue* (language) and *parole* (speech). Langue refers to the system of rules and conventions that is independent of, and pre-exists, individual users; parole refers to its use in particular instances. In order to isolate linguistic structures from their historical evolution, Saussure also introduced the dichotomy of *synchrony* and *diachrony*. Synchronic analysis studies a sign system at a given point of time, irrespective of its history. Diachronic analysis studies the evolution of a sign system in its historical development.

Despite these fruitful insights, semiotics became a major approach to cultural studies only in the late 1960s, partly as a result of the work of Claude Levi-Strauss in anthropology, Roland Barthes in literary criticism, and Algirdas Greimas in linguistics. Their textual analysis is synchronic and aims at delineating the codes and rules which underlie the production of texts by identifying invariants constituents units. The analysis of specific texts seeks to break down larger, more abstract units into "minimal significant units," then grouping these units by membership of common paradigms (or themes) and identifies the relationships that links the units.

However, contemporary social semiotics has moved beyond the structuralist concern with the internal relations of parts within a self-contained system, seeking to explore the use of signs in specific social situations. In this vein, Foucault (1970) argued that there were often distinct breaks in meaning between different historical periods, as though they were completely different systems of ordering differences in language without any logical connection. He particularly analyzed the ways in which changes in political power structures changed the way language, thought, and perception are ordered. Derrida (1978) maintained that meaning is always open to interpretations. One never arrives at a fixed meaning in the chain of differences since meaning is always deferred – it is never present in the sign but is always constituted of other signs. Umberto Eco (1976) started from the theories of Saussure and Peirce to find a common universal theory of semiotics. He argued that messages are not strictly linked to a locked and predetermined single meaning as readers contribute to construct meanings. Table 7.2 summarizes the main branches and figures of the semiotic history.

The semiotic analysis of texts: Why is it different from other textual analyses?

Even if semiotics it is far from just a mode of textual analysis, it is employed in this chapter as a tool to understand, interpret, and report texts in the field of SM. Actually, a multiplicity of qualitative research approaches share with semiotics the interest towards textual examination and explication. Given this circumstance, I retain that to clarify the differences between semiotics and other qualitative textual analysis is inevitable to avoid confusion.

I shall deal in particular with (a) *rhetorical analyses*, (b) *narrative* and *discourse analyses*, and (c) *critical discourse analyses*. As emphasized in the subsections reported below, all these analytic approaches are diverse from semiotics since only this research method focuses on the specific relationship between language and meanings.

Rhetorical analysis

Though held in low esteem by many writers as mere linguistic adornment or appearance, rhetoric was reformulated by the Greek philosopher Aristotle as the study of the available means of persuasion in any given situation. Aristotle proposed that the purpose of argumentation was not to discover verifiable absolute truths but rather to influence belief – what people thought was true. Argumentation therefore was based on probability. It meant demonstrating to an audience that the speaker's argument was more likely than other arguments and leaving the audience with the highest level of certainty that the argument was valid. He also identified ethos, pathos, and logos as keys to successful persuasion. Logos addresses the use of fact and logic whereas pathos addresses the use of emotion and ethos addresses the nature or character of the speaker. Unlike semiotics, rhetorical analysis means

TABLE 7.2 The history of semiotics: branches and major figures

Branches	Figures
Ancient Greece	Hippocrates (460–377 BC) establishes semiotics as a branch of medicine Plato (427–347 BC) addressed the difference between natural and conventional signs Aristotle (384–322 BC) focused on conventional signs and established a 3-part model of semiotics
Early modern	Henry Stubbes (1670) as defining the branch of medical science relating to the interpretation of signs/symptoms John Locke (1690) proposes importing semiotics into philosophy as a tool for allowing philosophers to understand the relationship between representation and knowledge
Structural linguistics	Charles Sanders Peirce (1890s), American pragmatist philosopher, begins developing a formal theory of semiotics Ferdinand de Saussure (1906), Swiss linguist, begins lecturing on his theories of semiology
Structuralism	Claude Lévi-Strauss (1950s), Belgian-French anthropologist, applies semiotics to cultural myths and social practices Roland Barthes (1950s), French literary critic, applies semiotics to all forms of social behavior Algirdas Greimas (1960s), French-Lithuanian literary scientist, applies semiotics to text analysis
Poststructuralism	Michel Foucault (1960s), French philosopher, explores the historical importance of semiotic systems Jacques Derrida (1960s), French-Algerian philosopher, deconstructs Saussurean linguistics definition examples Umberto Eco (1970s), Italian philosopher, started from the theories of Saussure and Peirce to find a common universal theory of semiotics

examining communication content to identify and assess its persuasive strategies (Selzer, 2004). While the focus at the time was on how an advocate or a politician might successfully argue for a cause, in SM field rhetorical analyses can be used to assess the persuasiveness of SM texts or firm strategies.

Roy Suddaby and Royston Greenwood (2005) described the role of rhetoric in legitimating profound institutional change. They found that such rhetorical strategies contain two elements. First were institutional vocabularies, or the use of identifying words and referential texts to expose contradictory institutional logics embedded in historical understandings of professionalism, one based on a trustee model and the other based on a model of expertise. A second element of rhetorical strategies was theorizations of change by which actors contest a proposed innovation against broad templates or scenarios of change. Gwendolyn Lee and Srikanth Parachuri (2008) analyzed how firms use media-associative rhetoric in their decisions to enter emergent and uncertain product-markets. Their panel study showed that firms enter such markets faster when the associative rhetoric has higher (versus lower) volume, positive (versus negative) tenor, firms (versus journalists/analysts) as the source of information, and generalizations (versus specific cases) as the focus.

Narrative analysis

Narrative analysis is the analysis of the formal properties of stories that people tell and the social role that stories play (Riessman, 1993). It generally attempts to identify a plot, the setting, characters, and the order of events in people's accounts of their lives. Narrative analysis pays specific attention to how stories play out over time and how events are sequenced from beginning to end (Labov and Waletzky, 1997). Researchers may be interested in how narratives are used to mark out the identities of a group and differentiate the group from others. They may focus on the formal properties of stories – that is, the plot, setting, characters, and order of events (Cortazzi, 2014). They may analyze how stories are reproduced, change over time, or change as a result of the settings in which they are told or are used politically to influence attitudes and behaviors. Researchers may also be interested in identifying key events or "triggers" that flag a vital learning experience or the point at which a firm changed its vision or competitive strategy. Pentland (1999) used concepts from narrative theory to create a framework to analyze structural features in narrative data. He argued that narrative can help researchers to build better process theory and better explanation in general. The organizational scholar David Barry and Michael Helmes (1997) use narrative theory to discuss the challenges strategists face in making strategic discourse both credible and novel and consider how strategic narratives may change within the "virtual" organization of the future. More recently, Garud, Dunbar and Bartel (2011) argued that by developing narratives, organizational actors create situated understandings of unusual experiences, negotiate consensual meanings, and engage in coordinated actions.

Discourse analysis

Discourse analysis focuses on how particular labels or concepts are developed and made powerful by the use of language (Brown, 1983). It has several roots – sociology of knowledge, cultural analysis, rhetoric, the psychology of human interaction, and conversation analysis. Predictably then, there are a variety of approaches to discourse analysis, but most scholars would agree that they share a common interest in language as a social practice more than in the language itself. They are interested in the frameworks within which ideas are formulated and the configurations of ideas and concepts that give meaning to physical and social realities (Gee, 2014).

Discourse analysis is best understood as a field of research or an interest area rather than a specific method. It has no specific, agreed procedure, but typically discourse analysis will involve starting with a research question, and selecting samples of news, videos, interview transcripts, social media, and such. Then comes coding, which unlike content analysis is qualitative, and analysis. Coding and analysis are basically a search for patterns and variations in content. They vary according to the researcher's perspective on the research and may change as the research and the analyst's thinking progress. Most analyses, though, are based on what the discourse appears to be doing rather than on categories of language or frequencies of occurrence, as with content analysis. In SM Sotirios Paroutis and Loizos Heracleous (2013) built on discourse analysis to investigate how the concept of strategy has been employed by practitioner. They also showed that the emphasis on strategy discourses differs over different periods in the institutional-ization process, and discussed the insights that can be gained from such deeper understanding of the role of language in this process.

Critical analysis

Critical discourse analysis aims to explore the relationships between language and power (Fairclough, 2013). The basic aim of critical discourse analysis, then, is to uncover the ideological assumptions behind public discourse and to link communication content with underlying power structures. The interest of the critical analysis is in injustice and inequality (Fairclough, 1992). In examining discourse in this light, the researcher may look for taken-for-granted assumptions, the use of evidence, style, the use of rhetoric, the type of medium used, the ways in which text and graphics interact, and omissions – what is not said as much as what is. Because the discourse of the powerful may be countered by minority discourse, the critical discourse analyst may study both in order to see how one influences the other. Unlike the content analyst who takes a primary interest in the frequency with which words occur, the critical analyst will take an interest in the words and phrases thought to be significant in promoting a viewpoint, not in their frequency. The potential benefits of the use of the critical discourse analysis to SM has been discussed by Nelson Phillips and his colleagues (Phillips *et al.*, 2008). Using the example of a case study of strategic change in a large banking and financial services institution, they explored the practical implications of applying critical discourse analysis in strategic management research.

Semiotic square and textual analysis

The basic assumption of structural semiotics is that language is an arbitrary, cultural construct because there is no necessary or natural relationship between the words of a given language and the concepts that they represent (Greimas, 1976). For example, there is nothing in the word "tree" that connects it to the concept of a tree. Similarly, the sounds or written lines that make up the word "cat" have only a cultural, conventional, and traditional connection to the actual cat that exists in the world. As a result, words have meaning only as parts of a system, with each word deriving its meaning solely from its difference from the other words in the system.

In this context, human beings own an innate ability to assign meanings to word by negation (to be and not to be) through differences and oppositions. The premise that language is a system of differences and oppositions is reflected in the structural presuppositions of the semiotic square (Figure 7.1).

The semiotic square, as concisely laid out by Greimas in *Du Sens I* (1970: 135–156), constitutes the elementary unit of signification in the Greimasian structuralist system and an elaboration of the simple semantic axis reuniting two contrary semes or semantic poles, as initially laid out in *Sémantique Structurale* (Greimas, 1966). The concepts that make up the semantic micro-universe of a semiotic square consist in object-terms (such as life and death), that is elementary semes that exist by virtue of their partaking of a relational structure.

The object-terms are relational entities and assume signification only by entering in various modes of relatedness with other object-terms. This very fundamental principle of the Greimasian semiotic approach sets it apart from the majority of semiotic theories that assume the sign as their point of departure. Greimas is not primarily concerned with the nature of elementary units of signification, but with the structuralist conditions of the possibility of signification.

In order to understand how the semiotic square functions as an elementary structure of signification or as a topographical approach to the logical organization of a semantic universe, the fundamental concepts of contrariety, contradiction, implication, schema and deixis must first be defined.

Contrariety, which forms the fundamental building block of the semantic axis and the vantage point for the construction of a semiotic square (Greimas, 1970), is the relation of mutual presupposition between the two terms of a semantic axis, where both terms are either present or absent. Two terms are contrary if (if and

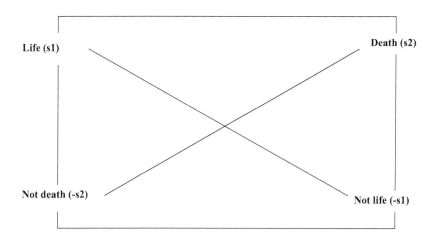

FIGURE 7.1 The structural presuppositions of the semiotic square

only if) the contradictory of each term implies the contrary of the other, for example death vs. life. In essence, contrariety constitutes a deflected or fuzzier form of contradiction. For example, the terms /beauty/ and /ugliness/ as the two contrary poles of the semantic axis «looks» are not exact contradictories, as there are multiple semantic layers in between, such as quasi-beautiful and quasi-ugly, as against the strict contradictory relationship between ugly vs non-ugly. However, if non-ugly is present as the contradictory of ugly then by implication beautiful as the contrary of ugly is also present. This qualifying feature of contrariety, as multiple semantic layers in between of the two contrary poles echoes the Aristotelian law of the excluded middle, that nothing can exist between two contradictories, but something may exist between contraries.

Contradiction denotes the relationship between terms of a binary logical category of assertion/negation. The presence of one term in this relationship presupposes the absence of the other. Contradiction defines the two schemas (S1-S1, S2-S2) of the semiotic square. For example, life and non-life are contradictory terms, where the presence of the one presupposes the absence of the other.

Implication consists in the assertive conditioning of the presupposing term, resulting in the appearance of the presupposed term. The relationship of presupposition is thus envisaged as logically anterior to implication.

Deixis constitutes one of the fundamental dimensions of the semiotic square, its inner logic that reunites through implication one of the terms of the axes of contrariety with the contradictory of the other contrary term. There are two types of deixis, positive and negative, which are not qualified as such axiologically prior to their placement on the square and the interpretation of the relationship between the terms ensuing thereupon. For example, life as the contrary of death is in a relationship of deixis with non-death as the contradictory term of its contrary. Deixis denotes an act of pointing and in terms of enunciation a spatiotemporal positioning of the object pointed to.

Schema is the dimension of the semiotic square reuniting two contradictory terms. A sharper distinction is drawn between a positive schema, where the first term belongs to the positive deixis and a negative schema, where the first term belongs to the negative deixis.

Thus, the semiotic square may be summed up as six systemic dimensions or three systemic pairs:

1. The contrary terms or semes s1 and s2 falling under the semic category S that organizes them into a semantic micro-universe and the contrary terms –s1 and –s2 under the inverse semantic micro-universe –S. This is the neutral axis, whose terms are organized in a neither/nor relationship.
2. The relationships of deixis denoted by the intra-square diagonal lines uniting by implication s1 with s2 and s2 with s1.
3. The schematic relationships denoted by the vertical lines reuniting in categorical terms the contradictories s1 with –s1 and s2 with –s2.

Greimas illustrates how all sorts of phenomena are organized by the above depicted semiotic logic. A good non-literary example is the logic of traffic lights in Europe. In Europe, the yellow light has two functions: when a yellow light follows green, you are expected to slow down and prepare to stop (as in the United States and Canada); when a yellow light follows a red light, you are warned to get ready to move forward. As Greimas explains, the green light (s_1) is, in this example, in a contrary relation to the red light (s_2). The green light represents "prescription" or a "positive injunction" (cross!); the red light represents an "interdiction" or a "negative injunction" (don"t cross!). In the European system of lights, we are also given both possible contradictory pairs ($-s_1$ and $-s_2$): when the yellow light follows green, the signal is a nonprescription (get ready to stop!); when the yellow light follows red, the signal is a noninterdiction (get ready to go!). If the yellow light stands alone without changing, it assumes the neutral position: both a nonprescription and a noninterdiction (get ready to stop if you see someone crossing but be ready to go if you see no one!). Greimas' point is that we are all constrained by the finite series of possibilities opened up by such semiotic oppositions:"An author, a producer of any semiotic object, operates within an epistemy, which is the result of his individuality and the society in which he is inscribed. Within this society it is possible for him to make a limited number of choices, which have as an initial result the investment of organized contents, that is, contents endowed with valencies (possibilities of relations)" (1976: 61).

Comparing the meanings of "strategy" according to Kenneth R. Andrews and Alfred D. Chandler

In this section I shall provide a practical illustration of how to use the semiotic framework introduced by Greimas (1966) and portrayed in the above sections. I shall focus on the *strategy concept*, which is central in our discipline even if the lack of a consensus definition (Hambrick and Fredrickson, 2001; Markides, 2004). In doing that, I shall build on the findings achieved by recent works on the evolution of SM and strategy concept (Furrer *et al.*, 2008; Nag *et al.*, 2007; Ronda-Pupo, Guerras-Martins, 2010 and 2012), and focus on the strategy as conceived by two of its founders, namely, Alfred D. Chandler and Kenneth R. Andrews. Such analysis encompasses two major assumption: (1) it defines strategy in terms of how authors themselves construct the meaning of strategy; (2) it defines strategy in terms of oppositions.

Actually, the meaning that Andrews and Chandler assigned to strategy is largely an expression of the academic knowledge of their time. Thus, one would expect Andrews' and Chandler's personal expressions of strategy to reflect the different context of their times. This study used academic books, in order to illustrate patterns of meaning, as these leaders themselves defined it. The search was for underlying regularities in the way these scholars constructed the meaning of firm strategy in relation to their environment.

The semiotic square of the strategy concept

In order to construct the semiotic square of the strategy concept, we need to proceed as follows:

1. Set up any opposition of contraries: in this phase, it is necessary to bank on received knowledge on the matter.
2. Project the sub-contraries.
3. Create the relationships of contrariety, deixis and schemata between concepts.
4. Examine texts for all ten semantic possibilities (the four terms and six combinations).

For each of the ten classes, it is necessary to assign the elements that manifest these possibilities. A single sentence – even an elaborate one like the SM papers – will not necessarily use all ten of the possible classes. The most frequent ones are the two contrary terms ("one or the other"), the complex term ("both"), and the neutral term ("neither one").

Different authors who have provided definitions on the concept of strategy have tended to give selective attention to the wide variety of issues relevant to strategy definition. Using implicit and explicit definitions from a set of scholars, Nag *et al.* (2007) identify seven key components of the concept of strategic management: performance, firms, strategic initiatives, environment, internal organization, managers/owners and resources. Although they employed a different approach based on co-word analysis, Ronda-Pupo and Guerras-Martins (2012) have identified similar main dimensions of the strategy concept in 91 definitions of strategy formulated between 1962 and 2008: firm, environment, actions, and resources. They have also highlighted that SM scholars' focus has shifted over time from achieving the firms' goals to improving its performance.

Previous research has also implicitly considered the main relationship of contrariety that governs strategy. More in detail, for Hoskisson *et al.* (1999) strategic management, which is mostly mirrored in the strategy concept, swings like a pendulum as it looks for the factor of success either inside the firm or in the environment. For these authors, the pendulum started in the 1960s when the focus was on analyzing internal strengths and weaknesses and the aim, therefore, was to look inside successful firms for those factors that underlay and had driven their performance.

We integrate all the findings of the previous studies in a semiotic square of the strategy concept (see Figure 7.2). The square depicts the components of strategy described above. Together, they comprise a system of meaning that defines strategy as multidimensional and context-dependent. The figure combines the interior and external aspect of strategy concept. Accordingly, the main relationship that governs the meaning of the strategy concept is determined by the tension between firm and environment. Firm, the first term of the square, implies resources, plans, actions, goals, managers/owners, and internal structure, whereas environment

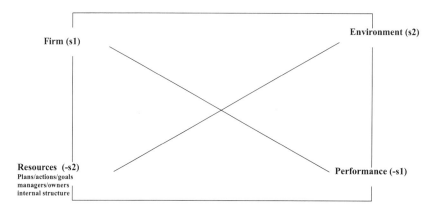

FIGURE 7.2   The semiotic square of the strategy concept

implies performance. The figure also suggests that at a lower level there is a second relationship of contrariety that governs the strategy meaning, which is between the interior aspects of firms and its performance.

Putting the semiotic square of the strategy concept in a diachronic perspective, it is possible to argue as follows. According to Ronda-Pupo and Guerras Martins (2014), during the 1960s and 1970s, strategy was seen as the way to link a firm to its environment in which both internal and external aspects were important. This was mirrored in the SWOT analysis that investigated both the interior of firms (strengths and weakness) and their exterior (opportunities and threats), or in the strategic matrices (BCG or McKinsey) which merged both approaches in a single tool.

Between the end of the 1970s and end of the 1980s, the search for the keys to success gravitated toward the external environment with the Porter's research on industry structure (Porter, 1980). The economics of organizations, through the contributions made by agency theory (Jensen and Meckling, 1976) and transactions cost theory (Williamson, 1975, 1985), shifted the focus of the strategy concept toward more of a middle position of the contrariety axes that addressed both the internal and external aspects in the search for success. Finally, the appearance and rise of the resource-based view (RBV), stimulated by the works of Wernerfelt (1984) and Barney (1991), once again moved the concept into the interior of firms.

The texts

In order to uncover the meanings of the strategy concept according to Alfred Chandler and Kenneth Andrews, I analyzed their most famous texts, i.e. *Strategy and*

Structure (Chandler, 1962) and *The Concept of Corporate Strategy* (Andrews, 1971). In his book, Chandler substantiated his structure follows strategy thesis based on four case studies of American conglomerates that dominated their industry from the 1920s onward. Chandler described how the chemical company Du Pont, the automobile manufacturer General Motors, the energy company Standard Oil of New Jersey, and the retailer Sears Roebuck managed a growth and diversification strategy by adopting the revolutionary multi-division form. The M-Form is a corporate federation of semi-independent product or geographic groups plus a headquarters that oversees the corporate strategy and coordinates interdependencies.

The second book I analyzed is the highly influential textbook *Business Policy: Text and Cases*, which was published in 1965, acknowledging Andrews as the author of the text portion; the text portion was published separately under Andrews' name in 1971. The innovative contribution of Andrews with his colleagues was to develop the concept of strategy as the organizing principle of the business policy course held at Stanford. Patterns of the meaning of strategy as reflected throughout the texts were coded according to the scheme reported below.

The coding scheme

In this semiotic analysis, words are used to understand meanings. Clusters of words representing recurring themes are the primary unit of analysis. All clusters of words referring to firm, environment, performance, and resources and other internal variables were extracted from the texts, regardless of their positions in the narratives.

The references were classified along two continua corresponding to the tensions depicted in the semiotic square of the strategy concept. The first continuum depicts the external dimension of firm as the positive value. Points along the continuum indicate the extent to which strategy is conceived at the environmental level. The second continuum depicts the internal dimension of strategy. Points along the continuum indicate the extent to which strategy is linked to performance.

Analysis and results

I analyzed 90 sentences in Chandler's book and 75 sentences in Andrews' book.

Strategy for Chandler

Of the 90 Chandler sentences, 23 sentences reflect the tension between firm and environment, while the remaining 67 sentences reflect the tension between interior firm assets and performance. Particularly, Chandler (1962: 13) defined strategy as the identification of long-term goals and objectives, and included the action and resources required to achieve them:

> Strategy is the determination of the basic long-term goals of an enterprise, and the adoption of courses of actions and the allocation of resources necessary to carry out these goals.
> Strategic growth resulted from an awareness of the opportunities and needs to employ existing or expanding resources more profitably.
>
> *(Chandler, 1962: 5)*

He also explained how strategy and structure are strongly linked in organizations. Structure was defined as the form firms assumed to achieve their strategy. This included the hierarchy, control and management mechanisms. Chandler's famous phrase was that "structure follows strategy," i.e. that the structure of organization should be defined with the aim of achieving the firm strategy.

In his studies of four large US firms (General Motors, Sears Roebuck, Du Pont, and Standard Oil), Chandler assessed how the companies responded to pressures in their environment. The alternative responses ranged from a defensive response that saw companies trying to protect their markets through strategies such as vertical integration to aggressive responses for example in diversifications of products and markets. Chandler concluded that Standard Oil, failed to appreciate that structure came from strategy and was thus slow to decentralize.

Chandler championed this type of study saying "only by comparing the evolution of large-scale multi-unit enterprises in different economies can organizational imperatives be identified and the impact of the cultural attitudes and values, ideologies, political systems, and social structures that affect these imperatives be understood" (53).

Strategy for Andrews

Of the 75 Andrews sentences, 25 sentences reflect the tension between firm and environment, while the remaining 50 sentences reflect the tension between interior firm assets and performance.

In the words of Kenneth Andrews "Business policy is the study of the functions and responsibilities of the senior management in a company, the crucial problems that affect the success of the total enterprise, and the decisions that determine its direction, shape its future and produce the results desired" (1971: 25). Additionally, Andrews affirms that "Strategy is the pattern of objectives, purposes or goals and major policies and plans for achieving these goals, stated in such a way as to define what businesses the company is in or is to be in and the kind of company it is or is to be" (28). This view of strategy recognizes the importance of the firm's goal while emphasizing the conscious development of corporate policies and plan as the means by which to achieve the overarching strategic aims.

Compared to Chandler's conception of strategy, Andrews focus his attention to the relationship between environment and performance and affirms,

"Corporate strategy defines the businesses in which a company will compete, preferably in a way that focuses resources to convert distinctive competence into competitive advantage ... Business strategy is the determination of how a company will compete in a given business, and position itself among its competitors" (18).

In a further sentence Andrews not only reinforces the notion of strategy as a determinant of organizational purpose, but explicitly incorporates the importance of stakeholders when stating as follows (35):

> Corporate strategy is the pattern of decisions in a company that determines and reveals its objectives, purposes, or goals, produces the principal policies and plans for achieving those goals, and defines the range of businesses the company is to pursue, the kind of economic and human organization it is or intends to be, and the nature of the economic and noneconomic contribution it intends to make to its shareholders, employees, customers, and communities.

He clearly distinguishes between *formulation* as a distinct activity deciding what to do and *implementation* where the decisions subsequently are carried out through concrete actions. Strategic alternatives to be decided upon are determined through identification of opportunities and risks in the business environment.

Andrews original model recognized the importance of personal values and social responsibility and he reasoned: "It is increasingly clear that government regulation is not a good substitute for knowledgeable self-restraint" (40).

Discussion of the results

The above illustrates the usefulness of a semiotic framework in identifying the complex nature of the meaning of strategy. The definition of these two scholars, namely Andrews and Chandler, indicate not only differences along each of the two value dimensions, but more important, they indicate differences in the relations between the dimensions.

Firms in the case of Chandler implied resources and organizational structures; management in the case of Andrews. Often the concept is put in relation to economic performance. The results of this analysis tell us nothing about the reasons for the different value combination. The differences in values may be attributed to personal traits. The differences may also reflect their different roles, Chandler closer to firm settings while Andrews to academic setting.

The results corroborate the findings of previous researches in SM such as Nag *et al.*, (2007) and Ronda-Pupo and Guerras-Martins (2013). Actually, the semiotic analysis deserves the merit not only to break down the meanings of the strategy concept but most importantly to uncover their interrelationships.

Concluding remarks: Criticisms and strengths of the semiotic analysis in SM

In this chapter the relative merits of the semiotic square as a static logical reconstruction of surface SM texts, but also as a dynamic platform that puts scholars in semiotic perspective, were laid out. By focusing on the Greimasian generative trajectory through which meanings emerge an attempt was made to demonstrate how meanings are uncovered in SM texts and progressively how constructs are formed through a reduction from surface to depth structures, alongside intermediate levels of the trajectory. In this vein, the major strength of a structural textual analysis as conducted in the above illustrative case lies in the power of semiotic squares to represent a complex, potentially infinite set of patterns with a finite, simple set of rules. To explain meanings we need to identify the generative structures that at the same time enable and constrain them.

In SM we generally have data from the surface (written firm strategies, letters to shareholders, interviews, etc.). These data are quite distant from their real meaning. Structuralist semiotics can help researchers look behind or beneath the surface of those data in order to discover the underlying organization of phenomena. The more obvious the structural organization of a text or code may seem to be, the more difficult it may be to see beyond such surface features (Chandler, 2007). Searching for what is "hidden" beneath the "obvious" can lead to fruitful insights. Actually, depending on the narrative situation at hand, multiple squares need to be constructed, coupled with a process of establishing relations among the squares' respective terms.

At this point the following limitation should be noted. By virtue of the fact that during the semantic investment of the square, formal object-terms assume particular values by recourse to a wider societal value-system, the model assumes a contingent character. The aim of the square is not to portray relationships in a universally binding and logical manner, but, as Patte puts it, "the way in which a culture (in a sociolectal semantic universe) or an individual (in an idiolectal semantic universe) perceives the relations among certain entities" (1982: 64).

Notes

1   The major rival to the term semiotics has been semiology. For some time, these two terms were used to be identified with the "two traditions" of semiotics. The linguistic tradition from Saussure to Hjelmslev and Barthes was usually defined as semiology. The general theory of signs in the tradition of the philosophers Peirce and Morris was called semiotics. Today, semiotics is generally accepted as a synonym of semiology or as a more general term, which includes semiology as one of its branches (Deely, 1990). The plural form semiotics (instead of semiotic) seems to have been adopted in analogy to forms such as semantics and physics.

2   For a detailed history of semiotics (and detailed references as well) please see Nöth (1995).

3   The history of investigation into the nature of signs is an important aspect of the history of philosophy in general, and contributions to the theory can be traced back to the

Greeks – from Heraclitus to the Stoics, from Plato to Aristotle – to the Hellenistic and Roman periods; the early Christian thinkers and church fathers (e.g. St. Augustine); medieval authors; humanists such as Dante Alighieri and philosophers, such as Francis Bacon.

4   The medical semiotics subdivides the field into three branches, *anamnestics*, the study of the patient's medical history, *diagnostics*, the study of the present symptoms of disease, and *prognostics*, concerning the predictions about future developments of a disease.

References

Andrews, K. R. (1971). *The Concept of Corporate Strategy*, revised edn. Homewood, IL: R.D. Irwin.

Barley, S. R. (1983). Semiotics and the study of occupational and organizational cultures. *Administrative Science Quarterly*, 28(3), 393–413.

Barr, P. S. and Glynn, M. A. (2004). Cultural variations in strategic issue interpretation: Relating cultural uncertainty avoidance to controllability in discriminating threat and opportunity. *Strategic Management Journal*, 25(1), 59–67.

Barry, D. and Helmes, M. (1997). Strategy retold: Towards a narrative view of strategic discourse. *Academy of Management Review*, 22(2): 429–452.

Barthes, R. (1964). *Elements of Semiology*. New York: Hill and Wang

Brannen, M.Y. (2004). When Mickey loses face: Recontextualization, semantic fit, and the semiotics of foreignness. *Academy of Management Review*, 29(4), 593–616.

Brown, G. (1983). *Discourse Analysis*. Cambridge: Cambridge University Press.

Chandler, A. D. (1990). *Strategy and Structure: Chapters in the History of the Industrial Enterprise*. Cambridge, MA: MIT Press.

Chandler, D. (2007). *Semiotics: The Basics*. Abingdon: Routledge.

Chesterton, G. K. (1912). *What's Wrong with the World*. London: Cassell.

Cinici, M. C. and Dunbar, R. L. (2012). Semiotic methods and the meaning of strategy in firm annual reports. In G. B. Dagnino (ed.) *Handbook of Research on Competitive Strategy*, 397–415. Cheltenham: Edward Elgar.

Cortazzi, M. (2014). *Narrative Analysis*. London: Routledge.

Deely, J. (1990). *Basics of Semiotics*. Bloomington: Indiana University Press.

Derrida, J. (1978): *Writing and Difference* (trans. Alan Bass). London: Routledge and Kegan Paul.

Eco. U. (1976). *A Theory of Semiotics*. Bloomington: Indiana Univeristy Press

Fairclough, N. (1992). *Discourse and Social Change*. Cambridge: Polity Press.

Fairclough, N. (2013). *Critical Discourse Analysis: The Critical Study of Language*. London: Routledge.

Fiol, C. M. (1989). A semiotic analysis of corporate language: Organizational boundaries and joint venturing. *Administrative Science Quarterly*, 34(2), 277–303.

Fiol, C. M. (1991). Seeing the empty spaces: Towards a more complex understanding of the meaning of power in organizations. *Organization Studies*, 12(4), 547–566.

Floch, J. M. (2001). *Semiotics, Marketing and Communication: Beneath the Signs, the Strategies*. Basingstoke: Palgrave Macmillan

Foucault, M. (1970): *The Order of Things*. London: Tavistock

Furrer O., Thomas H. and Goussevskaia A. (2008). The structure and evolution of the strategic management field: A content analysis of 26 years of strategic management research. *International Journal of Management Reviews*, 10(1): 1–23.

Garud, R., Dunbar, R. L., and Bartel, C. A. (2011). Dealing with unusual experiences: A narrative perspective on organizational learning. *Organization Science*, 22(3), 587–601.

Gee, J. P. (2014). *An Introduction to Discourse Analysis: Theory and Method*, 4th edn. London: Routledge.

Giudici, A. and Reinmoeller, P. (2012). Dynamic capabilities in the dock: A case of reification? *Strategic Organization*, *10*(4), 436–449.

Greimas, A. J. (1966). *Sémantique structurale*. Paris: Presses universitaires de France.

Greimas, A. J. (1970). *Du sens I*. Paris: Seuil.

Greimas, A.J. (1976). *On Meaning: Selected Writings in Semiotic Theory* (trans. Paul J. Perron and Frank H. Collins). Minneapolis: University of Minnesota Press.

Hambrick, D. C. and Fredrickson, J. W. (2001). Are you sure you have a strategy? *Academy of Management Executive* 15(4): 48–59.

Hoskisson, R. E., Hitt, M. A., Wan, W. P., and Yiu, D. (1999). Theory and research in strategic management: Swings of a pendulum. *Journal of Management* 25(3): 417–456.

Jensen, M. C. and Meckling, W. H. (1976). Theory of the firm: Managerial behavior, agency costs, and ownership structure, *Journal of Financial Economics*, 3, 305–360.

Khaire, M. and Wadhwani, R. D. (2010). Changing landscapes: The construction of meaning and value in a new market category – modern Indian art. *Academy of Management Journal*, 53(6), 1281–1304.

Labov, W. and Waletzky, J. (1997). Narrative analysis: Oral versions of personal experience. In Helm J. (ed.) *Essays on the Verbal and Visual Arts*, 12–44. Seattle: University of Washington Press. Reprinted in the *Journal of Narrative and Life History* 7, 3–38.

Lane, P. J., Koka, B. R., Pathak, S. (2006). The reification of absorptive capacity: A critical review and rejuvenation of the construct. *Academy of Management Review*, *31*(4), 833-863.

Lee, G. and Parachuri, S. (2008). Entry into emergent and uncertain product-markets: The role of associative rhetoric. *Academy of Management Journal*, 51(6): 1171–1188.

Liebenau, J. and Backhouse, J. (1990). *Understanding Information: An Introduction*. London: Palgrave Macmillan.

Liu, K. (2000). *Semiotics in information systems engineering*. Cambridge University Press.

Mainardes, E. W., Ferreira, J. J., and Raposo, M. L. (2014). Strategy and strategic management concepts: Are they recognised by management students? *Economics and Management*, 17(1), 43–61.

Markides, C. (2004). What is strategy and how do you know if you have one? *Business Strategy Review*, 15(2): 5–12

Mick, D. G., Burroughs, J. E., Hetzel, P., and Brannen, M. Y. (2004). Pursuing the meaning of meaning in the commercial world: An international review of marketing and consumer research founded on semiotics. *Semiotica*, (152-1/4), 1–74.

Morris, C. W. (1938): *Foundations of the Theory of Signs*. Chicago: Chicago University Press

Nag, R., Hambrick, D. C., and Chen, M. J. (2007). What is strategic management, really? Inductive derivation of a consensus definition of the field. *Strategic Management Journal*, 28(9), 935–955.

Nöth, W. (1995). *Handbook of Semiotics*. Bloomington: Indiana University Press.

Paroutis, S. and Heracleous, L. (2013). Discourse revisited: Dimensions and employment of first-order strategy disocurse during institutional adoption. *Strategic Management Journal*, 34: 935–956.

Patte, D. (1982). Greimas's model for the generative trajectory of meaning in discourses. *American Journal of Semiotics*, 1(3): 59–79.

Peirce, C. S. (1934). *Collected Papers: Volume V. Pragmatism and Pragmaticism*. Cambridge, MA: Harvard University Press.

Pentland, B. T. (1999). Building process theory with narrative: From description to explanation. *Academy of Management Review*, 24(4), 711–724.

Phillips, N., Sewell, G. and Jaynes, S. (2008). Applying critical discourse analysis in strategic management research. *Organizational Research Methods*, 11(4): 770–789.

Porter, M. E. (1980) *Competitive Strategy*. New York: Free Press.

Riessman, C. K. (ed.) (1993). *Narrative Analysis*. Newbury Park, CA: Sage.

Ronda-Pupo, G.A., Guerras-Martín, L.Á. (2010). Dynamics of the scientific community network within the strategic management field through the *Strategic Management Journal* 1980–2009: The role of cooperation. *Scientometrics*, 85(3), 821–848.

Ronda Pupo, G. A. and Guerras Martin, L. Á. (2012). Dynamics of the evolution of the strategy concept 1962–2008: A co word analysis. *Strategic Management Journal*, 33(2), 162–188.

Saussure, F. (de) (1916). *Course de linguistique générale*. Paris: Gallimard.

Selzer, J. (2004). Rhetorical analysis: Understanding how texts persuade readers. In Bazerman, C. and Prior, P. (eds) *What Writing Does and How it Does it: An Introduction to Analyzing Texts and Textual Practices*, 279-307. Mahwah, NJ: Lawrence Erlbaum Associates.

Sturrock, J. (1986): *Structuralism*. London: Paladin.

Suddaby, R. (2010). Editor's comments: Construct clarity in theories of management and organization. *Academy of Management Review*, 35(3): 346–357.

Wernerfelt, B. (1984). A resource-based view of the firm. *Strategic Management Journal*, 5(2): 171–180.

Williamson, O. E. (1975). *Markets and Hierarchies*. New York: Free Press.

Williamson, O. E. (1985). *The Economic Institutions of Capitalism : Firms, Markets, Relational Contracting*. New York: Free Press.

Recommended web resources

Daniel Chandler, University of Wales, "Semiotics for Beginners": www.aber.ac.uk/media/Documents/S4B/sem11.html. This site provides an introduction to semiotic analysis plus a glossary, references, and recommended readings.

Professor Charles Antaki's "Conversation Analysis Tutorial": www.staff.lboro.ac.uk/ssca1/sitemenu.htm. This site provides an introduction to conversation analysis plus examples of transcripts and notations.

"Qualitative Data Analysis on the Web": http://onlineqda.hud.ac.uk. This site from the School of Human & Health Sciences at the University of Huddersfield provides qualitative data analysis methods, resources, and a glossary.

www.signosemio.com. Check out this site for more information on theoreticians such as Jakobson.

"TalkBank": www.talkbank.org. At TalkBank you can find downloadable conversation analysis transcripts linked to audio or video recordings, and other resources.

Umberto Eco Website: www.umbertoeco.com. Eco is a semiotician, literary critic, and novelist, popularly known for his novel *The Name of the Rose*, among others. Check out his website on semiotics.

Appendix: "The semiotic toolkit" – Glossary of key semiotic terms

Presented here is a selection of key semiotic terms strictly connected to a structural textual analysis. For a complete semiotic glossary please consider the one provided by David Chandler in *Semiotic for Beginners* available on the following website: www.aber.ac.uk/media/Documents/ S4B/sem11.html.

Analogical sign

Analogical signs (such as paintings in a gallery or gestures in face-to-face interaction) are signs in a form in which they are perceived as involving graded relationships on a continuum rather than as discrete units (in contrast to digital signs). Note, however, that digital technology can transform analogical signs into digital reproductions which may be perceptually indistinguishable from the "originals."

Anchorage

Roland Barthes introduced the concept of anchorage. Linguistic elements in a text (such as a caption) can serve to "anchor" (or constrain) the preferred readings of an image (conversely the illustrative use of an image can anchor an ambiguous verbal text).

Arbitrariness

Saussure emphasized that the relationship between the linguistic signifier and signified is arbitrary: the link between them is not necessary, intrinsic, or natural. He was denying extra-linguistic influences (external to the linguistic system). Philosophically, the relationship is ontologically arbitrary: initially, it makes no difference what labels we attach to things, but of course signs are not socially or historically arbitrary (after a sign has come into historical existence we cannot arbitrarily change signifiers). Saussure focused on linguistic signs, whilst Peirce dealt more explicitly with signs in any medium, and noted that the relationship between signifiers and their signifieds varies in arbitrariness – from the radical arbitrariness of symbolic signs, via the perceived similarity of signifier to signified in iconic signs, to the minimal arbitrariness of indexical signs. Many semioticians argue that all signs are to some extent arbitrary and conventional (and thus subject to ideological manipulation).

Articulation of codes

Articulation refers to structural levels within semiotic codes. Semiotic codes have either single articulation, double articulation or no articulation. A semiotic code which has "double articulation" (as in the case of verbal language) can be analyzed into two abstract structural levels: a higher level called "the level of first articulation" and a lower level – "the level of second articulation."

Associative relations

This was Saussure's term for what later came to be called paradigmatic relations. The "formulaic" associations of linguistic signs include synonyms, antonyms, similar-sounding words, and words of similar grammatical function.

Binarism/dualism

The ontological division of a domain into two discrete categories (dichotomies) or polarities. "Binarism" is a more loaded term that critics have applied to what they regard as the obsessive dualism of structuralists such as Lévi-Strauss and Jakobson.

Hjelmslev argued against binarism. Derridean deconstruction demonstrates the inescapability of binary logic.

Binary oppositions (or digital oppositions)

Pairs of mutually-exclusive signifiers in a paradigm set representing categories which are logically opposed and which together define a complete universe of discourse (relevant ontological domain), e.g. alive/not-alive. In such oppositions each term necessarily implies its opposite and there is no middle term.

Bricolage

Lévi-Strauss's term for the appropriation of pre-existing materials which are ready-to-hand is widely-used to refer to the intertextual authorial practice of adopting and adapting signs from other texts.

Codes

Semiotic codes are procedural systems of related conventions for correlating signifiers and signifieds in certain domains. Codes provide a framework within which signs make sense: they are interpretative devices that are used by interpretative communities. They can be broadly divided into social codes, textual codes, and interpretative codes. Some codes are fairly explicit; others are much looser.

Codification

From a sociological point of view, codification is the historical social process whereby the conventions of a particular code become widely established. In textual analysis, it represents the act, process, or result of arranging texts in a systematic form or code.

Combination, axis of

A structuralist term for the "horizontal" axis in the analysis of a textual structure

Commonsense

Commonsense represents the most widespread cultural and historical values, attitudes, and beliefs within a given culture. It is generated by ideological forces operating through codes and myths. Commonsense does involve incoherences, ambiguities, paradoxes, contradictions and omissions; the role of ideology is to suppress these in the interests of dominant groups. Semiotics seeks to demonstrate that commonsense meanings are not givens, but are shaped by ideological forces.

Communication

From a semiotic perspective, communication involves encoding and decoding texts according to the conventions of appropriate codes. The centrality of codes to communication is a distinctive semiotic contribution which emphasizes the social nature of communication and the importance of conventions. While most semioticians are concerned with communicative meaning-making, some semioticians also study the attribution of meaning even where no intent to communicate exists or where no human agency was involved in producing what is perceived as a sign.

Complex sign

Saussure's term for a sign which contains other signs. A text is usually a complex sign.

Connotation

The socio-cultural and personal associations produced as a reader decodes a text. The term also refers to the relationship between the signifier and its signified. For Barthes, connotation was a second order of signification which uses the denotative sign (signifier and signified) as its signifier and attaches to it an additional signified. In this framework connotation is a sign which derives from the signifier of a denotative sign (so denotation leads to a chain of connotations).

Constructivism, (social) constructionism

A philosophical (specifically epistemological) stance (with diverse labels) on "what is real?" Constructivism can be seen as offering an alternative to the binarism involved in polarizing the issue into the objectivism of naive realists versus the radical subjectivism of the idealists. In contrast to realists, constructivists argue that "reality" is not wholly external to and independent of how we conceptualize the world: our sign systems (language and other media) play a major part in "the social construction of reality"; realities cannot be separated from the sign systems in which they are experienced.

Content analysis

A quantitative form of textual analysis involving the categorization and counting of recurrent elements in the form or content of texts. This method can be used in conjunction with semiotic analysis (semiotic textual analysis being a qualitative methodology).

Conventionality

A term often used in conjunction with the term arbitrary to refer to the relationship between the signifier and the signified. In the case of a symbolic system such as verbal language this relationship is purely conventional – dependent on social and cultural conventions (rather than in any sense "natural"). The conventional nature of codes means that they have to be learned (not necessarily formally). Thus some semioticians speak of learning to "read" photographs, television, or film, for instance.

Decoding

The comprehension and interpretation of texts by decoders with reference to relevant codes. Most commentators assume that the reader actively constructs meaning rather than simply "extracting" it from the text.

Deconstruction

This is a poststructuralist strategy for textual analysis which was developed by Jacques Derrida. Practitioners seek to dismantle the rhetorical structures within a text to demonstrate how key concepts within it depend on their unstated oppositional relation to absent signifiers (this involved building on the structuralist method of paradigmatic analysis). More broadly, deconstructive cultural criticism involves demonstrating how signifying practices construct, rather than simply represent social reality, and how ideology works to make such practices seem transparent.

Diachronic analysis

Diachronic analysis studies change in a phenomenon (such as a code) over time (in contrast to synchronic analysis). Saussure saw the development of language in terms of a series of synchronic states.

Discourse

A discourse is a system of representation consisting of a set of representational codes (including a distinctive interpretative repertoire of concepts, tropes, and myths) for constructing and maintaining particular forms of reality within the ontological domain (or topic) defined as relevant to its concerns. Representational codes thus reflect relational principles underlying the symbolic order of the "discursive field." Structuralists deterministically see the subject as the product of the available discourses. Constructivists allow for the possibility of negotiation or resistance. Poststructuralists deny any meaning (or more provocatively any reality) outside of discourses.

Encoding

The production of texts by encoders with reference to relevant codes. Encoding involves foregrounding some meanings and backgrounding others.

Epistemology

A branch of philosophy concerned with the theory of knowledge. The term refers to how "the world" can be known and what can be known about it.

Form and content

A distinction sometimes equated to Saussure's distinction between the signifier (seen as form) and the signified (seen as *content*). However, the metaphor of form as a "container" is problematic, tending to support the equation of content with *meaning*, implying that meaning can be "extracted" without an active process of interpretation and that form is not in itself meaningful. In "realistic" codes, content is foregrounded while form retreats to transparency.

Form and substance

Hjelmslev introduced the notion that both expression and content have substance and form. In this framework signs have four dimensions: substance of content; form of content; substance of expression; form of expression.

Formalism

Russian formalism was a structuralist, anti-realist aesthetic doctrine whose proponents included Victor Shklovsky. The Prague school linguists were also structural formalists. Formalism represented a linguistic focus on literary uses of language. As the name suggests, the primary focus of the formalists was on form, structure, technique or medium rather than on content. They saw literary language as language "made strange" and their model was poetry rather than prose. They were particularly interested in literary "devices" such as rhyme, rhythm, metre, imagery, syntax, and narrative techniques – favouring writing which "laid bare" its devices.

Genre

Conventional definitions of genres tend to be based on the notion that they constitute particular conventions of form and content which are shared by the texts which are regarded as belonging to them. However, an individual text within a genre rarely if ever has all of the characteristic features of the genre and texts often exhibit the conventions of more than one genre. Semiotic redefinitions of genre tend to focus on the way in which the formal features of texts within the genre draw on shared codes and function to "position" readers using particular modes of address. Postmodernist theorists tend to blur distinctions between genres.

Hermeneutics

Hermes was the Greek god who delivered and interpreted messages. The term hermeneutics is often used to refer to the interpretation of texts.

Ideology

There are no ideologically "neutral" sign systems: signs function to persuade as well as to refer. Modern semiotic theory is often allied with a Marxist approach which stresses the role of ideology. Ideology constructs people as subjects through the operation of codes. According to the theory of textual positioning, understanding the meaning of a text involves taking on an appropriate ideological identity.

Idiolect

A term from sociolinguistics referring to the distinctive ways in which language is used by individuals. In semiotic terms it can refer more broadly to the stylistic and personal subcodes of individuals.

Interpersonal communication

In contrast to mass communication ("one-to-many" communication), this term is typically used to refer to "one-to-one" communication, although this distinction tends to overlook the importance of communication in small groups (neither "one" nor "many"). It may be either synchronous or asynchronous. *Synchronous* interpersonal communication may involve: (a) both speech and non-verbal cues (e.g. direct face-to-face interaction, video links); (b) speech alone (e.g. telephone); or (c) mainly text (e.g. internet chat systems). *Asynchronous* interpersonal communication tends to be primarily through text (e.g. letters, fax, e-mail).

Interpretative community
Those who share the same codes are members of the same "interpretative community." Linguists tend to use the logocentric term, "discourse community." Thomas Kuhn used the term "textual community" to refer to epistemic (or epistemological) communities with shared texts, interpretations and beliefs. Constructivists argue that interpretative communities are involved in the construction and maintenance of reality within the ontological domain which defines their concerns. The conventions within the codes employed by such communities become naturalized amongst its members. Individuals belong simultaneously to several interpretative communities.

Isomorphism
The term is used to refer to correspondences, parallels, or similarities in the properties, patterns or relations of: (a) two different structures; (b) structural elements in two different structures; and (c) structural elements at different levels within the same structure.

Langue and *parole*
These are Saussure's terms. *Langue* refers to the abstract system of rules and conventions of a signifying system – it is independent of, and pre-exists, individual users. *Parole* refers to concrete instances of its use. To the Saussurean semiotician, what matters most are the underlying structures and rules of a semiotic system as a whole rather than specific performances or practices which are merely instances of its use. While Saussure did not concern himself with *parole*, the structure of *langue* is of course revealed by the study of *parole*.

Linguistic determinism
According to linguistic determinists our thinking (or "worldview") is determined by language – by the use of verbal language and/or by the grammatical structures, semantic distinctions, and inbuilt ontologies within a language. A more moderate stance is that thinking may be "influenced" rather than unavoidably "determined" by language: it is a two-way process, so that the kind of language we use is also influenced by the way we see the world. Critics who are socially-oriented emphasize the social context of language use rather than purely linguistic considerations; any influence is ascribed not to "Language" as such (which would be to reify language) but to usage in particular contexts and to particular kinds of discourse (e.g. a *sociolect*). Both structuralists and poststructuralists give priority to the determining power of the language system: language patterns our experience and the subject is constructed through discourse.

Materiality of the sign

Although signs may be discerned in the material form of words, images, sounds, acts, or objects, such things have no intrinsic meaning and become signs only when we invest them with meaning. Signs as such have no material existence: only the sign vehicle has material substance. Whilst nowadays the "signifier" is commonly interpreted as the material (or physical) form of the sign (something which can be seen, heard, touched, smelt or tasted), this is more materialistic than Saussure's own model. For Saussure, both the signifier and the signified were "form" rather than substance. However, the material form of the sign can itself be a signifier – the same written text might be interpreted somewhat differently depending on whether it was handwritten or word-processed, and it might even generate different connotations if it were in one typeface rather than another.

Meaning

Saussure's conception of meaning was purely structural, relational, and differential – the meaning of signs was seen as lying in their systematic relation to each other. In contrast, referential meaning is the representation of referents in signs and texts. In the transmission model of communication, meaning is equated with content. Similarly, for both formalists and structuralists, "the meaning of the text" is "immanent" – that is, it is regarded as lying within the text (socio-historical context, authorial intention and readers' purposes are excluded from consideration). Social semioticians reject this "literalist" notion – meaning does not reside within a text. They emphasize meaning-making practices and the interpretative importance of codes. Many semioticians would define meaning in terms of the denotative and connotative associations produced as a reader decodes a text with relation to textual codes.

Medium

The term "medium" is used in a variety of ways by different theorists, and may include such broad categories as speech and writing or print and broadcasting, or relate to specific technical forms within the *media of mass communication* (radio, television, newspapers, magazines, books, photographs, films, and records) or the *media of interpersonal communication* (telephone, letter, fax, e-mail, video-conferencing, computer-based chat systems).

Message

This term variously refers either to a text or to the meaning of a text – referents which literalists tend to conflate.

Metaphor

Metaphor expresses the unfamiliar (known in literary jargon as the "tenor") in terms of the familiar (the "vehicle"). The tenor and the vehicle are normally unrelated: we must make an imaginative leap to recognize the resemblance to which a fresh metaphor alludes. In semiotic terms, a metaphor involves one signified acting as a signifier referring to a rather different signified. Metaphors initially seem unconventional because they apparently disregard "literal" or denotative resemblance. Metaphor can thus be seen as involving a symbolic as well as an iconic quality. Metaphoric signifiers tend to foreground the signifier rather than the signified. Deconstructionists have sought to demonstrate how dominant metaphors function to privilege unmarked signifieds.

Motivation and constraint
The term "motivation" (used by Saussure) is sometimes contrasted with "constraint" in describing the extent to which the signified determines the signifier. The more a signifier is constrained by the signified, the more "motivated" the sign is: iconic signs are highly motivated; symbolic signs are unmotivated. The less motivated the sign, the more learning of an agreed code is required.

Narration or narrative voice
Narration is the act and process of producing a narrative. Modes of address differ in their narrative point-of-view. In academic writing, third person narrative has traditionally been regarded as more "objective" and "transparent" than first-person narrative; critics note that this style obscures authorial agency – "facts" and events appear to "speak for themselves."

Narrative
A narrative is a representation of a "chain" of events. In the orderly Aristotelian narrative form, causation and goals turn story (chronological events) into plot: events at the beginning cause those in the middle, and events in the middle cause those at the end.

Naturalization
Codes which have been naturalized are those which are so widely distributed in a culture and which are learned at such an early age that they appear not to be constructed but to be "naturally" given.

Paris school
This is a school of structuralist semiotic thinking established by Algirdas Greimas (1917–1992), a Lithuanian by origin. Strongly influenced by Louis Hjelmslev (1899–1966), it seeks to identify basic structures of signification. Greimas focused primarily on the semantic analysis of textual structures but the Paris School has expanded its rigorous (critics say arid) structural analysis to cultural phenomena such as gestural language, legal discourse, and social science. It is formalist in treating semiotic systems as autonomous rather than exploring the importance of social context.

Poststructuralism
While poststructuralism is often interpreted simply as "anti-structuralism," it is

worth noting that the label refers to a school of thought which developed *after*, out of, and in relation to structuralism. Poststructuralism built on and adapted structuralist notions in addition to problematizing many of them. Both schools of thought are built on the assumption that we are the subjects of language rather than being simply instrumental "users" of it, and poststructuralist thinkers have developed further the notion of "the constitution of the subject," challenging essentialist romantic individualism (the notion that we are autonomous and creative agents with stable, unified "personalities" and "original" ideas). For poststructuralists there are no fundamental "deep structures" underlying forms in an external world. Poststructuralist theorists include Derrida, Foucault, Lacan, Kristeva, and the later Barthes.

Primacy of the signifier
The argument that "reality" or "the world" is at least partly created by the language (and other media) we use insists on the *primacy of the signifier* – suggesting that the signified is shaped by the signifier rather than *vice versa*. Some theorists stress the materiality of the signifier. Others note that the same signifier can have different signifieds for different people or for the same person at different times. Lévi-Strauss emphasized the primacy of the signifier, initially as a strategy for structural analysis. Poststructuralist theorists such as Lacan, Barthes, Derrida, and Foucault have developed this notion into a metaphysical presupposition of the priority of the signifier, but its roots can be found in Saussure and structuralism.

Saussurean model of the sign
In Saussure's model, the sign consisted of *two* elements: a signifier and a signified (though he insisted that these were inseparable other than for analytical purposes). This dyadic model makes no direct reference to a referent in the world, and can be seen as supporting the notion that language does not "reflect" reality but rather constructs it. It has been criticized as an idealist model. Saussure stressed that signs only made sense in terms of their *relationships* to other signs within the same signifying system

Semantics
Morris divided semiotics into three branches: syntactics, *semantics* and pragmatics. *Semantics* refers to the study of the meaning of signs (the relationship of signs to what they stand for). The interpretation of signs by their users can also be seen as levels corresponding to these three branches – the *semantic* level being the comprehension of the preferred reading of the sign.

Semiology
Saussure's term *sémiologie* dates from a manuscript of 1894. "Semiology" is sometimes used to refer to the study of signs by those within the Saussurean tradition (e.g. Barthes, Lévi-Strauss, Kristeva, and Baudrillard), While "semiotics" sometimes refers to those working within the Peircean tradition (e.g. Morris,

Richards, Ogden, and Sebeok). Sometimes "semiology" refers to work concerned primarily with textual analysis while "semiotics" refers to more philosophically oriented work. Saussure's semiotics embraced only intentional communication – specifically *human* communication using conventionalized, artificial sign systems. Nowadays the term "semiotics" is widely used as an umbrella term to include "semiology" and (to use Peirce's term) "semiotic."

Sign

A sign is a meaningful unit which is interpreted as "standing for" something other than itself. Signs are found in the physical form of words, images, sounds, acts, or objects (this physical form is sometimes known as the sign vehicle). Signs have no *intrinsic* meaning and become signs only when sign-users invest them with meaning with reference to a recognized code. Semiotics is the study of signs.

Structuralism

Ferdinand de Saussure, the founder of modern linguistics, was a pioneer of structuralist thinking – his was the linguistic model which inspired the European structuralists. Other key structuralists include Nikolai Trubetzkoy, Roman Jakobson, Louis Hjelmslev, and Algirdas Greimas in linguistics, Claude Lévi-Strauss in anthropology, Louis Althusser in political science, Roland Barthes in literary criticism, and Jacques Lacan in psychoanalysis (although the theories of Barthes and Lacan evolved into poststructuralist ones). Michel Foucault, a historian of ideas, is often seen as a structuralist, although he rejected this label; his ideas are also closely allied with poststructuralism. Saussure's *Cours de linguistique générale* was published in 1916: although the words "structure" and "structuralism" are not mentioned, it is the source of much of the terminology of structuralism. Formalism was a key tributary leading to structuralism in the late 1920s and 1930s. The birth of European structuralism is usually associated with a conference of the Prague school linguists in The Hague in 1928. The first English translation of Saussure's *Course* was published in 1959, and structuralism flourished in academic circles in the 1960s and 1970s (though it continued to be influential in the 1980s). The primary concern of the Structuralists is with systems or structures rather than with referential meaning or the specificities of usage. Structuralists regard each language as a relational system or structure and give priority to the *determining* power of the language system (a principle shared by poststructuralists). They seek to describe the overall organization of sign systems as "languages" – as with Lévi-Strauss and myth, kinship rules, and totemism, Lacan and the unconscious and Barthes and Greimas and the "grammar" of narrative. The primary emphasis is on the *whole* system – which is seen as "more than the sum of its parts." Structuralists engage in a systematic search for "deep structures" underlying the surface features of phenomena (such as language, society, thought, and behavior). Their textual analysis is synchronic, seeking to delineate the codes and rules which underlie the production of texts by comparing those perceived as belonging to the same system (e.g. a genre) and identifying invariant constituent units. The analysis of specific texts seeks to break down larger, more abstract units into "minimal significant units" by means of the commutation test, then groups these units by membership of paradigms and identifies the syntagmatic relations which link the units. The search for underlying semantic oppositions is characteristic of structuralist textual analysis. Contemporary social semiotics has moved beyond structuralist analysis of the internal relations of parts within a self-contained system.

Text

Most broadly, this term is used to refer to anything which can be "read" for meaning Although the term appears to privilege written texts (it seems grapho-centric and logocentric), to most semioticians a "text" is an system of signs (in the form of words, images, sounds, and/or gestures). It is constructed and interpreted with reference to the conventions associated with a genre and in a particular medium of communication. The term is often used to refer to recorded (e.g. written) texts which are independent of their users (used in this sense the term excludes unrecorded speech). A text is the product of a process of representation and "positions" both its makers and its readers. Typically, readers tend to focus mainly on what is represented in a text rather than on the processes of representation involved (which usually seem to be transparent).

8

PUTTING NUMBERS TO WORDS IN THE DISCERNMENT OF MEANING

Applications of repertory grid in strategic management

Gerard P. Hodgkinson, Robert P. Wright, and Sotirios Paroutis

> It is not events themselves which influence or mould people, torment or terrify them, or make them deliriously happy. It is the meaning in which these events are invested by the individual which is the potent ingredient.
>
> *(Burr and Butt, 1992: 69)*

> And those who were seen dancing were thought to be insane by those who could not hear the music.
>
> *(Attributed to Friedrich Nietzsche)*

Introduction

Over the past three decades the management and organization sciences have witnessed the birth of highly exciting inter-disciplinary subfield: managerial and organizational cognition (MOC). Situated at the intersections of strategic management, organization theory, and organizational behavior, MOC researchers are drawing upon, and in some cases contributing to, a wide range of social science disciplines, from anthropology to behavioral economics, to psychology, to sociology, in order to advance fundamental and applied theory and research pertaining to strategic management processes, practices, and outcomes, spanning the individual, group, organizational, and inter-organizational levels of analysis (for overviews see Eden and Spender, 1998; Eggers and Kaplan, 2013; Hodgkinson, 2001a, 2001b; Hodgkinson and Sparrow, 2002; Narayanan, Zane, and Kemmerer, 2011; Porac, Thomas, and Badden-Fuller, 1989; Powell, Lovallo, and Fox, 2011; Walsh, 1995). This rapidly evolving body of work has created a perspective on strategic management that focuses on the (inter-) subjectivity and limitations of human information processing. The insights gained from this perspective have led scholars to raise a number of fundamental questions that challenge the very foundations of the strategy field, not least two of the foremost assumptions of neoclassical economics implicit in much of the field's classic writings, namely, the notions that: (1) all firms have equal access to information about the marketplace, and (2) they will invariably respond to such information in similar ways.

Traceable ultimately back to the seminal works of Barnard (1938) and Simon (1947), the basic principles of the cognitive perspective on strategic management can be summarized as follows:

- individuals are limited in their ability to process the rich variety of stimuli contained in the external world (in Simon's [1956] terms, they are constrained by "bounded rationality");
- consequently, they employ a variety of strategies in order to reduce the burden of information processing that would otherwise ensue, culminating in the development of simplified representations of reality that are encoded within the minds of individuals;
- once formulated, these "mental representations" act as filters through which incoming information is subsequently processed, which in turn may lead to biased and inappropriate decisions, but under certain circumstances may also form the basis of creative ideas and new insights.

The repertory grid technique (RGT) is one of a growing number of methods in use for externalizing actors' mental representations of strategic issues and problems and mapping strategic thought (for overviews of alternative approaches see Eden and Spender 1998; Hodgkinson and Healey, 2008; Hodgkinson and Sparrow, 2002; Huff, 1990; Huff and Jenkins, 2002; Wright, 2008). We focus on the RGT in this chapter because in our view it constitutes one of the most versatile and insightful approaches for mapping strategic thought presently available. However, its potential remains under-utilized vis-à-vis its strengths (Hodgkinson, Wright, and Anderson, 2015). Accordingly, our goal is to provide an overview of its theoretical and methodological origins and then show how, in departing from those origins, strategy scholars have used the RGT in a variety of innovative ways to advance strategic management theory, research, and practice, probing into a rich variety of fundamental cognitive processes of strategy formulation and implementation within and between levels of analysis. We conclude our overview with some suggestions for future methodological advances and substantive applications.

Background theory underpinning the initial development of the repertory grid technique

Underpinned by *personal construct theory* (PCT) the RGT originated in the field of clinical psychology (Kelly, 1955). PCT represents a major attempt to account for the way in which individuals construe meaning in order to make inferences about the world. According to PCT, individuals navigate their intra- and inter-personal worlds using a series of "personal constructs," which they employ in order to make sense of the stimuli, known as "elements," encountered variously as they go about their business. Emphasizing the uniqueness of individuals, as opposed to their commonalities, PCT is arguably one of the most prominent examples of an idiographic theory of individual differences. It is based on the fundamental premise that individuals behave in a manner akin to natural scientists in their everyday lives, formulating hypotheses about their worlds, which they then seek to "validate" through lived experience. To the extent that their hypotheses are confirmed, individuals' personal construct systems remain intact. In the event that their hypotheses are falsified, however, ordinarily they will set about the task of revising their construct systems, as we elaborate in further detail below. In this way, the labels people construct as individuals not only enable them to make sense of their past, but also help to guide their future actions.

Kelly (1955) developed PCT around a fundamental postulate which states that "a person's processes are psychologically channelized by the ways in which he anticipates events" (p. 46). Based on this postulate, Kelly articulated his theory through 11 corollaries; for example, he talks about the importance of people's construct systems of beliefs (the *construction corollary*), which are arranged in a hierarchical order (the *organization corollary*). Constructs are the language people use, and hence they represent the way they see/anticipate events by construing their replication. These constructs are always bi-polar in nature because Kelly (1955) believed that people make sense of the way they see the world based on similarities and differences (the *dichotomy corollary*). Hence, it is paramount to see constructs in their bi-polarity (not only as dualisms but also as *duality*), because simply focusing on either pole of a given construct, *per se*, misses the vitality of the relation between constructs (Butt, 2004). In fact, the juxtaposition of seemingly opposite poles does not denote the cancellation of possibilities, but rather the potential creation of new possibilities (Farjoun, 2010). Through these ongoing experiences and interactions, perpetually making choices in relation to others, objects, events, *and* situations (see Chen and Miller, 2011; Cooper, 2005; Ingold, 2000; Wright and Lam, 2002), as indicated above, people behave like "scientists," always practicing, testing, and re-testing (validating, invalidating, and revalidating) their fragmented views of the world. In this respect, Kelly believed that people's everyday engagement with the world as it presents itself in front of them is primarily pre-reflective (not always deliberate), but, nevertheless, intentional. Thoughts, feelings, and actions are intimately related, as constructs are embedded in actions themselves (Butt, 2004). The person Kelly (1955) theorized about is really a person-in-relation to significant others; through direct engagement with an inter-subjective world (Kelly, 1955: 503; Kalekin-Fishman and Walker, 1996) it is possible for people to construe the world in ways common to themselves and significant others (the *commonality corollary*). In fact, Kelly called his theory a Theory of *Personal* Constructs to emphasize the idea that people take responsibility for their own construct systems (the *individuality corollary*).

According to Wright, Paroutis, and Blettner (2013), grounding strategy research in PCT will enable scholars to advance the psychological analysis of strategic management by building theory that incorporates directly the dimensions/dualities that drive managers' judgments in the act of strategizing. Viewed from this standpoint, the goal of the RGT in strategic management research, as in wider spheres of application, is to analyze the systems of constructs used by individuals to understand, structure, and make sense of changes to their environment(s), thereby revealing their internal logic(s) of practicing in the world (cf. Sandberg and Tsoukas, 2011). However, as we shall see, the primary strength of the RGT lies in its inherent flexibility, and over the years it has come to enjoy considerable success in applied studies of social cognition, in a wide variety of domains well beyond its clinical roots and idiographic origins (cf. Forgas, 1976, 1978; Forgas, Brown, and Menyhart, 1980; Smith and Gibson, 1988; Smith, Hartley, and Stewart, 1978; Fransella, Bell, and Bannister, 2004; Stewart and Stewart, 1981). This is no less true in the strategic management field, where a willingness to move beyond the confines of PCT is opening up the possibilities of data collection and comparative analysis on a scale that would not be possible using conventional approaches to RGT.

Repertory grid technique and repertory grids

Overview of basic concepts (elements and constructs)

In the classic approach to administering the RGT, repertory grids take the form of a two-way classification of data, in which issues for investigation are integrated with the individual's views of the world, *based on lived experience* (for accounts of wider applications and a deeper appreciation of alternative designs and methods for analyzing repertory grids see Daniels, Markoczy, and de Chernatony, 1994; Easterby-Smith, 1980; Easterby-Smith, Thorpe, and Holman, 1996; Fransella, 2003; Hodgkinson and Sparrow, 2002; Huff, 1990; Jankowicz, 2003; Stewart and Stewart, 1981; Wright, 2006). Figure 8.1 illustrates a completed grid, following this classic approach, elicited from the deputy chairman of an organization in the course of an ongoing study of boards of directors being undertaken by the second author of this chapter. The object of the exercise is to enable participants to reflect on the importance of nine critical board-related activities. The grid itself comprises an empty matrix/grid, which is used to record the interview conversation (Centre for Person Computer Studies, 2009). In its empty state, the grid is deceptively structured with its matrix-like appearance. But the ultimate powers of the RGT lie in its flexibility and versatility, once the purpose of the interview is established and the domain of investigation is incorporated into the design of the grid interview.

Adopting the classic approach, four essential features of the grid exercise must be pilot tested before embarking on a substantive piece of work, namely, the elements, constructs, rating task, and the forced choice aspects:

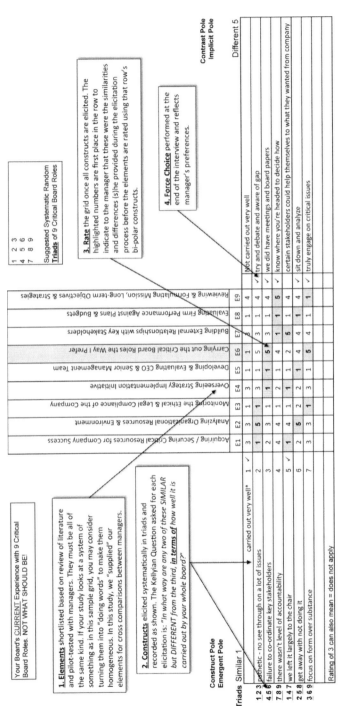

Using Kelly's (1955) Repertory Grid Technique

* This 'supplied' bi-polar construct was used at the end of the grid rating exercise as an overall cross-check for the board member's assessment of of each of the 9 critical board roles
✓ Checkmark indicates respondent's preferred construct pole when critical board roles are carried out well.
§ This completed grid is then input into a grid program (e.g. RepGrid5) to generate Principal Component Analysis, Construct Loadings, Construct Correlations and Cognitive Maps. If your grid study has multiple respondents and you want to compare between subjects, be sure to have your elements 'supplied' as a common denominator. You can then group individual grids in an Excel file to determine emerging knowledge structures, master constructs and then to calculate average ratings before inputting into a grid program.

FIGURE 8.1 Completed Repertory Grid elicited from an executive (Deputy Chairman), as part of a study on effective boards

1. Elements (listed vertically in the middle of the grid)

The elements are a key feature of the grid that determines the research area to be investigated (Bell, 1990; Bell, Vince, and Costigan, 2002). They can be either "supplied" or "elicited" from participants (using role titles or a series of short questions). Since the predominant focus is on the discernment of meaning, most researchers undertaking grid work will likely want to present common elements across sample groups to facilitate systematic comparison/analysis. In Figure 8.1, the (researcher supplied) elements are labelled as E1, E2, E3...E9. All grid elements must demonstrate a number of characteristics. *Homogeneity*: elements must consist solely of objects, people, events, or situations, not combinations of these categories; element heterogeneity is problematic when seeking to elicit constructs that are to be used to evaluate the complete set of elements in question (Wright and Lam, 2002). *Discrete and representative*: elements should provide reasonable coverage of the key aspects of whatever is being investigated. Although the number of elements can range from 8–24 (and even more in clinical settings), according to Stewart and Stewart (1981) about nine elements is an adequate number for most applications in business and management research. This is because any larger number will extend significantly the time taken to administer the grid for construct elicitation. *As short as possible*: elements must be specific and easily understood by the respondent. (Strictly speaking, participants must have experience of the elements, so as to render them personally meaningful.)

2. Constructs (elicited from respondent and listed along the rows from left to right)

Again following the classic approach to grid administration, construct elicitation is performed through a process known as triadic comparison of the elements. The researcher asks the *Kellyian Question* (often with a *qualifier* at the end) to focus the elicitation: "In what way are any two of these [elements] similar to one another, but also different from the third (*in terms of* ...)." The resultant bi-polar constructs represent the dimensions along which the individual strategist makes sense of his or her world. The individual's personal constructs help him or her to describe and differentiate the strategy elements as they view them on the basis of their lived experience. The constructs thus elicited are recorded verbatim (that is, in the participants' own words, unedited) on the repertory grid. The key here is to probe more deeply the meaning of the participants' (super-ordinate) constructs, through a process of laddering (Hinkle, 1965). This process entails asking repeatedly the participant what he or she means by the construct terms thus elicited, until further elaboration fails to yield additional clarity.

3. Rating the grid (the numbers recorded on the grid)

Once the researcher is satisfied that the construct elicitation process has reached saturation, the next stage is to ask the participant to rate (or "rank") the elements on a series of bi-polar rating scales, derived from the participant's bi-polar constructs. In the present case, shown in Figure 8.1, the nine strategy elements are to be evaluated using a series of 5-point semantic differential scales, derived from the personal constructs, as indicated. In the present example, which is typical of RGT applications in general, ratings of "1" and ratings towards "1" reflect judgments indicating that the element in question is described more appropriately by the construct description located at the left hand polar extreme element (singular) is the focus of this sentence. Ratings of "5" and ratings towards "5" indicate that the contrast poles, located towards the right hand side of the grid describe more appropriately the elements in question. The numbers to the left of each elicited bi-polar construct row, indicate which particular triadic combination of elements elicited the particular construct in question. In each case, the two digits underlined signify the particular combination of elements adjudged to be most alike during triadic comparison of the elements; technically speaking, the construct poles emerging from the pairs of elements adjudged more alike are known as the emergent poles, as opposed to the contrast poles, the latter referring to the construct poles arising from the participants' descriptions of how the third, least alike elements, differ from the two more similar ones within the triads in question.

In sum, the process of linking constructs to elements signifies the ways in which the constructs are used in relation to the elements, thus articulating the meaning of each side of the construct poles. Kelly (1955) called this process, "putting numbers to words." Longer scales can be used (for example 7-point or even 10-point scales), but on the basis of our experience the use of such longer scales is rarely advisable, not least because participants are typically unable to make full use of the complete range of scale points.

4. Forced choice of elicited strategic construct poles

Once the grid has been elicited and rated, participants are sometimes asked to indicate a preferred side of each construct pole, denoted by a tick. These choices are often revealing to participants and researchers alike.

Analysis of repertory grids

A detailed consideration of the analysis of repertory grids lies beyond the scope of the present chapter. In general, however, repertory grids can be subjected to a wide range of multivariate analysis visualization techniques including multidimensional scaling (MDS) and related principal components analysis (PCA) techniques and hierarchical cluster analysis (HCA) techniques. MDS and PCA techniques are especially powerful as basis for revealing the underlying psychometric structure of participants' representations of elements in multidimensional space (i.e. construct space), whereas HCA techniques are useful for revealing the underlying hierarchical structure of grid data.

A number of specialist computer supported tools are available to assist with the analysis of repertory grid data, either in web-form or as software packages.[1] Repertory grids can also be analyzed using standard statistical packages such as SPSS.

Figure 8.2 illustrates the output from Gaines and Shaw's (2010) *Rep5 Conceptual Representation Software*, as applied to the sample grid outlined in Figure 8.1. As illustrated, this particular software enables researchers to derive both spatial and hierarchical representations, through a combination of PCA and HCA techniques (for overviews and illustrated applications of a range of related approaches, see

(a) Spatial cognitive map (principal components analysis)

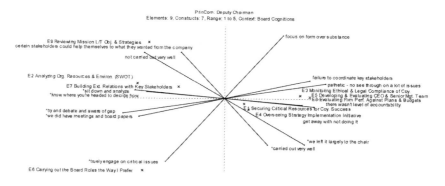

(b) Dendrogram (hierarchical cluster analysis)

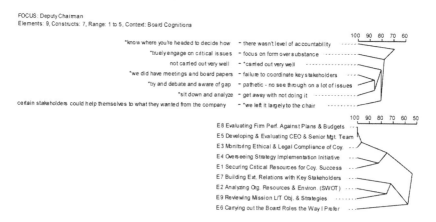

FIGURE 8.2   Sample output from the analysis of the repertory grid data elicited from an executive (Deputy Chairman), as part of a study on effective boards using the Rep5 Conceptual Representation Software

Daniels, Markoczy, and de Chernatony, 1994; Fransella *et al.*, 2004; Forgas, 1976, 1978; Forgas *et al.*, 1980; Ginsberg, 1989; Hodgkinson, 1997a, 2005; Hodgkinson *et al.*, 2015; Jankowicz, 1990, 2003; Smith and Gibson, 1988; Smith *et al.*, 1978; Stewart and Stewart, 1981).

Going beyond PCT

Although the RGT was developed by Kelly (1955) specifically to operationalize the theory of personal constructs, most researchers in the organization sciences have opted to separate the theory from the method and use just the technique (or modifications of it) as a powerful data collection tool in its own right, as an addition to the general kitbag of tools for externalizing actors' mental representations of organizational life (see for example Cammock, Nilakant, and Dakin, 1995; Hodgkinson, 1997a, 2005; Hodgkinson *et al.*, 2015; Huang, Wright, Chiu, and Wang, 2008). In the remainder of this chapter we illustrate how, in going beyond PCT, the RGT can be utilized as a versatile methodological tool for strategic management studies. Table 8.1 summarizes what we consider to be the principal benefits and drawbacks of moving increasingly beyond PCT, as an aid to would-be users who are considering how best to implement the RGT in the context of their own work.

RGT applications in strategic management research

In this section we highlight on a selective basis the wide range of alternative approaches to RGT that have been adopted across a diversity of topic areas in strategic management. Table 8.2 provides an overview of the relevant contributions from 2000 to 2013, while in the following subsections we consider in detail how the RGT has helped advance particular themes and debates in a given topic area. Inevitably, a wide range of considerations, well beyond the scope of this chapter, need to be factored in when arbitrating among the various alternative approaches and it is not our intention to be prescriptive in respect of these matters. Rather, our overarching goal is to demonstrate how and why the RGT is potentially so insightful for strategic management research and what it has contributed to particular topic areas to date.

Unpacking diversification strategy

In one of the earliest strategy-related applications, Dunn, Cahill, Dukes, and Ginsberg (1986) applied the RGT to an analysis of how seventeen criminal justice practitioners and non-practitioners interpreted criminal justice information in a large urban municipality. They concluded that, relative to other methods as a basis for understanding actors' frames of reference, the RGT is flexible, efficient, systematic and easily reproducible. Subsequently, Ginsberg (1989, 1990, 1994) further extended its application to the strategy field directly, through a series of

TABLE 8.1 Alternative conceptions of the repertory grid technique (RGT)

Approach	Definition	Advantages	Disadvantages
Original	The theoretical basis is personal construct theory (PCT) and the method follows closely all of the steps as outlined by Kelly (1955), the originator of the RGT	Provides a firm foundation for gaining deep insights into the thought processes of small numbers of individuals	The number of issues that can be studied is constrained Limited scope for methodological innovation Large scale comparisons are problematic
Original-developed	The theoretical basis is PCT and the method follows most steps postulated by Kelly but departs in the way some steps are interpreted and/or combined	The methodological departure could lead to new findings	The number of issues that can be studied is constrained The overall contribution attempted might not be perceived as novel enough
Independent	The theoretical basis departs significantly from PCT	The RGT is adapted in innovative ways to address a potentially more diverse set of research issues Potential to contribute new methodological and conceptual approaches, ones better suited to larger-scale data collection and comparative analysis	Researchers may need to work harder to legitimize their approach in the eyes of PCT traditionalists

publications that advanced understanding of the socio-cognitive microfoundations of diversification strategy, drawing in turn on Prahalad and Bettis's (1986) seminal work pertaining to the notion of the dominant logic. Responding directly to their call for the development and use of more creative methods to elicit top managers' cognitive maps, he advocated the RGT as the method of choice for probing into how executive teams construe their organizations' business portfolios.

Understanding the socio-cognitive dynamics of competitive positioning strategy

Much of the literature on competitive strategy, epitomized by the work of the positioning school (e.g. Oster, 1990; Porter, 1980), is predicated on the assumption that business environments are objective entities waiting to be discovered through

TABLE 8.2 Studies using the repertory grid technique in strategy research since 2000

Authors	Year	Study title/ indicative focus	Sample	Grid elements	Key contribution
Daniels, Johnson, and de Chernatony	2002	"Task and institutional influences on managers' mental models of competition."	N = 32 senior managers (18 executives + 14 middle managers) from within the UK Personal Financial Services Industry.	Used visual card sorts of named firms (i.e. the elements) to elicit managers' understanding of the bases of competition (i.e. the constructs).	Task and institutional environments were associated variously with convergence and divergence of participants' mental models.
O'Higgins	2002	"Non-executive directors on boards in Ireland: Co-operation, characteristics and contributions."	N = 26 prominent non-executive directors and chairman, all involved in the selection of fellow (non-executive) directors.	Effective (2), mediocre (2), and ineffective (2) role incumbents, ideal non-exec director role, and "self" (i.e. 8 elements in total).	Studied the selection criteria in use implicitly by decision makers in the appointment of non-executive directors, in an attempt to render explicit how and why certain people are chosen to serve on boards in this crucial governance role. Found that non-executives co-opted mainly through "old boys network," with remarkable homogeneity among participants in terms of their cognitive structures, leading the author to conclude that Irish boards lack diversity. The study also identified the key attributes that enable non-executive directors to fulfill their board roles in this context.

TABLE 8.2 continued

Authors	Year	Study title/ indicative focus	Sample	Grid elements	Key contribution
De Leon and Guild	2003	"Using repertory grid to identify intangibles in business plans."	N = 10 In-depth interviews with 5 venture capitalists and 5 entrepreneurs.	Elements were different business plans. Respondents asked to recall 6 business plans during past 18 months: 2 great hits, 2 average / marginal, and 2 rejected.	Identified the intangibles assessed by investors and communicated by entrepreneurs during investment decision making in the early stages of developing technology based ventures in Canada.
Spencer, Peyrefitte, and Churchman	2003	"Consensus and divergence in perceptions of cognitive strategic groups: Evidence from the health care industry."	N = 20 Hospital administrators in health care industry.	Supplied 20 element cards containing hospital names and asked respondents to sort them in terms of similarities.	Found convergence and divergence among administrators' cognitive maps, with core beliefs shared by the majority of participants. Cognitive strategic groups focus managers' attention and help them in deciding how to act and react in the marketplace.
Wright, Butler, and Priem	2003	"Asian cognitions of the strategic management process."	N = 34 Asian executives from 28 companies	12 researcher-supplied elements (e.g.: evaluating corporate governance, implementing strategy, liaising with top management team, formulating new strategies).	Identified through the use of "verb" elements how senior executives describe their strategy making experiences. The resulting cognitive maps were feedback to participants as a "psychological mirror" to enable deeper reflection on their views of the entire strategic management process.

TABLE 8.2 continued

Authors	Year	Study title/ indicative focus	Sample	Grid elements	Key contribution
Bourne and Jenkins	2005	"Eliciting managers' personal values: An adaptation of the laddering interview method."	N = 2 Demonstrates using 2 senior managers (project manager and division head).	Used a combination of work and non-work elements to reveal the participants' personal values.	Given constraints on researcher access to senior executives and the need to keep interviews short, the authors developed an easier and quicker way to complete the interview with meaningful elicitation of core personal values from senior executives, using a modified version of Hinkle's (1965) laddering technique.
Wright	2006	"Rigor and relevance using the repertory grid technique in strategy research."	N = 20 Board members from 17 listed companies.	9 verb elements that made up critical board roles of the board.	Demonstrated how boards of directors see, interpret, and make sense of their experiences. Recommendations for better boards, possibly using results from cognitive mapping and content analysis of board members' strategic constructs.
Wright, Paroutis, and Blettner	2013	"How useful are the strategic tools we teach in business schools?"	N = 46 practicing managers	Used 12 of the most popular strategic tools taught in business school capstone course; and added an additional element called "the type of strategy tool/ technique I prefer."	Identified the tools construed to be more or less useful in the language of practicing managers. Also identified core perceptual dimensions used to make judgment calls on a given tool's usefulness

formal analysis. Since the late 1980s, however, there has been growing recognition among strategic management and organizational behavior researchers that, ultimately, it is actors' perceptions of competitive positioning, filtered through their extant mental models, that form the basis for strategy formulation and, therefore, that these mental models are worthy of study (e.g. Calori, Johnson, and Sarnin, 1992, 1994; Daniels, Johnson, and de Chernatony, 2002; Hodgkinson and Johnson, 1994; Porac et al., 1989; Reger, 1990; Reger and Huff, 1993; Spencer, Peyrefitte, and Churchman, 2003). As Porac and Thomas observe:

> From a cognitive perspective, decision makers act on a mental model of the environment. Thus any explanation for strategic responses to competitive pressures must ultimately, take into consideration the mental models of competitive strategists ... before competitive strategies can be formulated, decision makers must have an image of who their rivals are and on what dimensions they will compete. Given the diverse range of organizational forms and decision makers' limited capacity to process complex inter-organizational cues, the task of defining "the competition" is both important and problematic.
>
> *(1990: 224–225)*

Perhaps not surprisingly, therefore, of all the topic areas in strategic management, this is the one that has witnessed the greatest volume of applications of RGT-related methods and methodological innovations. In one of the earliest studies, Walton (1986) investigated how top managers in the financial industry (based in New York) categorize successful and unsuccessful firms. As part of a phenomenological and multi-method design, he employed a variant of the RGT to examine top managers' descriptions of 10 firms. Incorporating their own firm, participants were each required to identify five successful firms and five less successful firms, which served as the stimulus elements in a series of individual level MDS analyses.

Adopting the classic triadic approach to construct elicitation, Reger (1987, 1990) undertook an exploratory study of strategists' mental models of competition among banks in the Chicago area. Using the names of 18 of the largest bank holding companies over the period 1982–1985 as the (researcher-supplied) elements, her 24 participants were required to explain how any two of three of the banks selected at random were strategically similar in the way they operated and carried out their business in the market, but also differed from the third bank in the relevant triad. In line with standard practice when using the triadic approach to construct elicitation, the exercise was repeated until each participant had reached saturation (i.e. no further new constructs were generated). Her findings provided a number of important insights into how the dimensions underpinning the competitive positioning strategies of key players were construed differentially by her informants.

Reger and Huff (1993) extended this line of inquiry to address the question of whether perceptions of competitive groups were shared widely within the banking sector or whether they were more idiosyncratic. Using the same dataset as Reger (1990), they found that construct differences notwithstanding, industry participants held convergent or shared mental representations in respect of how firms were grouped, in line with expectations derived from the theory of strategic groups, emanating from the work of the positioning school (e.g. McGee and Thomas, 1986).

In a further extension to this line of inquiry, Reger and Palmer (1996) compared the findings from Reger's Chicago (1990) study (based on data gathered in 1986) with a fresh wave of repertory grid data, gathered in 1989, from interviews with 25 upper-echelon managers in the Arizona financial intermediary industry. They also compared the findings of both of these field studies with the results of Walton's (1986) earlier repertory grid study of the New York financial industry, the main aim being to demonstrate how, until absolutely necessary, managers tend to rely on old/obsolete maps when seeking to navigate new environments, the phenomenon referred to as the cognitive inertia hypothesis (Porac and Thomas, 1990).

In a wide-ranging critique of the then emerging literature pertaining to the cognitive analysis of competitive position strategy, Hodgkinson (1997b) lamented the dearth of authentic longitudinal studies; that is, studies based on prospective research designs and appropriately large sample sizes, as required ultimately to validate the inertial effects of actors' mental models of competition suggested by the work of Reger and Palmer (1996) and hypothesized several years earlier by Porac and Thomas (1990). To this end, Hodgkinson (1997a, 2005) employed a questionnaire-based variant of the RGT, which entailed the use of a standardized list of researcher-supplied bi-polar construct scales in conjunction with a standardized list of competitor category stimulus elements to examine the extent to which UK residential estate agents' mental models of competition remained stable or changed in the face of significant shifts in the fortunes of the housing market, following the dramatic entrance of major corporate players. The participants were required to complete the questionnaire by generating their own lists of named competitors, which included their own firms, in response to the standardized list of competitor categories. In keeping with the earlier work of Reger and Huff (1993) and Reger and Palmer (1996) he found clear evidence of mental model convergence and stability across the sector as a whole, indicative of industry-level myopia and cognitive inertia.

Taken as a whole, the findings of the foregoing studies support the idea that within a given sector, the mental models of competitive strategists from rival organizations generally converge around a shared identity or "cognitive strategic group" (Peteraf and Shanley, 1997). However, a number of other studies, some of which have similarly employed variants of the RGT (e.g. Daniels, Johnson, and de Chernatony, 1994, 2002; Daniels, de Chernatony, and Johnson, 1995), others of which have employed alternative approaches to cognitive mapping (e.g. Calori, *et al.*, 1992, 1994; Hodgkinson and Johnson, 1994), present a more complex picture. Daniels, Johnson, and de Chernatony (1994), for example, investigated differences in and similarities between managers' mental models of competition in a study of the UK off-shore pump industry, employing a visual card sort technique in conjunction with the RGT. In contrast with Hodgkinson's (1997a, 2005) study, but in keeping with the work of Hodgkinson and Johnson's (1994) study of the UK grocery sector, which adopted an alternative approach to cognitive mapping, predicated on hierarchical categorization theory (Rosch *et al.*, 1976; Porac and Thomas, 1987), they uncovered evidence of mental model diversity among participants drawn from within and across rival organizations.

A number of more recent studies, again using a range of techniques including the RGT, have uncovered evidence suggesting that managers exhibit commonality and individuality simultaneously in their mental representations of competitive positioning (e.g. Daniels *et al.*, 2002; Simpson and Wilson, 1999; Spencer *et al.*, 2003). Unfortunately, as argued repeatedly by Hodgkinson and colleagues (e.g. Hodgkinson, 1997b, 2001a, 2001b, 2005, 2015; Hodgkinson and Sparrow, 2002) the fact that the overwhelming majority of cognitive studies in this topic area are based on small-scale, cross-sectional designs, combined with the fact there has been very little consistency in the methods deployed from one study to another, has meant that progress to date has been hampered in terms of systematic knowledge accumulation, not least due to a methods x sector confound. Perhaps these sorts of problems, arising from a desire to innovate new methods as a foundation for larger scale empirical endeavors as the field matures, are only to be expected in the early stages of the development of any new subfield. Nevertheless, it is a cause for concern that so little progress has been achieved in more than a quarter of a century of scholarship! (For a more detailed analysis of the pitfalls and possibilities of alternative approaches to the RGT and related methods in this topic area, see the interchange between Daniels and Johnson [2002], and Hodgkinson [2002]).

Strategic issue diagnosis

Strategic issue diagnosis has been an enduring problem in strategic management research. Strategic issues have important implications for organizational performance (Chattopadhyay, Glick, and Huber, 2001; Dutton and Dukerich, 1991). Founded on the basic idea of strengths, weaknesses, opportunities and threats (SWOT) analysis (Andrews, 1971), a body of work on issue diagnosis has problematized the question of how managers construe strategic issues. How strategists' interpret and make sense of strategic issues provides the impetus for their decisions and subsequent actions (Kiesler and Sproull, 1982; Sharma, 2000). Accordingly, making sense of how strategy practitioners understand strategic issues is a significant area of study especially in an increasingly uncertain world (Dutton, Fahey, and Narayanan, 1983; Plambeck and Weber, 2009).

The theoretical foundations of this topic stem from the work of Dutton and Jackson (1987), who like a number of scholars investigating the socio-cognitive dynamics of competitive positioning strategy (e.g. Hodgkinson and Johnson, 1994; Porac *et al.*, 1989; Porac and Thomas, 1990, 1994), use categorization theory

(Rosch *et al.*, 1976) to inform the analysis of managers' mental representations of strategic issues. Building on these theoretical foundations, empirical studies such as Jackson and Dutton's (1988) seminal paper on discerning strategic issue labels provided groundbreaking insights into the importance of cognitive processes for issue identification and how key decision makers classify the threats and opportunities facing their organizations. More generally, this line of work addresses how the interpretation of strategic issues is bound inextricably with questions of organizational identity, with attendant impacts on managerial action and organizational performance (see, e.g. Chattopadhyay *et al.*, 2001; Dutton and Dukerich, 1991; Thomas, Clark, and Gioia, 1993; Thomas and McDaniel, 1990).

Building on Walton's (1986) earlier study of competitor definition, Dutton, Walton, and Abrahamson (1989) elicited the constructs/dimensions used to sort strategic issues in a port authority. Their approach compared the 26 dimensions identified in three literatures to their empirical work using the RGT, to examine the degree of overlap in the dimensions strategic decision makers used when understanding strategic issues. They maintained that these dimensions influenced decision makers' attention. Their findings suggested that describing the meaning decision makers apply to issues may be equally important for understanding the links between cognition and individual and organizational actions. (For the most recent application of RGT in this area, see Hodgkinson *et al.* [2015].)

Understanding the role(s) of non-executive directors

Strategic management scholars have been interested in the nature and role of particular strategists sitting on corporate boards; from the CEO (Pearce and Zahra, 1991) to, more recently, the chief strategy officer (Angwin, Paroutis, and Mitson, 2009; Menz and Scheef, 2014; Paroutis and Pettigrew, 2005) and strategy teams more generally (Paroutis and Pettigrew, 2007). Although non-executive directors have been the focus of finance studies (Weisbach, 1988), it was the study of UK firms by McNulty and Pettigrew that pushed this agenda in strategic management research (McNulty and Pettigrew, 1999; Pettigrew and McNulty, 1995). Their work provides insights into the role and influence of non-executive directors and has shown that part-time board members do not simply ratify decisions made by all-powerful executives. They found that non-executive directors' involvement was influenced by changing norms about corporate governance, the history and performance of the company, the process and conduct of board meetings, and the nature and extent of informal dialogue with their executive counterparts between board meetings (McNulty and Pettigrew, 1999).

Methodologically, Stiles and Taylor (2001) advocated the need for more descriptive research at the board level that "tells it as it is," not as it should be or as we would like it to be (see also Pugliese *et al.*, 2009; Tricker, 1994). Other governance scholars have called similarly for more "fine-grained" research investigating boards and directors (Dalton *et al.*, 1998; Dalton *et al.*, 1999) and strategic leadership (Conger, 1988; Lord and Emrich, 2001; Walsh, 1995). More than 20 years have elapsed since Pettigrew (1992) argued similarly that research on boards should focus on the actual behaviors of boards, echoing Zahra and Pearce's (1990) concerns that relatively few studies of board governance are based on actual reports from and observations of the behavior of the directors themselves (see also Stiles, 2001). Challenging research that collects archival and cross-sectional survey data, Huse (2000) recommended more "venturesome" methods and designs to open up the black box of board dynamics. Against this rich backdrop, O'Higgins' (2002) work on what constitutes effective non-executive directors in the context of Irish Boards, using researcher-supplied role titles pertaining to effective and ineffective directors as elements, provides important first steps in the investigation of the mental models of incumbents occupying this critical role. The purpose of her study, through construct elicitation, was to reveal what dimensions are used by non-executive directors in their decision making concerning whether or not to sit on particular boards.

Entrepreneurial cognition

The rise of new scholarly journals such as the *Strategic Entrepreneurship Journal*, launched recently by the Strategic Management Society, reflects the increasing interest of strategy researchers in the topic of entrepreneurship. In an attempt to open the black box of decision making in what is yet another key area of scholarly endeavor crying out for greater precision, there have been growing efforts to study the cognitive foundations of entrepreneurial work (for an overview, see Gregoire, Corbett, and McMullen, 2011). In this regard, De Leon and Guild's (2003) study using the RGT has paved the way for larger scale investigations in future work. Applying the RGT to an analysis of how venture capitalists and entrepreneurs evaluated six business plans (two that were successful, two that were marginal, and two that were rejected), the findings helped reveal the importance of intangible criteria during the investment-decision process of early stage technology-based ventures. The authors highlighted the benefits of the technique, claiming it enabled them to elicit the constructs experts actually use to evaluate business proposals, without contaminating them unduly by forcing the participants to respond to researcher-imposed questions.

Understanding strategy-making activity and practice

The focus on strategic agents and their actions has become more prominent recently, following the rise of the strategy-as-practice perspective, which views strategy "as a socially accomplished, situated activity arising from the actions and interactions of multiple level actors" (Jarzabkowski, 2005: 6) and considers strategy not only as something an organization has but something that its members "do" (Jarzabkowski, 2005; Jarzabkowski, Balogun, and Seidl, 2007; Johnson, Melin, and Whittington, 2003; Whittington, 2006, 2007; Vaara and Whittington, 2012). Revealing what strategists actually do when they engage in strategy work and just as importantly, understanding the enablers and disablers of such work, could well provide important insights to help improve this important managerial practice. One approach to this line inquiry is to advance understanding of what strategy workers consider to constitute the strategy making process, juxtaposing the ideas of actors involved in such work against the key ideas in leading strategy textbooks (e.g. Grant, 2013; Hitt, Ireland, and Hoskisson, 2007; Johnson, Whittington, and Scholes, 2011; Porter, 1980, 1985) regarding the ostensive and performative aspects of strategy, strategizing, and strategic management (see, e.g. Angwin, Cummings, and Smith, 2007; Kachra and Schnietz, 2008; Paroutis and Heracleous, 2013; Paroutis, Heracleous, and Angwin, 2013).

Building on this idea, Wright *et al.*, (2003) and Wright (2004) employed the RGT in its classic form to elicit managers' mental representations of the strategy-making process. Using a set of verb elements Wright *et al.* (2003) identified the core perceptual dimensions (the labeling of the x and y-axis on a two dimensional cognitive map) and the language executives actually used to describe their experience in connection with a range of strategy-making activities. In a follow-up investigation, Wright (2004) compared the cognitive maps pertaining to the strategy-making process of managers from high- and low-performing firms, assessed by return on equity (ROE). He found marked differences in the way executives in these two types of firms think about their strategizing.

Concluding remarks

The body of work reviewed in this chapter demonstrates abundantly how the diverse family of approaches to knowledge elicitation and analysis known collectively as the repertory grid technique, or Rep Grid, has advanced the cognitive perspective on strategic management. As we have shown, the key strength of the RGT lies in its versatility, both in terms of elicitation and analysis, properties that have enabled scholars experimenting with a range of alternative approaches to advance the science and practice of strategic management across a broad spectrum of topic areas. However, as also implied, its potential remains underutilized, and there is much interesting further work yet to be completed, using this insightful collection of procedures (Hodgkinson *et al.*, 2015).

Going forward, as in the past, it is clear that scholars contemplating use of the RGT face a fundamental trade-off. In its classic, idiographic form, the Rep Grid provides a powerful basis for probing deeply into the mind of the strategist. Inevitably, however, that depth comes at the expense of comparability. As demonstrated by the work of Hodgkinson (1997a, 2005), such is the versatility of the method that it is possible to adapt it in ways that render it suitable for use in complex multilevel, longitudinal studies of the scale required ultimately to advance understanding of the socio-cognitive dynamics pertaining to many of the strategy field's most pressing problems. However, the comparability afforded by adapting the RGT to enable such nomothetic applications comes at the expense of the richness afforded by more traditional idiographic approaches, rooted in PCT. Unfortunately, there are no straightforward solutions to this dilemma, which all would-be adopters of the RGT must confront. The only firm prescriptive advice we can offer to prospective users is that they should first ascertain the approach that best addresses their own particular needs. In our experience, pilot testing is an essential requirement for this purpose.

It has been said that the creative use of the RGT is constrained only by the limitations of the human imagination (Fransella and Bannister, 1977; Stewart and Stewart, 1981). The work reviewed in this chapter bears out this observation. Our hope is that it will inspire current and future generations of strategic management scholars and wider organizational researchers to join us on what is clearly an exciting and productive journey.

Note

1   See, for instance: GridCor: www.terapiacognitiva.net/record/ gridcor.htm; GridSuite: www.gridsuite.de/; IdioGrid: www.idiogrid.com/; intanges: www.intanges.com/ relaunch/index.php?id=4&L=1; nextexpertizer: www.next-practice.com/ nextexpertizer; OpenRepGrid: www.openrepgrid.org/; Rep5: www.repgrid.com; Repertory Grid Tool: http://repertorygridtool.com/; sci:vesco: www.eac-leipzig.de/ scivescoweb; WebGrid 5: http://gigi.cpsc.ucalgary.ca:2000/.

References

Andrews, K. (1971). *The Concept of Corporate Strategy.* Homewood, IL: Irwin.

Angwin, D., Cummings, S., and Smith, C. S. (2007). *The Strategy Pathfinder: Core Concepts and Micro-cases.* Oxford: Blackwell Publishing.

Angwin, D., Paroutis, S., and Mitson, S. (2009). Connecting up strategy: Are senior strategy directors (SSDs) a missing link? *California Management Review*, Spring, 51(3): 74–94.

Barnard, C. I. (1938). *The Functions of the Executive.* Cambridge, MA: Harvard University Press.

Bell, R. C. (1990). Analytic issues in the use of repertory grid technique. In G. J. Neimeyer and R. A. Neimeyer (eds), *Advances in Personal Construct Psychology, Vol. 1* (25–48). New York: JAI Press.

Bell, R. C., Vince, J., and Costigan, J. (2002). Which vary more in repertory grid data: Constructs or elements? *Journal of Constructivist Psychology*, 15(4): 305–315.

Bourne, H. and Jenkins, M. (2005). Eliciting managers' personal values: An adaptation of the laddering interview method. *Organizational Research Methods*, 8(4): 410–428.

Burr, V., and Butt, T. (1992). *Invitation to Personal Construct Psychology.* England: Whurr Publishers.

Butt, T. (2004). Understanding, explanation, and personal constructs. *Personal Construct Theory and Practice*, 1: 21–27. Retrieved from www.pcp-net.org/journal/pctp04/ butt04.pdf

Calori, R., Johnson, G., and Sarnin, P. (1992). French and British top managers' understanding of the structure and the dynamics of their industries: A cognitive analysis and comparison. *British Journal of Management*, 3(2): 61-78.

Calori, R., Johnson, G., and Sarnin, P. (1994). CEO's cognitive maps and the scope of the organization. *Strategic Management Journal*, 15: 437–457.

Cammock, P., Nilakant, V., and Dakin, S. (1995). Developing a lay model of managerial effectiveness: A social constructionist perspective. *Journal of Management Studies*, 32(4), 443–474.

Centre for Person Computer Studies (2009). *RepGrid 5 Manual*. Canada: Centre for Person Computer Studies.

Chattopadhyay, P., Glick, W. H., and Huber, G. P. (2001). Organizational actions in response to threats and opportunities. *Academy of Management Journal*, 44: 937–955.

Chen, M-J. and Miller, D. (2011). The relational perspective as a business mindset: Managerial implications for East and West. *Academy of Management Perspectives*, 25(3): 6–18.

Conger, J. A. (1988). Qualitative research as the cornerstone methodology for understanding leadership. *Leadership Quarterly*, 9(1), 107–122.

Cooper, R. (2005). Peripheral vision: Relationality. *Organization Studies*, 26(11): 1689–1710.

Dalton, D. R., Daily, C. M., Ellstrand, A. E., and Johnson, J. L. (1998). Meta-analytic reviews of board composition, leadership structure, and financial performance. *Strategic Management Journal*, 19: 269–290.

Dalton, D. R., Daily, C. M., Johnson, J. L. and Ellstrand, A. E. (1999) Number of directors and financial performance: a meta-analysis. *Academy of Management Journal*, 42(6): 674–686.

Daniels, K., de Chernatony, L., and Johnson, G. (1995). Validating a method for mapping managers' mental models of competitive industry structures. *Human Relations*, 48(9): 975–991.

Daniels, K. and Johnson, G. (2002). On trees and triviality traps: Locating the debate on the contribution of cognitive mapping to organizational research. *Organization Studies*, 23(1): 73–81.

Daniels, K., Johnson, G., and de Chernatony, L. (1994). Differences in managerial cognitions of competition. *British Journal of Management*, 5: S21–S29.

Daniels, K., Johnson, G., and de Chernatony, L. (2002). Task and institutional influences on managers' mental models of competition. *Organization Studies*, 23(1): 31–62.

Daniels, K., Markoczy, L., and de Chernatony, L. (1994) Techniques to compare cognitive maps. In C. Stubbart, J. Meindl, and J.F. Porac (eds), *Advances in Managerial Cognition and Organizational Information Processing*, vol. 5 (141–164). Connecticut: JAI Press.

De Leon, E. D. and Guild, P. D. (2003). Using repertory grid to identify intangibles in business plans. *Venture Captial*, 5(2): 135–160.

Dunn, W. N., Cahill, A. G., Dukes, M. J., and Ginsberg, A. (1986). The policy grid: A cognitive methodology for assessing policy dynamics. In W. N. Dunn (ed.), *Policy Analysis: Perspectives, Concepts, and Methods* (355–375). Greenwich, CT: JAI Press.

Dutton, J. E. and Dukerich, J. M. (1991). Keeping an eye on the mirror: Image and identity in organizational adaptation. *Academy of Management Journal*, 34: 517–554.

Dutton, J. E. and Jackson, S. E. (1987). Categorizing strategic issues: Links to organizational action. *Academy of Management Review*, 12(1), 7690.

Dutton, J. E., Fahey, L. and Narayanan, V. K. (1983). Toward understanding strategic issue diagnosis. *Strategic Management Journal*, 4, 307–323.

Dutton, J. E., Walton, J. E., and Abrahamson, E. (1989). Important dimensions of strategic issues: Separating the wheat from the chaff. *Journal of Management Studies*, 26(4): 379–397.

Easterby-Smith, M. (1980). The design, analysis and interpretation of repertory grids. *International Journal of Man-Machine Studies*, 13: 3–24.

Easterby-Smith, M., Thorpe, R., and Holman, D. (1996). Using repertory grids in management. *Journal of European Industrial Training*, 20(3): 3–30.

Eden, C. and Spender, J. C. (eds) (1998). *Managerial and Organizational Cognitions: Theory, Methods and Research*. London, Sage.

Eggers, J. P. and Kaplan, S. (2013). Cognition and capabilities: A multi-level perspective. *The Academy of Management Annals*, 7(1): 295–340.

Farjoun, M. (2010). Beyond dualism: Stability and change as duality. *Academy of Management Review*, 35(2): 202–225.

Forgas, J. P. (1976). The perception of social episodes: Categorical and dimensional representation in two subcultural milieus. *Journal of Personality and Social Psychology*, 34: 199–209.

Forgas, J. P. (1978). Social episodes and social structures in an academic setting: The social environment of an intact group. *Journal of Experimental Social Psychology*, 14: 434–448.

Forgas, J. P., Brown, L. B., and Menyhart, J. (1980). Dimensions of aggression: The perception of aggressive episodes. *British Journal of Social and Clinical Psychology*, 19: 215–227.

Fransella, F. (ed.) (2003). *International Handbook of Personal Construct Psychology*. Chichester: Wiley.

Fransella, F., and Bannister, D. (1977). *A Manual of Repertory Grid Technique*. London: Academic Press.

Fransella, F., Bell, R., and Bannister, D. (2004). *A Manual for Repertory Grid Technique*, 2nd edn. Chichester: Wiley

Gaines, B. R. and Shaw, M. L. G. (2010). *Rep5 Conceptual Representation Software: Introductory Manual for Version 1.0*. Cobble Hill, BC: Centre for Person Computer Studies.

Ginsberg, A. (1989). Construing the business portfolio: A cognitive model of diversification. *Journal of Management Studies*, 26: 417–438.

Ginsberg, A. (1990). Connecting diversification to performance: A sociocognitive approach. *Academy of Management Review*, 15(3): 514–535.

Ginsberg, A. (1994). Minding the competition: From mapping to mastery [Special issue: Competitive Organizational Behavior]. *Strategic Management Journal*, 15: 153–174.

Grant, R. M. (2013). *Contemporary Strategy Analysis*, 8th edn. Chichester: Wiley.

Gregoire, D. A., Corbett, A. C., and McMullen, J. S. (2011). The cognitive perspective in entrepreneurship: An agenda for future research. *Journal of Management Studies*, 48(6): 1443–1477.

Hinkle, D. N. (1965). The change of personal constructs from the viewpoint of a theory of implications. Unpublished doctoral dissertation: Ohio State University.

Hitt, M. A., Ireland, R. D., and Hoskisson, R. E. (2007). *Strategic Management: Competitiveness and Globalization*. Mason, OH: Thomson South-Western.

Hodgkinson, G. P. (1997a). Cognitive inertia in a turbulent market: The case of UK residential estate agents. *Journal of Management Studies*, 34(6): 921–945.

Hodgkinson, G. P. (1997b). The cognitive analysis of competitive structures: A review and critique. *Human Relations*, 50: 625–654.

Hodgkinson, G. P. (2001a). The psychology of strategic management: Diversity and cognition revisited. In C. L. Cooper and I. T. Robertson (eds), *International Review of Industrial and Organizational Psychology*, Vol. 16 (65–119). Chichester: Wiley.

Hodgkinson, G. P. (2001b). Cognitive processes in strategic management: Some emerging trends and future directions. In N. Anderson, D. S. Ones, H. K. Sinangil, and C. Viswesvaran (eds), *Handbook of Industrial, Work and Organizational Psychology*, Vol.2 (416–460). London: Sage.

Hodgkinson, G. P. (2002). Comparing managers' mental models of competition: Why self-report measures of belief similarity won't do. *Organization Studies*, 23(1): 63–72.

Hodgkinson, G. P. (2005). *Images of Competitive Space: A Study of Managerial and Organizational Strategic Cognition*. Basingstoke: Palgrave Macmillan.

Hodgkinson, G. P. (2015). Reflections on the interplay between cognition, action and outcomes in industries and business markets: What have we learned so far and where might we go next? *Industrial Marketing Management*, 48(Special Issue), 12–25.

Hodgkinson, G. P. and Healey, M. P. (2008). Cognitions in organizations. *Annual Review of Psychology*, 59: 387–417.

Hodgkinson, G. P. and Johnson, G. (1994). Exploring the mental models of competitive strategists: The case for processual approach. *Journal of Management Studies*, 31(4): 525–551.

Hodgkinson, G. P. and Sparrow, P. R. (2002). *The Competent Organization: A Psychological Analysis of the Strategic Management Process*. Buckingham: Open University Press.

Hodgkinson, G. P., Wright, R. P., and Anderson, J. (2015). Emotionalizing strategy research with the repertory grid technique: Modifications and extensions to a robust procedure for mapping strategic knowledge. In G. Gavettie and W. Ocasio (eds.), *Advances in Strategic Management*, 32, 505–547: 'Cognition and Strategy'. Bingley, UK: Emerald.

Huang, X., Wright, R. P., Chiu, W. C. K., and Wang, C. (2008). Relational schemas as sources of evaluation and misevaluation of leader–member exchanges: Some initial evidence. *The Leadership Quarterly*, 19(3), 266–282,

Huff, A. S. (ed.). (1990). *Mapping Strategic Thought*. Chichester: Wiley.

Huff, A. S. and Jenkins, M. (eds). (2002). *Mapping Strategic Knowledge*. London: Sage.

Huse, M. (2000). Boards of directors in SMEs: A review and research agenda. *Entrepreneurship and Regional Development*, 12, 271–290.

Ingold, T. (2000). *The Perception of the Environment*. London, Routledge.

Jackson, S.E. and Dutton, J. E. (1988). Discerning threats and opportunities. *Administrative Science Quarterly*, 33, 370–387.

Jankowicz, A. D. (1990). Applications of personal construct psychology in business practice. *Advances in Personal Construct Psychology*, 1: 257–287.

Jankowicz, A. D. (2003). *The Easy Guide to Repertory Grids*. Chichester: Wiley.

Jarzabkowski, P. (2005). *Strategy as Practice: An Activity Based Approach*. Sage: London, UK.

Jarzabkowski, P., Balogun, J., and Seidl, D. (2007). Strategizing: The challenges of a practice perspective. *Human Relations*, 60(1): 5–27.

Johnson, G., Melin, L., and Whittington, R. (2003). Special issue on micro strategy and strategizing: Towards an activity-based view. *Journal of Management Studies*, 40(1): 3–22.

Johnson, G., Whittington, R., and Scholes, K. (2011). *Exploring Corporate Strategy*, 9th edn. Harlow: Prentice Hall.

Kachra, A. and Schnietz, K. (2008). The capstone strategy course: What might real integration look like? *Journal of Management Education*, 32: 476–508.

Kalekin-Fishman, D. and Walker, B. M. (1996). *The Construction of Group Realities: Cultures, Societies, and Personal Construct Theory*. Florida: Krieger Publishing.

Kelly, G. (1955). *The Psychology of Personal Constructs, Vol. 1*. London: Norton.

Kiesler, S. and Sproull, L. (1982) Managerial response to changing environments: Perspectives on problem sensing from social cognition. *Administrative Science Quarterly*, 27: 548–570.

Lord R. G. and Emrich C. G. (2001). Thinking outside the box by looking inside the box: Extending the cognitive revolution in leadership research. *Leadership Quarterly*, 11, 551–579.

McGee J. and Thomas, H. (1986) Strategic groups: Theory, research and taxonomy. *Strategic Management Journal*, 7(2): 141–160.

McNulty, T. and Pettigrew, A. M. (1999). Strategists on the board. *Organization Studies*, 20(1): 47–74.

Menz, M. and Scheef, C. (2014). Chief strategy officers: Contingency analysis of their presence in top management teams, *Strategic Management Journal*, 35(3): 461–471.

Narayanan, V. K., Zane, L. J., and Kemmerer, B. (2011). The cognitive perspective in strategy: An integrative review. *Journal of Management*, 37(1): 305–351.

O'Higgins, E. (2002). Non-executive directors on boards in Ireland: Co-option, characteristics and contributions. *Corporate Governance*, 10(1): 19–28.

Oster, S. M. (1990). *Modern Competitive Analysis.* Oxford: Oxford University Press.

Paroutis, S. and Heracleous, L. (2013). Discourse revisited: Dimensions and employment of first-order strategy discourse during institutional adoption. *Strategic Management Journal*, 34(8): 935–956.

Paroutis, S., Heracleous, L., and Angwin, D. (2013). *Practicing Strategy: Text and Cases.* London: Sage.

Paroutis, S. and Pettigrew, A. M. (2005). Making strategy in the multi-business firm. In S. Floyd, J. Roos, C. Jacobs, and F. W. Kellermanns (eds), *Innovating Strategy Processes* (97–110), Oxford: Blackwell.

Paroutis, S. and Pettigrew, A. M. (2007). Strategizing in the multi-business firm: Strategy teams at multiple levels and over time. *Human Relations*, 60(1): 99–135.

Pearce, J. A. and Zahra, S. A. (1991). The relative power of the CEOs and boards of directors: Associations with corporate performance. *Strategic Management Journal*, 12: 135–153.

Peteraf, M. and Shanley, M. (1997). Getting to know you: A theory of strategic group identity. *Strategic Management Journal*, 18 (Summer Special Issue): 165–185.

Pettigrew, A. (1992). The character and significance of strategy process research. *Strategic Management Journal*, 13: 5–16.

Pettigrew, A. M. and McNulty, T. (1995). Power and influence in and around the boardroom. *Human Relations*, 48(8): 845–873.

Plambeck, N. and Weber, K. (2009). Ambivalence and action responses to strategic issues. *Organization Science*, 20 (6): 993–1010.

Porac, J. F. and Thomas, H. (1987). Cognitive taxonomies and cognitive systematics. Paper presented at the Annual Meeting of the Academy of Management, New Orleans, August.

Porac, J. F. and Thomas, H. (1990). Taxonomic mental models in competitor definition. *Academy of Management Review*, 15(2): 224–240.

Porac, J. F. and Thomas, H. (1994). Cognitive categorization and subjective rivalry among retailers in a small city. *Journal of Applied Psychology*, 79: 54–66.

Porac, J. F., Thomas, H., and Baden-Fuller, C. (1989). Competitive groups as cognitive communities: The case of Scottish knitwear manufacturers. *Journal of Management Studies*, 26(4): 397–416.

Porter, M. E. (1980). *Competitive Strategy.* New York: Free Press.

Porter, M. E. (1985). *Competitive Advantage.* New York: Free Press.

Powell, T. C, Lovallo, D., and Fox, C. R. (2011). Behavioral strategy. *Strategic Management Journal*, 32(13): 1369–1386.

Prahalad, C. K. and Bettis, R. A. (1986). The dominant logic: A new link between diversity and performance. *Strategic Management Journal*, 7: 485–501.

Pugliese, A., Bezemer, P., Zattoni, A., Huse, M., Van Den Bosch, F.A.J., and Volberda, H.W. (2009). Boards of directors' contribution to strategy: A literature review and research agenda. *Corporate Governance: An International Review*, 17(3): 292–306.

Reger, R. K. (1987). Competitive positioning in the Chicago banking market: Mapping the mind of the strategist. Unpublished doctoral dissertation, University of Illinois at Urbana-Champaign.

Reger, R. K. (1990). Managerial thought structures and competitive positioning. In A. S. Huff (ed.), *Mapping Strategic Thought* (71–88). Chichester: Wiley.

Reger, R. K., and Huff, A. S. (1993). Strategic groups: A cognitive perspective. *Strategic Management Journal*, 14: 103–123.

Reger, R. K., and Palmer, T. B. (1996). Managerial categorization of competitors: Using old maps to navigate new environments. *Organization Science*, 7(1): 22–39.

Rosch, E., Mervis, C. B., Gray, W. D., Johnson, D. M., and Boyes-Braem, P. (1976). Basic objects in natural categories. *Cognitive Psychology*, 8, 382–439.

Sandberg, J., and Tsoukas, H. (2011). Grasping the logic of practice: Theorizing through practical rationality. *Academy of Management Review*, 36(2): 338–360.

Sharma, S. (2000). Managerial interpretations and organizational context as predictors of corporate choice of environmental strategy. *Academy of Management Journal*, 43(4): 681–697.

Simon, H. A. (1947). *Administrative Behavior*. New York: Macmillan.

Simon, H. A. (1956). Rational choice, and the structure of the environment. *Psychological Review*, 63, 129–138.

Simpson, B. and Wilson, M. (1999). Shared cognition: Mapping commonality and individuality. In J. A. Wagner III (ed.), *Advances in Qualitative Organizational Research*, Vol. 2, (73–96). Stamford, CT: JAI Press.

Smith, M. and Gibson, J. (1988). Using repertory grids to investigate racial prejudice. *Applied Psychology: An International Review*, 37: 311–326.

Smith, M., Hartley, J., and Stewart, B. (1978). A case of repertory grids used in vocational guidance. *Journal of Occupational Psychology*, 51: 97–104.

Spencer, B., Peyrefitte, J., and Churchman, R. (2003). Consensus and divergence in perceptions of cognitive strategic groups: Evidence from the health care industry. *Strategic Organization*, 1(2): 203–230.

Stewart, V. and Stewart, A. (1981) *Business Applications of Repertory Grid*. London: McGraw-Hill.

Stiles, P. (2001). The impact of the board on strategy: An empirical examination. *Journal of Management Studies*, *38*(5), 627–650.

Stiles, P. and Taylor, B. (2001). *Boards at Work: How Directors View Their Roles and Responsibilities.* New York: Oxford University Press.

Thomas, J. A. and McDaniel, J. R. (1990). Interpreting strategic issues: Effects of strategy and the information-processing structure of top management teams. *Academy of Management Journal*, 33 (2): 286–306.

Thomas, J. B., Clark, S. M., and Gioia, D. A. (1993). Strategic sensemaking and organizational performance: Linkages among scanning, interpretation, action, and outcomes. *Academy of Management Journal*, 36 (2): 239–270.

Tricker, R. (1994). Editorial. *Corporate Governance*, 2(1): 1–4.

Vaara, E. and Whittington, R. (2012). Strategy-as-practice: Taking social practices seriously. *Academy of Management Annals*, 6(1): 258–336.

Walsh, J. P. (1995). Managerial and organizational cognition: Notes from a trip down memory lane. *Organization Science*, 6: 280–321.

Walton, E. J. (1986). Managers' prototypes of financial firms. *Journal of Management Studies*, 23: 679–698.

Weisbach, M. S. (1988). Outside directors and CEO turnovers. *Journal of Financial Economics*, 20 (January-March): 431–460.

Whittington, R. (2006). Completing the practice turn in strategy research. *Organization Studies*, 27(5): 613–634.

Whittington, R. (2007). Strategy practice and strategy process: Family differences and the sociological eye. *Organization Studies*, 28: 1575–1586.

Wright, R. P. (2004). Top managers' strategic cognitions of the strategy making process: Differences between high and low performing firms. *Journal of General Management*, 30(1): 61–78.

Wright, R. P. (2006). Rigor and relevance using repertory grid technique in strategy research. In D. J. Ketchen and D. D. Bergh (eds), *Research Methodology in Strategy and Management*, Vol. 3 (295–348), Oxford: Elsevier and JAI.

Wright, R. P. (2008). Eliciting cognitions of strategizing using advanced repertory grids in a world constructed and reconstructed. *Organizational Research Methods*, 11: 753–769.

Wright, R. P., Butler, J. E., and Priem, R. (2003). Asian cognitions of the strategic management process. Paper Presented at the Strategic Management Society Mini-Conference, June, Hong Kong.

Wright, R. P. and Lam, S. S. K. (2002). Comparing apples with apples: The importance of element wording in grid applications. *Journal of Constructivist Psychology*, 15(2): 109–119.

Wright, R., Paroutis, S., and Blettner, D. (2013). How useful are the strategic tools we teach in business schools? *Journal of Management Studies*, 50(1): 92–125.

Zahra, S. A. and Pearce, J. A. (1990). Determinants of board directors' strategic involvement. *European Management Journal*, 8: 164–173.

PART III

Novel methodological approaches in strategic management research

9

QUALITATIVE COMPARATIVE ANALYSIS

Fuzzy set applications for strategic management research

Thomas Greckhamer

A key driver of the evolution of any discipline is the development of research methods that enable the exploration of (certain kinds of) research questions and theoretical arguments (Greckhamer, Koro-Ljungberg, Cilesiz, and Hayes, 2008; Hitt *et al.*, 1998; Ketchen, *et al.*, 2008). By the same token, configurational approaches have contributed important theoretical advances to strategy and organization studies by pointing to the exploration of viable phenomena. Configurations generally have been defined as "any multidimensional constellation of conceptually distinct characteristics that commonly occur together" (Meyer *et al.*, 1993: 1175) and that are meaningful collectively as opposed to individually (Dess *et al.*, 1993). Despite having a long history in and having become a vital part of strategic management research (Doty *et al.*, 1993; Ketchen *et al.*, 1997, 1993; Miller, 1986, 1996), the promise of configurational approaches has remained largely unfulfilled because of a dearth of advances in methodological tools needed to match their theoretical assumptions (Fiss, 2007; Fiss, Marx, and Cambré, 2013). As an important recent contribution towards fulfilling this promise, qualitative comparative analysis (QCA) has been added to the repertoire of research methodologies available to strategy scholars (e.g. Fiss, 2007, 2011; Greckhamer, Misangyi, Elms, and Lacey, 2008; Greckhamer and Mossholder, 2011; Kogut *et al.*, 2004).

QCA has been one of few genuine methodological innovations developed in the social sciences within the last decades (Gerring, 2001). Originally developed by Charles Ragin (1987, 2000, 2008), the bulk of research developing and applying QCA initially has been conducted in sociology and political science. In these disciplines, QCA has been used to explore a wide range of topics, including for example the conditions linked to autonomous rulers' propensity to start wars (Kiser *et al*, 1995), to the emergence of democracy in Europe during the interwar period (Berg-Schlosser and De Meur, 1994), to (collective or individual) workers' resistance (Boswell and Brown, 1999; Hodson and Roscigno, 2004), to an increase of public spending on active labor market policies by Western democratic governments (Vis, 2012), and to the experience of high food security versus insecurity in sub-Saharan countries (Brigham, 2011).

In recent years management has become the fastest growing field for QCA applications (Rihoux *et al.*, 2013). This is the case because QCA has revived the configurational literature in strategy and organization studies by reorienting it towards set theory and thereby overcoming the aforementioned mismatch between theory and methods that has limited empirical configurational research (Fiss, 2007). Indeed, QCA has the potential to greatly impact theory and research in strategy and despite its recent introduction to strategy research, Ketchen (2013) has argued that some of the strongest contributions to configurational strategy research to date have been offered by researchers utilizing QCA.

The purpose of this chapter is to contribute to facilitating applications of QCA's theoretical and methodological approach and to help strategy scholars stay abreast of its rapid development. Building on an introduction of its foundations, I explain and illustrate four functions of QCA and discuss their potential for strategy scholarship, followed by a discussion of current developments in this approach that are of particular interest to strategy scholars. In doing so, I illustrate the various ways in which strategy researchers might benefit from this evolving theoretical and methodological approach.

Foundations of qualitative comparative analysis

In his seminal introduction of qualitative comparative analysis (QCA), Charles Ragin (1987) observed that a unifying characteristic of virtually all empirical social research is that it involves some kind of comparison across cases. Key objectives for these case comparisons involve: (1) understanding what different types of cases may occur in a given study setting considering their key similarities and differences, and (2) understanding the complex causal relations underlying the occurrence of outcomes of interest. His initial and consequent development of QCA based on Boolean algebra and the theory of sets aimed at offering a formal set theoretic approach that maps both the diversity of cases (fulfilling the first key objective) and provides a systematic approach to analyzing the various paths by which an outcome may be reached (fulfilling the second key objective) (Ragin, 1987, 2000, 2008). From the outset QCA was aimed at synthesizing the strengths of qualitative and quantitative approaches and it has gained recognition across the social sciences for constituting an innovative way to bridge the frequently lamented divide between qualitative (i.e. focusing on in-depth studies examining specific cases) and quantitative (i.e. focusing on relationships between variables across many cases) research approaches (Marx *et al.*, 2013; Ragin, 1987; Rihoux, 2003).

The central innovation QCA has offered to social science research methodology is that it is based on a set theoretic (as opposed to a correlational) understanding of the social world and on Boolean algebra (as opposed to linear algebra); Boolean algebra provides a framework to study relations among sets (for a discussion of the set theoretic basis of QCA as well as a relevant introduction to Boolean algebra, see e.g. Ragin [1987, 2000]; Smithson and Verkuilen [2006]). A set theoretic approach describes case attributes in terms of sets and set relations; it assesses whether and to what degree a case is a member of a given set and then analyzes intersections between sets, rather than aiming to capture isolated dimensions of variation competing with one another to explain variation in the outcome (Ragin, 2000).

Fuzzy set QCA

Because in QCA's set theoretic approach both the outcomes researchers wish to study and key attributes suspected to be causally linked to these outcomes are conceptualized as sets, researchers have to determine the membership of their empirical cases in these sets. Hence, the process of determining set memberships, also referred to as the calibration of sets, is vital. With regard to the kinds of set memberships, QCA encompasses three specific techniques: crisp set- (csQCA), fuzzy set- (fsQCA), and multi value-QCA (mvQCA) (Rihoux and Ragin, 2009). These different approaches capture set membership through: (1) dichotomous or "crisp" sets where cases are either in or out of a set; (2) fuzzy sets where cases, in addition to full membership and full non-membership, may also have partial membership; or (3) multi value sets, which is an extension of csQCA and allows capturing multi-categorical nominal-scale conditions. In the remainder of this chapter I will focus on fsQCA (as csQCA follows the same logic); a discussion of mvQCA is beyond the scope of this chapter and readers are referred to the literature introducing it (e.g., Cronqvist and Berg-Schlosser, 2009; Vink and Vliet, 2009).

Unlike a crisp set, a fuzzy set has blurred boundaries, i.e. it represents a set with a gradual rather than an abrupt transition from membership to non-membership. This fuzziness is essential for human cognition because most terms we use to classify cases in the empirical world into sets are fuzzy (Zadeh, 1972), including for example the classes of tall men, old men, successful women, big cars, large firms, or competitive industries. The calibration of fuzzy (as well as crisp) sets requires decisions about criteria to determine membership in the set (Ragin, 2000, 2008). In the process of calibrating sets researchers begin with a careful definition of their respective sets and rely on previous theory and empirical knowledge to decide on the rules and the critical qualitative anchors that determine cases' membership in these sets. Whereas crisp sets require merely setting thresholds of full membership, fuzzy sets require setting thresholds of full membership, full non-membership, and intermediary degrees of membership. Fuzzy sets combine precision akin to quantitative measurement with substantive description that is emphasized by qualitative research.

For example, to define a fuzzy set capturing the extent to which corporations in a given industry are diversified, any competitor competing in it may be classified as fully out of the set of diversified corporations (e.g. a competitor exclusively competes in this industry), fully in the set of diversified corporations (i.e. the competitor surpassed a benchmark of diversification required for full membership in this set), or its membership may be assessed as partial (e.g. it may be "more out than in" or "more in than out" of the set of diversified corporations). This example illustrates that calibration can help researchers to learn more about their cases because it requires consideration of what constitutes full membership, full non-membership, and partial membership in the sets studied. It further illustrates that in QCA not all variation is equally relevant (Ragin, 2000); for example, once the set of diversified corporations has been calibrated, variation of diversification among those cases with full membership in the set of diversified corporations is no longer relevant. Depending upon the nature of defined sets and the information available about cases, researchers may consider different kinds of fuzzy sets. To begin with, continuous fuzzy sets allow for continuous membership scores in the range from 0 (= fully out of the set) to 1 (= fully in the set) and require the setting of thresholds for full, non-, and partial memberships. Additionally, researchers can also calibrate different kinds of multi-value fuzzy sets that in addition to full membership and full non-membership may for example distinguish the following membership scores and categories: .5 = neither in nor out (resulting in a three-value fuzzy set); .67 = more in than out; .33 = more out than in (resulting in a four-value fuzzy set); or .75 = more in than out, .50 neither in nor out, and .25 more out than in (resulting in a five-value fuzzy set) (see Ragin, 2000, 2008). Examples of key issues of calibration in the context of strategy research are found in the literature (Crilly, 2011; Fiss, 2011; Greckhamer, 2011; Greckhamer and Mossholder, 2011; Kogut et al., 2004).

QCA conceptualizes the connection of case attributes and outcomes (and hence the diversity of cases as well as the causal complexity underlying the occurrence of many empirical phenomena) in terms of set membership and subset relations and expresses these relations through the combinatorial logic of Boolean algebra (Fiss, 2007; Ragin, 2000, 2008). Logical *and* and logical *or* are the two basic operators for designating set relations. The operator *and* represents the intersection of sets (for example, highly performing firms in an industry may combine the characteristics of highly differentiated products *and* having abundant slack resources), whereas the operator *or* represents the union of sets (for example, firms with high performance may be either highly differentiated *or* have abundant slack resources). The Boolean negation *not* denotes the complement of a defined set and contains cases not in the defined set; for example, the set of *not* large firms encompasses all those cases that do not satisfy the criterion for membership in the set of large firms. To amplify the importance of carefully defining sets, I note that the set of not large firms is different from the set of small firms, because the calibration of the set of large firms would be informed by what it means to be a large firm in a respective empirical setting, whereas the calibration of the set of small firms would be informed by what it means to be a small firm in that setting. This also implies that the definition of what constitutes "large" firms and consequently the calibration of the according set may be very different, for instance, in empirical studies of the global automobile industry versus of the Austrian brewery industry.

The set theoretic relation of principal importance in QCA is the subset relation and it is easy to demonstrate subset relations for cases involving nested categories (Ragin, 2008). For example, Sunni Muslims are a subset of Muslims, who in turn are a subset of monotheists; wolves, foxes, and coyotes each are a subset of the family of canidae, which in turn are a subset of mammals; and large, diversified US firms are a subset of large US firms, which in turn are a subset of US firms. Subset relations of interest for causal analysis exist: (1) when cases that share a combination of causally relevant attributes (near) uniformly share the same outcome, or (2) when cases sharing the same outcome (near) uniformly share the same combination of causally relevant attributes. Provided proper substantive and theoretical knowledge exists, the first of these subset relationships may be interpreted as the combination of conditions being *sufficient* for the occurrence of the outcome (i.e. that it can produce a certain outcome on its own), whereas the second of these subset relationships may be interpreted as being *necessary* for the occurrence of the outcome (i.e. that it must be present for the outcome to occur).

For example, if all large and highly vertically integrated firms in an industry exhibit high performance, large and highly vertically integrated firms are a subset of highly performing firms in this industry and provided theoretical and substantive knowledge, this may be interpreted as a combination of these attributes being *sufficient* for high performance in this industry. Conversely, if all highly performing firms are large and vertically integrated, highly performing firms are a subset of firms that are large and vertically integrated; provided theoretical and substantive knowledge, this may be interpreted as large size and a high degree of vertical integration being *necessary* for high performance in this manufacturing industry.

QCA's approach to causality

QCA's alternative theoretical and methodological approach to causality is shaped by the notion of causal complexity (Ragin, 1987, 2000, 2008), which entails three elements (Schneider and Wagemann, 2012): equifinality, conjunctural causation, and asymmetric causation. Equifinality describes situations in which various (combinations of) causal attributes are linked to the same outcome. Conjunctural causation implies that attributes do not necessarily exert their impact on the outcome in isolation from each other. Asymmetric causation implies that researchers need to separately analyze the causal attributes for occurrence and non-occurrence of outcomes of interest; moreover, it implies that presence and absence of attributes may play crucially different roles in the occurrence of an outcome.

Whereas QCA systematically compares cases sharing certain outcomes in order to identify combinations of causal attributes linked to these outcomes, general linear regression approaches by design estimate the contribution of individual causes (i.e. independent variables) in explaining variation in the outcome (i.e. the dependent variable). For example, Greckhamer and colleagues (Greckhamer *et al.*,

2008b) have illustrated that QCA shifts the objective of inquiry from attempting to isolate the extent of relative individual contributions of various industry-, corporate-, and business-unit factors, to investigating what combinations of industry, corporate, and business-attributes may be consistently linked to outcomes such as superior performance. In short, QCA's alternative theoretical and methodological approach to causality differs fundamentally from the general linear regression approaches that dominate strategy research (Fiss, 2007, 2011; Greckhamer *et al.*, 2008b; Kogut *et al.*, 2004). Ragin (2013) provides a concise overview of the differences between QCA and general linear regression approaches and Vis (2012) provides an empirical comparison of analyzing causal relations with QCA and with general linear regression methodologies, respectively.

In order to enhance the interpretation of QCA results, Ragin (2006, 2008) has developed two key set theoretic measures – coverage and consistency – that constituted a key innovation for the further development of QCA (Marx *et al.*, 2013). Consistency captures the degree to which cases sharing a given configuration also display the outcome, thereby providing a measure for the degree to which the empirical evidence supports an argument that a set relation between configuration and outcome exists. Based on QCA's set theoretic assumptions, high consistency indicates support for the validity of the analyzed causal model whereas it is assumed that consistency will be low when the model is ill-specified. To illustrate this with a crisp set example, if 9 out of 10 cases sharing the combination of a highly munificent industry environment and abundant slack resources show high performance (and 1 does not), this results in a consistency score of .90 (i.e. 90 percent of cases in the configuration share the outcome) for this configuration. With fuzzy sets, cases with "strong" membership in a configuration (I will discuss below what constitutes strong membership) are most relevant for providing information about consistency. Generally, the calculation of consistency scores includes substantial penalties for large inconsistencies.

Determining adequate consistency, and thereby establishing the basis for inferring that a subset relation between a configuration of causal attributes and an outcome exists in the first place, is a precondition for calculating a configuration's coverage. For those configurations with adequate consistency, the set theoretic coverage measure assesses the degree to which a configuration of causal attributes accounts for instances of the outcome of interest; put differently, it gauges these configurations' relative empirical importance or relevance (Ragin, 2006, 2008). For crisp sets, a configuration's coverage captures the proportion of the cases falling into this configuration that represent the outcome of interest, whereas for fuzzy sets coverage captures the proportion of the sum of membership scores in the outcome (i.e. the scores expressing the degrees of cases' membership in this set) covered by the configuration. To again illustrate this measure with a crisp set example, assuming that 9 out of 27 cases showing high performance share the (already shown to be consistent) configuration highly munificent industry environment and abundant slack resources, then this configuration's (raw) coverage is .33 (i.e. 33 percent of the cases showing high performance combine a highly munificent industry environment and high slack resources). Coverage entails multiple variants; raw coverage is the overall coverage of a configuration that may overlap with that of others; unique coverage is that coverage it exclusively covers; and solution coverage is the combined coverage of all configurations consistently linked to the outcome. Thus, when QCA results include multiple consistent configurations, the researchers can gauge their relative empirical importance and the extent of their overlap by assessing their raw and unique coverage.

Utilizing QCA's multiple functions for strategic management research

QCA is a versatile theoretical and methodological approach that may serve diverse research purposes (Berg-Schlosser *et al.*, 2009; Marx *et al.*, 2013). To illustrate the potential of QCA for strategic management research, in this section I will demonstrate four different functions. The first two functions – using QCA's truth table to summarize empirical data and to explore contradictory configurations – primarily focus on exploring the diversity of cases; QCA's third and fourth functions – enabling researchers to test theories and hypotheses and to extend, refine, or redirect theoretical arguments towards configurational theorizing – primarily are concerned with studying causal complexity.

I illustrate the potential of each of these functions of QCA by presenting a limited hypothetical example focusing on theoretical drivers of high firm performance in a manufacturing industry. Assume that based upon the knowledge of the firms in this industry, we expect five attributes to be critical in understanding high performance. These are a firm's size, availability of slack resources, R&D intensity, degree of internationalization, and capital intensity. Assume further that after data were collected, they were calibrated – based upon the researcher's intimate knowledge with the research setting – into the sets of firms with: (1) abundant slack resources, (2) high R&D intensity, (3) large size, (4) highly internationalized operations, and (5) high capital intensity. Further note that I have utilized the fs/QCA software developed by Ragin and colleagues (Ragin *et al.*, 2009) for all calibration and analyses, which is one of two popular software packages for QCA applications (Ragin, 2008; Rihoux *et al.*, 2013).

Application 1: Describing and exploring (present and missing) data

To begin with, I illustrate QCA's perhaps most elementary type of application, using truth tables. In Boolean algebra, a truth table is a chart with 2^k rows (k = the number of included attributes) that displays all logically possible combinations of sets (Caramani, 2009); each of the truth table's rows constitutes a potential difference in kind among cases; in QCA truth tables are the key tool for analyzing the diversity of cases as well as causal complexity (Ragin, 2008). The first function of a truth table is to serve as a tool for summarizing empirical data in a manner that opens venues for theory (and typology) building as well as data exploration and synthesis. For example, truth tables have been used to explore and synthesize data combinations of industry and firm attributes that occur across industry sectors (Greckhamer et al., 2008b). Moreover, truth tables usually contain hypothetical combinations that lack empirical instances (Ragin, 1987, 2000), which underscores the limited diversity of many social and organizational phenomena, i.e. that the attributes of cases tend to occur in coherent patterns (e.g. Meyer et al., 1993). Greckhamer (2011) illustrates how these empirically non-existing configurations can be summarized to both build theory (and typologies) regarding logically possible but empirically not observed configurations and to construct the boundary conditions of empirical analyses.

To illustrate this first function of QCA, I turn to constructing the truth table of the hypothetical example introduced above. The complete truth table for this example would have 32 rows ($32=2^5$ logically possible Boolean combinations of 5 included attributes), with each row representing one logically possible combination. In constructing a truth table, each case is attributed to the configuration in which it has ("strong") membership (each case also has partial membership in other configurations that are incorporated in an fsQCA analysis); for fuzzy sets, this is determined by assigning a 1 to cases with a set membership score >0.5 and a 0 to cases with a set membership score <0.5. In Table 9.1, I present a truncated truth table that contains the 11 configurations represented by "strong" cases in the hypothetical sample and sorted by these configurations' consistency scores (in the truth table, the consistency scores of configurations is referred to as "raw consistency" to distinguish it from the consistency measures of configurations linked to the outcome through set theoretic analysis of the truth table; these raw consistency scores reflect data from cases both with strong as well

TABLE 9.1 Truncated truth table

Config. #	Abundant slack	High R&D intensity	Large size	High international-ization	High capital intensity	# of cases	High performance	Raw consistency
1	1	1	1	0	0	1	1	1.00
2	1	1	0	0	0	1	1	1.00
3	1	0	1	1	0	4	1	1.00
4	1	1	1	1	0	12	1	0.99
5	1	1	1	1	1	2	1	0.96
6	1	1	1	0	1	3	1	0.95
7	1	0	1	0	1	3	0	0.74
8	0	1	0	0	1	1	0	0.73
9	0	0	0	0	0	1	0	0.64
10	0	0	0	1	0	5	0	0.44
11	0	0	0	0	1	10	0	0.33

as with partial membership); the 21 remaining logically possible combinations of attributes, which are not represented by any cases in the data are not reported in this table for a more concise presentation (I will return to these when presenting Table 9.2). This truth table then illustrates the first and most elementary function of QCA, i.e. its utility to map and summarize the combinations of attributes of key interest to researchers that occur (and do not occur) as well as bringing to light similarities and differences among a sample's cases. This allows for data synthesis and typology building (Marx *et al.*, 2013; Ragin, 1987), and this function is further aided by the provision of information regarding whether or not the configuration is consistently linked to an outcome of interest.

Table 9.1 shows that the 43 cases in the sample fall into 11 configurations (in this table sorted by raw consistency), with two configurations (nos. 4 and 11) accounting for more than half and four configurations (nos. 3, 4, 10, and 11) accounting for almost three quarters of the cases. This information could also be used to calculate a Herfindahl index of diversity as well as a four-configuration concentration measure, for example to compare diversity of cases across industries or industry sectors (Greckhamer *et al.*, 2008b). The limited diversity in this (hypothetical) truth table illustrates the premise of configurational approaches that the attributes of cases tend to occur in coherent patterns, for example in phenomena of relevance to strategy and organizations researchers (Meyer *et al.*, 1993). The two most frequent configurations covering more than 50 percent of cases (i.e. configurations nos. 4 and 11 in Table 9.1) combine: (1) an abundance of slack resources, high R&D intensity, large size, and a high degree of internationalization as well as a lack of capital intensity; and (2) high capital intensity combined with an absence of slack resources, of R&D intensity, of large size, and of high internationalization. Moreover, the truth table shows that with respect to the two

TABLE 9.2 Logically possible configurations lacking strong cases in sample

	S1	S2	S3	S4	S5	S6	S7	S8
Abundant slack	⊗	⊗			●	●	●	●
High R&D intensity		●	⊗	●		⊗	⊗	
Large size	●			⊗	⊗		⊗	⊗
High internationalization			●	●		⊗		●
High capital intensity		⊗	●	●		●	⊗	
Consistency	1	1	1	1	1	1	1	1
Raw coverage	0.38	0.19	0.19	0.19	0.19	0.10	0.19	0.19
Unique coverage	0.24	0.05	0.10	0.05	0.05	0.05	0.00	0.00
Overall solution consistency				1.00				
Overall solution coverage				1.00				

Key: ● = Causal condition present
⊗ = Causal condition absent

most frequent configurations, configuration no. 4 is consistently linked to high performance (raw consistency = .99), whereas configuration no. 11 is fairly clearly linked to a lack of high performance (raw consistency = .33). Furthermore, four configurations are represented by only one case with strong membership, respectively. The truth table also builds on QCA's basic premise that two cases differing on only one key attribute may represent a difference in kind between the two configurations represented by these cases; for example, membership or non-membership in the set of large firms constitutes a difference in kind between configurations nos. 1 and 2 in Table 9.1. The truth table further implies that 21 logically possible configurations (not included in the table) are not represented by cases with strong membership. These configurations can be summarized through Boolean minimization (Ragin, 1987) as illustrated in an empirical study by Greckhamer (2011). In this illustrative example, the 21 configurations without empirical cases are summarized into 8 configurations (see Table 9.2).

For example, the first configuration combines large size and lack of slack resources, which implies that in this sample there are no large firms that lack slack resources, and barring the integration of counterfactuals (i.e. non-existing configurations), we should not draw any inferences regarding the performance outcome experienced by large firms lacking slack resources. Having the highest raw (=.38) and unique (=.24) coverage means that this configuration covers the largest number of non-existing configurations: specifically, it captures 8 of the 21 (=21*.38) non-existing configurations, uniquely representing 5 (=21*.24) of them. This unique feature of QCA that enable researchers to summarize areas of missing empirical evidence enables thought experiments and theory development regarding potential outcomes in these non-existent configurations as well as why these configurations may be missing from the sample; it also points researchers to potentially identifying cases representing these missing configurations.

Application 2: Identifying and exploring contradictory configurations

The truth table also enables researchers to examine the coherence of the data, which leads to QCA's second function of interest to strategy researchers, i.e. using it to identify and explore so-called "contradictory" configurations (Berg-Schlosser et al., 2009; Ragin, 2000, 2008). Contradictory configurations contain cases that share causal attributes but differ with respect to the outcome; they can be identified by examining the truth table. For example, assume that among seven firms in an industry that are large and vertically integrated, five experience high performance, whereas two cases belonging to this configuration do not experience high performance. Researchers could use this contradiction to increase their understanding of the cases as well as of the causal links between these attributes and performance; finding an explanation for this contradiction could help improve the originally proposed model linking them to high performance.

The marker for contradictions is configurations' raw consistency score in the truth table. Intermediate consistency scores (ranging from approximately 0.30 – 0.70) indicate contradictory configurations whose cases are divided with respect to the presence or absence of the outcome (Ragin, 2008). In the hypothetical example used here, Table 9.1 shows six configurations having (near perfect) raw consistency scores of .95 or higher, whereas five configurations represent different degrees of contradictions, with configurations nos. 9 and 10 most clearly having intermediate consistency scores (.64 and .44, respectively); configuration no. 11 is fairly clearly not linked to the outcome (consistency = .33), whereas configurations nos. 7 and 8 are at the cusp of the minimum consistency threshold (≥.75) above which a subset relationship with the outcome may be inferred (Ragin, 2008). Configuration no. 9 is represented by only 1 case with strong membership, whereas configuration no. 10 is represented by 5 cases. Contradictions of this kind weaken set theoretic consistency and make the drawing of inferences about causal relationships more difficult, implying that the causal model represented by the truth table is not capturing all paths to the outcome. Therefore, particularly when studying small numbers of cases, resolving contradictory configurations is considered an important part of building causal models.

A number of theoretically and empirically driven recommendations have been developed to provide guidance for resolving contradictions (and thereby improving causal models) (Ragin, 2008; Rihoux and Ragin, 2009); while these recommendations have originally been tailored to small-N QCA applications, they can also be extended to large-N studies (see Greckhamer *et al.*, 2013). In short, researchers may choose among the following strategies to deal with and resolve contradictory configurations such as the one identified in the above example: (1) review the criteria used to select cases to question whether all cases in the sample are actually part of the relevant population; (2) draw on extant theory to revise the causal model by removing or replacing one or more of the model's causal conditions; (3) reconsider how sets have been operationalized and calibrated, which may resolve contradictions; (4) develop a deeper understanding of the cases under study to both resolve the contradictions and to develop a better understanding of causal links between outcomes of interest and case attributes; (5) rely on a frequency criterion to determine what makes for theoretically relevant contradictions (e.g. up to four out of twenty cases or 20 percent not showing the outcome may be accepted as theoretically not significant contradiction), thereby leaving the task of exploring cases in greater depth for the future.

Additionally, irrespective of whether researchers deal with a small-N or large-N setting, identifying and resolving contradictions is more difficult in fuzzy sets as compared to crisp sets; this is the case because in crisp sets cases in a configuration either do or do not share the same outcome whereas in fuzzy sets set memberships and thereby contradictions may be partial. Even though cases with strong membership in a configuration are most relevant for and most strongly shape consistency, cases with partial membership do so as well. Hence, pinpointing and resolving the sources of contradictions may be less straightforward than would be the case with crisp set data, particularly for configurations that are represented by a relatively small number of strong cases in the data (e.g. configuration no. 9 in Table 9.1). However, the fact that consistency scores include substantial penalties for large inconsistencies may help researchers identify the relatively most relevant contradictory cases.

More generally, being mindful of contradictory configurations is an important part of building and improving researchers' understanding of the causal relationships of interest and ultimately of their causal models. Assessing and potentially resolving them is part of an iterative process of identifying cases and causal attributes potentially linked to the outcome of interest; this process is thus less likely to be reported in published research. Also, the ideal case of resolving all contradictions (in which case all configurations in a truth table would have a raw consistency score of close to 1 or close to 0, and the solution coverage of the causal model would be close to 1) appears unrealistic for most empirical research; pragmatically the pursuit of empirical research entailing causal models that retain contradictions is therefore appropriate for strategy researchers, provided it makes distinct contributions.

Application 3: Developing, refining, and/or redirecting theory

The remaining two functions of QCA are focused on causal analysis and interpretation of the truth table, which may either follow an inductive logic aimed at theory building or a deductive logic aimed at theory testing. Small-N QCA studies typically follow the trajectory of theory building, whereas large-N QCA studies can more readily accommodate the hypothetico-deductive logic of theory testing common in strategy and organization studies (Greckhamer *et al.*, 2013). I begin by discussing how QCA enables the development of new theory, the extension or refinement of existing theoretical arguments, or the redirection of theories towards configurational theorizing, by exploring causal configurations in empirical data; in doing so I illustrate the process of causal analysis and interpretation in QCA.

While researchers typically have strong theoretical reasons for the inclusion of causal attributes into their analyses, the actual development of configurational theories has remained rare. Empirical QCA results of patterns of consistent subset relationships across a sample of empirical cases and their interpretation are well suited to extend or refine theory by building arguments of configurational relationships among causal attributes. Because of the scarcity of configurational theories to be tested, this has been a common and very fruitful application of QCA in the strategy and organization literature. To give a few examples, Crilly (2011) utilized fsQCA to build the foundations for a mid-range theory combining environmental factors with an internal stakeholder perspective to explain the stakeholder orientations of corporations' overseas subsidiaries. Pajunen (2008) utilized fsQCA to explore how institutional factors influence the relative attractiveness of countries for multinational corporations' foreign direct investments (FDI); his results demonstrated that specific countries may not be attractive (or unattractive) because of a single institutional factor, thereby contributing to building of configurational theory as well as developing configurational policy recommendations. Greckhamer (2011) applied fsQCA to explore the link between combinations of cultural and macro-environmental attributes and cross-national differences in compensation, thereby extending theory regarding cross-national differences in compensation level and inequality.

In order to proceed with causal analysis, a researcher first has to complete the truth table by coding the outcome linked to the configurations, which requires a decision regarding the configurations that are consistently linked to the outcome (coded as 1) and those not consistently linked to it (coded as 0). In fsQCA, after considering any strategies to resolve contradictory configurations, researchers ultimately use configurations' raw consistency scores to make this decision, by setting a minimum consistency score for accepting that a configuration is associated with the presence of the outcome; consistency levels need to be at least ≥.75 to draw inferences regarding subset relationships, with recommended consistency levels being ≥.85 (Ragin, 2008). Additionally, researchers need to decide on a threshold for the strength of evidence for combinations of attributes, i.e. a minimum number of cases with strong membership that a given configuration has to have in order to be included in the empirical analysis of causal relations. The appropriate minimum level of cases depends on the study's objectives and the size of the analyzed sample; this decision involves the trade-off between the potential for deductive analysis and the inclusion of rare configurations (Greckhamer et al., 2013; Ragin and Fiss, 2008). For small-N samples the limit may be set to a minimum of 1 strong case, whereas for large-N studies it may be set to 3 or more cases.

These decisions can be illustrated by revisiting the truth table shown in Table 9.1; in this case it is easy to code configurations nos. 1–6 as consistently linked to the outcome, owing to the large gap in consistency scores between configurations nos. 6 and 7 (a formal application of the recommended threshold of consistency ≥.85 yields the same result). Also, due to the relatively small sample in this hypothetical example (n=43), the minimum threshold for inclusion into the truth table analysis was set as 1. Upon making these decisions, the truth table is finalized and ready for analysis.

As regards truth table analysis, current best practices enable researchers to distinguish complex, parsimonious, and intermediate solutions, based on how counterfactuals are integrated into the analysis (Ragin, 2008). Complex solutions refrain from integrating any assumptions concerning non-existing configurations as simplifying assumptions (i.e. assumptions used to simplify the Boolean statement manifested in the truth table); parsimonious solutions include all of them, no matter how plausible they appear; and intermediate solutions integrate "easy" counterfactuals that are consistent with existing knowledge (the opposite being "difficult" counterfactuals). Also, as noted above one cannot assume that the results of set theoretic analysis be symmetric, i.e. the causal configurations linked to an outcome's absence can be quite different from the inverse causes linked to its presence (Fiss, 2011; Greckhamer et al., 2008b; Ragin, 2008); therefore it is good practice to analyze the causal conditions linked both to the presence and the absence of the outcome of interest (in the simple example here, high firm performance and its absence).

I now illustrate the analysis of the sample hypothetical truth table presented above and start with reporting the results linked to the high performance outcome (see Table 9.3). In presenting my analysis, I follow current conventions of reporting a combination of intermediate and parsimonious solutions introduced by Ragin and Fiss (2008). Following this convention, attribute configurations that are part of both intermediate and parsimonious solutions are referred to as core conditions, whereas those present in intermediary but not in parsimonious solutions are referred to as complementary conditions; also, measures of coverage and consistency are reported for the intermediate solutions.

Table 9.3 shows the results of set theoretic minimization, portraying those configurations that are consistently linked to high performance in this hypothetical manufacturing industry. Key to interpreting these results are the set theoretic measures of consistency and coverage introduced above and reported in the table. The figure shows that three attribute configurations are consistently linked to high performance in this example (here sorted by unique and raw coverage). These three configurations (S1 and S2a–b) are equifinal paths to high performance in this industry and also represent a Boolean equation in which each configuration's elements are linked by a Boolean *and*, whereas the configurations are linked with each other by a Boolean *or*. The first configuration shows that firms combining the core conditions abundant slack resources and high R&D intensity with large size as complementary condition are consistently showing high performance. Solutions 2a and 2b share the same core conditions, indicating that firms combining an abundance of slack resources and a lack of internationalization as core conditions, supplemented by either high R&D intensity, or by large size and high capital

TABLE 9.3 Configurations for achieving high performance solution

	S1	S2a	S2b
Abundant slack	●	●	●
High R&D intensity	●		●
Large size	●	●	
High internationalization		⊗	⊗
High capital intensity		●	
Consistency	0.99	0.94	0.98
Raw coverage	0.60	0.66	0.61
Unique coverage	0.11	0.09	0.05
Overall solution consistency		0.95	
Overall solution coverage		0.82	

Key: ● = Core causal condition present
⊗ = Core causal condition absent
● = Complementary causal condition present
⊗ = Complementary causal condition absent

intensity as complementary conditions, are consistently showing high performance; configurations differing only in complementary conditions, such as solutions 2a and 2b, are also referred to as *neutral permutations* (Fiss, 2011).

Assessing these configurations' raw and unique coverage provides evidence for the solutions' relative empirical importance. As a reminder, coverage assesses the degree to which the configuration of causal attributes (here, for example the set of firms that are large, have abundant slack resources, and high R&D intensity) covers the outcome set (here, the set of firms with high performance) (Ragin, 2006). The first configuration covers 60 percent of firms' sum of membership scores in the set of high performance (raw coverage = .60), uniquely representing 11 percent thereof (unique coverage = .11); the second and third configurations have relatively similar raw but slightly lower unique coverages. Additionally, the relative difference between raw and unique coverages indicates that there is substantive overlap in coverage among these three solutions. Overall solution consistency and coverage for the combination of the three equifinal configurations show that this combination is consistently linked to high performance (solution consistency = .95) and covers more than 80 percent of the sum of membership scores in the set of high performance firms in the sample.

These empirical results may serve to inductively develop, refine, and/or redirect theory regarding the causes underlying performance of manufacturing firms by building configurational theoretical arguments (as opposed to theoretical arguments regarding the independent effects of any of the included attributes). For example, the results reported in Table 9.3 show that a key combination for high performance is abundant slack resources and lack of internationalization; presuming that the analyzed sample was constructed so as to be representative of the diversity of firms in this industry, this result could be used to build a configurational argument regarding the combination of these attributes. To give another example, the results suggest that among firms that are not internationalized and have abundant slack resources (S2a and S2b in Table 9.3), high R&D intensity versus large size combined with high capital intensity may substitute for one another in attaining high performance. Furthermore, the presence of abundant slack resources in all three paths to high performance could indicate that this condition is necessary for attaining high performance in this industry. However, the solutions presented in Table 9.3 do not encompass all cases of firms with high performance (solution coverage = .82). Provided a theoretical basis to expect this condition to be necessary for attaining high performance in this manufacturing industry, additional tests for necessity could be conducted. In order to solidify the theoretical arguments based on these results, configurational arguments to build new theory or to extend or redirect existing theory as input for future research could be built. Because the results of this simple example are hypothetical, I refrain from building theoretical arguments in greater detail.

As noted above, whether the results can be generalized to the industry and possibly beyond it depends on the nature of the sample. Therefore, any researcher aiming to build (or test) theory by means of QCA should consider that the extent to which QCA's set theoretic findings of relations supporting claims of necessity and sufficiency can be generalized beyond the study's sample depends upon the initial construction of the sample. In short, if generalizability is desirable, researchers should aim to construct the study sample with an eye towards representing the diversity of the population or alternatively should include the population of cases (Greckhamer, *et al.*, 2013).

As noted earlier, because of the asymmetric nature of QCA's set theoretic analysis, researchers should also consider reporting the configurations linked to the absence of the outcome of interest. Hence, continuing my example I report the analysis results of configurations consistently linked to the absence of high performance in Table 9.4. As this table shows, in this hypothetical example two configurations sharing a lack of slack resources as sole core condition (i.e., neutral permutations) are consistently linked to the absence of high performance; moreover, cases that complement this core condition with not being large and either a high degree of internationalization and a lack of capital intensity or a lack of R&D intensity and a lack of internationalization, are consistently not performing highly. Both of these paths have substantial raw and unique coverage, suggesting that they are both empirically salient paths to the absence of high firm performance in this industry. These results suggest that lack of slack resources may be a necessary condition for achieving not high performance, but again these two paths do not cover all cases showing lack of high performance (solution coverage = .70). While due to the hypothetical nature of this example I do not pursue this further here, in an actual empirical study these results could provide the basis for building, extending, or refining theories and move towards building configurational theories of firm performance.

TABLE 9.4 Configurations for achieving not high performance solution

	S1a	S1b
Abundant slack	⊗	⊗
High R&D intensity		⊗
Large size	⊗	⊗
High internationalization	●	⊗
High capital intensity	⊗	
Consistency	0.95	0.96
Raw coverage	0.48	0.37
Unique coverage	0.33	0.22
Overall solution consistency	0.95	
Overall solution coverage	0.70	

Key: ⊗ = Core causal condition absent
● = Complementary causal condition present
⊗ = Complementary causal condition absent

Application 4: Testing configurational hypotheses

The fourth and perhaps most promising QCA application for strategy researchers is the possibility to test configurational hypotheses. Indeed, hypothetico-deductive large-N QCA applications present one of the most promising future directions to utilize QCA's set theoretic approach in strategy and organizations research as well as the social science research more generally (Greckhamer *et al.*, 2013). QCA's capacity for theory testing is particularly promising because rather than theorizing independent effects of single causes in an isolated manner, QCA's configurational approach both enables and guides researchers to test truly configurational theories (and hypotheses) regarding combinations of causal attributes hypothesized to be necessary or sufficient for the occurrence of an outcome. The key to utilizing QCA for testing hypotheses is for researchers to specify clearly configurational hypotheses predicting causal relationships of sufficiency or necessity, which consequently can be tested through set theoretic analysis. Once hypotheses are formulated based on extant theory, they can be tested through set theoretic analysis; for large enough datasets these tests can also be combined with statistical testing of probabilistic criteria (Ragin, 2000).

The challenges for utilizing QCA for theory testing are mainly of a theoretical (as opposed to methodological) nature. Because of the interdependence of theory building and the methodological tools to test theory, unsurprisingly strategy and organizations research has primarily been concerned with building (and consequently testing) theories concerned with the (strengths and directions of) relationships of individual causes with outcomes (Fiss, 2007; Greckhamer *et al.*, 2013). However, a few studies using QCA to test configurational theory exist in the literature. For example, Fiss (2011) provides an instructive example for using QCA to test configurational theory by testing the link between Miles and Snow's (1978) generic typology of organizational configurations and firm performance. To give another example Schneider, Schulze-Bentrop, and Paunescu (2010) utilize fsQCA to investigate the institutional sources of national competitive advantage in high-technology manufacturing; examining configurations of institutional features representing characteristic forms of capitalism linked to export performance, they specifically test hypotheses derived from theoretical arguments regarding institutional complementarities and institutional arbitrage.

For purposes of demonstration utilizing this chapter's running example, assume that based on previous theory we have formulated a number of hypotheses (as discussed above, the degree of generalization drawn from an empirical study and reflected in tested hypotheses should be consistent with the characteristics of the study's sample as well as theoretical arguments of generalizability; in the examples here I formulate hypotheses about the studied industry).

Hypothesis 1: Abundant slack resources are necessary for high performance in this manufacturing industry.

Hypothesis 2: A combination of high R&D intensity and abundant slack resources is sufficient for high performance in this manufacturing industry.

Hypothesis 3: A combination of abundant slack resources, large size, and a high degree of internationalization, is sufficient for high performance in this manufacturing industry.

To evaluate whether these hypotheses are supported by our analyses, I return to the results presented in Table 9.3. These results provide empirical support for Hypothesis 1, with abundant slack resources being a core condition in each of the three configurations consistently linked to high performance (however also see discussion above regarding conducting separate necessity tests if for theoretical reasons researchers expect and predict relations of necessity). Hypothesis 2 is partially supported by the results because the configurations of firms combining high R&D intensity and abundant slack resources with large size (S1) or lack of internationalization (S2b), are both subsets of the set of firms combining high R&D intensity and abundant slack resources, which Hypothesis 2 predicted to be linked to high performance (and which constitutes the combination of core conditions in S1 as well as a core and complementary condition in S2b). The set theoretic relation hypothesized in Hypothesis 3 is clearly not supported by the findings reported in Table 9.3. As with other hypothetico-deductive research, the key of QCA studies testing hypotheses is the theoretical support underlying the formulated hypotheses and the nature and quality of the sample (including the extent to which it represents the population's diversity of cases), in addition to proper execution of the empirical study.

Current trends of importance for strategic management researchers

In the previous section I have illustrated the four main types of applications of QCA that are available for strategy researchers to explore the diversity of cases and study complex causality. In this section I briefly highlight two issues currently at the forefront of developments in QCA that should be of particular interest for this community of scholars: developing QCA as alternative to general linear approaches for analyzing large-N datasets as well as for analyzing multilevel phenomena.

QCA and the analysis of large-N datasets

QCA has originally been conceived as an approach for the analysis of small-N datasets (i.e. encompassing approximately 12–50 cases) and the bulk of its applications has remained in these settings (Marx *et al.*, 2013; Ragin, 2000). However, recently QCA's potential and unique contributions for research analyzing large-N datasets has been recognized and developed (Greckhamer *et al.*, 2013). Specifically, recent strategy research has demonstrated QCA's potential to constitute a viable methodological alternative for the analysis of large-N datasets both to build and redirect (Greckhamer *et al.*, 2008b) as well as to test theory (Fiss, 2011); the work of Ragin and colleagues (Amoroso and Ragin, 1999; Ragin and Bradshaw, 1991; Ragin and Fiss, 2008) constitutes examples of large-N QCA studies in other disciplines. QCA's evolution with regard to the analysis of large-N datasets is important for strategy research because a majority of the field's mainstream research utilizes some form of general linear regression analysis and/or analysis of variance (Ketchen *et al.*, 2008); this arguably is due to the lack of methodological alternatives for analyzing large-N datasets (more than 50 cases), which have taken center stage in strategy research.

Greckhamer *et al.* (2013) outline QCA's potential for widespread application in research involving large-N settings to either complement or substitute general linear regression approaches, noting that while remaining configurational in its theoretical and methodological approach, applying QCA to large-N research settings inevitably involves a departure from some of the underlying ideas of the original small-N QCA approach. Specifically, these authors contrast small-N and large-N QCA applications with respect to objectives and underlying theoretical assumptions, processes and decisions researchers have to make in building the causal model, sample selection, and data analysis and interpretation. Consequently, Greckhamer *et al.* (2013) provide guidance for theoretical and methodological implications of using QCA in large-N settings. Relatedly, Fiss, Sharapov, and Cronquist (2013) explore the intersection of and potential complementarities between QCA and mainstream regression analysis techniques. Large-N applications of QCA are vital for its future prospect in strategy research because these settings enable researchers to utilize all the functions of QCA discussed in the previous section, particularly those concerned with building, redirecting, and testing configurational theories.

QCA and the analysis of multilevel issues

Addressing multilevel issues has become an issue of high priority in management and strategy research (Hitt *et al.*, 2007). For example, it is now well established that firm performance varies across industries, strategic groups, corporations, and businesses, and that these levels of analysis are related in a nested manner (Misangyi *et al.*, 2006; Short *et al.*, 2007). At the same time, similar to analyzing large-N datasets, strategy researchers have lacked alternatives to specialized regression approaches (including HLM) to study multilevel phenomena. Therefore, recent developments to utilize QCA as such an alternative are vital for strategy researchers.

Using QCA as alternative theoretical and methodological approach for analyzing causal relationships between industry, firm, and corporate effects and firm performance, Greckhamer *et al.* (2008b) demonstrate that QCA can be used to analyze causal relationships spanning multiple levels of analysis. Instead of parsing out the independent contributions of various industry-, corporate-, and business-unit level effects to performance, this study shows how QCA enables examination of the *combinations* of industry-, corporate-, and business-unit attributes that may be necessary and/or sufficient for attaining superior or inferior performance. Rather than asking, for example, "how much does corporate strategy matter?", it demonstrates how the use of QCA enables moving the question to "how do corporate factors combine with industry and business-unit factors to matter?" for business-unit performance.

Lacey and Fiss (2009) elaborate on QCA"s potential to study multilevel phenomena, conceptualizing the theoretical foundations of a set theoretic approach to multilevel issues as alternative to general linear regression approaches such as HLM. For example, expanding on the firm performance issue studied by Greckhamer *et al.* (2008b) discussed above, these authors note that the effects of an industry sector's characteristic could be qualitatively different for corporations with high diversification and high capital intensity than for those corporations with high diversification and low capital intensity, implying that causal attributes located at different levels may interact with each other and therefore should properly be considered part of configurations spanning levels. In short, Lacey and Fiss (2009) detail how QCA's set theoretic approach to multilevel issues and to conceptualizing cases as configurations across levels differs from conventional statistical approaches to multilevel analysis (variance decomposition methods and variance disaggregation methods such as HLM); going forward, applications of QCA for studying multilevel phenomena is a promising direction for strategy research because of the salience of multilevel challenges in the field.

Discussion

Research methods are significant for legitimate knowledge production in a discipline and the legitimacy of the knowledge produced hinges upon the use of a discipline's conventional practices (Elgin, 1996; Greckhamer, Koro-Ljungberg *et al.*, 2008). At this point in the evolution of strategic management research, general linear regression approaches constitute conventional practice whereas QCA is the relative "newcomer" methodology. Therefore, researchers using QCA might face a range of criticism of their work. Mahoney (2004) distinguishes three kinds of QCA critics. First, *uninformed dismissers* reject the QCA approach without being well informed about its assumptions and logics. Second, *informed skeptics*, after understanding QCA and its assumptions and practices conclude that other approaches are more powerful and/or appropriate for their research; for example they may conclude that regression analysis is a more powerful tool for studying causal relations. However, as Ketchen (2013: 309) has noted to researchers pursuing configurational approaches, the fact that configurational research encounters challenges in gaining acceptance "has the positive effect of forcing us to work harder to build compelling insights." This leads us to the third kind of QCA critic identified by Mahoney: *critical innovators* who identify issues or problems with QCA but are motivated to improve this approach by providing full or partial solutions to these problems.

To explain how QCA's relatively novel approach constitutes a viable alternative to mainstream strategy methodologies, in this chapter I have illustrated the four types of applications QCA offers and have complemented these illustrations by highlighting current developments of particular interest to strategy researchers. With these illustrations I have aimed to show that QCA is an alternative mode of inquiry that complements more conventional research approaches in strategy, particularly those rooted in general linear approaches; it has a demonstrated potential to inform and redirect central areas of strategy research and thereby to contribute to the development of the discipline, its theories, and its empirical insights (e.g. Fiss, 2007, 2011; Greckhamer *et al.*, 2008b; Greckhamer and Mossholder, 2011; Kogut *et al.*, 2004).

Finally, it is important to remember that the QCA approach is not inherently superior to other approaches, hence strategy researchers should judge whether choosing QCA or general linear regression approaches (or other methodologies, for that matter) is most suitable for their research project at hand. For this purpose, they should be able to judge the respective approach's relative merits and demerits. Most importantly, QCA and general linear regression approaches are built upon fundamentally different conceptions of causality (Ragin, 1987, 2000); while neither of these is superior, they have the potential to complement one another, hence the relative dominance of regression approaches is unnecessarily limiting empirical research (Katz *et al.*, 2005). Comparing the relative advantages and disadvantages of QCA and regression analysis, Vis (2012) illustrates that QCA has the advantages of addressing multiple conjunctive causality and being able to identify combinations of multiple causes linked to an outcome, which leads to greater horizontal complexity (i.e. to greater insights into alternative paths to an outcome) as compared to general linear regression analysis. On the other hand, regression analyses have the advantages of enabling researchers to test theories that emphasize a specific causal factor and to estimate the average net impact of this independent variable on the dependent variable.

References

Amoroso, L. M. and Ragin, C. (1999). Two approaches to understanding control of voluntary and involuntary job shifts among Germans and Foreigners from 1991 to 1996. *Vierteljahreshefte zur Wirtschaftsforschung, 68*(2), 222–229.

Berg-Schlosser, D. and De Meur, G. (1994). Conditions of democracy in Interwar Europe: A Boolean test of major hypotheses. *Comparative Politics, 26*(3), 253–279.

Berg-Schlosser, D., De Meur, G., and Rihoux, B. (2009). Qualitative comparative analysis (QCA) as an approach. In B. Rihoux and C. Ragin (eds), *Configurational Comparative Methods: Qualitative Comparative Analysis and Related Technique*, 1–18. Los Angeles: Sage.

Boswell, T. and Brown, C. (1999). The scope of general theory: Methods for linking deductive and inductive comparative history. *Sociological Methods and Research, 28*(2), 154–185.

Brigham, A. M. (2011). Agricultural exports and food insecurity in sub-Saharan Africa: A qualitative configurational analysis. *Development Policy Review, 29*(6), 729–748.

Caramani, D. (2009). *Introduction to the Comparative Method with Boolean Algebra*. Thousand Oaks, CA: Sage.

Crilly, D. (2011). Predicting stakeholder orientation in the multinational enterprise: A mid-range theory. *Journal of International Business Studies, 42*, 694–717.

Cronqvist, L. and Berg-Schlosser, D. (2009). Multi-value QCA (vmQCA). In B. Rihoux and C. Ragin (eds), *Configurational Comparative Methods: Qualitative Comparative Analysis and Related Techniques*, 69–86. Los Angeles: Sage.

Dess, G., Newport, S., and Rasheed, A. M. A. (1993). Configuration research in strategic management: Key issues and suggestions. *Journal of Management, 19*(4), 775–795.

Doty, D. H., Glick, W. H., and Huber, G. P. (1993). Fit, equifinality, and organizational effectiveness: A test of two configurational theories. *Academy of Management Journal, 36*, 1196–1250.

Elgin, C. Z. (1996). *Considered Judgment*. Princeton, NJ: Princeton University Press.

Fiss, P. (2007). Towards a set-theoretic approach for studying organizational configurations. *Academy of Management Review, 32*(4), 1180–1198.

Fiss, P. (2011). Building better causal theories: A fuzzy set approach to typologies in organization research. *Academy of Management Journal, 54*(2), 393–420.

Fiss, P., Marx, A., and Cambré, B. (2013). Configurational theory and methods in organizational research: Introduction. *Research in the Sociology of Organizations, 38*, 1–22.

Fiss, P., Sharapov, D., and Cronqvist, L. (2013). Opposites attract? Opportunities and challenges for integrating large-N QCA and econometric analysis. *Political Research Quarterly, 66*(1), 191–197.

Gerring, J. (2001). *Social Science Methodology: A Criterial Framework*. Cambridge: Cambridge University Press.

Greckhamer, T. (2011). Cross-cultural differences in compensation level and inequality across occupations: A set-theoretic analysis. *Organization Studies, 32*(1), 85–115.

Greckhamer, T. and Mossholder, K. (2011). Qualitative comparative analysis and strategic managment research: Current state and future prospects. In D. Ketchen and D. Bergh (eds), *Building Methodological Bridges: Research Methodology in Strategy and Management* (Vol. 6), 189–218. Bingley, UK: Emerald.

Greckhamer, T., Koro-Ljungberg, M., Cilesiz, S., and Hayes, S. (2008a). Demystifying interdisciplinary qualitative research. *Qualitative Inquiry, 14*(2), 307–331.

Greckhamer, T., Misangyi, V., Elms, H., and Lacey, R. (2008b). Using qualitative comparative analysis in strategic management research: An examination of combinations of industry, corporate, and business-unit effects. *Organizational Research Methods, 11*(4), 695–726.

Greckhamer, T., Misangyi, V., and Fiss, P. (2013). The two QCAs: From a small-N to a large-N set-theoretic approach. *Research in the Sociology of Organizations, 38*, 49–75.

Hitt, M., Beamish, P., Jackson, S., and Mathieu, J. (2007). Building theoretical and empirical bridges across levels: Multilevel research in management. *Academy of Management Journal, 50*(6), 1385–1399.

Hitt, M., Gimeno, J., and Hoskisson, R. (1998). Current and future research methods in strategic management. *Organizational Research Methods, 1*(6), 6–44.

Hodson, R. and Roscigno, V. J. (2004). Organizational success and worker dignity: Complementary or contradictory. *American Journal of Sociology, 110*(3), 672–708.

Katz, A., Hau, M. V., and Mahoney, J. (2005). Explaining the great reversal in Spanish America: Fuzzy-set analysis versus regression analysis. *Sociological Methods Research, 33*(4), 539–573.

Ketchen, D. (2013). We try harder: Some reflections on configurational theory and methods. *Research in the Sociology of Organizations, 38*, 303–309.

Ketchen, D., Boyd, B., and Bergh, D. (2008). Research methods in strategic management: Past accomplishments and future challenges. *Organizational Research Methods, 11*(4), 643–658.

Ketchen, D., Combs, J. G., Russell, C. J., Shook, C., Dean, M. A. *et al.* (1997). Organizational configurations and performance: A meta-analysis. *Academy of Management Journal, 40*(1), 223–240.

Ketchen, D., Thomas, J. B., and Snow, C. C. (1993). Organizational configurations and performance: A comparison of theoretical approaches. *Academy of Management Journal, 36*, 1278–1313.

Kiser, E., Drass, K. A., and Brustein, W. (1995). Ruler autonomy and war in early modern Western Europe. *International Studies Quarterly, 39*(1), 103–138.

Kogut, B., MacDuffie, J. P., and Ragin, C. (2004). Prototypes and strategy: Assigning causal credit using fuzzy sets. *European Management Review, 1*(2), 114–131.

Lacey, R. and Fiss, P. (2009). Comparative organizational analysis across multiple levels: A set-theoretic approach. *Research in the Sociology of Organizations, 26*, 91–116.

Mahoney, J. (2004). Reflections on Fuzzy-Set/QCA. *Newsletter of the American Political Science Association, 2*(2), 17–21.

Marx, A., Rihoux, B., and Ragin, C. (2013). The origins, development, and application of qualitative comparative analysis: The first 25 years. *European Political Science Review, 6*(1), 115–142.

Meyer, A. D., Tsui, A. S., and Hinings, C. R. (1993). Configurational approaches to organizational analysis. *Academy of Management Journal, 36*(6), 1175–1195.

Miller, D. (1986). Configurations of strategy and structure: Towards a synthesis. *Strategic Management Journal, 7*, 233–249.

Miller, D. (1996). Configurations revisited. *Strategic Management Journal, 17*, 505–512.

Misangyi, V., Elms, H., Greckhamer, T., and LePine, J. (2006). A new perspective on a fundamental debate: A multi-level approach to industry, corporate, and business-unit effects. *Strategic Management Journal, 27*(6), 571–590.

Pajunen, K. (2008). Institutions and inflows of foreign direct investment: A fuzzy-set analysis. *Journal of International Business Studies, 39*, 652–669.

Ragin, C. (1987). *The Comparative Method: Moving Beyond Qualitative and Quantitative Strategies.* Berkeley: University of California Press.

Ragin, C. (2000). *Fuzzy-Set Social Science.* Chicago: University of Chicago Press.

Ragin, C. (2006). Set relations in social research: Evaluating their consistency and coverage. *Political Analysis, 14*(3), 291–310.

Ragin, C. (2008). *Redesigning Social Inquiry: Fuzzy Sets and Beyond.* Chicago: University of Chicago Press.

Ragin, C. (2013). New directions in the logic of social inquiry. *Political Research Quarterly, 66*(1), 171–174.

Ragin, C. and Bradshaw, Y. (1991). Statistical analysis of employment discrimination: A review and critique. *Research in Social Stratification and Mobility, 10*, 199–228.

Ragin, C., Davey, S., and Drass, K. (2009). *FS/QCA 2.5.* Tucson, AZ: Department of Sociology, University of Arizona.

Ragin, C. and Fiss, P. (2008). Net effects versus configurations: An empirical demonstration. In C. Ragin (ed.), *Redesigning Social Inquiry: Fuzzy Sets and Beyond,* 190–212. Chicago: University of Chicago Press.

Rihoux, B. (2003). Bridging the gap between qualitative and quantitative worlds? A retrospective and prospective view on qualitative comparative analysis. *Field Methods, 15*(4), 351–365.

Rihoux, B., Álamos-Concha, P., Bol, D., Marx, A., and Rezsöhazy, I. (2013). A comprehensive mapping of QCA applications in journal articles from 1984 to 2011. *Political Research Quarterly, 66*(1), 175–184.

Rihoux, B. and Ragin, C. (2009). *Configurational Comparative Methods: Qualitative Comparative*

Analysis (QCA) and Related Techniques. Los Angeles: Sage Publications.

Schneider, C. and Wagemann, C. (2012). *Set-Theoretic Methods for the Social Sciences.* Cambridge: Cambridge University Press.

Schneider, M. R., Schulze-Bentrop, C., and Paunescu, M. (2010). Mapping the institutional capital of high-tech firms: A fuzzy-set analysis of capitalist variety and export performance. *Journal of International Business Studies, 41,* 246–266.

Short, J., Ketchen, D., Palmer, T., and Hult, G. T. (2007). Firm, strategic group, and industry influences on performance. *Strategic Management Journal, 28*(2), 147–167.

Smithson, M. and Verkuilen, J. (2006). *Fuzzy Set Theory: Applications in the Social Sciences.* Thousand Oaks, CA: Sage Publications.

Vink, M. P. and Vliet, O. v. (2009). Not quite crisp, not yet fuzzy? Assessing the potentials and pitfalls of multi-value QCA. *Field Methods, 21*(3), 265–289.

Vis, B. (2012). The comparative advantages of fsQCA and regression analyses for moderately large-N analyses. *Sociological Methods and Research, 41*(1), 168–198.

Zadeh, L. A. (1972). A fuzzy-set-theoretic interpretation of linguistic hedges. *Journal of Cybernetics, 2*(3), 4–34.

10

NEUROSCIENTIFIC METHODS FOR STRATEGIC MANAGEMENT

Sebastiano Massaro[1]

In the past decade, social disciplines have looked with increasing interest at neuroscience. From anthropology (Adenzato and Garbarini, 2006) to law (Greene and Cohen, 2004; Jones and Shen, 2012), from politics (Connolly, 2002) to sociology (Franks, 2010), the integration of neuroscientific aspects into social studies has become a phenomenon of considerable interest. Business scholarship has not been immune from this trend with contributions crossing leadership (Ghadiri, Habermacher, and Peters, 2012), marketing (Ariely and Berns, 2010; Lee, Broderick, and Chamberlain, 2007) and strategy (Powell, 2011), among others. Accordingly, universities have created dedicated centers of research; journals and conferences have started to offer substantial space to the role of neuroscience in management; and several researchers have developed international partnerships aiming to extend these cutting-edge approaches.[2]

Although some scholars have questioned the appropriateness and viability of neuroscience to effectively advance social analyses and business research (e.g., Bennett, Hacker, and Bennett, 2003; Gul and Pesendorfer, 2008; Lindebaum and Zundel, 2013), the intensification and effects of this type of studies cannot be denied. Indeed, knowing more on how our brain works can help to advance our understanding of human cognition, emotions, behavior, and decision making, both inside and outside organizations.

In this work, I argue that to better appreciate how neuroscience can inform research in management, understanding the rationale of relevant neuroscience methods, is a fundamental step currently missing in the scholarship.[3] Only through this knowledge, will management scholars fully appreciate the potential of the related research and possibly incorporate further these instruments into their exploratory equipment.

By mainly concentrating on brain-imaging methods, this chapter provides an opening review, for both those researchers who are new to neuroscience, and those multidisciplinary-oriented scholars who are seeking to refresh their knowledge on the topic. Following an introductory excursus on the early applications of these methods to management studies, I will explain how they can be classified, and supply a core description of relevant techniques. Moreover, I will offer some evidence related to management scholarship, and in particular to strategy, one of the fields most attentive to neuroscience (e.g., Powell, 2011; Powell, Lovallo, and Fox, 2011). Finally, the chapter will pinpoint critical considerations for management research related to employing neuroscience approaches.

The partnership between neuroscience and management

The idea of coupling descriptions of human behaviors and the brain has actively engaged researchers for centuries (for a history of neuroscience see, e.g., Finger [2001]).Yet, the experimental partnership between cognitive neuroscience and social disciplines – nowadays often called social cognitive and affective neuroscience – has acquired wider resonance only in the past couple of decades, thanks to the emergence of *functional neuroimaging of behavior* (Raichle, 2003; 2009a), the combination of neuroimaging and behavioral research approaches. This research area generally refers to the use of technologies measuring hemodynamic, electromagnetic, or biophysical properties and changes in the brain and in the nervous system, following an experimental behavioral manipulation, task or stimulus, to provide visual metrics (e.g. graph, image, scan) of the underlying brain regions and neural functions. The resulting outcomes enable inferences about the relationships between neural substrates and behavioral or mental processes associated.[4]

One of the first techniques used to measure brain activity, *electroencephalography* (EEG), emerged in the 1930s when Berger (1929) demonstrated that electrical activity from the brain could be measured by placing conducting material on the scalp and amplifying the consequential signal. After Dawson (1951) developed a method of signal averaging, management research suggested EEG's use to investigate the neural basis of performance decrements in the workplace (Scott, 1966). The successive, essentially misleading, idea that the left hemisphere of the human brain would control *only* logic, analytical ability, sequential perception, and language, while the right hemisphere spatial and simultaneous perception, imagination, and intuition (for a review see, e.g., Gazzaniga and LeDoux [1978]) further inspired management inquiries. Mintzberg (1976) addressed the challenge of coupling neuroscience information with management research when he imprecisely claimed that "right-brain is holistic and the left-brain logical," suggesting differences in the brain hemispheres were compelling for business studies, training, and practice. Afterwards, such claims offered room to a body of management neuromythology supported by a rather lay dissemination (Hines, 1987). Those outcomes allowed, for instance, to argue that executives tend to use more right brain processing than analysts, and vice versa (Doktor, 1978), and contributed to setting the basis for the development of frameworks seeking to enhance managers' analytical and intuitive skills (Robey and Taggart, 1982).

Although EEG offered preliminary management-related findings obtained by examining brain activity, it is with the advent of tomographic techniques that the actual imaging takeover began.[5] In 1973, Godfrey Hounsfield (1973) introduced a breakthrough technique: *X-ray Computed Tomography* (CT). It had immediate impact; not only did it revolutionize medical clinical practice, facilitating screening and diagnosis, but it also provoked behavioral scientists to consider new ways of imaging the brain (Garvey and Hanlon, 2002; Raichle, 2009b; Rogers, 2003).

Subsequently, another type of tomography, *Positron Emission Tomography* (PET), enabled creating autoradiographs of brain functions (Tilyou, 1991). This ushered in the beginning of the "hemodynamic era" for functional brain-imaging: by injecting a radioactive pharmaceutical in a subject, it was possible to quickly measure blood flow changes and associate them with measurements of brain function (Phelps and Mazziotta, 1985). PET also made possible "experimentalizing" a strategy of *cognitive subtraction* with functional neuroimaging (Donders, 1969; Petersen *et al.*, 1988), which, although often questioned (Friston *et al.*, 1996; Sartori and Umiltà, 2000), has represented a pillar for numerous studies. Cognitive subtraction mostly relies on assumptions of *linearity* and *pure insertion*: an elicited mental component evokes an "extra" physiological activation that is the same regardless of preexisting mental and physiological contexts (Price and Friston, 1997). This suggests that functional imaging of behavioral processes can then be derived by subtraction of a control task from an experimental assignment, so that differences in brain activity can be attributed to selected mental components (Friston *et al.*, 1996). Due to its logistics (i.e. requirement for local presence of a particle accelerator) and concerns for participants' health (i.e., use of radioactive material) PET has not arisen as the technique of choice for most of management inquiries. However, it has been employed to identify neural substrates of phenomena such as planning (Dagher *et al.*, 1999), and risk-avoiding and ambiguity-avoiding behaviors (Smith *et al.*, 2002).

More recently, another neuroimaging technique has offered the ability to apprise where activity is occurring in the brain while we are performing experimental behavioral tasks or we are at rest. This is *functional Magnetic Resonance Imaging* (fMRI), which grounds on nuclear magnetic resonance physics (Bloch, 1946; Lauterbur, 1973; Purcell, Torrey, and Pound, 1946). The revolution in neuroscience arrived in 1992, when researchers associated Magnetic Resonance Imaging with brain activity-related changes in blood oxygenation. The signal arising from the unique combination of brain physiology and nuclear physics became known as the *Blood Oxygen Level Dependent* (BOLD) signal (Ogawa, Lee, and Tank, 1990).[6] There rapidly followed several evidences of BOLD signal changes in humans during "brain activation," giving official birth to fMRI (Bandettini *et al.*, 1992; Kwong *et al.*, 1992; Ogawa *et al.*, 1992). fMRI has dominated functional brain imaging of behavior research ever since, and has been the neuroimaging technique bringing the greatest promises to management research. For instance, some encouraging contributions have been those applied to strategic games (e.g., Sanfey *et al.*, 2003) and those investigating the neural underpinnings associated with strategic insight and intuition (e.g., Volz and von Cramon, 2006).

Classifications: Between resolution and functionality

To fully appreciate how neuroscience techniques can attempt to "open the black box of the brain," it is important to classify them under a systemic outlook, according to their distinctive characteristics. Experimental methods in neuroscience have traditionally been organized according to a matrixed perspective that considers and emphasizes the distinct spatial and temporal resolutions of each technique (Churchland and Sejnowski, 1988), as shown in Figure 10.1a.[7]

The concept of *resolution* is an essential prerequisite for understanding the essence of each neuroimaging procedure. Simply speaking, it allows providing answers for questions such as "how good is a brain scan image?" The response is commonly disentangled into concepts of spatial or temporal resolution, which are respectively the abilities to discriminate between two points in space and time (Menon *et al.*, 1998). A high spatial resolution determines a sharp image, while a low one gives a "pixely" appearance to the image; for example, when two spatially close (i.e., a few millimeters) anatomical structures are distinguishable in an image, this has a higher resolution than one when they are not discernable. Spatial resolution depends on the properties of the system that creates the images, such as gradient strength and digitalizing rate (Bandettini, 2002), being therefore limited by hardware and acquisition protocols. Several techniques provide spatial information of the human brain with high resolution, including fMRI and PET.

However, understanding the neuroscience of mental processes requires information not only on the spatial localization of brain activities, but also on their temporal evolution. Analyses with a temporal resolution of milliseconds can be conducted by electroencephalographic (EEG) and magnetoencephalographic (MEG) methods, which are based on the electric or magnetic activity caused by movements of ions inside and outside cellular membranes (e.g., Kristeva *et al.*, 1979). These methods provide almost real-time information on brain activity; yet, EEG has lower spatial localization and resolution.

The importance of understanding the properties of each method is fundamental. Limited resolutions bound practical applications of the techniques. Moreover, each technique allows a different examination of the neural functions specifically on the basis of its intrinsic characteristics. Some might believe the results obtained exploiting different resolutions of several techniques could just converge in an overall explanation of the neural processes. This claim however is inaccurate. Several other influences determine an experimental outcome, such as whether the process is recording physiological brain activity, or instead interfering with it, or stimulating the brain to change a behavioral response. Therefore, the appropriate methods and levels at which to examine brain function largely depend on the research question being addressed (Stewart and Walsh, 2006).

Organizational scholars have drawn from this resolution-based classification, arguing its ease in depicting the relative advantages and disadvantages of each method: as seen in Figure 10.1b, this categorization has helped delineating the

(a)

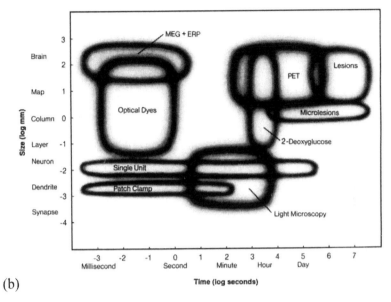

(b)

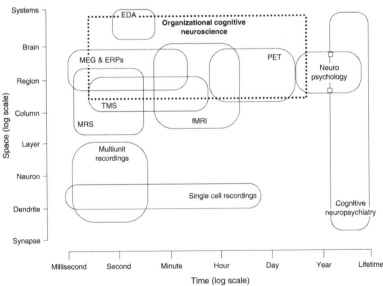

FIGURE 10.1 Spatial and temporal resolutions of neuroscience techniques

Notes: The vertical axes show the spatial extent of the techniques; the horizontal axes represent the
time intervals over which information can be collected with each technique. Recordings from
the central nervous system are often limited in resolution by the properties of nervous tissue
and of the specific method.

Sources: (a) Churchland and Sejnowski, 1988; (b) Senior, Lee, and Butler, 2011.

preliminary experimental boundaries of *organizational neuroscience* (Becker, Cropanzano, and Sanfey, 2011; Senior, Lee, and Butler, 2011).

Kable (2011) has suggested a complementary framework to organize neuroscience techniques when applied to social sciences, on the ground of their underlying testing rationale. *Association tests* are those experimental methods that implicate a manipulation of a psychological state or behavior, the simultaneous measurements of the neural activity, and the following analysis of the correlation between the two. These include classic fMRI, PET, EEG, and MEG approaches. *Necessity tests* are instead those that involve a disruption of the neural activity and aim to show how this manipulation impairs a specific mental function. *Sufficiency tests* are those enhancing a neural activity and seeking to establish that this process results in a specific behavior or mental state. Necessity and sufficiency tests, such as lesion studies, neuropharmacological or Transcranial Magnetic Stimulation (TMS) experiments, are able to directly probe the causality between neural and mental states.

Overall, it is quite straightforward to argue that knowledge of these classifications represents an important apparatus for scholars who both seek to understand the technicalities, and also inquire what different kinds of evidence they should gather to allow the most appropriate inferences about brain functions.

The techniques

The main neuroimaging techniques examined in this chapter include functional Magnetic Resonance Imaging (fMRI), Positron Emission Tomography (PET), and electroencephalography (EEG). These methods generally allow identifying brain areas displaying increased activity, in comparison to controls, while the subjects are performing specific tasks.

Functional Magnetic Resonance Imaging (fMRI)

Functional Magnetic Resonance Imaging (fMRI) is probably the most known and widely applied neuroscience methodology in business research (Dimoka *et al.*, 2012). To understand the foundation of fMRI it is first necessary to appreciate the underlying principles of Magnetic Resonance Imaging (MRI). MRI exploits the fact that protons (atomic hydrogen nuclei) of our body in the presence of an external magnetic field behave like compass needles, aligning in parallel to that field (Le Bihan, 1996). Simply put, after electromagnetic pulses are applied to these protons (and then switched off), they emit detectable and characteristic radio signals, allowing a computer to reconstruct images of the inner organs (for a review, see Brown and Semelka [2010]). Imposing the magnetic field and pulses and acquiring the resulting signals requires specific equipment, consisting of an MRI magnet, a system of coils and signal amplifier systems (Figure 10.2). An MRI scanner is a cylindrical tube whose core is constituted by a very powerful electro-magnet (Chapman, 2006); a typical magnet, well-suited for fMRI research, has field strength of 3 Teslas (T).[8]

Functional MRI uses these principles to detect the magnetic signal from hydrogen nuclei in water (H_2O). It relies on differences in magnetic properties between venous (oxygen-poor) and arterial (oxygen-rich) blood, which allow revealing the changes in blood oxygenation and flow that occur in response to neural activity, the so-named *neurovascular coupling* (Logothetis *et al.*, 2001; Logothetis and Wandell, 2004). When a brain area is more active it requires more oxygen, and as a consequence blood flow increases to the active area (Fox and Raichle, 1986; Uludag *et al.*, 2004). By using the BOLD signal (Ogawa *et al.*, 1990) fMRI allows researchers to examine activation maps showing which parts of the brain are involved in a particular mental process (Bandettini *et al.*, 1992; Ogawa *et al.*, 1992; Kwong *et al.*, 1992).

Nonetheless, the extent, dynamics, and underlying mechanisms of neurovascular coupling are not yet fully understood (Attwell and Iadecola, 2002; Magistretti and Pellerin, 1999) and the BOLD signal depends on several parameters, so its biophysical link with neuronal activation is not yet entirely straightforward (Malonek *et al.*, 1997). Moreover, the fact that fMRI experiments elicit a BOLD signal does not indicate that subjects necessarily had psychological events associated with that part of the brain (Poldrack, 2006).

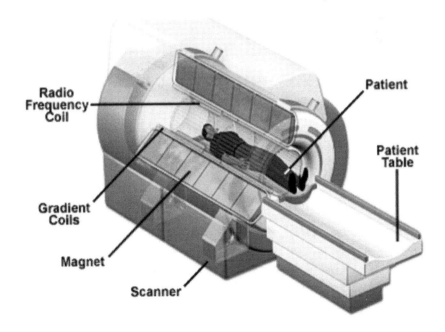

FIGURE 10.2 Main components of an MRI scanner

Source: http://www.themesotheliomalibrary.com

These concerns have lead to some research issues for fMRI research, which however can rely on high spatial (typically 3 millimeters) and high temporal (about 2 seconds) resolution (Song, Huettel, and McCharty, 2006).[9] For instance, the spatial localization of the BOLD signal can be distant from the actual site of neural activity, because the signal source includes various vascular networks sized from capillaries to large draining veins, and the physiological delay necessary for the mechanisms triggering the vascular response to work limits the temporal resolution of the technique (Le Bihan *et al.*, 2006). Research is constantly improving resolution parameters, yet these may be ultimately limited by our physiology. For example, the brain vascular supply is not regulated on the scale of individual neurons and might then be restricted to 0.5-1.5 mm (Menon and Kim, 1999).

Nonetheless, recent work has suggested that *water diffusion MRI* (for a review, see Beaulieu [2002]), could among other methods, overcome some of these limits: changes in the magnitude of diffusion of water molecules within cerebral tissue during neuronal activation would likely reflect transient changes in the microstructure of the neurons, which can then be imagined (Le Bihan, 2003). Although this suggestion has been challenged (Yacoub *et al.*, 2008), capturing such effects would have a remarkable consequence on neuroimaging applications in behavioral reserach, since they would be directly linked to neuronal events in contrast to blood flow effects, which are secondary.

Despite these and other concerns, fMRI has been extensively recruited in social sciences (e.g. Camerer, 2003; Crockett *et al.*, 2008; Damasio, 1994; Glimcher and Rustichini, 2004). Not surprisingly, it has also been the technique of choice to investigate several strategic management paradigms.

For example, fMRI studies have significantly contributed to investigating the neural basis for cooperation. Cooperation, the willful contribution of personal effort to the completion of interdependent tasks, including jobs, has been a mainstay in the management literature (e.g., Barnard, 1938; March and Simon, 1958; the whole special issue of the *Academy of Management Journal* 38(1) [1995]). McCabe and colleagues (2001) employed fMRI in two-person reciprocity games in which participants were facing both human and computer counterparts. They found that cooperation with humans was highly correlated with increased activation of brain regions responsible for joint attention and mutual gains, and decreased activation of regions associated with immediate reward gratification. This study prompted further exploration of other aspects key for management research, such as the role of fairness and trust in the workplace. For instance, equity theory (Adams, 1963; 1965) suggests that perceptions of fairness are job-related motivational grounds that can influence responses of job performers. Research has argued that fair treatment has positive effects on individual employee attitudes (e.g., satisfaction and commitment) and individual behaviors (e.g., absenteeism and citizenship behavior) (Colquitt *et al.*, 2001; Moorman, 1991), while unfair treatment conveys opposite behaviors and attitudes (Cohen-Charash and Mueller, 2007). Research has measured the neural responses and identified key correlates underlying social exchanges and sense of fairness in volunteers playing different strategic games, such as the prisoner dilemma, the ultimatum game, or the reciprocal trust game. For instance, King-Casas and colleagues (2005) found that reciprocity expressed by one social actor strongly predicts trust expressed by his or her partner, a behavioral finding mirrored by an increased activation in the dorsal striatum as compared to control conditions.

In recent years, functional magnetic resonance imaging studies have begun to covered other strategic management paradigms, embracing topics spanning from exploration and exploitation (Daw et al., 2006) to escalation of commitment. For example, research has widely established how the inability to plan ahead often results in escalation of commitment, myopia of learning, or unnecessary risk taking (Levinthal and March, 1993). Escalation of commitment is that situation whenever a manager, or any decision maker, keeps committing considerable resources to a course of action in the hope of achieving a positive outcome, but instead experiences disappointing results (Staw, 1981; Brockner, 1992). Campbell-Meiklejohn and colleagues (2008) highlighted neural correlates of this complex behavior: in comparison to control conditions, decisions not to escalate were associated with increased activity in the anterior cingulate, left anterior insula, posterior cingulate, and parietal cortices, but decreased activity in the ventro-medial prefrontal cortex. Decisions to escalate were associated with a decrease of activity in the anterior cingulate, right anterior insula, and inferior frontal gyrus, but there was no increase in activity in comparison with the control condition, which instead suggested increased activity in the ventro-medial prefrontal cortex.

The burst of wide applicability in presenting such imaging research outcomes has perhaps raised the bitterest criticisms around fMRI results, despite scholars having highlighted actual limitations of the methodology (Logothetis, 2008; Poldrack, 2012). As seen above, spatial resolution barriers would not allow to map the intimate nature of individual neurons (i.e., in a voxel there are about 5.5 millions neurons) and directly distinguish between functional activities relevant to the task, irrelevant to the task, and noise. The averaging of imaging, which often leads to ignoring differences between individuals, random effect analysis, and statistical issues are other arguments often brought up to underlie problems of research reproducibility (Vul et al., 2009; the whole *Perspectives on Psychological Science* issue 4(3), [2009] is a must read, dedicated to the issue of correlations in psychological research using fMRI). Recent investigations have started to address these concerns and suggest that increased reproducibility can be achieved through the combined results from multicenter fMRI studies (Stöcker et al., 2005), the development of neuroimaging databases, the use of consistent protocols (Liu et al., 2004), similar machineries, homogeneous sampling, and multiple comparisons correction methods (Poldrack et al., 2011).

In any case, these considerations per se should not prevent management scholars from exploring the use of this methodology, since the debate is a current challenge accompanying the daily routine of every neuroimaging scientist. For one, an analysis of the rise of brain imaging methods from a socio-historical point of view (Beaulieu, 2000), has revealed that neuroscientists have a love-hate relationship with their images: these are useful for blending data and convenient for communicating results to a large audience; however, they hold incredible exposure to the most disparate criticisms.

Positron Emission Tomography (PET)

Positron Emission Tomography (PET) was one of the first techniques used to exploit the links between neural activity and metabolism to study brain functions (Phelps and Mazziotta, 1985; Raichle and Snyder, 2007). It is an analytical nuclear imaging technique, able to provide high spatial resolution images of functional processes occurring in the brain, and it has traditionally been used to make *in vivo* measurements of the anatomical distribution and rates of specific biochemical reactions (Gulyas *et al.*, 2002). The term nuclear signifies that the technique relies on radioactively labeled molecules (tracers). Similar to MRI, PET requires dedicated instrumentation, which includes a ring of detectors located around the patient's head (Turkington, 2001) (Figure 10.3).

In a typical PET experiment, a short-lived radioisotope of a biologically relevant element (carbon, nitrogen, oxygen, fluorine) is produced locally using a low-energy particle accelerator (i.e., a cyclotron). It is then synthetically bound to a biomolecule, usually glucose or oxygen, or to a drug, to form a physiological radiotracer able to emit positrons (positively charged particles of the mass of an electron). This radiotracer is then injected intravenously into the subject, so that it can bind to a specific receptor or enter into specific metabolic pathways. During the natural process of radioactive decay the positron is emitted and travels for a short distance within the brain, then collides with an electron. This impact produces two coincidental rays (gamma rays), which can be measured by the

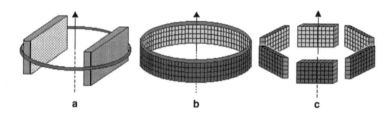

      a   b   c

(a) a rotating gantry

(b) circular

(c) polygonal rings

FIGURE 10.3   Examples of PET detectors

Source: Humm, Rosenfeld, and Del Guerra, 2003

detectors around the subject's head (Ter-Pogossian and Herscovitch, 1985). When two opposite detectors on the ring simultaneously recognize a gamma ray, a computerized system records this as a coincidence event. The computer records all of the coincidence events that occur during the imaging period and then reconstructs cross-sectional images. Bi- and three-dimensional images are often accomplished with the aid of an X-ray CT scan performed on the subject during the same session, in the same machine (Pelizzari *et al.*, 1989). Since the tracer accumulates in the brain in direct proportion to the blood flow, the greater the flow, the greater the radioactive count rate. Thus, the distribution and intensity of the uptake of the positron-emitting radiotracer indicates the underlying neural activity, and the *regional cerebral blood flow* (rCBF) works as the dependent variable (Raichle, 1979; Raichle, Martin, and Herscovitch, 1983).

PET presents several disadvantages in comparison to fMRI. Above all, it involves the use of ionizing radiations, which have potential harmful effects on the research subjects. Moreover, it affords relatively poorer spatial (4 millimeters) and temporal (30–40 seconds) resolutions and generally involves one to two measurements per subject, with each measurement reflecting neural activity averaged over one minute (Kato, Taniwaki, and Kuwabara, 2000).

Nonetheless, PET has provided intriguing insights on topics central to strategic management. One of the most productive lines of research developed around the concept of planning. Planning has been a growing topic in strategy inquiries since the 1950s (Payne, 1957), and has been identified as a variable able to both impact firm performance and have a role in strategic decision making (Ansoff, 1991; Armstrong, 1982; Mintzberg, 1994). Strategic planning decisions emerge from complex interactions among individuals with subjective interests and perception; understanding the respective neural correlates can inform further on both planning processes and theories. Several neuroimaging studies have independently addressed the issue. Associating PET studies with the Tower of London (TOL) task – an adaptation of the Tower of Hanoi (Anzai and Simon, 1979), which consists of moving colored balls within a limited number of moves in order to achieve a given goal configuration – researchers shed a light on the anatomic and physiological correlates of planning processes. Longer planning times and fewer moves to complete a problem are associated with significantly higher regional cerebral blood flow in the left prefrontal cortex, whereas execution time is negatively correlated with both left and right prefrontal rCBF (Baker *et al.*, 1996; Dagher *et al.*, 1999).

With the preponderant emergence of fMRI, more widely accessible and cheaper, the use of PET in social sciences has seemingly plateaued. Nevertheless, PET may still hold a relevant role for management scholarships. This technique measures blood flow in absolute terms (while fMRI measures changes in blood oxygenation), permitting therefore a more precise comparison between subjects, sessions, and brain regions (Minoshima *et al.*, 1994). Therefore, there is considerable reliability for research investigating associations within subjects across different tasks.

Moreover, PET has the unique ability to measure cerebral metabolism, hence associate differences in molecular synthesis with difference in behavior (Phelps and Mazziotta, 1985). For instance, in the striatum, differences in the synthesis of dopamine, a molecule frequently implicated in impulsive behaviors, has been associated with differences in reversal learning (Cools *et al.*, 2009). This phenomenon is connected to decisions made under emotional situations and conflicts (Fellows and Farah, 2003; Kovalchik and Allman, 2005), which are circumstances often experienced across several management levels (Huy, 2002).

Electroencephalography (EEG)

While measuring regional cerebral flow can provide a detailed anatomical mapping of active brain areas, the time resolution of the related methods is generally too slow to reveal the rapid flux of neuronal communication. Conversely, surface recordings of the electric fields emanating from active populations of neurons offer a higher degree of temporal resolution (on the order of milliseconds), but yield a less complete picture of anatomical sources. This method, called electroencephalography (EEG), is the oldest non-invasive method to measure brain activity (Nunez, 1995).

The existence of electrical currents in the brain was discovered by Richard Caton (1875), and the first electroencephalographic experiment was performed in 1929 by Hans Berger (1929), in which he discovered the *alpha rhythm*, waves with a uniform rhythm typical of a subject awake in a quiet resting state (Adrian and Matthews, 1934). Since this pioneering discovery, researchers have conducted thousands of experiments, leading to advances in both the recording systems and the understanding of brain functions (Freeman and Quiroga, 2013). Nowadays, it is acknowledged that our brain produces several types of brainwaves with different frequencies, and each of them is associated with particular mental states. As an example, *beta waves* have a frequency of 15–38 Hz and are characteristic of individuals who are fully awake and alert (Nunez, 1995).

EEG employs advanced signal processing methods to infer data about the brain through the scalp and skull (Niedermeyer and Lopes da Silva, 1995). It develops around the concept that neurons are excitable cells, which transmit information through electrical or chemical signals via dedicated structures called *synapses*. Populations of neurons are connected into networks and communicate with each other repeatedly by sending electrical impulses. The technique specifically measures the resulting electrical currents that flow underneath the scalp while short extensions of certain cortical neurons (the dendrites of pyramidal neurons) are excited (Atwood and Mackay, 1989). When the brain processes an event, thousands of these cells are activated at the same time, causing a fluctuation in voltage. In order to measure these signals a cap with several electrodes is placed on the subject's head. By quantifying the differences between the electrodes, the flow and strength of the electric field can be inferred (Tyner *et al.*, 1989). Since the signals that reach the scalp are very small (usually in the range of 1 to 100 μV) they are then amplified and converted into a digital form (Luck, 2005). However, because EEG detects electrical signals at the scalp, it can only measure activity coming from the cortex, making almost impossible evaluating direct activation in deeper lying structures (Bronzino, 1995). Moreover, EEG has a very high temporal resolution, hence allowing for very fast measurement within milliseconds. However, the low spatial resolution makes it challenging to precisely localize the source of the signal.

To be able to extract the correct electrical signal associated with a behavioral experimental task and distinguish it from the background noise, a functional EEG study requires multiple averaged measurements. By averaging signals, researchers can indicate that a certain task causes a specific activation of the measured brain region at a specific time stamp. Simply put, the resulting response is called event-related potential (ERP) (Squires *et al.*, 1976).

The preparation of a standard EEG setup takes a relatively long time (Lebedev and Nicolelis, 2006); however, an EEG assessment can be accomplished while people are seated and engaged in everyday activities, including conversations associated with the type of task the experiment involves. Being relatively inexpensive, non-invasive, and non-harmful for the participants of a study, EEG has been one of the most applied techniques in management studies.

Already in the 1980s, Robey and Taggart (1981; 1982) sought to establish a linkage between measures of managerial styles and brain activity recorded with EEG. Drawing on the insights on hemispheric dominance and on the initial claims of Doktor (1978) they argued relationships between cerebral dominance and scales able to assess distinct strategic leadership types. More recently, Waldman and colleagues (2011) focused on inspirational management and its association with electrical brain activity, by recording subjects' beta waves in terms of coherence. In this way they were able to measure the coordinated activity between multiple parts of the brain when the subjects were presented a visual task on activities related to inspirational leadership (Figure 10.4). They showed that coherence in the right frontal areas of the brain could offer the basis for social visionary communication, which helps to build followers' perceptions of charismatic leaders. Although this research pipeline has ambitious potential, with some authors foreseeing the eventuality to train managers to "replicate such brain patterns," its results shall be understood with caution (as reported in Dvorak and Badal [2007]).

EEG has been employed to understand several other management constructs, such as punishment behavior. This topic has received increasing attention from management researchers (Simons, 1991), as it is associated with important variables such as power, reward, cooperation, and fairness. For instance, when managers are considered to have punished others unfairly, they not only impair their own reputations, but also risk eliciting negative attitudes and counterproductive behaviors, weakening the perceived legitimacy of their authority (Ball, Treviño, and Sims, 1994). Knoch and colleagues (2010) disclosed that the right lateral prefrontal cortex may play a central role in punishment behavior: subjects with an active PFC region seem most likely to punish an unfair proposal, even though the action has disadvantages for themselves, and vice versa.

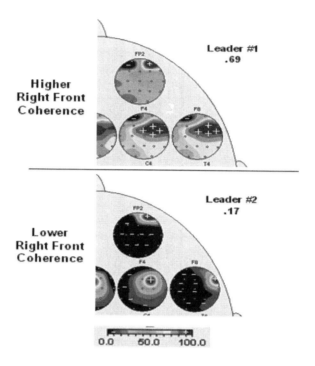

FIGURE 10.4 Spectral analysis of right front coherence in leadership research

Notes: The gradient shows the levels of coherence on 3 right frontal electrode locations, including areas at 0% (indicated by the minus signs), areas at 100% (indicated by plus signs), and in between. Dark regions with a + represent areas with high degrees of coherence (75% or higher); dark regions with minus signs characterize areas with low coherence (25% or lower). The numeric values indicate the summed averaged coherence scores for such brain regions in different leaders.

Source: Waldman, Balthazard, and Peterson, 2011

Lesion studies, VLSM, TMS, and MEG

It is central to highlight that while the techniques examined so far can identify brain activation, they cannot independently determine which of these areas are indispensable for performing the experimental task. This information can instead be provided by neuropsychological studies.

Among them, *lesion studies* are the oldest approaches to the study of mental functions. Already in 1861, Paul Broca (1861) suggested a relation between language and the brain's left hemisphere, setting the basis for localizing human brain function by studying the correlation between a behavioral disorder and the site of a brain injury. This approach has been the milestone for a long tradition of neuropsychological research, grounding the rationale of *cognitive dissociation*

(Caramazza, 1986; Shallice, 1988). Single dissociation occurs when damage in a brain region causes a disruption in one specific mental function but not in another, allowing inference that those functions are independent of each other (Kolb and Whishaw, 2009). Alternatively, double dissociation is conceivable when a subject with brain damage shows poor performance on one task and good performance on another task, while other patients show the opposite performance. This allows inference that the two related mental processes function independently of each other. Several researchers have criticized the logic or some of its applications, arguing, for example, that double dissociations do not necessarily imply a difference in processing mechanisms between tasks (Bullinaria and Chater, 1995; Chater and Ganis, 1991).

Despite these criticisms and the advancements provided by modern neuroimaging techniques, management research can still gather important investigative elements from lesion studies (Rorden and Karnath, 2004). One approach, for example, is that of grouping subjects according to the lesions' locations and comparing the performance of each group. This can be exemplified in attention studies. Attention is a topic of great interest in strategic management, since it fosters questions not only in problem solving (Bower, 1986; Newell and Simon, 1972), but also in aspects such as strategic issue diagnosis (Dutton, Fahey, and Narayanan, 1983), and organizational mindfulness (Levinthal and Rerup, 2006; Weick and Sutcliffe, 2006). In parallel, neuroscience studies on attention have proposed the existence of three systems of attention: orienting, alerting, and executive control (Posner *et al.*, 2007). Research has compared their efficiencies between differently brain-damaged subjects (frontal, temporal, and parietal lesions) and healthy controls using the Attention Network Test (ANT) (Raz and Buhle, 2006). A reduced efficiency of the executive network was found in patients with frontal lobe and parietal lobe injuries, patients with parietal lobe injuries showed a deficit in the orienting network, and analysis of lateralization indicated the right hemisphere superiority to the alerting system.

Subjects with brain damages, as those recruited for that research, can easily be enrolled from different sources (i.e., ischemic, tumor removal, degenerative diseases patients). However, aside from the fairly obvious ethical concerns, there are some practical implications in conducting large-scale lesions studies in management, since they require dedicated infrastructure and personnel. Moreover, a major drawback of this approach is that brain damage is not under easy experimental controls (Brett, Johnsrude, and Owen, 2002). This ongoing uncertainty means that it is difficult to control for phenomena such as brain reorganization, different severity of lesion, and more generally individual differences.

A combination of imaging and lesion studies could prove useful to overcome these difficulties and advance management investigations (Shallice, 2003). *Voxel-based Lesion-Symptom Mapping* (VLSM) is a relatively recent method for analyzing the relationships between behavioral deficits in a neurological population and lesion sites associated with those deficits. The major advantage of VLSM over classic lesion studies is that it allows researchers to examine such data without articulating behavioral and lesion sites' boundaries (e.g., parietal patients vs. frontal patients) (Bates *et al.*, 2003). For instance, Driscoll and colleagues (2012) have elucidated the neural bases of self-reported emotional empathy comparing a group of Vietnam combat veterans who had traumatic brain injuries with a group of non-brain-injured veterans, by using VLSM on computed tomographic scans. Empathy is essential for managing relations in organizations, and research has suggested that the ability to understand others' emotions enables a manager to foster strategic management (Nonaka and Toyama, 2007).

Another method alternative to classical lesion studies is offered by *Transcranial Magnetic Stimulation* (TMS). However, differently from classic lesion studies, this approach does not involve permanent brain damage. Transcranial magnetic stimulation is a non-invasive technique that electromagnetically induces very brief electrical current pulses through a coil placed above the brain area to be stimulated; this produces weak electrical currents in the underlying neurons (Walsh and Cowey, 2000). TMS thus holds a unique role in understanding how the brain works, because it can be used to disengage a brain area for a minimal time, allowing scientists to understand its functional role (Pascual-Leone, Bartes-Faz, and Keenan, 1999). TMS has a temporal resolution of milliseconds, while the spatial resolution depends on the coil and the target area, which can be located thanks to a navigator device (Stewart and Walsh, 2006).

Although promising, the neurophysiological effects of TMS are not fully understood, often leading to difficulties in interpretation of the results; it may have excitatory, as well as inhibitory effects on brain regions, and differences in TMS stimulation parameters can influence experimental results (Rorden and Karnath, 2004). Moreover, current TMS systems are able to directly disrupt regions only near the scalp, usually evoke slight changes in behavior, and may induce epileptic seizures if applied at high intensities (Sack and Linden, 2003). These limitations make the technique not yet ideal for investigating long-term and social effects, such as those characterizing organizations. Thus, one of the most promising research directions is to explore *multimodal imaging modalities*, the combined use of two or more experimental techniques able to complement each other (e.g., TMS and fMRI) (Siebner and Rothwell, 2003; Babiloni *et al.*, 2004).

Another neuroimaging method that might receive increasing resonance in management studies is *magnetoencephalograpy* (MEG). It uses signals emerging from the scalp and measures fluctuations in the magnetic field as a result of changes in neural activity (Hämäläinen *et al.*, 1993). Since the fields have strength of only 50–500fT (about 100 million times weaker than the Earth's magnetic field), MEG instrumentation requires the use of special devices placed on the subject's head (superconducting SQUID-based magnetometers), and a magnetically shielded room (Vrba and Robinson, 2002). Magnetoencephalography is specular to TMS: while MEG detects magnetic fields generated by neural currents, TMS induces currents in the brain via magnetic fields. Moreover, MEG provides elevated temporal resolution and, due to poor signal degradation, results in high spatial discrimination of neural contributions (Pascual-Marqui, Michel, and Lehmann,

1994). Finally, it allows for absolute measures, which are not dependent on the choice of a reference, introducing new opportunities to further investigation of strategic management topics.

Other neuroscience methods in management research

While this work has largely concentrated on neuroimaging technologies, it is necessary to mention that several other neuroscientific approaches (e.g., those measuring autonomic parameters, neurogenetics, and neuropharmacology techniques) can provide important information for management and strategy inquiries.

For instance, a method with the potential to offer novel insights in strategic management research is that of *eye-tracking*. Eye-movement data usually consist of eye fixations, when the gaze position is relatively still so that the foveae remain directed at a particular point in space and information is extracted from the stimulus (Pieters, 2008). The rationale of this method is then aimed at determining the spatial point at which a viewer's foveae are directed and the extent of time they remain focused there. For instance, eye-tracking has been employed in the evaluation of facial perception, which is an important antecedent to successful social and business communication, since human social inferences are derived largely from viewing facial expression (Schulte-Mecklenbeck, Kühberger, and Ranyard, 2011). Similarly, it can be employed to provide insights in the processing of risky decisions (Glöckner and Herbold, 2011).

Research in strategy could also be further supported by *neurogenetics* experimental procedures, investigating the basis of cognition, sociality, and behavior. Such method has already been applied to business disciplines, for instance to entrepreneurship (Nicolau and Shane, 2010). This type of studies generally relies on comparisons between twins or examines allelic differences, suggesting that genetic variances translate into functional differences. Neurogenetics may be particularly useful for strategy research by linking polymorphisms of selected genes affecting neurotransmitter systems, or by employing genome-wide approaches to investigate mental functions and behavioral phenotypes. For instance, research on exploration and exploitation has shown that basal ganglia support learning to exploit decisions that have yielded positive outcomes in the past, while the prefrontal cortex is associated to strategic exploratory decisions when the magnitude of potential outcomes is unknown. Distinct genetic processes sustain these differences: genes controlling striatal dopamine function (*DARPP-32* and *DRD2*) are associated with exploitation, while a gene controlling prefrontal dopamine function (*COMT*) is associated with "directed exploration" (Frank *et al.*, 2009).

Although the sampling collecting procedures for these studies are quite simple (a saliva or blood sample is usually sufficient), these analyses require advanced expertise and facilities. Moreover, due to the intimate nature of the approach, research findings are at high risk of producing serious ethical concerns or stigmatization (i.e., associating specific polymorphisms to supposed deviant attitudes or to targeted populations) (Illes and Racine, 2005).

Finally, *neuropharmacological* studies rely on the rationale that specific compounds excite or inhibit particular neurotransmitter actions (neurotransmitter loading or depletion), thereby influencing a subject's behavior. Also in this case, these approaches hold important concerns, in particular in relation to cognitive enhancement (Bostrom and Sandberg, 2009). Examples of this methodological approach are studies, which employ neuropeptides such as oxytocin and vasopressin (Heinrichs, von Dawans, and Domes, 2009). For example, research has proposed a role for oxytocin in modulating trust, thus influencing cooperative relations. Administration of intranasal oxytocin increased the amount of money that a social actor was ready to offer to a "trustee," who could return either a smaller or larger sum back to the person (Kosfeld *et al.*, 2005). However, oxytocin did not increase monetary distributions when the feedback was determined by a random draw, indicating that these results are specific to the social interaction between the two actors. In support to this research, imaging studies revealed that oxytocin decreased amygdala activity, independently from the experimental scenario, providing further insights into the neural mechanisms by which this neuropeptide regulates cooperation (Petrovic *et al.*, 2008).

Ethics, hype, and hope

Despite its complexity and technicalities, neuroscience research has engaged the interest and curiosity of several audiences, including non-expert scholars (Frazzetto and Anker, 2009). Since the 1990s we have seen the rise of a neuroculture (Rolls, 2012), with "neuro" concepts increasingly assimilated in the social sciences, including management research.

In response to this phenomenon, some scholars have argued that managerial, organizational, and strategy frameworks involve dynamic systems, multilevel analyses, depend on environment, interaction with people, tasks, and structures, and these paradigms cannot be fully appreciated with neuroscientific methods currently available (Powell, 2011). Others have associated neuroimaging research with phreonological cults (Dobbs, 2005; Simpson, 2005; Uttal, 2001), pointing out methods, such as fMRI, inform about the location of neural activities, yet offer a very plastic snapshot of the complex mental and behavioral processes occurring in the brain (Coltheart, 2006; Page, 2006). On the other hand, researchers have responded that functional neuroimaging allows for broader and more complex explanations, and have proposed connectivist and network frameworks (Cowell, Huber, and Cottrell, 2009; Rogers *et al.*, 2007; Rubinov and Sporns, 2010).

Moreover, neuroimaging methods were primarily conceived for clinical applications, and only later have been applied to behavioral and management inquiries. What could happen if some incidental pathological abnormality emerges during a management study? What if a non-clinical researcher thinks there is an abnormality, which is instead just an ordinary physiological variant, and worries the subject unreasonably?

These ethical issues are not insignificant (Grossman and Bernat, 2004). An unexpected finding may turn the naive desire of a volunteer to have a picture of his or her brain into a major incident with severe consequences impacting both health and everyday life (Kirschen, Jaworska, and Illes, 2006). And if it is unethical not to provide result interpretations, detecting pathological abnormalities is a relatively frequent event, especially with functional neuroimaging systems (Katzman, Dagher, and Patronas, 1999). Therefore, in order to minimize the impact of incidental findings, research protocols should include informed consent and adhere to detailed guidelines (Illes *et al.*, 2004) and research outputs should be examined and reported by qualified personnel able to flag minor normal variants as well as pathologies (Illes *et al.*, 2004).

Despite these vibrant considerations and debates, it is possible to claim that learning about the brain can help to understand further people's behaviors in firms and organizations; thus neuroscience methods can add to the understanding of management and strategy frameworks' elements on the basic neural process involved. To this end, knowledge on the techniques presented in this chapter represents a key instrument to acquire new awareness about those paradigms, and to ascertain the basis for a durable and doable association between neuroscience and management research. Nevertheless, researchers should not only understand and recognize both these tools' potentials and limitations, but also be careful about getting into the hype of including a "brain-talk" or neuroimage with any and every research output. For instance, there is growing evidence that an untrained audience too often trusts catchy neuroscience claims blindly (Racine, Bar-Ilan, and Illes, 2005; Weisberg *et al.*, 2008). Once research results are publicized, especially when linked to personality or social constructs, non-experts often relate with lay interpretations of these outcomes. Although this phenomenon should not be confused with the merits of sound research (Beck, 2010), it is also true that the way in which some findings are presented tends to be vigorously loaded (Racine *et al.*, 2010). Extensively incorporating brain region labels and scans, perhaps supported by amateurish statistics or imprecise anatomical knowledge, may become just rhetoric, if not supported by clear experimental and scientific agendas and precise methodological disclosure (Illes, 2006; McCabe and Castel, 2008; Weisberg *et al.*, 2008). Similarly, management scholars shall rethink the epistemological urge of outlining new "neuro" disciplines (Bennett, Hacker, and Bennett, 2003; Legrenzi and Umiltà, 2011). For one, here I have provided an introductory review on how experimental neuroscience for management and strategy must necessarily be considered as a set of instruments, suggesting that also uprising "neuromanagement" discussions must not disengage from the fuller understanding of the underlying neuroscience.

The hope in and the competitive advantage of neuroscience and management is thus an integrated framework, established through systematic understanding of neuroscientific methods, multidirectional communication, and planned collaborations between scholars as the most appropriate means to achieve a fuller knowledge on human strategic behavior.

Notes

1   I would like to thank Sigal Barsade, James Berry, Giambattista Dagnino, Martin Kilduff, and Simcha Jong for their useful suggestions.
2   Examples of these evidences include e.g. the Zhejiang University's Neuromanagement Laboratory; dedicated sessions at the Academy of Management Meetings; the Open Research Area NESSHI (www.nesshi.eu/) and the Human Brain (https://www.humanbrainproject.eu/) projects.
3   An all-inclusive analysis of the neuroscience methods would have to be book-length to cover each of the techniques presented in this chapter. A few examples of neuroscience-specific texts able to exhaustively address these topics, which however do not touch management paradigms, are: Cabeza and Kingstone, 2001; Senior, Russell, and Gazzaniga, 2006; Toga and Mazziotta, 2002.
4   The notion of functional neuroimaging of behavior employed in this work seeks to highlight the differences with the use of these techniques in clinical practice (i.e., clinical functional neuroimaging). I will interchangeably use the terms mental and behavioral to broadly encompass cognitive, emotional, and affective processes. Readers must note that there is direct inference when the investigator infers something about the role of particular brain regions in cognitive function. Reverse inference, which is instead not recommended, occurs when the investigator infers the engagement of particular cognitive functions based on activation in particular brain regions (Poldrack 2006).
5   Tomographic techniques are those methods that allow imaging a body by sections through a penetrating wave. They allow imaging of a slice through, rather than a projection of a three-dimensional structure (Natterer and Ritman, 2002).
6   Technically a T2* relaxation time.
7   This work does not review classic electrophysiological techniques (e.g., single- and multi-unit recordings, patch clamp; for more information on these methods, see Bretschneider and de Weille, 2006), and methods that currently have received marginal applications in the strategic management scholarship (e.g., Magnetic Resonance Spectroscopy [MRS]). Moreover, the work will solely cover neuroscience methods in humans, hence excluding those applications carried out in primates (for more information on this, see Murray and Baxter, 2006).
8   3 Teslas are roughly 60 thousand times greater than the Earth's magnetic field.
9   MRI and fMRI are also characterized by high *contrast resolution*, which is the ability to distinguish the differences between two arbitrarily similar but not identical tissues, such as white and grey matter (Bushberg *et al.*, 2002).

References

AA.VV. (2009) *Perspectives on Psychological Science*, 4(3).
AA.VV. (1995) *Academy of Management Journal*, 38(1).
Adams, J. S. (1963) "Toward an understanding of inequity", *Journal of Abnormal Social Psychology*, 67(5): 422–436.
Adams, J. S. (1965) "Inequity in social exchange," in L. Berkowitz (ed.) *Advances in Experimental Social Psychology*, 267–269, New York: Academic Press.
Adenzato, M. and Garbarini, F. (2006) "The As if in cognitive science, neuroscience and anthropology: A journey among robots, blacksmiths and neurons", *Theory & Psychology*, 16(6): 747-759.
Adrian, E. D. and Matthews, B. H. (1934) "The Berger rhythm: Potential changes from the occipital lobes in man," *Brain*, 57(4): 355-385.
Ansoff, H. I. (1991) "Critique of Henry Mintzberg"s The design school: reconsidering the basic premises of strategic management," *Strategic Management Journal*, 12(6): 449–461.

Anzai, Y. and Simon, H. A. (1979) "The theory of learning by doing," *Psycholgical Review*, 86(2): 124–140.

Ariely, D. and Berns, G. S. (2010) "Neuromarketing: The hope and hype of neuroimaging in business," *Nature Reviews Neuroscience*, 11(4): 284–292.

Armstrong, J. S. (1982) "The value of formal planning for strategic decisions: Review of empirical research," *Strategic Management Journal*, 3(3): 197–211.

Attwell, D. and Iadecola, C. (2002) "The neural basis of functional brain imaging signals," *TRENDS in Neurosciences*, 25(12): 621–625.

Atwood, H. L. and MacKay, W. A. (1989) *Essentials of Neurophysiology*, New York: Decker.

Babiloni, F., Mattia, D., Babiloni, C., Astolfi, L., Salinari, S., Basilisco, A., and Cincotti, F. (2004) "Multimodal integration of EEG, MEG and fMRI data for the solution of the neuroimage puzzle," *Magnetic Resonance Imaging*, 22(10): 1471–1476.

Baker, S. C., Rogers, R. D., Owen, A. M., Frith, C. D., Dolan, R. J., Frackowiak, R. S. J., and Robbins, T. W. (1996) "Neural systems engaged by planning: A PET study of the Tower of London task," *Neuropsychologia*, 34(6): 515–526.

Ball, G. A., Trevino, L. K. and Sims, H. P. (1994) "Just and unjust punishment: Influences on subordinate performance and citizenship," *Academy of Management Journal*, 37(2): 299–322.

Bandettini, P. A. (2002) "fMRI: The spatial, temporal, and interpretive limits of functional MRI," in Davis, K., Charney, D., Coyle, J. and Nemeroff (eds), *Neuropsychopharmacology: The Fifth Generation of Progress*, 343–356, Philadelphia: Lippincott Williams and Wilkins.

Bandettini, P. A. (2009) "What's new in neuroimaging methods?," *Annals of the New York Academy of Sciences*, 1156(1): 260–293.

Bandettini, P. A., Wong, E. C., Hinks, R. S., Tikofsky, R. S. and Hyde, J. S. (1992) "Time course EPI of human brain function during task activation," *Magnetic Resonance in Medicine*, 25(2): 390–397.

Barnard, C. I. (1938) *The Functions of the Executive*, Cambridge, MA: Harvard University Press.

Bates, E., Wilson, S. M., Saygin, A. P., Dick, F., Sereno, M. I., Knight, R. T., and Dronkers, N. F. (2003) "Voxel-based lesion–symptom mapping," *Nature Neuroscience*, 6(5): 448–450.

Beaulieu, A. (2000) "The Space inside the skull: Digital representations, brain. mapping and cognitive neuroscience in the decade of the brain," Ph.D. Dissertation, Science and Technology Dynamics, University of Amsterdam, the Netherlands.

Beaulieu, C. (2002) "The basis of anisotropic water diffusion in the nervous system: A technical review," *NMR in Biomedicine*, 15(7–8): 435–455.

Beck, D. M. (2010) "The appeal of the brain in the popular press," *Perspectives on Psychological Science*, 5(6): 762–766.

Becker, W. J., Cropanzano R., and Sanfey A. G. (2011) "Organizational neuroscience: Taking organizational theory inside the neural black box," *Journal of Management*, 37(4): 933–961.

Bennett, M. R., Hacker, P. M. S., and Bennett, M. R. (2003) *Philosophical Foundations of Neuroscience,* Oxford: Blackwell.

Berger, H. (1929) "Uber das Elektrenkephalogramm des Menschen," *Arch. Psychiatrie Nerv.*, 87: 527–570.

Bloch, F. (1946) "Nuclear induction," *Physical Review*, 70(7–8): 460.

Bostrom, N. and Sandberg, A. (2009) "Cognitive enhancement: Methods, ethics, regulatory challenges," *Science and Engineering Ethics*, 15(3): 311–341.

Bower, J. L. (1986) *Managing the Resource Allocation Process*, Vol. 3, Cambridge, MA: Harvard Business Press.

Bretschneider, F. and De Weille, J. R. (2006) *Introduction to Electrophysiological Methods and*

Instrumentation, London: Elsevier.

Brett, M., Johnsrude, I. S., and Owen, A. M. (2002) "The problem of functional localization in the human brain," *Nature Reviews Neuroscience*, 3(3): 243–249.

Broca, P. (1861) "Perte de la parole, ramollissement chronique et destruction partielle du lobe antérieur gauche du cerveau," *Bulletin Society Anthropology*, 2: 235–238.

Brockner, J. (1992) "The escalation of commitment to a failing course of action: Toward theoretical progress," *Academy of Management Review*, 17(1): 39–61.

Bronzino, J. D. (ed.) (1995) *The Biomedical Engineering Handbook*, Vol. 1, Boca Raton, FL: CRC Press.

Brown, M. A. and Semelka, R. C. (2011) *MRI: Basic Principles and Applications*, Hoboken, NJ: Wiley.

Bullinaria, J. A. and Chater, N. (1995) "Connectionist modeling: Implications for cognitive neuropsychology," *Language and Cognitive Processes*, 10(3–4): 227–264.

Bushberg, J. T., Seibert, J. A., Leidholdt, Jr, E. M., and Boone, J. M. (2002) *The Essential Physics of Medical Imaging*, Philadelphia, PA: Lippincott Williams & Wilkins.

Cabeza, R. and Kingstone, A. (eds) (2001) *Handbook of Functional Neuroimaging of Cognition*, Cambrdige, MA: MIT Press.

Camerer, C. F. (2003) *Behavioral Game Theory: Experiments in Strategic Interaction*, Princeton, NJ: Princeton University Press.

Campbell-Meiklejohn, D. K., Woolrich, M. W., Passingham, R. E., and Rogers, R. D. (2008) "Knowing when to stop: The brain mechanisms of chasing losses," *Biological Psychiatry*, 63(3): 293–300.

Caramazza, A. (1986) "On drawing inferences about the structure of normal cognitive systems from the analysis of patterns of impaired performance: The case for single-patient studies," *Brain and Cognition*, 5(1): 41–66.

Caton, R. (1875) "Electrical currents of the brain," *Journal of Nervous and Mental Disease*, 2(4): 610.

Chapman, B. L. (2006) "Gradients: The heart of the MRI machine," *Current Medical Imaging Reviews*, 2(1): 131–138.

Chater, N. and Ganis, G. (1991) "Double dissociation and isolable cognitive processes," *Behaviour*, 5(9): 668–672.

Churchland, P. S. and Sejnowski, T. J. (1988) "Perspectives on cognitive neuroscience," *Science*, 242(4879): 741–745.

Cohen-Charash, Y. and Mueller, J. S. (2007) "Does perceived unfairness exacerbate or mitigate interpersonal counterproductive work behaviors related to envy?," *Journal of Applied Psychology*, 92(3): 666–680.

Colquitt, J. A., Conlon, D. E., Wesson, M. J., Porter, O. L. H., and Ng, K. Y. (2001) "Justice at the millennium: A meta-analytic review of 25 years of organizational justice research," *Journal of Applied Psychology*, 86(3): 425–445.

Coltheart, M. (2006) "What has functional neuroimaging told us about the mind (so far)?," *Cortex*, 42: 323–331.

Connolly, W. E. (2002) *Neuropolitics: Thinking, Culture, Speed*, Minneaoplis, MN: University of Minnesota Press.

Cools, R., Frank, M. J., Gibbs, S. E., Miyakawa, A., Jagust, W., and D'Esposito, M. (2009) "Striatal dopamine predicts outcome-specific reversal learning and its sensitivity to dopaminergic drug administration," *The Journal of Neuroscience*, 29(5): 1538–1543.

Cowell, R. A., Huber, D. E., and Cottrell, G. W. (2009) "Virtual brain reading: A connectionist approach to understanding fMRI," Paper presented at the 31st Annual Meeting of the Cognitive Science Society.

Crockett, M. J., Clark, L., Tabibnia, G., Lieberman, M. D., and Robbins, T. W. (2008) "Serotonin modulates behavioral reactions to unfairness," *Science*, 320(5884): 1739–1739.

Cushman, F. and Greene, J. D. (2012) "Finding faults: How moral dilemmas illuminate cognitive structure," *Social Neuroscience*, 7(3): 269–279.

Dagher, A., Owen, A. M., Boecker, H., and Brooks, D. J. (1999) "Mapping the network for planning: A correlational PET activation study with the Tower of London task," *Brain*, 122(10): 1973–1987.

Damasio, A. R. (1994) *Descartes' Error: Emotion, Reason, and the Human Brain*, London: Penguin Books.

Daw, N. D., O'Doherty, J. P., Seymour, B., Dayan, P., and Dolan, R. J. (2006) "Cortical substrates for exploratory decisions in humans," *Nature*, 441, 876–879.

Dawson, D. G. (1951) "A summation technique for detecting small signals in a large irregular background," *Journal of Physiology*, 494: 251–326.

Dimoka, A., Banker, R. D., Benbasat, I., Davis, F. D., Dennis, A. R., Gefen, D., and Weber, B. (2012) "On the use of neuropyhsiological tools in IS research: Developing a research agenda for NeuroIS," *MIS Quarterly*, 36(3): 679–702.

Dobbs, D. (2005) "Fact or phrenology?," *Scientific American Mind*, April 1–8: 24–31.

Doktor, R. (1978) "Problem solving styles of executives and management scientists," *TIMS Studies in the Management Sciences*, 8(2): 123–134.

Donders, F. C. (1969) "On the speed of mental processes," *Acta Psychologica*, 30: 412–431.

Driscoll, D. M., Dal Monte, O., Solomon, J., Krueger, F. and Grafman, J. (2012) "Empathic deficits in combat veterans with traumatic brain injury: A voxel-based lesion-symptom mapping study," *Cognitive and Behavioral Neurology*, 25(4): 160–166.

Dutton, J. E., Fahey, L. and Narayanan, V. K. (1983) "Toward understanding strategic issue diagnosis," *Strategic Management Journal*, 4(4): 307–323.

Dvorak, P. and Badal, J. (2007) "This is your brain on the job," *The Wall Street Journal*, September 20. Retrieved at: http://online.wsj.com/news/articles/SB119024585835733168

Fellows, L. K. and Farah, M. J. (2003) "Ventromedial frontal cortex mediates affective shifting in humans: Evidence from a reversal learning paradigm," *Brain*, 126(8): 1830–1837.

Finger, S. (2001) *Origins of Neuroscience: A History of Explorations into Brain Function*, New York: Oxford University Press.

Fox, P. T. and Raichle, M. E. (1986) "Focal physiological uncoupling of cerebral blood flow and oxidative metabolism during somatosensory stimulation in human subjects," *Proceedings of the National Academy of Sciences*, 83(4): 1140–1144.

Frank, M. J., Doll, B. B., Oas-Terpstra, J. and Moreno, F. (2009) "Prefrontal and striatal dopaminergic genes predict individual differences in exploration and exploitation," *Nature Neuroscience*, 12(8): 1062–1068.

Franks, D. D. (2010) *Neurosociology: The Nexus Between Neuroscience and Social Psychology*. New York: Springer.

Frazzetto, G. and Anker, S. (2009) "Neuroculture," *Nature Reviews Neuroscience*, 10(11): 815–821.

Freeman, W. J. and Quiroga, R. Q. (2013) *Imaging Brain Function with EEG: Advanced Temporal and Spatial Analysis of Electroencephalographic Signals*, New York: Springer.

Friston, K. J. (2005) "Models of brain function in neuroimaging," *Annual Review of Psychology*, 56: 57–87.

Friston, K. J., Price, C. J., Fletcher, P., Moore, C., Frackowiak, R. S. J., and Dolan, R. J. (1996) "The trouble with cognitive subtraction," *Neuroimage*, 4(2): 97–104.

Garvey, C. J. and Hanlon, R. (2002) "Computed tomography in clinical practice," *BMJ: British Medical Journal*, 324(7345): 1077.

Gazzaniga, M. and LeDoux, J. (1978) *The Integrated Mind*, New York: Plenum.

Ghadiri, A., Habermacher, A., and Peters, T. (2012) "Neuroleadership: The backdrop," in *Neuroleadership: A Journey Through the Brain for Business Leaders*, 1–15, Berlin: Springer.

Glimcher, P. W. and Rustichini, A. (2004) "Neuroeconomics: The consilience of brain and decision," *Science*, 306(5695): 447–452.

Glöckner, A. and Herbold, A. K. (2011) "An eye tracking study on information processing in risky decisions: Evidence for compensatory strategies based on automatic processes," *Journal of Behavioral Decision Making*, 24(1): 71–98.

Greene, J. and Cohen, J. (2004) "For the law, neuroscience changes nothing and everything," *Philosophical Transactions of the Royal Society*, 359(1451): 1775–1785.

Grossman, R. I. and Bernat, J. L. (2004) "Incidental research imaging findings Pandora's costly box," *Neurology*, 62(6): 849–850.

Gul, F. and Pesendorfer, W. (2008) "The case for mindless economics," in Caplin, A. and Schotter, A. (eds), *The Foundations of Positive and Normative Economics*, 3–39, Oxford: Oxford University Press.

Gulyas, B., Halldin, C., Sandell, J., Karlsson, P., Sóvágó, J., Kárpáti, E., and Farde, L. (2002) "PET studies on the brain uptake and regional distribution of [11C] vinpocetine in human subjects," *Acta Neurologica Scandinavica*, 106(6): 325–332.

Hämäläinen, M., Hari, R., Ilmoniemi, R. J., Knuutila, J., and Lounasmaa, O. V. (1993) "Magnetoencephalography: Theory, instrumentation, and applications to noninvasive studies of the working human brain," *Reviews of Modern Physics*, 65(2): 413.

Heinrichs, M., von Dawans, B., and Domes, G. (2009) "Oxytocin, vasopressin, and human social behavior," *Frontiers in Neuroendocrinology*, 30(4): 548–557.

Hines, T. (1987) "Left brain/right brain mythology and implications for management and training," *Academy of Management Review*, 12: 600–606.

Hounsfield, G. N. (1973) "Computerized transverse axial scanning (tomography): Part 1. Description of system," *British Journal of Radiology*, 46(552): 1016–1022.

Humm, J. L., Rosenfeld, A. and Del Guerra, A. (2003) "From PET detectors to PET scanners," *European Journal of Nuclear Medicine and Molecular Imaging*, 30(11): 1574–1597.

Huy, Q. N. (2002) "Emotional balancing of organizational continuity and radical change: The contribution of middle managers," *Administrative Science Quarterly*, 47(1): 31–69.

Illes, J. (ed.) (2006) *Neuroethics: Defining the Issues in Theory, Practice and Policy*, New York: Oxford University Press.

Illes, J. and Racine, E. (2005) "Imaging or imagining? A neuroethics challenge informed by genetics," *The American Journal of Bioethics*, 5(2): 5–18.

Illes, J., Moser, M. A., McCormick, J. B., Racine, E., Blakeslee, S., Caplan, A., and Weiss, S. (2009) "Neurotalk: improving the communication of neuroscience research," *Nature Reviews Neuroscience*, 11(1): 61–69.

Illes, J., Rosen, A. C., Huang, L., Goldstein, R. A., Raffin, T. A., Swan, G., and Atlas, S. W. (2004) "Ethical consideration of incidental findings on adult brain MRI in research," *Neurology*, 62(6): 888–890.

Jones, O. D. and Shen, F. X. (2012) "Law and neuroscience in the United States," in Spranger, T. M. (ed.) *International Neurolaw: A Comparative Analysis*, 349–380, Berlin: Springer.

Kable, J. W. (2011) "The cognitive neuroscience toolkit for the neuroeconomist," *Journal of Neuroscience, Psychology, and Economics*, 4(2): 63–84.

Kato, M., Taniwaki, T. and Kuwabara, Y. (2000) "The advantages and limitations of brain function analyses by PET," *Clinical Neurology*, 40(12): 1274.

Katzman, G. L., Dagher, A. P., and Patronas, N. J. (1999) "Incidental findings on brain magnetic resonance imaging from 1000 asymptomatic volunteers," *JAMA: the Journal of the American Medical Association*, 282(1): 36–39.

King-Casas, B., Tomlin, D., Anen, C., Camerer, C. F., Quartz, S. R., and Montague, P. R.

(2005) "Getting to know you: Reputation and trust in a two-person economic exchange," *Science*, 308(5718): 78–83.

Kirschen, M. P., Jaworska, A., and Illes, J. (2006) "Subjects' expectations in neuroimaging research," *Journal of Magnetic Resonance Imaging*, 23(2): 205–209.

Knoch, D., Gianotti, L. R., Baumgartner, T. and Fehr, E. (2010) "A neural marker of costly punishment behavior," *Psychological Science*, 21(3): 337–342.

Kolb, B. and Whishaw, I. Q. (2009) *Fundamentals of Human Neuropsychology*, New York: Macmillan.

Kosfeld, M., Heinrichs, M., Zak, P. J., Fischbacher, U., and Fehr, E. (2005) "Oxytocin increases trust in humans," *Nature*, 435(7042): 673–676.

Kovalchik, S. and Allman, J. (2006) "Measuring reversal learning: Introducing the Variable Iowa Gambling Task in a study of young and old normals," *Cognition & Emotion*, 20(5): 714–728.

Kristeva, R., Keller, E., Deecke, L., and Kornhuber, H. H. (1979) "Cerebral potentials preceding unilateral and simultaneous bilateral finger movements," *Electroencephalography and Clinical Neurophysiology*, 47(2): 229–238.

Kwong, K. K., Belliveau, J. W., Chesler, D. A., Goldberg, I. E., Weisskoff, R. M., Poncelet, B. P., and Turner, R. (1992) "Dynamic magnetic resonance imaging of human brain activity during primary sensory stimulation," *Proceedings of the National Academy of Sciences*, 89(12): 5675–5679.

Lauterbur, P. C. (1973) "Image formation by induced local interactions: examples employing nuclear magnetic resonance," *Nature*, 242(5394): 190–191.

Le Bihan, D. (1996) "Functional MRI of the brain principles, applications and limitations," *Journal of Neuroradiology*, 23(1): 1–5.

Le Bihan, D. (2003) "Looking into the functional architecture of the brain with diffusion MRI," *Nature Reviews Neuroscience*, 4(6): 469–480.

Le Bihan, D., Urayama, S. I., Aso, T., Hanakawa, T., and Fukuyama, H. (2006) "Direct and fast detection of neuronal activation in the human brain with diffusion MRI," *Proceedings of the National Academy of Sciences*, 103(21): 8263–8268.

Lebedev, M. A. and Nicolelis, M. A. (2006) "Brain–machine interfaces: Past, present and future," *TRENDS in Neurosciences*, 29(9): 536–546.

Lee, N., Broderick, A. J., and Chamberlain, L. (2007) "What is 'Neuromarketing?' A discussion and agenda for future research," *International Journal Of Psychophysiology*, 63(2): 199–204.

Legrenzi, P. and Umiltà, C. (2011) *Neuromania: On the Limits of Brain Science*, New York: Oxford University Press.

Levinthal, D. A. and March, J. G. (1993) "The myopia of learning," *Strategic Management Journal*, 14(S2): 95–112.

Levinthal, D. and Rerup, C. (2006) "Crossing an apparent chasm: Bridging mindful and less-mindful perspectives on organizational learning," *Organization Science*, 17(4): 502–513.

Lindebaum, D. and Zundel, M. (2013) "Not quite a revolution: Scrutinizing organizational neuroscience in leadership studies," *Human Relations*, 66(6): 857–877.

Liu, J. Z., Zhang, L., Brown, R. W., and Yue, G. H. (2004) "Reproducibility of fMRI at 1.5 T in a strictly controlled motor task," *Magnetic Resonance in Medicine*, 52(4): 751–760.

Logothetis, N. K. (2008) "What we can do and what we cannot do with MRI," *Nature*, 453(7197): 869–878.

Logothetis, N. K. and Wandell, B. A. (2004) "Interpreting the BOLD signal," *Annual Review of Physiology*, 66: 735–769.

Logothetis, N. K., Pauls, J., Augath, M., Trinath, T., and Oeltermann, A. (2001) "Neurophysiological investigation of the basis of the fMRI signal," *Nature*, 412(6843):

150–157.

Luck, S. J. (2005) "Ten simple rules for designing ERP experiments," in T.C. Handy (ed.), *Event-Related Potentials: A Methods Handbook*, 16–32, Cambridge, MA: MIT Press.

Magistretti, P. J., Pellerin, L., Rothman, D. L., and Shulman, R. G. (1999) "Energy on demand," *Science*, 283(5401): 496–497.

Malonek, D., Dirnagl, U., Lindauer, U., Yamada, K., Kanno, I., and Grinvald, A. (1997) "Vascular imprints of neuronal activity: Relationships between the dynamics of cortical blood flow, oxygenation, and volume changes following sensory stimulation," *Proceedings of the National Academy of Sciences*, 94(26): 14826–14831.

March, J. G. and Simon, H. A. (1958) *Organizations*, Oxford: Wiley.

McCabe, D. P. and Castel, A. D. (2008) "Seeing is believing: The effect of brain images on judgments of scientific reasoning," *Cognition*, 107(1): 343–352.

McCabe, K., Houser, D., Ryan, L., Smith, V., and Trouard, T. (2001) "A functional imaging study of cooperation in two-person reciprocal exchange," *Proceedings of the National Academy of Sciences*, 98(20): 11832–11835.

Menon, R. S. and Kim, S. G. (1999) "Spatial and temporal limits in cognitive neuroimaging with fMRI," *TRENDS in Cognitive Sciences*, 3(6): 207–216.

Menon, R. S., Gati, J. S., Goodyear, B. G., Luknowsky, D. C. and Thomas, C. G. (1998) "Spatial and temporal resolution of functional magnetic resonance imaging," *Biochemistry and Cell Biology*, 76(2-3): 560–571.

Minoshima, S., Koeppe, R. A., Frey, K. A. and Kuhl, D. E. (1994) "Anatomic standardization: linear scaling and nonlinear warping of functional brain images," *Journal of Nuclear Medicine*, 35(9): 1528–1537.

Mintzberg, H, (1976) "Planning on the left and managing on the right," *Harvard Business Review*, 54(4): 49–58.

Mintzberg, H. (1994) "The fall and rise of strategic planning," *Harvard Business Review*, 72(1): 107–114.

Moorman, R. H. (1991) "Relationship between organizational justice and organizational citizenship behaviors. Do fairness perception influence employee citizenship?," *Journal of Applied Psychology*, 76(6): 845–855.

Murray, E. A. and Baxter, M. G. (2006) "Cognitive neuroscience and nonhuman primates: Lesion studies," in Senior, C. E., Russell, T. E., and Gazzaniga, M. S. (eds), *Methods in Mind*, 43–69. Cambrdige, MA: MIT Press.

Natterer, F. and Ritman, E. L. (2002) "Past and future directions in x ray computed tomography (CT)," *International Journal of Imaging Systems and Technology*, 12(4): 175–187.

Newell, A. and Simon, H. A. (1972) *Human Problem Solving*, Vol. 14, Englewood Cliffs, NJ: Prentice-Hall.

Nicolaou, N. and Shane, S. (2009) "Born entrepreneurs? The genetic foundations of entrepreneurship," *Journal of Business Venturing*, 23: 1–22.

Niedermeyer, E. and Lopes da Silva, F.H. (eds) (1999) *Electroencephalography: Basic Principles, Clinical Applications, and Related Fields*, 4th edn, Baltimore: Williams & Wilkins.

Nonaka, I. and Toyama, R. (2007) "Strategic management as distributed practical wisdom (phronesis)," *Industrial and Corporate Change*, 16(3): 371–394.

Nunez, P. L. (1995) *Neocortical Dynamics and Human EEG Rhythms*, New York: Oxford University Press.

Ogawa, S., Lee, T. M., Kay, A. R., and Tank, D. W. (1990) "Brain magnetic resonance imaging with contrast dependent on blood oxygenation," *Proceedings of the National Academy of Sciences*, 87(24): 9868–9872.

Ogawa, S., Tank, D. W., Menon, R., Ellermann, J. M., Kim, S. G., Merkle, H., and Ugurbil,

K. (1992) "Intrinsic signal changes accompanying sensory stimulation: functional brain mapping with magnetic resonance imaging," *Proceedings of the National Academy of Sciences*, 89(13): 5951–5955.

Page, M. (2006) "What can't functional neuroimaging tell the cognitive psychologist?," *Cortex*, 42(3): 428–443.

Pascual-Leone, A., Walsh, V., and Rothwell, J. (2000) "Transcranial magnetic stimulation in cognitive neuroscience–virtual lesion, chronometry, and functional connectivity," *Current Opinion in Neurobiology*, 10(2): 232–237.

Pascual-Marqui, R. D., Michel, C. M., and Lehmann, D. (1994) "Low resolution electromagnetic tomography: A new method for localizing electrical activity in the brain," *International Journal of Psychophysiology*, 18(1): 49–65.

Payne, B. (1957) "Steps in long-range planning," *Harvard Business Review*, 35(2): 95–101.

Pelizzari, C. A., Chen, G. T., Spelbring, D. R., Weichselbaum, R. R., and Chen, C. T. (1989) "Accurate three-dimensional registration of CT, PET, and/or MR images of the brain," *Journal of Computer Assisted Tomography*, 13(1): 20–26.

Petersen, S. E., Fox, P. T., Posner, M. I., Mintun, M., and Raichle, M. E. (1988) "Positron emission tomographic studies of the cortical anatomy of single- word processing," *Nature*, 331(6157): 585–589.

Petrovic, P., Kalisch, R., Singer, T., and Dolan, R. J. (2008) "Oxytocin attenuates affective evaluations of conditioned faces and amygdala activity," *The Journal of Neuroscience*, 28(26): 6607–6615.

Phelps, M. E. and Mazziotta, J. C. (1985) "Positron emission tomography: human brain function and biochemistry," *Science*, 228(4701): 799–809.

Pieters, R. (2008) "A review of eye-tracking research in marketing," in Naresh, K. M. (ed.), *Review of Marketing Research*, Vol. 4, 123–214, Bingley, UK: Emerald Group Publishing Limited.

Poldrack, R. A. (2006) "Can cognitive processes be inferred from neuroimaging data?," *TRENDS in Cognitive Sciences*, 10(2): 59–63.

Poldrack, R. A. (2012) "The future of fMRI in cognitive neuroscience," *Neuroimage*, 62(2): 1216–1220.

Poldrack, R. A., Kittur, A., Kalar, D., Miller, E., Seppa, C., Gil, Y., and Bilder, R. M. (2011) "The cognitive atlas: Toward a knowledge foundation for cognitive neuroscience," *Frontiers in Neuroinformatics*, 5: 5–17.

Powell, T. C. (2011) "Neurostrategy," *Strategic Management Journal*, 32(13): 1484–1499.

Powell, T. C., Lovallo, D., and Fox, C. R. (2011) "Behavioral strategy," *Strategic Management Journal*, 32(13): 1369–1386.

Price, C. J. and Friston, K. J. (1997) "Cognitive conjunction: A new approach to brain activation experiments," *Neuroimage*, 5(4): 261–270.

Purcell, E. M., Torrey, H. C., and Pound, R. V. (1946) "Resonance absorption by nuclear magnetic moments in a solid," *Physical Review*, 69(1–2): 37.

Racine, E., Bar-Ilan, O., and Illes, J. (2005) "fMRI in the public eye," *Nature Reviews Neuroscience*, 6(2): 159–164.

Racine, E., Waldman, S., Rosenberg, J., and Illes, J. (2010) "Contemporary neuroscience in the media," *Social Science & Medicine*, 71(4): 725–733.

Raichle, M. E. (1979) "Quantitative in vivo autoradiography with positron emission tomography," *Brain Research Reviews*, 1(1): 47–68.

Raichle, M. E. (2003) "Functional brain imaging and human brain function," *The Journal of Neuroscience*, 23(10): 3959–3962.

Raichle, M. E. (2009a) "A paradigm shift in functional brain imaging," *The Journal of Neuroscience*, 29(41): 12729–12734.

Raichle, M. E. (2009b) "A brief history of human brain mapping," *TRENDS in Neurosciences*, 32(2): 118–126.

Raichle, M. E. and Snyder, A. Z. (2007) "A default mode of brain function: A brief history of an evolving idea," *Neuroimage*, 37(4): 1083–1090.

Raichle, M. E., Martin, W. R., Herscovitch, P., Mintun, M. A., and Markham, J. (1983) "Brain blood flow measured with intravenous $H_2(15)O$. II. Implementation and validation," *Journal of Nuclear Medicine*, 24(9): 790–798.

Raz, A. and Buhle, J. (2006) "Typologies of attentional networks," *Nature Reviews Neuroscience*, 7(5): 367–379.

Robey, D. and Taggart, W. (1981) "Measuring managers' minds: The assessment of style in human information processing," *Academy of Management Review*, 6(3): 375–383.

Robey, D. and Taggart, W. (1982) "Human information processing in information and decision support systems," *MIS Quarterly*, 6(2): 61–73.

Rogers, B. P., Morgan, V. L., Newton, A. T., and Gore, J. C. (2007) "Assessing functional connectivity in the human brain by fMRI," *Magnetic Resonance Imaging*, 25(10): 1347–1357.

Rogers, L. F. (2003) "Helical CT: The revolution in imaging," *American Journal of Roentgenology*, 180(4): 883–883.

Rolls, E. T. (2012) *Neuroculture: On the Implications of Brain Science*, New York: Oxford University Press.

Rorden, C. and Karnath, H. O. (2004) "Using human brain lesions to infer function: A relic from a past era in the fMRI age?," *Nature Reviews Neuroscience*, 5(10): 812–819.

Rubinov, M. and Sporns, O. (2010) "Complex network measures of brain connectivity: Uses and interpretations," *Neuroimage*, 52(3): 1059–1069.

Sack, A. T. and Linden, D. E. (2003) "Combining transcranial magnetic stimulation and functional imaging in cognitive brain research: Possibilities and limitations," *Brain Research Reviews*, 43(1): 41–56.

Sanfey, A. G., Rilling, J. K., Aronson, J. A., Nystrom, L. E., and Cohen, J. D. (2003) "The neural basis of economic decision-making in the ultimatum game," *Science*, 300(5626): 1755–1758.

Sartori, G. and Umiltà, C. (2000) "How to avoid the fallacies of cognitive subtraction in brain imaging," *Brain and Language*, 74(2): 191–212.

Schulte-Mecklenbeck, M., Kühberger, A., and Ranyard, R. (2011) "The role of process data in the development and testing of process models of judgment and decision making," *Judgment and Decision Making*, 6(8): 733–739.

Scott Jr., W. E. (1966) "Activation theory and task design," *Organizational Behavior and Human Performance*, 1(1): 3-30.

Senior, C. E., Russell, T. E., and Gazzaniga, M. S. (2006) *Methods in Mind*, Cambridge, MA: MIT Press.

Senior, C., Lee, N., and Butler, M. (2011) "PERSPECTIVE – Organizational Cognitive Neuroscience," *Organization Science*, 22(3): 804–815.

Shallice, T. (1988) *From Neuropsychology to Mental Structure*, New York: Cambridge University Press.

Shallice, T. (2003) "Functional imaging and neuropsychology findings: How can they be linked?," *Neuroimage*, 20(S1): 46–54.

Siebner, H. and Rothwell, J. (2003) "Transcranial magnetic stimulation: New insights into representational cortical plasticity," *Experimental Brain Research*, 148(1): 1–16.

Simons, R. (1991) "Strategic orientation and top management attention to control systems," *Strategic Management Journal*, 12(1): 49–62.

Simpson, D. (2005) "Phrenology and the neurosciences: Contributions of FJ Gall and JG Spurzheim," *ANZ Journal of Surgery*, 75(6): 475–482.

Smith, K., Dickhaut, J., McCabe, K., and Pardo, J. V. (2002) "Neuronal substrates for choice under ambiguity, risk, gains, and losses," *Management Science*, 48(6): 711–718.

Song, A. W., Huettel, S. A., and McCarthy, G. (2006) "Functional neuroimaging: Basic principles of functional MRI," in Cabeza, R. and Kingstone, A. (eds) *Handbook of Functional Neuroimaging of Cognition*, 21–52, Cambridge, MA: MIT Press.

Squires, K. C., Wickens, C., Squires, N. K., and Donchin, E. (1976) "The effect of stimulus sequence on the waveform of the cortical event-related potential," *Science*, 193(4258): 1142–1146.

Staw, B. M. (1981) "The escalation of commitment to a course of action," *Academy of Management Review*, 6(4): 577–587.

Stewart, L. and Walsh, V. (2006) "Transcranial magnetic stimulation in human cognition," in Senior, C. E., Russell, T. E., and Gazzaniga, M. S. (eds), *Methods in Mind*, 1–27, Cambridge, MA: MIT Press.

Stöcker, T., Schneider, F., Klein, M., Habel, U., Kellermann, T., Zilles, K., and Shah, N. J. (2005) "Automated quality assurance routines for fMRI data applied to a multicenter study," *Human Brain Mapping*, 25(2): 237–246.

Tang, Y. Y. and Posner, M. I. (2009). "Attention training and attention state training," *Trends in Cognitive Sciences*, 13(5): 222–227.

Taggart, W., Robey, D., and Kroeck, K. (1985) "Managerial decision styles and cerebral dominance: An empirical study," *Journal of Management Studies*, 22(2): 175–192.

Ter-Pogossian, M. M. and Herscovitch, P. (1985) "Radioactive oxygen-15 in the study of cerebral blood flow, blood volume, and oxygen metabolism," *Seminars in Nuclear Medicine*, 15(4): 377–394.

Tilyou, S. M. (1991) "The evolution of positron emission tomography," *Journal of Nuclear Medicine*, 32(4): 15N–26N.

Toga, A. W. and Mazziotta, J. C. (eds) (2002) *Brain Mapping: The Methods*, Vol. 1, San Diego: Elsevier.

Turkington, T. G. (2001) "Introduction to PET instrumentation," *Journal of Nuclear Medicine Technology*, 29(1): 4–11.

Tyner, F. S., Knott, J. R., and Mayer Jr, W. B. (1989) *Fundamentals of EEG Technology: Clinical Correlates*, Philadelphia: Lippincott Williams and Wilkins.

Uludag, K., Dubowitz, D. J., Yoder, E. J., Restom, K., Liu, T. T., and Buxton, R. B. (2004) "Coupling of cerebral blood flow and oxygen consumption during physiological activation and deactivation measured with fMRI," *Neuroimage*, 23(1): 148–155.

Uttal, W. R. (2001) *The New Phrenology: The Limits of Localizing Cognitive Processes in the Brain*. Cambridge, MA: MIT Press.

Volz, K. G. and von Cramon, D. Y. (2006) "What neuroscience can tell about intuitive processes in the context of perceptual discovery," *Journal of Cognitive Neuroscience*, 18(12): 2077–2087.

Vrba, J. and Robinson, S. E. (2002) "SQUID sensor array configurations for magnetoencephalography applications," *Superconductor Science and Technology*, 15(9): R51.

Vul, E., Harris, C., Winkielman, P., and Pashler, H. (2009) "Puzzlingly high correlations in fMRI studies of emotion, personality, and social cognition," *Perspectives on Psychological Science*, 4(3): 274–290.

Waldman, D. A., Balthazard, P. A., and Peterson, S. J. (2011) "Leadership and neuroscience: Can we revolutionize the way that inspirational leaders are identified and developed?," *Academy of Management Perspectives*, 25(1): 60–74.

Walsh, V. and Cowey, A. (2000) "Transcranial magnetic stimulation and cognitive neuroscience," *Nature Reviews Neuroscience*, 1(1): 73–80.

Weick, K. E. and Sutcliffe, K. M. (2006) "Mindfulness and the quality of organizational attention," *Organization Science*, 17(4): 514–524.

Weisberg, D. S., Keil, F. C., Goodstein, J., Rawson, E., and Gray, J. R. (2008) "The seductive allure of neuroscience explanations," *Journal of Cognitive Neuroscience*, 20(3): 470–477.

Willingham, D. T. and Dunn, E. W. (2003) "What neuroimaging and brain localization can do, cannot do and should not do for social psychology," *Journal of Personality and Social Psychology*, 85(4): 662.

Yacoub, E., Uludag, K., Ugurbil, K., and Harel, N. (2008) "Decreases in ADC observed in tissue areas during activation in the cat visual cortex at 9.4 T using high diffusion sensitization," *Magnetic Resonance Imaging*, 26(7): 889–896.

PART IV

Research design and execution in strategic management

11

A MULTI-INDICATOR APPROACH FOR TRACKING FIELD EMERGENCE

The rise of Bologna Nanotech[1]

Simone Ferriani, Gianni Lorenzoni, and Damiano Russo

Introduction

A significant challenge of strategic management as a scholarly discipline is the rapidly evolving nature of its research. The fluidity of many strategic issues requires strategy scholars to employ a variety of research methodologies to keep advancing the extant body of knowledge. As pointed out by Hitt *et al.* (1998), different types of research methods are likely to be adopted by strategic management researchers tackling different research questions. Among such questions and issues, the emergence of highly clustered areas of firms and related organizational actors has been of growing interest within the strategic management literature. There are various reasons why the emergence of organizational fields represents an important area of strategic and organizational inquiry. First, given that it typically takes several decades for a field to move from initiation to take-off (Klepper and Grady 1990), it is very important to understand the nature of the institutional underpinnings and antecedents that sustain commitment during the lengthy period when success may appear doubtful and the field identity is fragile and unclear. Second, knowledge about the process by which new fields emerge is invaluable both to industrial policy makers and to corporate managers and entrepreneurs (Van de Ven and Garud 1989). New fields shape local development and competitiveness and are the basis of the growth of vibrant regional economies. Yet, the approaches followed to trace the origin of these institutions have relied primarily on ex-post functional accounts of genesis and emergence. As noted by Powell and colleagues (2012): "Most research on the emergence of high-tech clusters samples on successful cases, and works backwards to trace a narrative, often highlighting the role of specific individuals or groups." A limitation to this approach is that it risks predetermining the outcomes, casting an aura of inevitability to the evolutionary whole process. In fact, the use of the current state of an institution to illuminate its prior state is tantamount to treating the institution "time zero" as an exogenous fact. If some institutional state sits antecedent to a theory, that theory then cannot shed light on the emergence of the state.

Our goal in this chapter is to address this important yet relatively unattended issue by analyzing the conditions underpinning the emergence of an organizational field in nanotechnology. To this aim we propose a methodology based on a variety of indicators that offer an holistic representation of the multiple forces that cohere into a recognized area of institutional and economic life, engaged in common activities and subject to similar regulatory processes. Recent work in this area suggests that the nanotech field is characterized by classic agglomerative forces resulting in the clustering of scientific knowledge and technical expertise. These areas are typically centered around universities and government labs where business research units can take advantage of a rich and dense "invisible college" of scientists and researchers working to push the frontiers of the field outward.

We probe nanotechnology emergence at a local level using an original real-time mapping procedure based on multiple parameters. In so doing we seek to validate the feasibility and usability of our approach and illustrate how such method can inform policy efforts aimed at understanding spatial trajectories of particular industrial sectors. Conceptually, our perspective on field emergence is close to the tradition of work on the accumulative theory of change (Etzioni 1963), which emphasizes change as the intertwining of motivations and purposeful activities at the level of individual firms and the collective level of multiple actors that interact and socially construct the field in cumulative way. Following Van De Ven and Garud (1989), we therefore emphasize the detection of individual actors with the potential of triggering the emergence of the field. The virtue of this unit of analysis is that it directs our attention not simply to competing firms, like the population approach of Hannan and Freeman (1977), or to networks of organizations that interact, like the inter-organizational network approach of Laumann *et al.* (1978), but to the totality of relevant actors acting autonomously and collectively at the same time. We therefore use a combination of multiple measures (i.e. publications, patent applications, research projects portfolio) to illustrate the features and magnitude of the emerging field. After mapping field emergence at the Italian level we move to an in-depth analysis of the Bologna case, which is coming across as one of the most prominent and vibrant European nanotech locations, despite the complete absence of government support.

In the following, we discuss the methodological approach used to map field emergence in the nanotech domain and present our findings. Our exploratory analysis suggests that the appearance of the nanotech field is the result of the cumulative achievements of a plurality of new firms and actors which, through individual and collective action, attempt to mobilize the stakeholders and infuse them with the emerging field's norms and values. Interestingly, this field seems to have emerged in an almost completely tacit and "invisible" fashion, without public recognition nor clear institutional legitimation, but through a process of local formation centered on scientific excellence and global expansion based on scientists' networks.

Methodology

The nanotechnology field

The field of nanotechnology is emergent and undergoing rapid growth, prompting much interest in understanding its development. Unlike other high-tech fields, nanotechnology is mainly characterized by a technological approach rather than a singular technology. However, because this field is an evolving research domain that covers multiple scientific disciplines (including physics, chemistry, biology, biotechnology, engineering, electronics and materials), there is no established approach to clearly identify its boundaries. In order to get around this problem and measure nanotechnology emergence, we had to employ an original multiple-indicators approach to capture the inherent diversity of this domain. Below, after motivating our unit of analysis, we provide a detailed illustration of the multiple parameters we employed to map the emergence of the nanotechnology field in Italy.

Unit of analysis

Regions are very complex social entities, encompassing multiple types of social and business activity and existing within several levels of geographic location. Regions exist at many levels, for example, cities, counties, states or provinces, and nations, though they are often not defined by political boundaries. For example, neighborhoods such as Greenwich Village and the Upper West Side in New York City are commonly understood as distinctive regions, though they are not circumscribed by formal, political boundaries.

More broadly, work and residential activities often spill across political boundaries, leading to perceptions of "greater" metropolitan regions, for example, the New York Tristate Area, the Research Triangle in North Carolina and Silicon Valley in northern California. Thus, the specification of a region, which may be accurate for analytical purposes at any of these geographic levels, depends on the interests of observers. In this chapter, we focus on metropolitan regions – e.g. greater Rome, greater Bologna – as physically distinct locations that are embedded in larger social, business, and political environments, but which are also separate from other metropolitan regions. Despite globalization, metropolitan regions remain primary milieus for concentrations of people, organizations, the arts and industries and permit comparison of the social and industrial features that characterize and differentiate them.

A broad literature has stressed the importance of metropolitan areas as units of geographical investigation in high-technology settings in general (Harrison *et al.* 1996; Feldman and Audretsch 1999; Acs 2002) and also more specifically in nanotechnology (Robinson *et al.* 2007). In line with this work, we have included in our analysis both highly populated cities (Rome, Milan, Naples) and smaller urban centers (Vicenza, Venice, Faenza, Parma) which share nanotechnology-linked activities with nearby major scientific poles (Padua, Bologna).

Overall, we identified 20 metropolitan areas satisfying at least one of the following conditions: (a) presence of research centers institutionally recognized as being Nanotech Centres of Excellence or Nanotech Districts (e.g. Milan, Turin, Cosenza, Trieste, Perugia, Lecce, Pisa, Padua); (b) presence of 2 or more public research institutes engaged in nanotechnology research (Rome, Bologna, Genoa, etc.); and (c) presence of plants of multinational firms highly involved in nanotechnologies in other European countries, such as ST Microelectronics, for example, (Catania, Naples, surroundings of Milan). To probe into the consistency of the emerging field, we then focused on a variety of parameters defined through multiple and complementary sources.

The parameters

To probe the emergence of nanotechnology, we employed a multidimensional approach. Most published research on American and European Nanodistricts (Zucker and Darby 2005; Kahane *et al.* 2006; Bassecoulard *et al.* 2007) focuses just on one or two indicators, typically publications and patents. The only exceptions to this trend are represented by recent works by Heinze (2006) and Youtie and Shapira (2008). Heinze included in his analysis empirical indicators like the volume of investments, public attention cycles on economic and general press, inter-organizational networks and prize winners, as well as publications and patents. Youtie and Shapira (2008) identified nascent Nanodistricts in southern American metropolitan areas by employing ten indicators related to four categories: knowledge generation, human capital, R&D funding, and patenting. But while both these studies emphasize the importance of a multidimensional perspective, they focus solely on indicators that represent science and technology, while the "industry" dimension remains largely unattended. In particular, what is missing from this body of literature is information about the presence and magnitude of entrepreneurial activities. This shortcoming is not trivial, as new firms with core competence in specific technological fields bridge scientific and technological problems with the needs imposed by the market (cost reductions, respect of standards, etc.). Ignoring this aspect means missing an important component of the phenomena. After all, scholars define Nanodistrict as a "regional area where research institutions and firms active in developing nanotechnology are located" (Youtie and Shapira 2008: 211). In addition to more conventional parameters adopted in prior research (Zucker and Darby 2005; Robinson *et al.* 2007; Youtie and Shapira 2008; Shapira and Youtie 2008), we therefore employed the number of new nanotechnology-based firms (created by scientists from public scientific research centers) and the number of "star scientists." While the former are directly connected with the vibrancy of an industry, the latter provide fruitful insights on the relationship between the world of public research laboratories and the market. As Zucker *et al.* (2002) illustrate in the case of biotechnology, star scientists "wear two hats," one as professor at a university and one as a leader or lab head at a firm (143). Star scientists play a central role both in developing and commercializing knowledge. Moreover, they are often responsible for affecting field formation by orchestrating academic as well as cosmopolitan networks (Murray 2004).

The other parameters that we considered in our analysis are related to science and technology outputs. These are the number of scientific publications, patent applications and European research applications granted. Jointly, these four parameters provide a rich understanding of the key forces underpinning the emergence of the field. Scientific articles published in international journals are largely acknowledged as the central outcome of science and as the more reliable source to appreciate the quantity and quality of scientific knowledge production within the field. Patents, by contrast, are one of the most widely used measures of inventiveness. They represent an independent source of data on inventions that are new and have the potential to be applied. The last parameter, European Research Project portfolio,[2] represents both science and technology and captures collaborative research efforts undertaken by local research groups. In the context of Italy, European grants constitute a particularly relevant source of funding, especially so for public research centers. The lack of significant investments from large anchor firms or venture capitalists, and the government's policy to channel resources only to a few geographical areas acknowledged at the institutional level as technological districts, dramatically reduces large-scale funding opportunities, making Europe the only viable alternative for gathering resources. Besides, the number of European research projects is a useful indicator for capturing the capabilities of local research groups/units to sustain and develop leading-edge scientific research at the international level (see Figure 11.1).

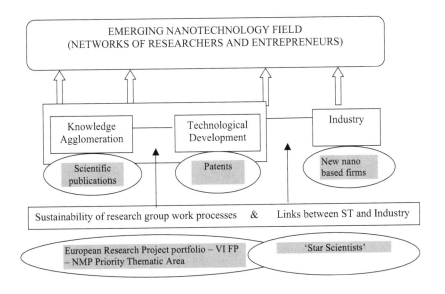

FIGURE 11.1 Overview of parameters selected and related source of data

Data

The data mining procedure employed to build the sample is described below.

Publications

Nanotechnology publications were identified using well-established procedures in bibliometric literature. Nanoscience and nanotechnology publications were identified for every geographic agglomerate through the following Boolean string (Mogoutov and Kahane 2007):

> **TS**=((NANO* OR A*NANO* OR B*NANO* OR C*NANO* OR D*NANO* OR E*NANO* OR F*NANO* OR G*NANO* OR H*NANO* OR I*NANO* OR J*NANO* OR K*NANO* OR L*NANO* OR M*NANO* OR N*NANO* OR O*NANO* OR P*NANO* OR Q*NANO* ORR*NANO* OR S*NANO* OR T*NANO* OR U*NANO* OR V*NANO* OR W*NANO* OR X*NANO* OR Y*NANO* OR Z*NANO*) **NOT** (NANO2 OR NANO3 OR NANO4 OR NANO5 OR NANOSECOND* OR NANOLITER*)) **AND CI = (***name of the city***)**

This procedure rests on a computerized method that takes into account the evolution of the terminology that typifies this research field and at the same time excludes unimportant or misleading terms. We run the search on the text of the title, abstract, subject, and keywords in order to identify the nanotech-related scientific publications. At the same time, we connected each publication with specific metropolitan areas based on the affiliation of the authors.[3] The data source is ISI-Thomson Web of Science, one of the most popular and comprehensive databases for this kind of analysis. It includes bibliometric data on publications from more than 8700 international journals in the fields of science and medicine, starting from 1987. The data mining was conducted on August 3, 2007 and updated after a year and half.

Patent applications

The nanotech patent applications were selected by using a methodology described by the European Patent Office (EPO). In 2006, an experts' team from the European Patent Office identified and classified with the tag Y01N all the documents contained in the database of EPO that satisfied certain nanotechnological requisites (Scheu 2006). We conducted the data mining combining the tag Y01N with the following keywords related to the field "applicant": "CONSIGLIO" and "CNR" for Italian National Research Council, "UNIVERSITA" for university, "ISTITUTO" and "ENTE" for institute and "POLITECNICO" for polytechnic. All the data was extracted from the EPO database (as of December 10, 2008) using the esp@cenet search engine for the observation period January 2003–June 2007. This search resulted in information on 32 patents. Next, we repeated the data mining procedure by joining only the names of the different patent inventors previously identified with the TAG Y01N. This further step was necessary due to the cultural behavior of not indicating the affiliated institution as applicant in the patent application, largely diffused among Italian academic scientists (Baldini *et al.* 2006) Finally, in order to improve sample representativeness, we also employed a third type of algorithm. We tracked down all the scientists working for research centers recognized as "Nanotech Centres of Excellence" by MIUR. A comprehensive list of scientists' names was then obtained by searching through the research centers' websites. We identified 47 patent applications directly ascribable to the above inventors. Finally, for each of the 47 patent applications, we gathered further information regarding: (i) geographical origin of the institution; (ii) patent office of filing; and (iii) sub-categories of category Y01N.

European research projects portfolio

To map the EU project portfolio, we used the label that identifies the NMP thematic area of the 6th European Framework Programme (EFP).[4] We collected this data in September 2007 when the calls of the 6th EFP were closed and we focused our attention only on projects involving at least one Italian partner. The source for this data was the Ministry for Education, University and Research (MIUR), which provided us the full list of research projects supported (245 in total).

New firms

To build this sample, we selected only new firms that used the label "nanotechnology" to construct their external image through products, services, denominations, advertisements, etc. The main sources of data were a study on Italian players in nanotechnology carried out by Chiesa and De Massis in 2006 and the findings of a survey conducted by the Italian Association for Industrial Research (AIRI) in 2006. Finally, we searched the internet, especially the institutional websites, to gain a better insight on the phenomena.[5]

"Star scientists in action"

We gauged the presence of "star scientists" using the data related to science, technology, and industry previously introduced. The procedure consisted of three steps. First, we identified all the scientists working in Italian public institutes who had published in international journals more than 25 papers related to nanotechnology during the period 2004–2008. In this way, we collected data on a sample of 79 scientists. Next, we checked the productivity of this sample in terms of number of patent applications filed in the same period (18 scientists in total) and in relation to the number of entrepreneurial initiatives started (3 scientists in total). We considered as "star scientists" only those scientists who had contributed to the development of nanotechnology through the simultaneous engagement in scientific, technological, and entrepreneurial activities (projects). This definition emphasizes not only their scientific inventiveness but also their capability in manipulating and dynamically recombining the same or similar bodies of knowledge in order to generate diversified outputs (papers, patents, firms).

Findings: In search of Italian emergent nanotech fields

Scientific excellence agglomerations

We counted 9651 publications co-authored by at least one researcher affiliated with an Italian institution over the period 1998–2008.[6] Within this sample, we assessed the top scientific agglomerations (localized in the metropolitan areas previously selected) on the basis of two dimensions: the concentration of nanotech-related publications per metropolitan area (x axis), and their impact on the scientific community (y axis). To gauge the impact of publications, we used the H-index.[7] This index is based on the scientist's most-cited papers and the number of citations that he or she received from other publications. The index can also be applied to the productivity and impact of a group of scientists, such as a department or university or country. The results shown in Figure 11.2 suggest that there is a positive relation between these two theoretical dimensions.

This analysis shows that the area between the city of Bologna, Modena, Faenza, and Parma has the highest concentration of nanotech-related scientific papers and it is characterized by the highest impact on the scientific community (H factor 52).[8] Within this cluster, Bologna is the most prominent city (735).

We found concentrations of scientific publications above the average (577) in the metropolitan areas of Rome (1232), Milan (989), Padua (711), Trieste (706), and Turin (654). Among these, Padua (h-index=30) is characterized by the lowest impact on the international scientific community while Rome, Milan, and Turin have the highest number of research institutes.[9] Interestingly, Florence displays a moderate scientific production (4 percent of grand total) but a relatively high impact (38). In order to better distinguish the scientific agglomerations on the basis of their disciplinary specialization (over the early period 2003–2008[10]), we also regrouped the publications by sub-fields.[11] It turned out that most agglomerations are centered on a specific sub-field with the exception of Bologna, Milan and Rome metropolitan areas where we recorded a higher rate of scientific production in all the sub-fields. For instance, Catania, Lecce, and Naples have a relatively high percentage of publications specializing in nanoelectronics, likely a consequence of ST Microelectronics' influence. Padua, Trieste, and Turin are characterized by a particularly high concentration of publications in the sub-field of NanoMaterials; while Florence, Genoa, Naples, and Pisa appear more specialized in the nanobio and medicine fields. These results are displayed on Figure 11.3.

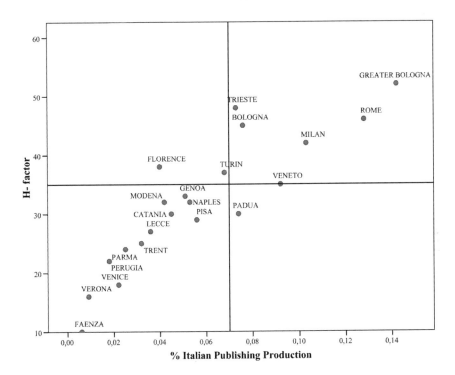

FIGURE 11.2   Map of Italian scientific excellence agglomerations in nanotech field (1998–2008)

Source: ISI THOMPSON, our elaborations

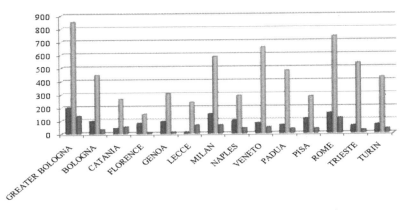

FIGURE 11.3   Nanotech Papers agglomerations by sub-field and metropolitan area (2003–2008)

Source: ISI THOMPSON, our elaborations

Scientific inventiveness

We recorded the presence of patenting activities in all of 20 metropolitan areas with the exception of Padua, Venice, Verona, Modena, Parma, Perugia, and Naples. The results from patent analysis confirm the leadership of Bologna, Milan, Rome, and Trieste. Tracking patents in relation to the filing office allows us to measure the economic impact in potential terms. A common and widespread method used by patent scholars consists of assessing patent impact in relation to the breadth of the geographical protection (exclusive use of what it is protected). Accordingly, we categorized as high impact patents those patents registered in all 3 main international offices (EPO, USPTO, WIPO). Results are showed in Figure 11.4.

Bologna (8 of 12) and Trieste (6 of 7) are the areas with the highest number of high impact patents, while Lecce, Catania, and Torino did not register any. Rome has 7 patents but only 2 are high impact (see Table 11.1). We also refined our investigation considering the technological domains associated with the selected

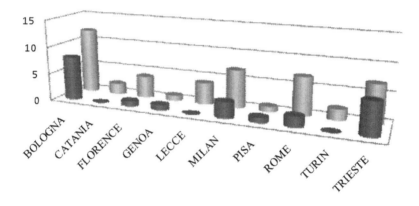

■ N. high impact Patents   ▧ N. different Patents

FIGURE 11.4   High impact patents

Source: Esp@cenet, our processing

TABLE 11.1 Nanotechnology

Y01N2	Nanobiotechnology
Y01N4	Nanotechnology for information processing, storage and transmission
Y01N6	Nanotechnology for materials and surface science
Y01N8	Nanotechnology for interacting, sensing and actuating
Y01N10	Nanotechnology for optics
Y01N12	Nanomagnetics

Source: Sheu 2006

nanotech patents. The main technologies domains were identified on the basis of the 6 sub-classes that are included in category Y01N (see Figure 11.5).

Results show that Italian patents tend to concentrate in sub-categories Y01N6 (34 per cent) and Y01N4 (27 percent) and Y01N2 (18 percent). At the local level, the analysis reveals a high level of technological diversification for the Bologna, Milan, and Rome areas. Despite the small size of the sample, it is apparent that some areas tend to concentrate on a specific technological domain. For example, Torino and Trieste are focused on nanomaterials while Lecce specializes in sub-fields related to nanoelectronics

Research projects

Both private and public Italian research groups have taken into great account European fundraising opportunities to support their research in nanotechnology. Among public research labs, we counted 172 different EU-supported research projects and we recorded a higher rate of concentration in Bologna, Milan (both 19 percent), and Rome (11 percent). Moreover, we analyzed the variety of research groups in relation to their institutional affiliation (university, government research center, and scientific hospital). Under this lens, the metropolitan area of Bologna appears characterized by the highest rate of variation in terms of different research institutions represented. Conversely, in the case of Milan and Rome, the number of research projects supported is strongly concentrated within specific faculties or departments.

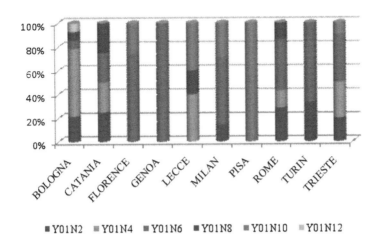

FIGURE 11.5   Nanotech patents applications distribution by sub-category (2003–2008)

Source: Esp@cenet, our processing

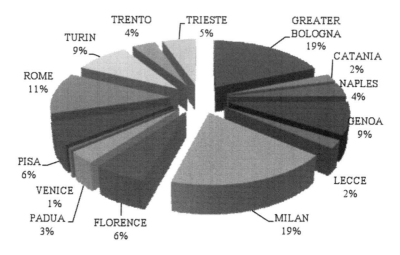

FIGURE 11.6   EU research projects supported by metropolitan area

Source: MIUR, our processing

Entrepreneurship

We were able to identify 18 nanotechnology-related ventures created by scientists affiliated to Italian public research institutions. This result is relevant because it sheds light on two interesting aspects. First, the government initiatives have stimulated a very low rate of entrepreneurship; second, 56 percent of the firms identified are located around the same area, Bologna (see Table 11.2).

To summarize, the triangulation of evidence obtained reveals that at the macro level, the metropolitan areas of Bologna, Milan and Rome are the most significant in terms of nanotechnology-related outcomes. Moreover, the cases of Bologna and Rome were both characterized by the absence of top-down institutional actions and are not included in the list of publicly-recognized nanotech districts.

Public research institutes involved in nanotechnologies at the local level

In this section we move the focus from the measure of STI outcomes and agglomerations to the identification of institutional actors involved in the nanotech field at local level and on the intensity of their relationships in network of collaborations. In particular, for each metropolitan area, we analyze the performance of universities, government research centers, and scientific hospitals. In this way, we seek to provide a better understanding of the role of the different research institutions in the process of field emergences.

TABLE 11.2 List of Italian *de novo* firms

Firms	Location	Industrial applications	Foundation year	Parent Institution
Organic Spintronics	Bologna	Materials	2003	CNR
MEDITECKNOLOGY	Bologna	NanoBio	2004	CNR
Nanodiagnostic	San Vito di Spilamberto (Modena)	Toxicology	2004	UNI
NanoSurfaces	Granarolo dell'Emilia (Bologna)	Materials	2004	UNI-IND
Scriba Nanotecnologie	Bologna	Materials	2005	CNR
IPECC S.r.l.	Faenza	Materials	2005	CNR
2SN	Bologna	Energy	2007	CNR
OSJ	Bologna	Energy	2007	CNR
NANO4BIO	Bologna	NanoBio	2008	CNR
PROART	Bologna	NanoMedicine	2008	CNR-IRCSS
NANOVECTOR S.r.l.	Torino	NanoMedicine	2001	UNI
ADAMANTIO S.r.l.	Torino	Materials	2006	UNI
CYANINE Technologies	Torino	Instrumentation	2006	UNI
SINGULAR ID	Padova	Materials	2006	IND
ANANAS NANOTECH	Padova	Pharmaceutical	2007	UNI
NANO Center for Advanced Technologies	L'Aquila	Materials	2007	UNI
Advanced Nanomaterials Research s.r.l.	Messina	Materials	2006	UNI
TETHIS S.r.l.	Milano	Materials	2004	UNI

Source: Chiesa De Massis 2006; Airi Census 2006, 2007; institutional web site

Productivity of Italian public research institute by typology

At national level, universities (80.3 percent of total) play a more critical role than government research centers (31.7 percent) and scientific hospitals (1.5 percent). However, this trend is not always confirmed at local level, as the Trieste and Catania cases show. Moreover, we didn't always find a direct relationship between concentration of publications and international impact. For instance, the University of Padua (650) and the University of Bologna (508) both distinguish themselves for very high scientific production. But while Bologna also displays the highest scientific impact (H=40), the University of Padua has a relatively low H (30). The map in Figure 11.7 shows that there are three groups of universities in relation to

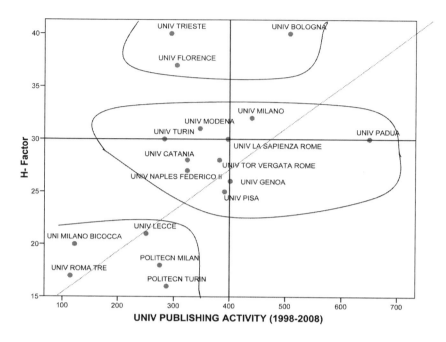

FIGURE 11.7 Scientific excellence map of Italian Universities in nanotech field (1998–2008)

Source: ISI THOMPSON, our elaborations

their impact. Of these, the group composed of the universities of Bologna, Trieste, and Florence is characterized by an outstanding level of scientific impact compared with the rest of the Italian context. The analysis of authors' affiliation at the faculty and department level shows an interesting pattern. The scientific contribution of the University of Bologna in the nanotechnology field is associated with the work of researchers from a high number of different faculties and departments. In contrast, in the cases of the University of Florence and Trieste, only a restricted number of departments are significantly involved (Faculty of Chemistry in Florence and Faculty of Physics in Trieste) in terms of scientific productivity.

The metropolitan areas of Bologna and Trieste are characterized by outstanding scientific excellence also with respect to government research centers (Figure 11.8). High levels of scientific impact are registered also in the areas of Rome, Catania, Milan, Naples, and Genoa, between territorial divisions of the Italian National Research Council (CNR).

The map in Figure 11.9 provides a valuable insight on the relevance of scientific agglomeration processes enacted within the main Italian public research institutions (CNR and university) both with respect to the institutional level (x axis) and the geographical level (y axis). It focuses on the scientific production of the Italian National Research Council's territorial division. Thus, this map can be

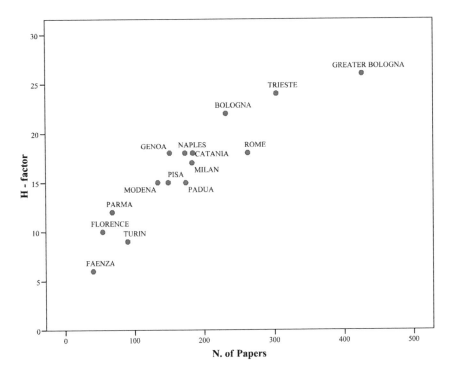

FIGURE 11.8 Scientific excellence map of CNR territorial divisions in nanotech field (2003–2008)

Source: ISI THOMPSON, our elaborations

seen as complementary to the previous ones shown in Figures 11.7 and 11.8, as it provides a comparison on the magnitude of engagement in the nanotechnology field of the main Italian research institutes at the local level. The map suggests that the contribution of local university units and C.N.R. divisions to the local scientific agglomeration is more balanced within the area of Bologna, Modena, Parma, Genoa, and Naples. Instead, universities play the greater role in the areas of Padua, Florence, and Turin, while in Trieste and Catania, CNR divisions are critical actors.

Finally, we analyzed the publishing activity of scientific research hospitals (IRCCS), even if they account only for a small portion of the total.[12] The presence of this type of scientific labs enriches the salience and variety of actors involved in the nanotech field. First, research activities are directly connected to applications at local level through clinical work practices. Second, research activities are focused only on a very specific sub-field, namely nanomedicine. Results show that only few centers (Table 11.3) have been involved in nanotech-related scientific production over the last ten years.

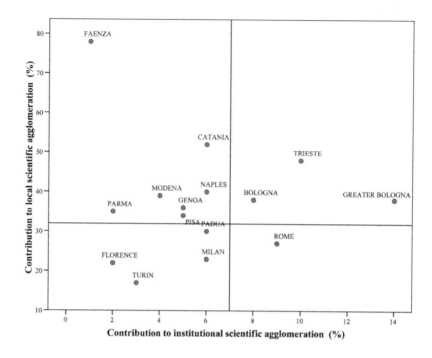

FIGURE 11.9   Map of Italian National Research Council territorial divisions contribution on local scientific production in nanotech field (2003–2008)

Source: ISI THOMPSON, our elaborations

TABLE 11.3   Top 5 Italian scientific research hospital labs (IRCCS) for publishing productivity in nanotech field (1998–2008)

ID	Legal status	Location	Paper
Orthoped Inst Rizzoli★	Public	Bologna	18
S. Giovanni Di Dio Centre	Private	Brescia	10
Nat Inst Cancer Research	Public	Genoa	9
Gaslini Inst	Public	Genoa	7
San Raffaele Center	Private	Milan	6

Note: ★ Orthopaedic Institute Rizzoli intensified its scientific production after 2005 resulting in 80 percent of its papers being published in the last four years.
Source: ISI THOMPSON, our processing

The analysis of the contribution of local institutions on the emergence of the field is completed by the analysis on patenting activity (Figure 11.10) and European projects portfolio (Figure 11.11). In both cases, only the metropolitan area of Bologna confirms the heterogeneity of institutions involved in the process.

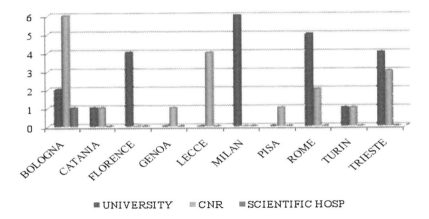

FIGURE 11.10   Distribution of nanotech patents by type of research institute and metropolitan area

Source: Esp@cenet, our elaboration

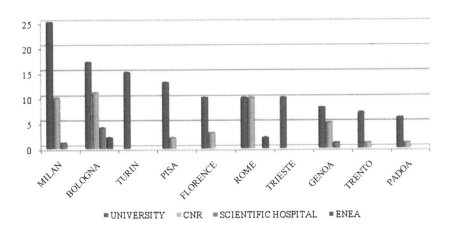

FIGURE 11.11   Distribution of EU research projects by type of research institute and metropolitan area

Source: MIUR, our processing

The Bologna case attracted our curiosity not only for the highest levels of nanotech-related outputs but also for its heterogeneity. We have demonstrated this heterogeneity in terms of plurality of research institutes involved, variety of disciplinary domains covered and typologies of output derived from research activities (publications, patents, research project portfolio, entrepreneurship). This evidence is consistent with star scientists' analysis. Table 11.4 shows the results from the analysis of "top" scientists' productivity. It suggests that within some metropolitan areas such as Trieste, Lecce, Catania, Florence, and Turin, only a few departments are highly involved in the process of field emergence. Moreover, these departments seem to rest on the actions of a few key actors, as indicated by the analysis of the standard deviation of scientists' H-factor. In contrast, a greater number of departments are represented by top scientists within the metropolitan areas as Bologna, Rome, and Milan, where standard deviation in H-factor is much lower. Second, only three scientists have been able to perform successfully in publishing, patenting, and entrepreneurial activities over the last six years. Two of them work in public research centers in Bologna.[13]

Collaboration networks of neighboring institutions

In this final section we show some evidence on the intensity of relationships between scientists belonging to different research institutes located in the same metropolitan area in order to have some sense of the magnitude of the proximity

TABLE 11.4 The presence of "star" scientists

	N. of highly prolific scientists (> 25 papers)	N. of departments represented	Mean of scientists' H-factor	St. Dev. scientists H-factor	N. of highly prolific scientists in publishing and patenting activity	N. of highly prolific scientists in publishing, patenting and entre-preneurial activity
Rome	9	6	9	1,8	2	0
Greater Bologna	9	6	10,2	1,6	3	2
Milan	7	5	9,1	1,1	4	0
Padua-Venice Verona	12	4	9,7	1,8	0	0
Turin	3	3	6,7	3,1	0	0
Trieste	5	3	12	12	2	0
Naples	4	3	11	1,2	0	0
Catania	8	3	8,4	3,3	2	0
Genoa	6	3	10	1,3	1	0
Florence	8	2	10,6	4,4	1	0
Lecce	7	1	11,6	4,6	3	1
Pisa	1	1	8	–	0	0

Source: ISI THOMPSON, our processing

effect. The measures are based on the analysis of scientific publications co-authorships (Figure. 11.12), patents' co-inventorship (Figure 11.13), and research consortia partnership in EU projects (Table 11.5). For scientific collaborations, our analysis encompassed only the cases of Rome, Milan, and Bologna because they account for the greater concentrations of publications and they are comparable in terms of number of research institutes involved (3 universities,[14] CNR, and IRCCS). In general, our analysis shows that the percentage of scientific collaborations decreased over the last six years even if each area experienced a dramatic increase in the number of nanotechnology publications. Against this tendency, the Bologna case represents an exception since starting from 2005 it features an increasing number of scientific collaborations. Similar findings emerged from the analysis of European projects partnerships. We counted the highest rate of cross-institutional relationships (24 percent) within the Bologna metropolitan area.

Even if the sample of patent applications is small, it seems possible to distinguish between two different typologies of patenting behavior. In one case, the technological agglomeration (based on the number of filed patent applications) is mainly the result of occasional events. Here the local networks of collaboration associated with each patent application are disconnected, as the inventors have published only one patent application during the last six years. In the second case, the technological agglomeration is the result of repeated events by the same actors. Here the network of patenting collaborations is more connected. While the Rome, Milan, Turin, and Catania areas are mostly characterized by disconnected networks and occasional patenting events, the metropolitan areas of Bologna, Trieste, and Lecce are characterized by repeated events and connected networks of collaboration.

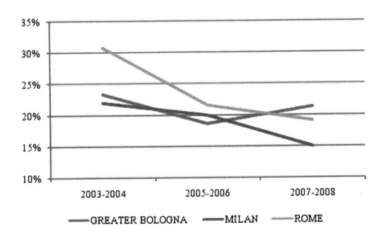

FIGURE 11.12 Trend of scientific collaborations between scientists affiliated with different institutes located in the same metropolitan area (2003–2008)

Source: ISI THOMPSON, our processing

TABLE 11.5 Concentration of partnership in EU projects between different research
institutions located in the same metropolitan area (2002–2006)

	Nr. EU research projects	Nr. EU research projects involving more than one research institute from the same metropolitan area
Greater Bologna	34	8
Catania	4	1
Florence	11	1
Genoa	16	0
Lecce	4	0
Milan	34	4
Naples	7	0
Padua	6	0
Venice	1	0
Pisa	11	1
Rome	21	3
Turin	16	1
Trento	7	1
Trieste	10	0

Source: MIUR, our processing

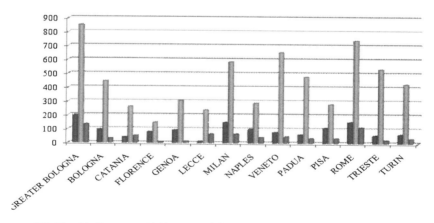

■ N. Nanobio Papers   ■ N. Nanomaterials Papers   ■ N. Nanoelectronics Papers

FIGURE 11.13   Concentration of collaboration networks in co-patenting at local level
(2003-2008)

Source: Esp@cenet, our processing

Discussion

Our understanding of how vibrant localized fields emerge, take hold and then transform regional economies remains remarkably limited. Markusen (1996) draws a distinction between fields that are sticky and thus able to hold on to new ideas and translate them into competitive regions and places that are slippery and thus not able to benefit in the long term from innovation and investment. But while provocative and intriguing, her characterization fails to explain how fields emerge in the first place and subsequently transform themselves from being slippery to sticky. Yet it is precisely the process of variation that needs to be understood to explain field emergence. As Rosenberg (1983) suggests, even radical innovations require many complementary institutional and technological "ingredients" before they are ready for commercialization. It is a process that unfolds over a long time and through the accumulation of many small steps that make emergence possible. In this study, we sought to outline a simple descriptive methodological approach to track some of these steps, in an attempt to shed more light on the terrain in which the Bologna nanotech field is taking shape, against the broader Italian landscape. To this end, we have introduced an original methodology based on an array of indicators in multiple categories of scientific collaboration, knowledge generation, research funding and entrepreneurship. Such a measurement approach goes beyond the traditional use of publications and/or patents alone to provide a multidimensional perspective on the forces underpinning the emergence of the field.

Our analysis suggests that various forces are converging to signal the ensuing identity of the Bologna nanotech field: knowledge communities composed of diverse (yet complementary) academic disciplines, academic entrepreneurs, and star scientists. Beginning with the initiation period, paths of independent scientists and entrepreneurs (acting on their own diverse intentions and ideas) have gradually intersected. These intersections have provided occasions for interaction, revealing areas of interdependence and co-operation. As a result, the novel field has acquired a significant (yet still largely unrecognized from an institutional standpoint) scientific prominence at the national level, and a visible position at the international level. The plurality of actors is especially significant at the academic level, but new ventures are growing rapidly too (this is particularly important because nanotechnology is not a technological innovation per se but the application of nanometre tools and methods to different technical domains). Compared with other national and international nanotechnology fields, the Bologna case is especially striking for the broad spectrum of disciplines that are involved in the making of the field. Chemistry, physics, material sciences, as well as the life sciences are all uniformly represented within this field. This heterogeneity is nurtured and sustained by extensive collaborations across different research institutes (universities, governmental research centers, scientific hospitals) and knowledge communities. These features mark a departure from major nanodistricts at the European level too, where the range of disciplines and application domains is considerably narrower than in Bologna. It also points to the existence of specific capabilities to move and manage knowledge horizontally across domain boundaries and "trading zones" as well as vertically, from science to technology and from technology to market (Galison 1999; Kellogg *et al.* 2006)

We previously argued that the cluster emerged spontaneously. As we move towards the conclusion, this statement needs more articulation. In particular, while our evidence and findings make it apparent that Bologna is hosting a rapidly-emerging field in nanotechnology, it has to be stressed that this field is still overlooked by local authorities, which lag behind and are slow in providing it with institutional standing. In fact, this area has not been officially recognized by the government. This is in striking contrast with other European cases, where local government agencies and political actors are heavily involved in endorsing the domain through the financing of large-scale facilities as well as mobilization of resources and constituencies. That was not the case with Bologna, where co-ordination has so far taken place only through individual actors' driven (intended as well as unintended) interactions and partisan mutual adjustments (Astley and Van de Ven 1983). In other words, the construction of the field has mainly resulted from the combination of opportunistic and collectivistic efforts of independent actors in the common pursuit of scientific and technological innovation. Our evidence suggests that, lying behind these collectivistic efforts is an "invisible college" of actors capable of self-organizing into networks of scientific exchange and reciprocal support (Merton 1973; Murray 2004). In the case of a field such as nanotechnology, these networks span the core discipline in which the inventor has trained but also bridge disciplines and domains, as we could appreciate from analyzing the extent of co-authorships across institutions as well as the collabo-rations across large-scale research projects. These exchanges have enhanced the mutual awareness of the various actors involved in the structuring of the field, despite initial uncertainty and lack of some initial conditions often associated with the emergence of new fields.

Also, unlike these and other well-known technology-orientated clusters in Europe (i.e. nanoelectronics in Grenoble, biotech in Munich, photonics in Jena and Berlin), the development of the Bologna nanotech field does not appear to be associated with the presence of a large lead-organization fostering the activities of similar or complementary firms. Instead, our findings indicate that most of the active companies are small entrepreneurial ventures whose main stakeholders are local medium-sized companies in search of complementary investment opportu-nities. We surmise that this fragmentation is the result of an alternative yet complementary development model to the anchor-tenant hypothesis, one that rests on the repeated entrepreneurial efforts of a few serial entrepreneurs who exploit the broad applicability of nanotechnologies to multiple industrial domains. Thus, although the emergence of the field can be considered spontaneous, in that there was no direct top-down public interventions, several enabling pre-conditions facilitated the coming together of all the elements

Conclusions and avenues for future research

As we move towards the conclusion of this chapter we hope our multi-indicator approach can help lay the basis for methodological orientations especially sensitive to the great organizational diversity that field emergence entails. The argument we offer does not hinge on specific types of arrangements or building blocks, in fact it is broad and flexible enough to accommodate multiple pathways. The analysis is still preliminary, and further micro-level inquiry is needed in order to unpack the interplay between agency at the micro level and field emergence. For instance, enriching our multi-indicator methodology with a discursive perspective might help illuminate how shared symbols provide entrepreneurs resources to legitimate heterogeneous visions. This appears an especially promising avenue for research given that it allows one to study embryonic fields (Bartel and Garud 2009). Along this line, additional qualitative analysis should be devoted to probe into the behavior and role of academic entrepreneurs (Murray 2004) in bridging the science-technology market process (Lubik and Garnsey 2008). Similarly, attention should be paid to institutional players who can confer labels and meaning to the field through mobilization of resources, public initiatives, speeches, etc. (Lounsbury and Glynn 2001). Finally, while at this embryonic stage of development the nature of linkages among actors remains largely invisible, future social network analysis investigating the social fabric of the field could add significantly to our understanding of how social structure shape the proximity advantage.

Certainly, this is not the last word on this topic. It is our hope that this empirically informed theorizing will inspire others to take a more detailed look. It is only through the employment of methods that allow an appreciation of the nuances of field emergence and development that we may begin to inform policy.

Notes

1   We gratefully acknowledge financial assistance from the European Commission through project FRIDA (FP7-grant agreement no.: 225546). An earlier version of this study was also supported by Fondazione Carisbo. We are especially thankful to Gianni Lorenzoni, Charles Baden-Fuller, Vincent Mangematin, and Erik Stam for insightful comments and discussion on previous versions of the manuscript. The authors are responsible for errors and omissions.

2   With the aim of "integrating and strengthening the European Research Area," the Framework Programme promoted by the European Commission offers for all European researchers an incentive to develop specific research agendas and a major fundraising opportunity. It favours the formation of research groups independently from national policy, because it provides the opportunity to recruit new researchers, improve the laboratory equipments, and gain access to a network of complementary laboratories and technological facilities. Moreover, it creates the conditions for fruitful co-operation between research groups from different institutions and countries.

3   In the case of publication co-authored by scientists affiliated with institutes located in different metropolitan areas, we counted the same publication as many times as the number of different metropolitan areas represented by authors' affiliation. On the contrary, in the case of publication co-authored by scientists affiliated with different institutes located in the same metropolitan area, we counted the same publication only once.

4 NMP is the acronym for "Nanotechnology and nanosciences, knowledge-based multifunctional materials and new production processes and devices". With a budget of EUR 1,429 million for 2002–2006.

5 www.cnr.it/sitocnr/IlCNR/Valorizzazionerisultati/Spinoff/SocietaSpinoff.html

6 At a European level, Italian publishing productivity is higher than the productivity of Spain (7857) Switzerland (4804) Netherlands (4260) Belgium (3072) and Ireland (1407) while it is lower than Germany (24824) France (17382) and England (12083).

7 The H-index was suggested by Jorge E. Hirsch, a physicist at UCSD, as a tool for determining theoretical physicists' relative quality. In practice, according to this index, a scholar or a group of scholars with an index of h has/have published h papers each of which has been cited by others at least h times.

8 The research area in Bologna is 45 km away from the University of Modena, 55 km away from the CNR Institute (ISTEC) in Faenza, and 99 km away from the University of Parma.

9 In Rome and Milan there are three universities while in Turin there are two.

10 Of the publications edited in the last ten years, 78,3 percent are concentrated within the period from 2003–2008.

11 We have adopted the procedure indicated by Porter *et al.* (2008) to identify the publications belonging to each of these three sub-fields.

12 www.ministerosalute.it/ricsan/organizzazione/sezorganizzazione.jsp?id=73&label=ir1 for a full list.

13 These two scientists are Fabio Biscarini and Massimiliano Cavallini. The former has been awarded the 2007 EU Descartes Prize for Transnational Collaborative Research and the latter has been awarded the 2006 EURAY Prize.

14 Tor Vergata, La Sapienza, and Roma Tre in Rome; University of Milan, Bicocca, and Politecnique in Milan; Alma Mater Studiorum, University of Modena, and University of Parma in Bologna Cluster.

References

Acs, Z. J. (2002). *Innovation and the Growth of Cities*. Cheltenham: Edward Elgar.

Almeida, P., Kogut, B. (1997). The exploration of technological diversity and the geographic localization of innovation. *Small Business Economics*, 9(1), 21–31.

Astley, W. G. and Van de Ven, A. H. (1983). Central perspectives and debates in organization theory. *Administrative Science Quarterly*, 28, 245–273.

Baldini, N., Grimaldi, R. and Sobrero, M. (2006). Institutional changes and the commercialization of academic knowledge: A study of Italian universities' patenting activities between 1965 and 2002. *Research Policy*, 35, 518–532.

Bartel, C. A. and Garud, R. (2009) The role of narratives in sustaining organizational innovation. *Organization Science*, 20: 107–117.

Bassecoulard, E., Lelu, A. and Zitt, M. (2007). Mapping nanosciences by citation flows: A preliminary analysis. *Scientometrics*, 70(3), 859–880.

Breschi, S., Malerba, F. (2005). *Clusters Networks and Innovation*. Oxford: Oxford University Press.

Chiesa, V. and De Massis, A. (2006). *La nanoindustria. Analisi dei principali player italiani nelle nanotecnologie*. Rome: Aracne Ed.

Di Maggio, P. and Powell, W. (1983). The iron cage revisited: Institutional isomorphism and collective rationality in organizational fields. *American Sociological Review*, 48, 147–160.

Etzioni, A. (1963). The epigenesis of political communities at the international level. *American Journal of Sociology*, 68, 407–421.

Feldman, M. (2001). The entrepreneurial event revisited: Firm formation in a regional context. *Industrial Corporate Change* 10 861–891.

Feldman, M. (2004). Resources in emerging structures and processes of change. *Organization Science*, 15, 295–309.

Feldman, M. and Audretsch, D. B. (1999). Innovation in cities: Science-based diversity, specialization and localized competition. *European Economic Review*, 43, 409–429.

Galison, P. (1999). Trading zone: Coordinating action and belief. In M. Biagioli (ed.), *The Science Studies Reader* (137–160). New York: Routledge.

Garnsey, E. and Heffernan, P. (2005). High tech clustering through spin out and attraction: The Cambridge case. *Regional Studies*, 39(8), 1127–1144.

Granqvist, N., Grodal, S. and Woolley, J. (2009). Executives labelling strategies in emerging domains of activity: Constructing and using nascent market labels. *Academy of Management Best Paper Proceedings of the Academy of Management Conference.*Chicago

Hannan, M.T. and Freeman, J. (1977). The population ecology of organizations. *American Journal of Sociology*, 82, 929–964

Harrison, B., Kelley, M.R. and Grant, J. (1996). Innovation firm behavior and local milieu: Exploring the intersection of agglomeration firm effects and technological change. *Economic Geography*, 72 (3), 233–258.

Heinze, T. (2006). Mapping the evolution of Nano S & T: Analytical and empirical tools. Workshop on mapping the emergence of nanotechnologies and understanding the engine of growth and development, Prime, NanoDistrict Workshop, March 1–3, Grenoble, France.

Hitt, M. A., Gimeno, J., and Hoskisson, R. E. (1998). Current and future research methods in strategic management. *Organizational Research Methods*, 1, 6–44.

Iammarino, S. and Cantwell, J. (2001). EU regions and multinational corporations: Change, stability and strengthening of technological comparative advantages. *Industrial and Corporate Change*, 10(4), 1007–1037.

Kahane, B., Theoret, C., Mogoutov, A. and Larédo, P. (2006). Dynamics of "Nano" science: A remake of the IT or bio "waves"? Prime, NanoDistrict Workshop, March 1–3, Grenoble, France.

Kellogg, K. C., Orlikowski, W. J. and Yates J. (2006). Life in the trading zone: Structuring coordination across boundaries in postbureaucratic organizations. *Organization Science*, 17, 22–44.

Klepper, S. and Graddy, E. (1990). The evolution of new industries and the determinants of market structure. *RAND Journal of Economics*, 21(1), 27–44.

Laumann, E. O., Galaskiewicz, J. and Marsden, P.V. (1978). Community structure as inter-organizational linkages, *Annual Review of Sociology*, 4, 455–484.

Lounsbury, M. and Glynn, M. A. (2001). Cultural entrepreneurship: Stories, legitimacy, and the acquisition of resources. *Strategic Management Journal*, 22(6), 545–564.

Lubik S. and Garnsey, E. (2008). Commercialising nano-innovations from university spin-out companies. *Nanotechnology Perceptions*, 4(3), 225–238.

Maine, E. and Garnsey, E. (2006). Commercializing generic technology: The case of advanced materials ventures. *Research Policy*, 35 (3), 375–393.

Marcus, A. A., Anderson, M. H. (2008). Commitment to an emerging organizational field, institutional entrepreneurship, and the perception of opportunity: An enactment theory. *Industry Studies Conference Paper*. Available at: http://ssrn.com/abstract=1135691

Markusen, A. (1996). Sticky places in slippery space: A typology of industrial districts. *Economic Geography*, 72, 293–313.

Merton, R. K. (1973). *The Sociology of Science: Theoretical and Empirical Investigations.* Chicago: University of Chicago Press.

Mogoutov, A. and Kahane, B. (2007). Data search strategy for science and technology emergence: A scalable and evolutionary query for nanotechnology tracking. *Research Policy*, 36, 893–903.

Murray, F. (2002). Innovation as co-evolution of scientific and technological networks: Exploring tissue engineering. *Research Policy*, 31 (8–9), 1389–1403.

Murray, F. (2004). The role of academic inventors in entrepreneurial firms: Sharing the laboratory life. *Research Policy*, 33, 643–659.

Pisano, G. P. (2006). *Science Business the Promise, the Reality & the Future of Biotech Business*. Boston: Harvard Business School Press.

Porter, A. L., Youtie, J., Shapira, P., and Schoeneck, D. (2008). Refining search terms for nanotechnology. *Journal of Nanoparticle Research*, 10 (5), 715–728

Powell, W. W., Packalen, K., and Whittington, K. B. (2012). Organizational and institutional genesis: The emergence of high-tech clusters in the life sciences. In Padgett, J. and Powell, W. W. (eds), *The Emergence of Organizations and Markets* (434–465), Princeton, NJ: Princeton University Press.

Rao, H. (2009). *Market Rebels*. Princeton, NJ: Princeton University Press

Robinson, D. K. R., Rip, A., and Mangematin, V. (2007). Technological agglomeration and the emergence of clusters and networks in nanotechnology. *Research Policy*, 36, 871–879.

Rosenberg, N. (1983). *Inside the Black Box: Technology and Economics*. Cambridge: Cambridge University Press.

Shapira, P. and Youtie, J. (2008). Emergence of nanodistricts in the United States: Path dependency or new opportunities? *Economic Development Quarterly*, 22, 187–199.

Scheu M., Veefkind, V., Verbandt, Y., Molina Galan, E., Absalom R., and Förster, W. (2006). Mapping nanotechnology patents: The EPO approach. *World Patent Information*, 28, 204–211.

Scott, A. J. (2006), Entrepreneurship, innovation and industrial development: geography and the creative field revisited. Small Business Economics, 26, (1), 1-24.

Scott, R. W. (2001). *Institutions and Organizations*, 2nd edn. Thousand Oaks, CA: Sage Publications.Stam, E. (2007) Why butterflies don"t leave: Locational behavior of entrepreneurial firms. *Economic Geography*, 83(1), 27–50.

Van de Ven, A. H. and Garud, R. (1989). A framework for understanding the emergence of new industries, in Rosenbloom, R. S. and Burgelman, R. (eds), *Research on Technological Innovation, Management, and Policy* (195–225). Greenwich, CT: JAI Press.

Youtie, J. and Shapira, P. (2008). Mapping the nanotechnology enterprise: A multi-indicator analysis of emerging nanodistricts in the US South. *Journal of Technology Transfer*, 33(2) 209–223.

Zucker, L. G., Darby, M. R., and Armstrong, J. S. (2002). Commercializing knowledge: University science, knowledge capture, and firm performance in biotechnology. *Management Science*, 48(1), 138–153.

Zucker, L. G. and Darby, M. R. (2005). Socio-economic impact of nanoscale science: Initial results and NanoBank. *NBER Working Paper No. W11181*. Available at: www.nber.org/papers/w11181

12

DATA COLLECTION PROTOCOL IN STRATEGIC MANAGEMENT RESEARCH

Opportunities and challenges

Giorgia M. D'Allura

The primary purpose of collecting and analyzing data in academic and scientific research is to support the process of intellectual discovery (Hitt, 2009). Nonetheless, data gathering and data analysis are oftentimes collective actions conducted by multiple units or partners located in different geographical locations that design their own research and conduct their own empirical investigation. This process frequently produces a collection of data, analyses, and results that are not comparable to each other for the different methodological assumptions, as well as the way the process of investigation is run. Conversely, one of the aims of scientific research is to collect data that allow the comparison of different studies and different contexts so as to advance the knowledge on the particular issue under investigation. In fact, data collection and analysis is an ongoing, continuous cycle of intellectual discovery, learning, and inquiry that allows the refinement of ideas so as to have the potential to transform the knowledge and understanding of a specific issue. The specific tool that supports the research process and the opportunity to compare academics and scientific research is, as mentioned earlier, the data collection protocol.

If we juxtaposed the research methods used in strategic management with the ones used in other fields of research, such as biomedical sciences, we would see that in more traditional fields of study, far from being a researcher's personal choice as it usually occurs in management (Pocock, 1983a; Evans, Thornton, and Chalmers, 2006), ensuring results comparability in research is a compulsory issue for any researcher. Arguably, vis-à-vis such rigorous research fields, strategic management research limitation is epitomized by the condition that each article published in the major *Strategic Management Journal* usually presents its own methods, that very rarely makes adequate reference to previous studies in terms of data collection and interpretation processes. Actually, this way of conducting research in strategic management oftentimes produces results that are far from being comparable. As a consequence, if "the primary purpose of collecting and analyzing data in academic and scientific research is to support the process of intellectual discovery" (Hitt, 2009), the way to carry out research hinders the advancement of knowledge in strategy.

In this vein, this chapter supports further the opportunity to generate knowledge about data collection protocols in order to robustly stimulate strategic management awareness of the importance of using and sharing data collection protocols.

Part of my task in this chapter is to make clear the origins of the theme and the reasons why it is relevant to use data collection protocols in strategic management investigation. By doing so, I shall explain the advantages of using DCPs, especially in the context of research projects conducted by multiple units, teams, and partners that have dissimilar backgrounds and are located in different physical spaces.

Following this argument, I will illustrate the process of developing a data collection protocol by discussing the various sections that need to be included in a DCP document. Then I will discuss the what, why, and when to use a DCP in strategic management. In order to illustrate the relevance of the data collection protocol in strategic management research, at the end of this chapter I include an appendix reporting a data collection protocol concretely generated in the context of a specific project (whose name, for preserving anonymity, has been abridged). The research project was a project developed in management and the social sciences and funded by the European Commission a few years ago. More specifically, the project's data collection protocol puts forward the content and rules regarding the collection of data to assess the firms' role in networks existing in four significant industrial contexts (i.e. biotech, medical, nanotech, and aircraft) over Europe. The goal of this data collection protocol is to allow researchers to identify and collect various kinds of information and data by exploiting active databases and other secondary sources as well as to define a common data collection procedure to be used during the fieldwork study performed by the seven EU and non-EU based partners that were involved in the project.

Origins of data collection protocols and reasons to use them in strategic management research

A data collection protocol is a document that simply outlines the goals of the research project, the research methods that will be followed, and the methods for analyzing data. The document includes information on research methods, ethics, and time constraints. More specifically, an appropriate data collection protocol includes the project's research objectives, methodology, and the definition of the units of analysis, together with ethical considerations, the plan for the analysis of results, the preliminary bibliography, and the actionable timetable (Pocock, 1983c).

Needless to say, the one area where use of data collection protocols in a most prominent fashion are the biomedical sciences, where DCPs are usually the ones that define the timing, content, and the other rules relating to data acquisition and collection; i.e., the assessments conducted at particular occasions during episodes of care. In this domain, data collection protocols must enable data to be collected for two main purposes (Pocock, 1983b; Gallin, 2007). First, the data will be used in describing and explaining the reasons for the utilization of services during the episode of care. Second, the data will be used in evaluating the outcomes of the episode of care. The data collected will also be used for other secondary purposes. For example, to describe the pathways to and from care, and to more fully describe the socio-demographic profile of patients receiving care.

Applying this process to strategic management research, a data collection protocol is expected to report the content and the other rules related to data collection, illustrating in this manner the rules of engagement to handle missing data and to interpret the results eventually obtained (Bradstreet, 1991; Butler, 2007; Pocock, 1983d; Wooding, 1984). More specifically, an appropriate data collection protocol includes – as I suggested earlier – the definition of the project's research objectives, its methodology, the units of analysis, ethical considerations, the plan for the analysis of results, a preliminary reference list, and the research timetable. Figure 12.1 illustrates how the DCP in strategic management is to be developed moving out from DCP's goals in the biomedical sciences.

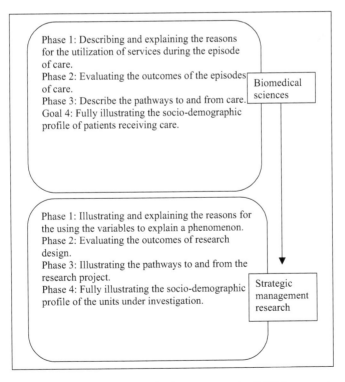

FIGURE 12.1 From the DCP in biomedical sciences to the DCP in strategic management

After all, data collection protocols are expected to drive the data collection process in strategic management research. This occurs for two main reasons. First, the data will be used in describing and explaining the reasons for turning out at the organization level. Second, the data will be used to describe the pathways to extend the results of the research to other contexts. More specifically, in order to achieve this goal, researchers need to follow the four main phases related to the corresponding objectives of the DCP (see Figure 12.1). With the aim of analyzing the four phases in depth, we observe the following.

Phase 1: Illustrating and explaining the reasons to use specific variables to explain a phenomenon

Researchers usually have the autonomy to choose the variables that they deem help-ful to advance our understanding of a specific phenomenon. DCP focuses researchers' attention on the description and explanation of the reasons that lead us to use a specific variable. This circumstance requires researchers to discuss in groups or teams how to choose the research variables and, finally, open the discussion with the wide community of researchers that review what has been done in previous research. In this context, the DCP is considered the first product of research. For this reason, it should be considered for review by peer reviewers and advisors so as to circumvent errors and/or problems that other research programs and projects may incur.

Phase 2: Evaluating the outcomes of the research design

The DCP includes the opportunity to evaluate in advance the outcomes of the research design. It opens up the discussion among the research team on the outcomes expected. Following the collective discussion, research design should be reviewed by other researchers that the key research team invites to advise them about the way they are running the whole research process in its launching stage.

Phase 3: Illustrating the pathway to and from the research project

This phase of the DCP is an operational one since it supports the research team to win efficiency by organizing the research project into sub-phases, illustrating the time and the goals that need to be achieved in each phase, as well as the resources that are required. Moreover, this phase helps improving team productivity by introducing an efficiency-driven way (or tailor made approach) to conduct research.

Phase 4: Fully describing the socio-demographic profile of the analytical unit(s) under investigation. Researchers are called for investing time and effort in describing the features of the unit(s) of analysis of their research project

Sometimes, due to journal format requirements researchers need to reduce the extent of this important section of explanation in their papers; i.e. illustrating the socio-demographic profile of the analytical unit(s) under investigation. Other times the database used would not allow the research team to dig deeper as concerns socio-demographic profiles of analytical units. However, the description of the unit(s) under investigation is particularly relevant to explain the sources of the research outcomes. In order to support this reflection, we recall that the strategic management field has at least one of its sub-fields that present the relevant issue: the area of family business studies. According to Littunen and Hyrsky (2000), there is "no widely accepted definition of a family business." Various definitions have been reported in the literature and, more specifically, each publication presents its own definitional proposal. As a result, the definitional gap as concern family business research's key unit of analysis increases the probability of obtaining results that are unreliable or show a low reliability level. Thus, in such instances the DCP may help researchers to clarify the definition of the unit of analysis upfront in their research projects, thereby allowing them to obtain results that facilitate the comparison among different contexts.

Advantages in using the data collection protocol in strategic management research

As follows the description of the four key phases of the DCP discussed above, we observe that, while the use of the data collection protocol finds its origins in the biomedical sciences, the reasons why it is helpful to use a data collection protocol in strategic management research is not yet investigated. Multiple are the benefits and the advantages of using DCPs in strategic management. First, the opportunity of pursuing the specific research objectives of the field of study in a consistent fashion. In fact, if the advantage of DCP in the biomedical sciences is related to the necessity of achieving universal recognition and application of the scientific results related to patient care, because individual care is the main goal of the biomedical sciences, as social science strategic management has different goals. Accordingly, we focus attention on the specific goals of strategic management research and on the reasons why it is relevant that the results achieved in the field may be available for comparison around the world.

Strategic management investigates the main initiatives taken by the firms' top management as concerns the allocation of resources and the achievement of performance in environments that are internal and external to the firm (for an extended review on the concept of strategic management, see Bracker [1980]). More specifically, strategic management focuses on defining an organization's mission, vision, and objectives for developing strategies and plans, that are aimed to achieve such objectives, and then on allocating pools of resources to execute the strategies, plans, and programs earlier envisioned (Jemison, 1981). Thus, the role of strategy theory in acquiring knowledge about business reality reconnects to the comprehension of the strategic choices being made by the individuals and individual teams within the organizations. One of the main consequences of this search of strategic management scholars relates to the theoretical background and methodological tools that are required in the knowledge acquiring process. Understanding individual choices requires the use of an interdisciplinary approach including lenses and methodological assumptions about the nature of reality, the role of theory, and the significance of empirical experimentation. This is the reason why strategy scholars traditionally come from a variety of backgrounds (e.g. industrial economics organization, sociology, consumer behavior, organizational behavior, marketing, business and economic history; Devinney and Siegel [2012]) and often present dissimilar methodological assumptions.

Consistent with the role and different assumptions existing in strategic management research (vis-à-vis, for instance, mainstream economics), empirical research provides a range of challenges for scholars in strategic management. First, scholars are often expected to choose between using quantitative and qualitative research methods. Second, within each research method, researchers have different options. In this landscape, the opportunity to build and share a data collection protocol is the opportunity to manage in a consistent fashion and easily juxtapose data collected in different contexts and areas. Consequently, knowledge production in the strategy field pays a cost related to each scholar's freedom to design his/her own research and make inference and advance conclusions.

At this point of our analysis, we need to consider that freedom of choice in research is certainly a conquest of reason and great benefit to researchers, but it is also a cost. Actually, the freedom of choice approach in strategic management may produce fragmented results and, consequentially, lags and delays in advancing knowledge in the field. Reasonably, we ought to consider that fragmentation in results limits the possibility of comparing empirically contextual experiences and that this condition turns it difficult to extract a set of managerial implications that may be span across contexts.

Actually, the use of DCP in strategic management studies suggests that, as scholars and researchers, we should start to think differently. Since strategic management as a field of study needs to increase its popularity among organizations and managers, building and sharing a data collection protocol is a good opportunity in the direction to enhance investigation results, as well as in obtaining robust results that are applicable in business practice (Bourgeois, 1984; Smircich and Stubbart, 1985). Moreover, from an academic perspective, I believe that the debate about the issue of relevance can be circumvented by means of sharing similar experiences in the data collection process. The practice of sharing the data collection protocol would also avoid the risk of repeating the same errors, thereby accelerating the pace of the knowledge production process in strategic management.

Consistent with these arguments, I imagine that we need to work actively on sharing data collection protocols in strategic management studies, thereby attempting to disseminate this "new" way of thinking that, as reported earlier, has widely been used in the biomedical sciences. In that field, the extensive use of DCPs is related to the condition that researchers need to present results and outcomes that are universally recognized and may be universally applied. Similarly, we should deem the development of DCPs as an opportunity to institute a best practice scheme in future strategic management research, especially when it is run by research teams. With this aim in mind, in the next section I will present the data collection protocol development process so as to establish a milestone in this direction.

Data collection protocol development process

Following the identification of the four key phases/objectives in the definition of the DCP, the interest turns to the process of developing a data collection protocol in strategic management. The process I explain in the following pages takes shape from those four phases considering that they require a set of specific research activities to be performed. Figure 12.2 represents the translation of the phases into actions. The result of this process and the decisions being taken by the research team form the content of the DCP. In more detail, a typical data collection protocol in strategic management studies should deal with the following issues that are to turn into the main sections of the DCP document:

(A) Linked with the first phase: Section 1: Purposes of the Survey/Field Observations/Section 2: Data Sources/Section 3: References
(B) Linked with the second phase: Section 4: Data Analysis Strategies/Section 5: Potential Challenges and Solutions/Section 6: Data Coding
(C) Linked with the third phase: Section 7: Data Collection Schedule
(D) Linked with the fourth phase: Section 8: Sampling

Based on the enumeration reported above, I suggest that the background work being performed to produce the DCP leads to the first product of the research process: the launch of the same DCP! In fact, this document allows researchers to formalize their investigation objectives, phases, and the overall process illustrating how they intend to achieve their investigational goals in the specific project they are pursuing. Actually, the DCP contains the thorough description of all the methodological decisions that the researchers are expected to take. More specifically, each DCP action formalizes the methodological decisions underlying the research project. In this vein, the production of a DCP should be considered as a central inescapable part of the strategic management research process as a whole.

In the initial part of their research project, researchers need to analyze the previous contributions advanced by the literature in their subject matter and take their definitional decisions. Thus, the DCP is a document that is going to be the starting reference point for further research. In the following, I discuss the typical content of the main sections of a DCP.

Section 1: Purpose of the research

In the first section of the document, I suggest to describe the purpose of the analysis. The goal is to clarify the project's research question(s), along with the

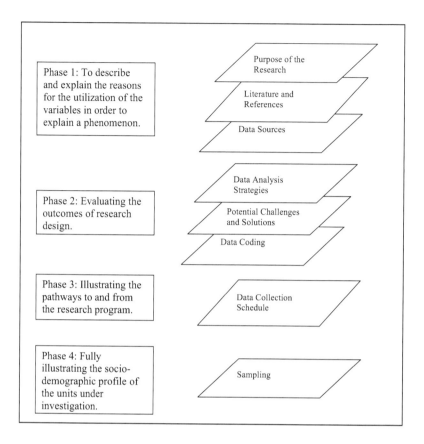

FIGURE 12.2 DCP in strategic management: Goals and research activities

Source: Our elaboration

decision about the methods selected to achieve the final aim of the research. Moreover, in this section researchers should describe in brief the result reported in the literature of their project's subject area, so as to clarify the reasons for using the specific variables selected to analyze the phenomenon under investigation. The sources of information for this activity are the key journals, books, database, and/or panels of experts in the theme. In this section, I suggest to carefully motivate the reasons to start new investigation efforts and its actual relationship with the ones previously performed. Then, researchers should depict and juxtapose the various approaches used in previous studies (if any) and motivate the research approach they have selected. In discussing the subject matter, it is important to report and discuss critically the evidence already published, as well as to make it clear how the approach chosen meets the objectives of the research. Generally speaking, if the researcher is not sure about what to expect from an experiment, a qualitative approach might be the method to prefer, at least to start anew with a novel research project. Nonetheless, generating scenarios on what to expect from an experiment might help the researcher to develop a hypothesis that can be tested. In this instance, in order to verify the hypotheses engendered, the researcher would need to perform quantitative data analysis. This method is also useful for establishing cause-and-effect relationships among dependent and independent variables. In this vein, I suggest that the initial section of the DCP should specify and discuss the reasons why researchers have chosen the specific methods of analysis.

Section 2: Literature review and references

In a DCP, I consider important to include a section showing the preliminary references of the research to be performed. This is relevant to motivate the decision about the research subject. In addition, a good section of references will definitely turn helpful to highlight the strength of the hypotheses advanced in the research. Finally, after specifying the purpose and the choice of methods, in this section I suggest the researcher perform a thorough literature review so as to motivate the role and possible impact of the research project in advancing knowledge in the strategic management field. The reference section will be reported at the end of the DCP, as usually occurs in contemporary academic papers.

Section 3: Data sources

Since it affects the nature of information sources (such as interviews, observations, archival data; Gorden [1980]), the choice of the research methods is also relevant for the data acquisition process. Thus, I advise on the opportunity in a DCP to have a third section in which the researcher describes the sources of information and the data collection process. Generally speaking, qualitative research is a kind of research that focuses on generating detailed information. It differs from quantitative research in that much of the data cannot be directly linked to a numerical value.

Qualitative and quantitative research methods represent two different methods of collecting and analyzing information, and therefore of how strategic management research may progress (Clarke, 1999; Creswell, 2003). Specifically, in the case of performing interviews, it is relevant to choose the set of questions to administrate. This task will certainly require researchers to invest their time. I suggest thinking intensely about the purpose of each question before setting it into words and describing the choice in this section. The experience in empirical investigation highlights that improperly worded questions can yield inaccurate results. A major suggestion is to describe the range of options considered and the final decision taken in this regard. In the development of the questions, it is relevant to ask for advice from peers and senior colleagues so as to revise the outline of the section before launching the investigation. Moreover, it would be useful to run a pilot study including the preliminary results in this section of the DCP. In this vein, before launching the investigation it would be advisable to locate a small sample of individuals available to take the survey or questionnaire. At this point, the researcher may modify the document format to make it more visually attractive to the respondents. I suggest describing accurately the process. Finally, the adjustments and amendments that may possibly be advanced to the section should be reported in the final section on potential challenges and solutions.

Section 4: Data analysis strategy

Data analysis is the process of bringing order, structure, and interpretation in the mass of collected data. It is a messy, ambiguous, time consuming, creative, and fascinating process. It does not proceed in a linear fashion, especially when making reference to qualitative research. Thus, this section of the DCP should describe the initial decisions taken about data analysis so as to evaluate the outcomes of the research design. Generating categories of data to collect, or cells in a matrix, can be an important focusing device for the study (see the appendix).

Focusing on qualitative research, data collection and analysis typically go hand-in-hand to build a coherent interpretation of the data. The researcher is guided by an initial concept developing understandings, but may shift or modify them as he/she collects and analyzes the data. Turning on quantitative research, as it is easy to understand, the process is strictly guided by the statistical/econometric model considered. In both cases, these decisions need to be described in this section of the DCP.

Section 5: Potential challenges and solutions

The DCP also needs clarification as concerns the potential challenges that the researchers involved in the data collection may be called to face and pre-emption of the decisions to take in this regard. Moreover, this section requires an explanation of the range of possible solutions to handle missing data. This section needs to be carefully developed to circumvent troubles in the phase of data analysis. Generally speaking, I assume that researchers should be able to determine the most practical, efficient, feasible, and ethical methods for collecting data as the research progresses. In this section, they provide a detailed description of the potential challenges and the solutions to follow.

Section 6: Data coding

Coding of data is the formal representation of analytic thinking. The tough intellectual work of analysis generates categories and themes. The researchers then apply some coding scheme to those categories and themes. Codes may take several forms: abbreviations of key words, colored dots, and numbers. The specific choice is left to the researchers that need to illustrate the kind of data coding they have chosen and why they did so in this section.

Section 7: Data collection schedule

In order to clearly recognize the bits and pieces of information needed, the DCP also includes a section showing the timing and outline of the data collection process of the research project as a whole. In this vein, the schedule contains a detailed picture of the set of activities to perform and their timing so as to accomplish the various phases of the research as effectively as possible. The data collection schedule is also relevant to manage the tasks in the research teams involved.

Section 8: Sampling

Sampling is the important tool used for selecting the participant units/individuals to the empirical research. More specifically, participant selection has a different flavor as concerns quantitative research vs. qualitative research (Adler and Adler, 1998). Since it is interested in finding a statistically representative sample of a population, quantitative research selects a sample by random selection. According to Polkinghorne (2005), participants rich with experience should be sought out and not randomly selected. Conversely, qualitative research selects a sample by considering the nature of the experiments (Marshall and Rossman, 2006). In this part of the data collection protocol, researchers should report their decision about the sampling, explain the reasons why they decided in that way, and clarify how to proceed in the collection of the data. This part is one of the most relevant of the whole DCP shaping process, if we consider that the results obtained at the end are strongly related to this part of the research. Accordingly, errors in the collection of the data will have strong impact on the research as concerns the type of results and their overall significance.

At this point of this general reflection about how to perform a DCP in strategic management research, I wish to underscore that its shaping significantly affects the project's research design process as a whole and the result that will be produced.

In the following section, I shall discuss the usefulness of the DCP in strategic management research.

Discussion

Researchers, policy makers, and the general public need data to understand economic and firm development. Higher quality data tend to generate more significant actions and better understanding of the business reality. Researchers and scholars perform research by collaborating with the wide community to increase the quality levels of gathering data. They are also expected to improve the quantity, quality, and credibility of the results accomplished so as to improve our understanding of business reality.

Data quality will be increased by implementing basic entry verification and by other researchers that repeat and improve measurements for the issue under investigation. Implementing an *adaptive* DCP based on shared research and participatory sensing facilitate accurate knowledge production on behalf of researchers and scholars. Thus, DCP generation and sharing needs to be increased to improve both methodological awareness and results of strategic management research.

While some consensus exists among statistician that data collection protocols are of substantial value, accurate planning of DCP piloting phases as described above is often neglected (Short and Pigeon, 1998). Accordingly, this area needs to be developed (Hogg, 1991).

Many of the concepts mentioned in this chapter deal with *minimizing bias and maximizing precision*. An appropriate DCP design requires a clear definition of the objectives of the research project and, more specifically, a crystal-clear definition of the hypotheses to test. Statistical analyses deal with random errors due to sample or random variation in the outcome variables. The interpretation of these measures and the comparisons with other research in the same stream are to be considered as the major contribution of DCP development in strategic management research. Actually, a well-designed DCP reflects the scientific and methodological integrity of the research.

Likewise, while strategic management analysis encompasses issues related to the decision-making process, statistical inspection is difficult in this case. Compared to the biomedical sciences, strategic management as a social science does not offer treatment to people thereby observing its results in terms of health fallouts. The field, instead, was born to monitor the behavior of individuals and organizations under dynamic conditions. This is methodologically and statistically challenging. Thus, strategic management research's first step implies the generation of a set of hypotheses and then to appropriately design the study to test those hypotheses. Once hypotheses have been developed, the study aims, design, methodology, methods, and analyses call to be formulated. Accordingly, a well-conceived the DCP needs to clearly deal with issues related to the study conduct, set up, organization, monitoring, publication policy, and timelines, reported in appropriate sections as described above in the preceding section.

Regular review of peers is also essential during the DCP development process. Moreover, all materials and documentation should be kept alive, including protocol versions, meeting minutes, and correspondence discussing protocol related issues. The aim of these activities is that the final, comprehensive DCP document should elicit a systematic approach to the development of scientific research which is acceptable on scientific, organizational, and ethical grounds. Otherwise, scientific research would be nothing more than a niche product that is not useful to improving organizational performance. This turns in a dissipated way to conduct research that, as researchers and scholars, we ought to avoid (Emanuel, 2007).

I consider that in strategic management research the time has come to create the right conditions for activating more intense exchange and cross fertilizations between strategy researchers and methodologists and statisticians/econometrician so as to improve the conception and delivery of DCPs and of research project results. Considering that DCPs support the increase of both the quantity and quality of research (observing the results spreading out from the biomedical sciences), I suggest to initiate their wider use in strategic management. While DCPs have heretofore been essentially used almost exclusively in research projects involving research teams located in different spaces, I would like to see DCPs developed for all strategic management research projects. This condition would echo what occurs in the biomedical sciences, where researchers are used to developing DCPs for definite diseases, such as a specific form of cancer, and then improve them over the time with the much-needed interdisciplinary collaboration with social methods research scholars. By adopting a longitudinal research approach that is useful for the understanding and knowledge development in strategic management studies, such research strategy would also support the collaboration between research teams working at different times and/or in different locations.

Conclusion

Composing a protocol for strategic management research is a complex, intellectual, creative task, which may be fulfilled by a strategic management research team with the collaboration of experts in methods research issues. DCP is the document that carefully synchronizes knowledge in these areas matching the scientific literature in the issue under investigation.

In the last few years, the development of guidelines in the biomedical sciences has tremendously helped develop standards for protocol writing in clinical research. This, in turn, has improved the methodology, conduct, and quality of clinical trials, with a fast-growing ethical emphasis on all the participants (Friedman, Furberg, and DeMets, 2010; Wang and Bakhai, 2006). Drawing on the literature at hand, in this chapter I have considered the challenges and the advantages of using DCPs in strategic management studies.

Actually, in my study I have detected that little is known about data collection protocols in the strategic management field. However, DCPs are relevant tools that need more promotion in strategic management studies so as to speed up the development of the field. Specifically, I consider three main advantages outspreading from the wider application of DCPs:

(1) the development of a DCP for a specific theme in strategic management allows the comparison of research conducted in different times and space;
(2) DCP sharing circumvents errors in the process of data collection thereby increasing the opportunities to improve the research projects results. This condition will reduce the costs related to problems in the data collection process;
(3) the practice of developing DCPs enhances the research process since it fosters researchers to share ideas and experiences in a way not occurring in cases of brainstorming or research meeting.

Actually DCPs incentivize the sharing of guidelines, procedures, and results so as to support researchers to produce comparable results and circumvent errors. In this vein, DCP sharing is also an ethical issue for strategic management researchers that intend to enhance investigation results by shunning costs related to errors solved in previous work.

The DCP I present in the appendix to this chapter was created in the context of an EU-funded project. More specifically, it puts forward the content and rules that concerns the data collection to assess the role of firms in the network and network dynamics in the key industrial contexts under scrutiny (i.e., biotech, nanotech, and aerospace). As reported earlier, the development process helped researchers to generate a set of hypotheses important for both advancing the research project and producing actionable results.

References

Adler, P. and Adler, P. (1998) "Observational Techniques," in N. K. Denzin and Y. Lincoln (eds) *Collecting and Interpreting qualitative Materials*, Thousand Oaks: Sage.

Bourgeois III, L. J. (1984) "Strategic Management and Determinism," *Academy of Management Review*, 9(4): 586–596.

Bracker, J. (1980) "The Historical Development of the Strategic Management Concept," *Academy of Management Review*, 5(2): 219–224.

Bradstreet, T. E. (1991) "Some Favorite Data Sets from Early Phases of Drug Research," in *Proceedings of the Section on Statistical Education*, American Statistical Association, 190–195.

Butler, S. L. (2007) "Clinical Research: A Patient Perspective," in J. I. Gallin and F. P. Ognibene (eds) *Principles and Practice of Clinical Research*, Amsterdam: Elsevier, 193–203.

Clarke, A. (1999) *Evaluation Research: An Introduction to Principles, Methods and Practice*, London: Sage.

Creswell, J. W. (2003) *Research Design: Qualitative, Quantitative, and Mixed Methods Approaches*, 2nd edn, Thousand Oaks: Sage.

Devinney, T. M. and Siegel, D. S. (2012) "Perspectives on the Art and Science of Management Scholarship," *Academy of Management Perspectives*, 26(1): 6–11.

Emanuel, E. J. (2007) "Researching a Bioethical Question," in J. I. Gallin and F. P. Ognibene (eds) *Principles and Practice of Clinical Research*, 2nd edn, Amsterdam: Elsevier, 31–42.

Evans, I., Thornton, H., and Chalmers, I. (2006) *Testing Treatments: Better Research for Better Healthcare*, London: The British Library Publishing.

Fontana, A. and Frey, J. (1994) "Interviewing: The Art of Science," in N. K. Denzin and Y. S. Lincoln (ed.) *The Handbook of Qualitative Research*, Thousand Oaks: Sage.

Friedman, L. M., Furberg, C., and DeMets, D. L. (2010). *Fundamentals of Clinical Trials*, Vol. 4, New York: Springer.

Gallin, J. I. (2007) "A Historical Perspective on Clinical Research," in J. I. Gallin and F. P. Ognibene (eds) *Principles and Practice of Clinical Research*, 2nd edn, Amsterdam: Elsevier, 1–15.

Gorden, R. L. (1980) *Interviewing: Strategy, Techniques, and Tactics*, Homewood, IL: Dorsey.

Hitt, M. A. (2009) "Editorial Judgments, Quality Scholarship, and the Academy of Management"s journals," *Organizational Research Methods*, 12(2): 253–258.

Hogg, R. V. (1991) "Statistical Education: Improvements are Badly Needed," *The American Statistician*, 45(4): 342–343.

Jemison, D. B. (1981) "The Importance of an Integrative Approach To Strategic Management Research," *Academy of Management Review*, 6(4): 601–608.

Littunen, H. and Hyrsky, K. (2000) "The Early Entrepreneurial Stage in Finnish Family and Nonfamily Firms," *Family Business Review*, 13(1): 41–54.

Lofland, J. and Lofland, L. (1995) *Analysing Social Settings: A Guide to Qualitative Observation and Analysis,* Belmont, CA: Wadsworth.

Marshall, C. and Rossman, G. B. (2006) *Designing Qualitative Research*, 4th edn, Thousands Oaks, CA: Sage.

Miles, M. B. and Huberman, A. M. (1994) *Qualitative Data Analysis*, 2nd edn, Newbury Park, CA: Sage.

Morgan, D. L. (1997) *Focus Groups as Qualitative Research*. Thousand Oaks, CA: Sage.

Morgan, D. L. (2002) "Focus Group Interviewing," in J. F. Gubrium and J. A. Holstein (eds) *Handbook of Interview Research: Context and Method*, Thousand Oaks, CA: Sage.

Patton, M. Q. (1990) *Qualitative Evaluation and Research Methods*, 2nd edn, Newbury Park, CA: Sage.

Pocock S. J. (1983a) "The Rationale of Clinical Trials," in S. J. Pocock (ed.) *Clinical Trials: A Practical Approach*, Chichester: John Wiley & Sons, 1–13.

Pocock, S. J. (1983b) "The Historical Development of Clinical Trials," in S. J. Pocock (ed.) *Clinical Trials: A Practical Approach*, Chichester: John Wiley & Sons, 14–27.

Pocock, S. J. (1983c) *Clinical Trials: A Practical Approach*, Chichester: John Wiley & Sons.

Pocock, S. J. (1983d) "Organization and Planning, Evaluation of Patient Response," in S. J. Pocock, *Clinical Trials: A Practical Approach*, Chichester: John Wiley & Sons, 28–49.

Polkinghorne, D. E. (2005) "Language and Meaning: Data Collection in Qualitative Research," *Journal of Counseling Psychology*, 52(2): 137–145.

Shadish, W. R., Cook, T. D., and Cambell, D. T (2002) *Experimental and Quasi-Experimental Designs for Generalized Causal Inference*, Boston: Houghton.

Short, T. H. and Pigeon, J. G. (1998) "Protocols and Pilot Studies: Taking Data Collection Projects Seriously," *Journal of Statistics Education*, 6(1). Available at: www.amstat.org/publications/jse/v6n1/short.html

Smircich, L. and Stubbart, C. (1985) "Strategic Management in an Enacted World," *Academy of Management Review*, 10(4): 724–736.

Wang, D. and Bakhai, A. (2006) *Clinical Trials: A Practice Guide to Design, Analysis and Reporting*, London: Lippincott.

Wooding, W. M. (1994) *Planning Pharmaceutical Clinical Trials: Basic Statistical Principles*, New York: John Wiley & Sons.

Appendix

Data collection protocol: An example from a EU-funded project

To preserve requisite anonymity and at the same time offer the interested readership an illustration useful for their own research, we report below an abridged version of the data collection protocol prepared for a wide-ranging research project in management and the social science, involving seven different research units and about thirty researchers within the European Union and beyond. The project was successfully evaluated and thus funded under the scheme of the European Committee seventh Framework Program in the year 2008.

Table of contents

Introduction

The data collection protocol defines the content and rules relating to the collection of data to assess network dynamics in the industries under investigation. The specific details of the procedure to follow aim to produce an outcome from each partner of the project that is comparable with the other outcomes, even if there are some specific differences related to the different industries under investigation (i.e. nanotech, biotech, aircraft). More specifically, social networks data consist in firm relations that will be measured by checking a set of actors that are present in the specific regional area under scrutiny. Thus, the goal of the Data Collection Protocol is to identify and collect the data available through existing databases and other secondary sources and to define a common data collection protocol to be used during the fieldwork (WP4). In order to understand the role of firms and networks in regional development, project partners will observe three specific industry contexts in seven different regions. For each of these settings the first step of work package 2 is the identification of reliable data sources and key actors. As regards secondary data, various databases relevant to each specific setting will be used (please refer to Appendix Table 12.1 for a summary of secondary sources already identified). As regards primary sources, interviews will be conducted with the actors involved in the process (i.e., the entrepreneurs and managers of the institutions involved in the firm networks and the other relevant stakeholders located in the geographic areas) by means of a questionnaire jointly defined by the seven partners.

Our preliminary analysis suggests some of the firms we will be looking at including a range of companies when researching regional development in biotech, nanotech, and aerospace industries...

In order to ensure that the field data collected from interviews and surveys are comparable and consistent across settings, the project will make use of a shared data collection protocol. A data collection protocol is commonly defined as a predefined procedural method in the design and implementation of experiments. In natural sciences, it is widely used to generate standards that create a crucial knowledge base for successful replication of results by others in the field. A common semi-structured research protocol will therefore be used to allow the output of the individual case studies to be contrasted. This will allow the causal factors identified in the literature review to be evaluated, providing consistent inputs to work packages 5 and 6. In this perspective the project's data collection protocol is aimed at:

1) Establishing a common field-data collection procedure;
2) Establishing the common themes to be addressed by the questionnaires:
   a. Qualitative questions;
   b. Quantitative questions;
3) Establishing the performance indicators to be collected through the question-naires;
4) Establishing the sociometric questions to be asked in order to uncover the relational structure of each industry-region;
5) Establishing data collection requirements specific to each partner.

In summary, WP3 will move along the following four steps:

<u>Step 1</u> – Identification of data sources;
<u>Step 2</u> – Definition of research boundaries (sample size, units of analysis, etc.);
<u>Step 3</u> – Definition of data collection protocols;
<u>Step 4</u> – Databases and secondary sources inquiry.

Step 1 and 2 will be performed individually by each partner. In order to achieve Step 3, the project partners will be led by the steering committee which will meet at the end of month 3 (M2) to review data sources and again on month 6 to finalize the protocol for data collection (M3). Step 3 will be carried out by each partner according to the nature and size of the databases (it is estimated that the collection of secondary data will run from month 3 to month 9).

Social networks data features

(a) Levels of analysis

It is well known, that social network analysis can be studied at a number of different levels. Following they are describe in the context of the project:

APPENDIX TABLE 12.1 Identified databases and other secondary sources

	Secondary sources (i.e. database on publication, patent, firms, et.)	Clusters under review (or to be reviewed)	Firms
Nanoelectronics/ Semiconductors	• ISI Web of Science; • Nanoproject Datatbase; • Il Sole24Ore Database on industries and firms data; • AIDA Database on sectoral and company information; • esp@cenet database on European and Worldwide patents		
Biotech/ Biomedical	• Daily registration and deregistration records of the German Commercial Register ("Bundeszentralregister"); (b) "Yearbooks of the German Biotechnology Industry" by Biocom AG; (c) Sourcing of archival data from industry newsmagazines such as "TRANSCRIPT", FT, or Handelsblatt. (d) Longitudinal records from the German Patent and Trademark Office. e) AIDA - Comprehensive database of Italian firms' financial data f) esp@cenet database on European and Worldwide patents; g) Archival time series available from Consobiomed (the association of biomedical companies of the database, i) data on alliances RECAP database, j) data on firms' regulatory filings from Companies House (London), k) database of international pressing cuttings on the biotech industry (University of Nottingham)	Biomedical Valley	Various
Aircraft industries	• Polish Central Statistical Office, as far as industry and region indicators are concerned (year books, regional data bank) and Polish Patent Office; • Internal documentation of the Aviation Valley Association members - data collection focusing on formalized ties with other regional network members	Aviation Valley	

a.1 The individual actors

Given that in this project we aim to understand the role of firms in shaping the development of firm influencing local development (RQ1), we will focus our attention on the firm level. Thus, the individual level of our analysis is strictly focused on the firms that each unit will identify.

Further, at this level of analysis, according with RQ2, we will observe the resources and capabilities that firms mobilize in order to activate and enable local development. Second, according with RQ8, we will investigate the force that influences firms' decision to localize in particular regions and how they contribute to different types of regional capability building.

a.2 The pair of actors

According to RQ6, in order to understand if the kind of linkages that organizations have within the local cluster is relevant, we will focus our attention on the relations that firms have with:

- public centers of research;
- universities;
- private centers of research;
- policy makers.

During the course of this step of analysis, we will focus our attention on the dyadic relationship between the firms and each actor observed and considered relevant with the aim of our project.

a.3 The subset of actors

Following the step above and in order to understand better the linkages that organizations have within the local cluster, we will focus our attention on the relations that firms have with a subset of actors selected among:

- public center of research;
- universities;
- private center of research;
- policy makers.

In this step of analysis, we will focus our attention on the subset relationship among the firm and the actors observed in the dyadic level.

a.4 The network as a whole

Finally, we will observe the network as a whole. Most importantly, in this step of analysis the modeling unit will be under investigation in order to understand:

- what is the position that firms occupy within the network (RQ5);
- if there are structures that are more conducive to regional development (RQ4);
- what are the configurations that underlie the functioning of successful regions (RQ3).

In sum, the project will refer to four level of analysis in order to achieve the goal set by the following research questions (Appendix Table 12.2):

APPENDIX TABLE 12.2 Level of analysis

Level of analysis	Research questions
The individual actor level	RQ1: "What is the role of firm in shaping the development of local networks and influencing regional development?" RQ2: "What kind of resources and capabilities do firms mobilize in order to enable local development?" RQ8: "What influences how firms are attracted to particular regions and how they contribute to different types of regional capability building?"
The dyadic level	RQ6: Does it matter whether linkages are with organizations within the local cluster or do firms do better by reaching out beyond their neighborhood?"
The subset of actors level	RQ6: Does it matter whether the linkages are with organizations within the local cluster or do firms do better by reaching out beyond their neighborhood?"
The network as a whole level	RQ5: "What position do firms occupy within these structures?" RQ4: "Are there network structures that are more conducive to regional development?" RQ3: "What network configurations underlie the functioning of successful regions?"

Finally, by the Statistical Analysis of Networks we will answered to the following questions (Appendix Table 12.3):

APPENDIX TABLE 12.3 Statistical analysis of networks

Type of analysis	Research question
Statistical analysis	RQ7: "Do firms, if any, that bridge across local clusters perform better than locally embedded ones" RQ9: "How are these behaviors influenced by policy?" RQ10: "How can policy be better designed to encourage more equitable and sustainable regional development?"

(b) Unit of observation

The unit of observation is the entity on which measurements are taken. Under the project, the data will be collected by observing, interviewing and questioning individual actors about the ties from these actors to other actors in the set.

The individual actors that we aim to interview are:

1. first, the workers of the firm;
2. second, the workers of the other unit mentioned from the firm's workers;
3. third, other individual named by the firm's workers.

The list of individual will be generate by the Questionnaires Number 1.

(c) Boundary specification

The study populations in the project has vertical and horizontal boundaries. The vertical boundary concerns the job ranks to include. The horizontal boundary concerns the organizational groups to include.

In order to specify the boundaries on the set of units to be included in the network, the project partners will follow the rules indicate below:

- Identification of the ego network, following the project review.
- Identification of the vertical boundaries. This step is just to define core people who should be included in the study population. The key to the vertical boundary is to include all the job ranks in which people are in large part the author of their job because they are expected to find ways to create innovation. Specifically if the firm (EGO) is: (a) an individual – the person to contact is only the EGO; (b) a firm – the person to get in touch with are the directors of the R&D, production, marketing and sale departments. These people will be asked to name the people with whom they regularly discuss their work and with whom they are in contact because of the work. If those named colleagues come from lower ranks, the vertical boundaries will include also the lower ranks. The tool to define the network boundary is the open questionnaire (Burt, 1984).
- Identification of the horizontal dimension. This step is to include all unit that have a direct effect on the production of knowledge and of innovation. Specifically, it the firm's element named colleagues come from other divisions, the horizontal boundaries will include the other divisions. If those named colleagues come from other organization, these organization will take part of the horizontal dimensions of the network. The tool to define the network boundary is the open questionnaires (Burt, 1984).
- Identification of the second-order zone (Barnes, 1969). Using the open-ended questionnaires, we will ask the names of the individuals with which they are in contact by one intermediary.

- Finally, we shall add to the open questionnaires the recall methods to identify other external units that should be included in the network. Thus, each partner will prepare a list of the organizations present in the area and ask if the EGO elements know them and what is the relationship with them. This step will expand the network to include people/units who provide indirect connection around the target population and that enhance knowledge and innovation process. Both the opened questionnaires and the "recall method" will allow project researchers to assess the role of the organizations that are in the area and the relationship with the EGO.

(d) Sampling

The sampling of the ego network we will process by the project's network survey includes two kinds of questions:

- name generators;
- name interpreters.

Generator elicits the names of the EGO defined as described above. By the name generator we will obtain a complete list of alters. The name generator for the project's survey are five:

- Who is your immediate supervisor?
- With whom do you most often discuss company new project?
- Who are essential sources of support for your job?
- Who are the people with whom you had the most frequent and substantive work contact over the last six months?
- Who are the people with whom you had the most frequent and substantive research project contact over the last six months?

Considering the people with whom you like to spend your free time. Over the last six months, who are the people you have been in touch with most often for informal social activities?

After a name is generated, there are five name interpreters:

- For how many years have you been in touch with the person?
- For how many years have you work with the person?
- How often do you have direct contact with the person?
- How close are you with the person?
- How often do you have work collaborate with the person?

(e) Data sources

Project researchers will collect the data by using multiple sources such as:

- questionnaires;
- interviews;
- archival data.

Questionnaires

The project partner will collect data by questionnaire. This data collection method is the most commonly used in applied research. We will use it also because the actors in our sampling are people. In fact, we believe that the data about the relations in the network under investigation can be reported only by the individual that are involved in the network.

The project's questionnaire contains questions about the firm's tie to other actors. Further, the question formats that we will use are described follows:

Questions for firms: Free recall, free choices, rating and complete ranking

Given that the project researchers do not know prior the members in the set, they will ask to the firm''s actors the name of the individual they usually work with. Thus, researcher will ask to the respondents to name those people with whom the fill in the specific tie investigate such as: informal collaboration; work collaboration; research project collaboration.

The format of these questions addressed to the firm will generate the list of names of the network's actors. The choice about the actors to nominate from the respondent is free. Thus, project researchers do not predetermine how many other actors the respondent will nominate. It is important that the firm is not constrained to choose the actors because the goal of the project is, according to RQ3, to understand in depth the network configurations that underlie the functioning of successful regions.

Further, moving more deeply from RQ3 to RQ10, in order to measure the strength intensity of relations, project researchers will ask to the respondents to assign a value and to rank all the actors nominated. We will require each respondent to assign a value to each tie. Then, to rank them from the major important.

Finally, with this step of analysis project researchers will produce valued relations of the actors from the firm perspective. Moreover, this first step of analysis will produce the list of actors that the project researchers will investigate in the forward steps.

Questions for network actors: Roster, fixed choice, rating and complete rankings

Given that project aims, according to RQ1 and RQ5, to understand what is the role of firms in shaping the development of local networks and influencing regional development (RQ1), and at analyzing the positions that firms occupy within these structures, the second step of the social network analysis is to interview the actors named from the firm's individual. In this direction, based to the list made from the interview with the firm (roster recall), researcher shall ask the respondents to nominate five actors among the ones present in the roster. Thus, the actors will make a fixed choice in order to understand the most relevant ties perceived from the actors of the networks.

Further, in order to verify the firm's perspective and to dig more deeply in RQ10, project researchers will ask the respondents to assign a value and to rank all the actors choose in the questionnaire. As done with the firms, we will require each respondent to assign a value to each tie. Then, they will be asked to rank them from the most important to the least important. Thus, with this step of analysis, researchers will be able to drawn the map of the most valued relations among the actors.

Finally, the comparison between the firm's perspective and the actors' perspective will give a prior assessment of the strength of tie inside the network under investigation.

Interviews

Even if the cost of face-to-face interviews is high and, then, occasionally used to gather network data, in order to deeply achieve the project's goals, researchers will interview the actors face-to-face. In fact, according to Burt (1984, 1985), face-to-face interviews is fundamentally to gather high quality data in ego-centered networks as the ones we are investigating.

Archival data

According to RQ1, RQ9 and RQ10, the project aims to:

1. understanding the role of firms in shaping the development of local networks and influencing regional development (RQ1);
2. assessing how firm's behaviours are influenced by policy (RQ9);
3. verifying how policy can be better designed to encourage more equitable and sustainable regional development (RQ10).

Thus, project researchers will also observe network evolution through the time. In order to assess the role of EGO to the development of the network and how and why do these structure changed over time, researchers will observe the network in three point of time:

- to date,
- in the year in which the EGO was firstly established in the area,
- in the middle of these two periods of time.

In doing the assessment above, project researchers will measure the actors ties by examining measurement taken from records of interactions such as:

a. previously patent of the actors;
b. previously innovation products and process of the actors;
c. previously publication of academic and researchers linked to the actors;
c. past political intervention to the regional area under investigation.

According to Burt and Lin (1977), project researchers will observe the social networks by collecting archival data from:

1. journal articles;
2. newspapers;
3. minute of executive meetings;
4. patent databank.

How to handle missing data

If archival data are unfortunately not available on a population, the measure of the network will go for completing the network with perceived relations.

13

DESIGNING AND PERFORMING A MIXED METHODS RESEARCH IN STRATEGIC MANAGEMENT

Jose Francisco Molina-Azorin

Introduction

Mixed methods research (the combined use of quantitative and qualitative methods within a single study) has developed rapidly in the last few years. Although researchers have combined qualitative and quantitative data for many years (Plano Clark, 2010), current conceptualizations of mixed methods research did not emerge until the 1980s (Rossman and Wilson, 1985; Bryman, 1988; Greene *et al.*, 1989). This methodological approach is becoming increasingly articulated and recognized, along with qualitative research and quantitative research, as the third methodological movement (Tashakkori and Teddlie, 2003). Therefore, mixed methods research has emerged as a methodological approach with a recognized name and distinct identity (Denscombe, 2008).

The scientific fields with more tradition in using, studying, and developing this research approach are education, sociology, psychology, and health sciences. Scholars from these fields have published specific books on mixed methods research (Tashakkori and Teddlie, 2003; Niglas, 2004; Mertens, 2005; Brewer and Hunter, 2006; Creswell and Plano Clark, 2007; Greene, 2007; Bergman, 2008; Plano Clark and Creswell, 2008; Ridenour and Newman, 2008; Andrew and Halcomb, 2009; Morse and Niehaus, 2009; Teddlie and Tashakkori, 2009; Tashakkori and Teddlie, 2010; Creswell and Plano Clark, 2011). Moreover, the two founding coeditors of the *Journal of Mixed Methods Research* are researchers in the field of education (John Creswell and Abbas Tashakkori) and the current coeditors (Dawn Freshwater and Michael Fetters) are scholars in the field of health sciences. Besides, special issues about mixed methods are published in journals from these fields, empirical articles that employ a mixed methods approach usually use the term "mixed methods" in the title, and literature reviews that analyze the prevalence and application of this methodological approach are carried out.

As noted by Creswell and Plano Clark (2007), mixed methods research has only been carefully used and examined in a handful of disciplines (as stated above, especially in education, sociology, psychology, and health sciences). In the case of management in general, and strategic management in particular, there has been less use and analysis of this approach, maybe as a consequence of less knowledge of its main foundations and characteristics. Although there are calls for using mixed methods in management and strategy research (Armstrong and Shimizu, 2007; Hitt et al., 1998), there is a lesser attention devoted to this approach than in the other fields. For example, there is not any specific book on mixed methods research in our field. Moreover, there is not any special issue on mixed methods in strategy research. In addition, although there are articles in the field of strategic management that have used a mixed methods approach (as examined later in this chapter), the expression "mixed methods" is not usually used in the title of these mixed methods studies. Furthermore, the literature base of this methodological approach is not included in the references sections of these mixed methods articles (Molina-Azorin, 2011). Then, it seems likely that the advantages, purposes, and designs of mixed methods research may be unknown to strategy scholars.

The scant diffusion of mixed methods research in strategic management, and in business disciplines in general, may be due to a number of reasons. One factor may be the predominance of positivistic approaches linked to quantitative methods in management and strategy research, and consequently the lesser attention to qualitative and interpretative methods. Another reason may be related to the difficulty in learning both qualitative and quantitative approaches. Thus, usually scholars have been inclined to specialize on single methods.

The purpose of this chapter is to describe methodological advances in mixed methods research made by other fields that can be relevant to strategy research. The chapter examines how strategic management research may take advantage of benefits and potential of this methodological approach. An important objective of this paper is to help strategy scholars to become more familiar with mixed methods research, providing the literature base and describing why and how to use this approach. This article is relevant for strategy researchers who want models of how other scholars effectively apply this approach. In this regard, several examples of mixed methods studies published in the field of strategic management are examined.

This chapter is organized as follows. First, briefly I point out some ideas about research methods in strategic management. Next, the foundations and main characteristics of mixed methods research are indicated, emphasizing why and how to design and conduct a mixed methods study. The following section analyzes several examples of strategy research that have used a mixed methods approach. Then, how mixed methods research may help to improve strategy research addressing some important issues is examined. Finally, the last section offers a summary of the main conclusions.

Research methods in strategic management

Summer *et al.* (1990) noted that the openness and creativity of the strategic management field requires an understanding and use of a variety of research methods. Our field relies on an array of complex methods drawn from various disciplines, and therefore a plurality and diversity of methods is being applied (Hitt *et al.*, 1998; Ketchen *et al.*, 2008).

Using the traditional classification that distinguishes between quantitative and qualitative research, strategy scholars have used both types of methods (Duncan, 1979; Hatten, 1979; Hitt *et al.*, 1998; Hoskisson *et al.*, 1999). From an historical point of view, qualitative inductive case-based studies dominated the early history of strategic management. But as the field embraced industrial organization economics, important changes in the methodology of strategic management research occurred. Thus, strategy scholars advocated that strategic management needed quantitative empirical research to show relationships between variables, and the field had to emphasize scientific generalizations based on study of broader sets of firms (Hitt *et al.*, 1998; Hoskisson *et al.*, 1999). Then, positivistic deductive empirical research became predominant. Concern with explanation and prediction, rather than prescription, was strongly advocated by scholars with the aim to elevate the field to a more rigorous academic discipline.

Although both quantitative and qualitative approaches are employed, the use of quantitative designs dominates (Rouse and Daellenbach, 1999; Phelan *et al.*, 2002). This higher prevalence of quantitative research is reflected in the number of articles published using a quantitative approach. In this regard, Molina-Azorin (2012) reviewed all articles published in *Strategic Management Journal* from 1980 to 2006. A total of 1,431 articles were published in this period: 345 nonempirical (24.1 percent), 835 quantitative (58.4 percent) 86 qualitative (6 percent) and 165 mixed methods articles (11.5 percent). Considering only the empirical papers (1,086 articles), 76.9 percent were quantitative, 7.9 percent were qualitative and 15.2 percent were identified as mixed methods studies. In addition, there are many methodological reviews carried out about aspects related to quantitative research (see Ketchen *et al.*, 2008). In any case, qualitative research is also relevant in strategic management. Barr (2004) indicated that although the use of qualitative methods in strategy research has lagged significantly behind the use of more quantitative approaches, significant contributions to strategy theory and practice have come from qualitative studies. Moreover, methodological reviews have also been carried out with regard to qualitative methods (Gibbert *et al.*, 2008; Ridder *et al.*, 2009). In sum, quantitative and qualitative articles are found in the strategic literature, and discussions and critical reviews about the use of quantitative and qualitative approaches have been carried out.

Regarding mixed methods research, calls for the use of mixed methods research have been carried out in the strategic management field (Hitt *et al.*, 1998; Boyd *et al.*, 2005; Armstrong and Shimizu, 2007; Molina-Azorin, 2007, 2012). Hitt *et al.* (1998) indicated that research projects may realize the benefits and advantages of both quantitative and qualitative research approaches by integrating them in a single project. Boyd *et al.* (2005) pointed out that qualitative research complements quantitative research, and in tandem quality research of both types can move forward the strategic management field more rapidly. Armstrong and Shimizu (2007) believed that using both qualitative and quantitative methods best contributes to isolating potentially unobservable resources and testing the resource-based view. Molina-Azorin (2007) reviewed the use of mixed methods research in a specific strategic theory, namely the resource-based view, and Molina-Azorin (2012) carried out a systematic review of the application of mixed methods research designs in the *Strategic Management Journal*, examining the impact of this methodological approach in terms of citations. The findings showed that mixed methods articles tended to receive more citations than mono-method articles.

An objective of this chapter is to help strategy researchers to become more familiar with mixed methods, providing the literature base about this approach and describing why, when and how to use this type of research. Next, these main foundations and characteristics of mixed methods research are examined.

Foundations of mixed methods research

Definition and purposes of mixed methods research: Why to use mixed methods research?

Johnson *et al.* (2007) asked several researchers to define mixed methods and, as a result of their review, they offered a composite definition: mixed methods research is the type of research in which a researcher or team of researchers combines elements of qualitative and quantitative research approaches (e.g. use of qualitative and quantitative viewpoints, data collection, analysis, inference techniques) for the broad purposes of breadth and depth of understanding and corroboration (Johnson *et al.*, 2007: 123). These authors indicated a continuum of several types of mixed methods studies, with the identification of pure mixed, qualitative dominant and quantitative dominant as the three types that fall into their mixed methods definition.

The overall purpose and central premise of mixed methods studies is that the use of quantitative and qualitative approaches in combination provides a better understanding of research problems and complex phenomena than either approach alone (Creswell and Plano Clark, 2007). This can be considered the main benefit or advantage of mixed methods research.

Better understanding can be obtained, for example, by triangulating one set of results with another and thereby enhancing the validity of inferences. Thus, if we use several different methods for investigating the phenomenon of our interest, and the results provide mutual confirmation, we can be more sure that our results are valid (Jick, 1979; Niglas, 2004). Other purposes, reasons or rationales for combining qualitative and quantitative methods can be indicated. Greene *et al.* (1989) point out four additional purposes: complementarity (elaboration or clarification of the results from one method with the findings from the other method), development (when the researcher uses the results from one method to help develop the use of the other method), expansion (seeking to extend the breadth and range of inquiry by using different methods for different inquiry components), and initiation (seeking the discovery of paradox and contradiction, new perspectives of frameworks, the recasting of questions or results from one method with questions or results from the other method).

Bryman and Bell (2007) also present a wide variety of purposes in mixed methods research: triangulation (the findings from one method are cross-checked against the results deriving from the other type); qualitative research facilitates quantitative research (providing hypotheses and aiding measurement – the in-depth knowledge of social contexts acquired through qualitative research can be used to inform the design of survey questions for structured interviewing and self-completion questionnaires); quantitative research facilitates, qualitative research (preparing the ground for qualitative research through the selection of people to be interviewed, or companies to be selected as case studies); static and processual features (whereas quantitative research can study the static features and regularities of a phenomenon, qualitative research can focus on more processual character-istics); qualitative research may facilitate the interpretation of the relationship between variables (a qualitative study can be used to help explain the factors underlying the broad relationships that are established in the quantitative part); and studying different aspects of a phenomenon (for example, the relationship between macro and micro levels, or different stages of a longitudinal study). All these purposes can be considered as benefits and advantages of mixed methods research.

When to use mixed methods research?

Mixed methods research is not intrinsically superior to research that relies on a single method. An important consideration prior to designing and conducting a mixed methods study is whether mixed methods, as compared to other designs, best addresses the research problem. Creswell and Plano Clark (2007) pointed out some situations in which mixed methods is the preferred approach to addressing the research problem. First, when only one approach to research (quantitative or qualitative) is inadequate by itself to address the research problem, a need exists for both quantitative and qualitative approaches. One type of evidence may not tell the complete story, or the researcher may lack confidence in the ability of one type of evidence to address the problem. Second, a problem exists when the quantitative results are inadequate to provide explanations of outcomes, and the problem can best be understood by using a qualitative part to enrich and explain the quanti-tative results. Then, mixed methods research is the preferred design. Third, a problem exists when qualitative research can provide an adequate exploration of a question, but such an exploration is not enough, and then a quantitative research is needed to further understand the question, but this quantitative part also requires the previous qualitative exploration. Thus, qualitative research can explore initially to best identify variables and theories to test, as well as aid in the identification of items and scales to help develop a quantitative instrument. Mixed methods research provides a good method for these situations.

Edmondson and McManus (2007) also pointed out the conditions under which mixed methods research is most helpful. These authors propose that the two methods can be combined successfully in cases where the goal is to increase validity of new measures through triangulation and/or to generate understanding of the mechanisms underlying quantitative results in at least partially new territory. Moreover, the state of current theory and literature influences when hybrid research strategies are appropriate. Thus, just as quantitative methods are appropriate for mature theory and qualitative methods for nascent theory, intermediate theory is well served by a blend of both. This blend works to support provisional theoretical models. The combination of qualitative data to help elaborate a phenomenon and quantitative data to provide preliminary tests of relationships can promote both insight and rigor, when appropriately applied.

Teddlie and Tashakkori (2003) indicated three areas in which mixed methods studies may be superior to mono-method approaches. First, mixed methods research can answer research questions that the other methodologies cannot. Although there is no necessary and perfect connection between purpose and approach, quantitative research has typically been more directed at theory testing or verification, while qualitative research has typically been more concerned with theory building or generation. A major advantage of mixed methods research is that it enables the researcher to simultaneously answer confirmatory and exploratory questions, and therefore generate and verify theory in the same study. Second, mixed methods research provides better (stronger) inferences. Several authors have postulated that using mixed methods can offset the disadvantages that certain of the methods have by themselves. Johnson and Turner (2003) refer to this as the fundamental principle of mixed methods research: methods should be mixed in a way that has complementary strengths and non-overlapping weaknesses. Third, mixed methods provide the opportunity for presenting a greater diversity for divergent views. Divergent findings are valuable in that they lead to a re-examination of the conceptual frameworks and the assumptions underlying each of the two (qualitative and quantitative) components.

Mixed methods designs: How to use mixed methods research?

An important issue in mixed methods research is how to use this methodological approach, or in other words, how to design and perform a mixed methods study. Methodologists writing about mixed methods research have devoted a great deal of attention to classifying the different types of mixed methods designs. Creswell and Plano Clark (2007) presented a list of 12 classifications of mixed methods designs. The different types and various classifications speak to the evolving nature of mixed methods research. Next, three aspects related to mixed methods designs are examined. First, two of the main characteristics that are considered in most classifications of mixed methods designs are indicated. Second, a parsimonious and functional classification of four major mixed methods designs is analyzed. Finally, some guidelines and recommendations for designing and conducting a mixed methods study provided by methodologists in this field are examined.

Mixed methods designs based on implementation of data collection and priority

Two main factors that help researchers to design and conduct a mixed methods study are implementation of data collection and priority (Morse, 1991; Morgan, 1998; Tashakkori and Teddlie, 1998; Creswell, 2003). Implementation of data collection refers to the sequence the researcher uses to collect both quantitative and qualitative data. The options consist of gathering the information at the same time (concurrent, simultaneous, or parallel design) or introducing the information in phases (sequential or two-phases design). In concurrently gathering both forms of data, the researcher seeks to compare them to search for congruent findings. When the data are introduced in phases, either the qualitative or the quantitative approach may be gathered first, but the sequence relates to the objectives being sought by the researcher. Thus, when qualitative data collection precedes quantitative data collection, the intent is to first explore the problem under study and then follow up on this exploration with quantitative data that are amenable to studying a large sample so that results might be inferred to a population. Alternatively, when quantitative data precede qualitative data, the intent is to test variables with a large sample and then to explore in more depth with a few cases during the qualitative phase.

Regarding priority, the mixed methods researcher can give equal priority to both quantitative and qualitative research, emphasize qualitative more, or emphasize quantitative more. This emphasis may result from research questions, practical constraints for data collection, the need to understand one form of data before proceeding to the next or the audience preference. Mixed methods designs can therefore be divided into equivalent status designs (the researcher conducts the study using both the quantitative and the qualitative approaches about equally to understand the phenomenon under study) and dominant–less dominant studies or nested designs (the researcher conducts the study within a single dominant paradigm with a small component of the overall study drawn from an alternative design).

These two dimensions and their possible combinations can lead to the establishment of several designs which are represented using the notation proposed by Morse (1991). In her system, the main or dominant method appears in capital letters (QUAN, QUAL) whereas the complementary method is in lowercase letters (quan, qual). The notation "+" is used to indicate a simultaneous design, and the arrow "→" stands for sequential design. Thus, the following four groups and nine types of mixed methods designs can exist using these two dimensions (Johnson and Onwuegbuzie, 2004):

I – Equivalent status/simultaneous design: QUAL+QUAN.
II – Equivalent status/sequential designs: QUAL→QUAN; QUAN→QUAL.
III – Dominant/simultaneous designs: QUAL+quan; QUAN+qual.
IV – Dominant/sequential designs: qual→QUAN; QUAL→quan; quan→QUAL; QUAN→qual.

Triangulation, exploratory, explanatory, and embedded designs

There are other classifications of mixed methods designs. Creswell and Plano Clark (2007) pointed out that although authors have emphasized different features and used different names, there are actually more similarities than differences among these classifications. These authors indicate four main types of mixed methods designs: triangulation, exploratory, explanatory, and embedded designs.

The purpose of a triangulation mixed methods design is to simultaneously collect both quantitative and qualitative data, merge the data, and use the results to understand a research problem. The researcher gathers both quantitative and qualitative data, compares results from the analysis of both data, and makes an interpretation as to whether the results from both data support or contradict each other. The triangulation design is usually a one-phase design in which researchers implement the quantitative and qualitative methods during the same timeframe and with equal weight. It generally involves the concurrent, but separate, collection and analysis of quantitative and qualitative data so that the researcher may best understand the research problem.

The purpose of an exploratory mixed methods design is the procedure of first gathering qualitative data to explore a phenomenon, and then collecting quantitative data to explain relationships found in the qualitative data. Therefore, this design is a two-phase (sequential) mixed methods design. In this case, the results of the first method (qualitative) can help develop or inform the second method (quantitative). This design is based on the premise that an exploration is needed for one of several reasons: measures or instruments are not available, the variables are unknown, or there is no guiding framework or theory. Therefore, researchers use this design when existing instruments, variables and measures may not be known or available for the population or context under study. It is also appropriate when a researcher wants to generalize results to different groups, to test aspects of an emergent theory or to explore a phenomenon in depth and then measure its prevalence.

The explanatory design is also a two-phase mixed methods design and it consists of first collecting quantitative data and then collecting qualitative data to help explain or elaborate on the quantitative results. Then, this design starts with the collection and analysis of quantitative data. The second, qualitative phase of the study is designed so that it follows from the results of the first quantitative phase. The rationale of this approach is that the quantitative data and results provide a general picture of the research problem, but more analysis through qualitative data collection is needed to refine, extend or explain the general picture. For example, this design is well suited to a study in which a researcher needs qualitative data to explain significant (or non-significant) results, outlier results, or surprising findings. This design can also be used when a researcher wants to form groups based on quantitative results and follow up with the groups through subsequent qualitative research or to use quantitative participant characteristics to guide purposeful sampling for a qualitative phase. In sum, there are two main variants of the explanatory design: the follow-up explanations design and the participant selection design. Although both models have an initial quantitative phase followed by a qualitative phase, they differ in the connection of the two phases, with one focusing on results to be examined in more detail and the other on the appropriate participants to be selected.

Finally, the embedded design is a mixed methods design in which one data set provides a supportive, secondary role in a study based primarily on the other data type. The premises of this design are that a single data set is not sufficient, that different questions need to be answered, and that each type of question requires different types of data. Scholars can also use this design when they need to include qualitative or quantitative data to answer a research question within a largely quantitative or qualitative study. The embedded design mixed the different data set at the design level, with one type of data being embedded within a methodology framed by the other data type. Moreover, this design can use either a one-phase or a two-phase approach for the embedded data.

Recommendations for designing and conducting a mixed methods study

Along with studying the types of mixed methods designs, another aspect that may help address the question about how to use mixed methods research is to indicate some guidelines and recommendations provided by methodologists in this field. Creswell *et al.* (2003) and O'Cathain *et al.* (2008) suggest some guidelines for the good application and reporting of mixed methods studies. Researchers should pay significant attention to the explicit clarification of several relevant aspects. Specifically, scholars must clearly identify the core reasons and rationale for collecting and combining both forms of data in a single study, describing the justification for using a mixed methods approach. In addition, researchers must describe the design in terms of the purpose, priority and sequence of the quantitative and qualitative parts, and insights gained from mixing or integrating methods must be also indicated.

Hanson *et al.* (2005) also offer some recommendations for designing, implementing, and reporting a mixed methods study. Thus, they recommend that researchers attend closely to design and implementation issues, particularly to how and when data are collected (e.g. concurrently or sequentially). The study's purpose plays an important role here. They also recommend that researchers familiarize themselves with the analysis and integration strategies used in the published mixed methods studies. Moreover, in preparing a mixed methods manuscript, they recommend that, early on, researchers foreshadow the logic and progression of their studies by stating the study's purpose and research questions in the introduction. Clear, well-written purpose statements and research questions that specify the quantitative and qualitative aspects of the study help focus the manuscript. Additionally, these authors recommend that, in the introduction, researchers explicitly state a rationale for mixing quantitative and qualitative methods and data (e.g., to triangulate results, to develop or improve one method with the other, to extend the study's results). Another recommendation is that, in the methods section, researchers specify the type of mixed methods research design used.

Creswell and Plano Clark (2007) strongly recommend that researchers carefully select a single design. This will make the study more manageable and simpler to implement. These authors indicate that the key factors that researchers should consider when choosing a mixed methods design are the research problem, the quantitative and qualitative skills that they possess, the available resources and the expectations of audiences. In addition, the choice of a research design relates to three decisions: the timing of the use of collected data (implementation of data collection), the relative weight of the quantitative and qualitative parts (priority), and the approach to mixing the two datasets. We have pointed out some ideas regarding the first two decisions previously. With regard to the third decision, these authors indicate that there are three overall strategies for mixing quantitative and qualitative data: the two data types can be merged (the researcher takes the two data sets and explicitly brings them together or integrated them), one can be embedded within the other (so that one type of data provides a supportive role for the other dataset), or they can be connected (the analysis of one type of data leads to, and thereby connects to, the need for the other type of data).

Teddlie and Tashakkori (2006) point out that mixed methods designs have an opportunistic nature. Thus, a mixed methods research study may have a predetermined research design, but new components of the design may evolve as researchers follow up on leads that develop as data are collected and analyzed. Therefore, researchers should mindfully create designs that effectively answer their research questions (Johnson and Onwuegbuzie, 2004). The use of figures and visual models may help the researcher to plan and present the study (Ivankova *et al.*, 2006).

Examples of mixed methods studies in strategy research

Some mixed methods articles published in the field of strategic management are examined in this section. This analysis can be relevant for strategy scholars who desire a better understanding of mixed methods research and want models of how other scholars apply this approach. Thus, analysis of examples of mixed methods studies in the strategy field will be examined, emphasizing the main purposes and designs used.

Tripsas (1997) employed the triangulation mixed methods design (QUAN+QUAL) in her study about the process of creative destruction and the performance of incumbents versus new entrants in the typesetter industry. The quantitative data included the entry date of every firm in the industry and, for those firms that exited, the exit date. Detailed data for 95 percent of the products introduced by these firms covers product performance characteristics, price, and unit sales over time. This quantitative data were supplemented with qualitative data about how organizations responded to new technology, including in-depth case studies of multiple firms. These qualitative data come from a combination of primary and secondary sources. Both quantitative and qualitative parts confirmed that established firms were handicapped by their prior experience in that their approach to new product development was shaped by that experience.

Elbanna and Child (2007) indicated that a two-stage study was conducted in which the first stage provided exploratory insights and the second stage investigated hypotheses on the impact of strategic decision-making process dimensions on strategic decision effectiveness and the moderating role of broader contextual variables in Egypt. Specifically, the authors pointed out that given the contradictory conclusions of previous research, the effect of context and the absence or paucity of reported investigations on strategic decision making in the Egyptian setting, an exploratory approach appeared to be warranted as a foundation for hypothesis testing. This exploratory first stage was then conducted in advance of the main quantitative study for the following purposes: to clarify concepts and develop measures, to assist the development of hypotheses, and to expose practical problems in carrying out the research. Therefore, this paper employed an exploratory sequential design, being development the main mixed methods purpose of this work. Semi-structured interviews were conducted in the qualitative part, and questionnaires and regression analysis were employed in the quantitative part.

Sharma and Vredenburg (1998) also carried out an exploratory mixed methods study in the Canadian oil and gas industry, examining the relationship between environmental strategy and firm capabilities. In this case, the specific design can be considered as a QUAL→QUAN design (sequential, equivalent status of the two parts). The first phase involved comparative case studies through in-depth interviews and analysis of documents. This exploratory study was intended to examine linkages between environmental strategies and the development of capabilities. This first phase ends with two hypotheses. The second phase (quantitative) involved testing the emergent linkages through a mail survey-based study of 99 firms in this industry. The final written report is structured in two main parts: the exploratory study includes several sections (qualitative data collection, qualitative data analysis and results with the proposed hypotheses) and then the confirmatory study is presented (with a quantitative data collection, quantitative analysis section and the results). The mixed methods purpose is development: the qualitative phase helps to know the industry, and develop theory, hypotheses and the measurement instrument used in the quantitative phase.

The work by Davies et al. (2010) is an example of explanatory mixed methods design. These authors examined the gaps between employee and customer perceptions of corporate reputation and the influence of these gaps on the performance of service organizations. The main part of the study is quantitative. Data about perceptions were obtained through structured questionnaires to employees and customers, and regression analysis was used. Qualitative interviews with employees and customers helped illustrate the mechanisms behind the studied hypotheses. In addition, after the quantitative analysis, the authors presented the quantitative findings to senior managers in participating companies, and the authors held a series of focus group discussions with some managers. These discussions help elaborate, explain, and clarify the quantitative results. Therefore, the main mixed methods purpose in this work is complementarity.

Another example of explanatory mixed methods design is the work by Dyer and Hatch (2006). These authors examined the role of network knowledge resources in influencing firm performance, using a sample of US automotive suppliers selling to both Toyota and US automakers. The first quantitative part of this study tested the hypothesis that a buyer that provides greater knowledge transfers to its supplier network will develop the suppliers' production capabilities such that the suppliers' operations for that particular buyer will be more productive. A survey was sent to the plant managers at suppliers in the Toyota's US supplier association. The quantitative findings confirmed that Toyota's supplier network does produce components of higher quality and at lower cost for Toyota than for their largest US customers. Then, the second part (qualitative) was to explore why the supplier performs better as a member of one network (i.e. Toyota's) than another network (i.e. GM, Ford, or Chrysler). Thus, in this part interviews were done at 13 suppliers to explore and explain quantitative results.

As stated above, there are two variants of the explanatory design: the follow-up explanations design and the participant selection design. The works by Davies *et al.* (2010) and Dyer and Hatch (2006) can be considered as examples of the follow-up explanations design. Regarding the participant selection design (when groups are formed based on quantitative data, members of these groups are selected and then these members are studied through qualitative research), Rouse and Daellenbach (1999) advocated this mixed methods design in order to analyze the firm internal resources than can be sources of competitive advantages. Their article is not empirical, but they proposed a design that begins with a quantitative four-step firm selection process: (1) selecting a single industry; (2) clustering firms by strategic type or group within this industry; (3) comparing performance indices within strategic groups; and (4) identifying those firms within each strategic group that are the high and low performers. Then, these firms would be selected as research subjects using in-depth fieldwork or ethnographic study methods. This qualitative approach which takes the researcher into the organization is essential to gain an in-depth knowledge and understanding of the organization and its processes, given the contention that sustainable competitive advantages are organizational in origin, tacit, highly inimitable, socially complex, embedded in process, and often driven by culture.

Contributions of mixed methods to strategy research

Mixed methods designs may contribute to address some specific research issues related to the improvement and development of strategy research. Next, I highlight three issues: the relevance of context in strategy research, the simultaneous analysis of outcomes and processes, and the relevance of strategy research to practice.

Context-specific research

Regarding the relevance of context in strategic management, taking into account that firm strategies, resources, and competitive advantages are context-specific, the task of finding a better answer to quantitative research questions could be made easier if, prior to the quantitative inquiry, a qualitative phase were carried out with the aim of acquiring a deeper understanding of the industry context. This would make possible a better knowledge of the strategies in that industry as well as the specific variables and permit the design of a better measuring instrument.

For example, with regard to the resource-based view, Priem and Butler (2001) argue that little work has been done with respect to evaluating strategic resources in appropriate contexts, emphasizing that researchers should focus on one industry. Mixed methods studies with the purpose of development and with a sequential design where the qualitative phase is carried out before the quantitative one, may help solve this aspect.

Examining a single industry arguably reduce the generalizability of the results but support more accurate measurement of firm-specific resources and their impact on specific firm performance adequate for the industry analyzed. In fact, the qualitative part may play an important role for determining appropriate independent (strategies, resources, capabilities, competences) and dependent (competitive advantage, performance) variables.

Simultaneous analysis of outcomes and processes

Theory building in strategy research would benefit from a greater integration between process- and outcome-oriented research. Mixed methods studies should be encouraged because they can yield richer insights regarding both aspects. Giving more attention to process-research could help to improve our understanding of content related issues. Thus, process studies can clarify which variables are important and why they might influence the outcomes researchers seek to explain.

Whereas the quantitative part of a mixed methods study may focus on the statistical effects of some independent variable (for example, firm resources) on some dependent variable (for example, competitive advantage or firm performance), the qualitative part may focus on processual characteristics. In this regard, qualitative research is adequate whether it is focused on process rather than on the results or outcomes obtained, which it is more appropriate for quantitative research. Then, a mixed methods study can examine at the same time, for example, the impact of capabilities on performance and how these capabilities emerge and develop inside the firm studying the process of evolution.

Relevance to practice

The application of mixed methods research may facilitate and enhance the interpretation of the results obtained in order to emphasize the practical implications of a study. With regard to this practical impact, mixed methods can be used to understand the extent to which a study's results are significant in practice by including practitioners' own discourses.

Aguinis *et al.* (2010), with the goal to bridge the science-practice gap, pointed out that to demonstrate a study's practical significance, there is a need to describe quantitative results in a way that makes sense for practitioners. They suggested that this can be achieved by including practitioners in each research project as part of a qualitative study. Therefore, these authors implicitly defend mixed methods research where a quantitative study is completed with a subsequent qualitative part where practitioners become participants. After the application of a quantitative study, a qualitative part is particularly appropriate because its goal is to understand and describe phenomena. Also, qualitative research gives voice to the participants and places importance on their understanding and interpretation of a given research study.

Conclusions

Mixed methods research is not the panacea for all research problems in strategy research. Moreover, there are several barriers to carrying out mixed methods studies (Bryman, 2007; Creswell and Plano Clark, 2011). Mixed methods studies require extensive time, resources, and effort. Mixed methods studies are a challenge because they are perceived as requiring more work and financial resources, and they take more time. Increased time demands arise from the time it takes to implement the quantitative and qualitative parts of the study (Niglas, 2004). In addition, mixed methods research also requires that researchers develop a broader set of skills that span both the quantitative and the qualitative. Another barrier is related to the challenges of publishing mixed methods studies. The need to describe and discuss two sets of data collection, data analysis and findings may make it difficult to publish mixed methods studies due to the word and page restrictions that journals impose on authors. Furthermore, the research question and context dictate the choice of the appropriate research methods, and then different methods (quantitative, qualitative and mixed methods) are appropriate for different situations and questions.

In any case, although mixed methods research is not a panacea, there are several barriers to designing and conducting these studies, and sometimes it is more appropriate to carry out a pure quantitative or pure qualitative research, mixed methods designs may provide important and useful contributions to the extant methodologies and research issues in strategic management. Moreover, we must also take into account that the knowledge about mixed methods research can stimulate a researcher to better define and analyze innovative problems and research questions in strategy research. Mixing methods therefore offers enormous potential for exploring new dimensions.

I would like to provide some arguments and implications related to how mixed methods research might gain legitimization among strategy scholars and how the diffusion of this methodological approach can be improved. As noted above, Molina-Azorin (2012) found that mixed methods articles in strategy research tended to receive more citations than mono-method articles. Moreover, mixed methods may add value to strategic management addressing specific issues related to the improvement and development of strategy research (see previous sections). Therefore, authors are advised to recognize that the use of a mixed methods approach in their articles may help differentiate these studies from other empirical articles, and then the application of a mixed methods approach may improve the likelihood that these studies will receive more attention.

An implication for academic institutions is that the application of mixed methods research requires that strategy scholars develop a diversity of research capacities. The need for such skills has implications for how strategy researchers need to be trained. To improve the implementation of mixed methods studies, academic institutions should increase their concern for education about this type of research. That is, along with quantitative and qualitative research courses, universities and Ph.D. programs should also provide specific training on mixed methods through specific courses. In addition, academic institutions must take into account that it is not easy to conduct and publish mixed methods studies and, at the same time, to publish a large number of articles. Then, attention should be paid to this issue in evaluation and promotion decisions.

As the application of a mixed methods approach is related to citation counts, an implication for journals is that they should encourage the publication of mixed methods articles. Moreover, editors should assign reviewers who have a solid understanding of mixed methods to review manuscript submissions that use this methodological approach. Furthermore, a barrier to conducting mixed methods research is related to the challenges of publishing these studies, especially constraints such as page limits in journals. By limiting space, journals may discourage publication of mixed methods research, and then journals should be flexible regarding manuscript length.

The advancement of strategic management requires an understanding and application of a variety of research methods, and mixed methods research may play an important role in this use of diverse methods. Mixed methods research shows great promise for addressing strategy topics and specific issues, but only if researchers understand the design options that accompany this methodological choice. Knowledge of the literature base of mixed methods research and analysis of empirical papers that use a mixed methods approach can help strategy researchers to design and conduct this type of studies. In this chapter, this literature base and examples of mixed methods studies in the field of strategic management have been provided. I hope that this chapter may help to strategy scholars to improve their understanding of mixed methods research.

Bibliography

Aguinis, H., Werner, S., Abbott, J., Angert, C., Park, J., and Kohlhausen, D. (2010) "Customer-centric science: Reporting significant research results with rigor, relevance, and practical impact in mind," *Organizational Research Methods*, 13: 515–39.

Andrew, S. and Halcomb, E. (eds) (2009) *Mixed Methods Research for Nursing and the Health Sciences,* Chichester: Wiley-Blackwell.

Armstrong, C. E. and Shimizu, K. (2007) "A review of approaches to empirical research on the resource-based view of the firm," *Journal of Management*, 33: 959–86.

Barr, P. (2004) "Current and potential importance of qualitative methods in strategy research," in D. Ketchen and D. Bergh (eds) *Research Methodology in Strategy and Management*, Vol. 1, Oxford: Elsevier, 165–188.

Bergman, M. (ed.) (2008) *Advances in Mixed Methods Research,* London: Sage.

Boyd, B., Gove, S., and Hitt, M. (2005) "Construct measurement in strategic management research: Illusion or reality?," *Strategic Management Journal*, 26: 239–57.

Brewer, J. and Hunter, A. (2006) *Foundations of Multimethod Research*, Thousand Oaks, CA: Sage.

Bryman, A. (1988) *Quantity and Quality in Social Science Research*, London: Routledge.

Bryman, A. (2007) "Barriers to integrating quantitative and qualitative research," *Journal of Mixed Methods Research*, 1: 8–22.

Bryman, A. and Bell, E. (2007) *Business Research Methods*, 2nd edn, Oxford: Oxford University Press.

Creswell, J. (2003) *Research Design: Qualitative, Quantitative and Mixed Methods Approaches*, 2nd edn, Thousand Oaks, CA: Sage.

Creswell, J. W. and Plano Clark, V.L. (2007) *Designing and Conducting Mixed Methods Research*, Thousand Oaks, CA: Sage.

Creswell, J. W. and Plano Clark, V. L. (2011) *Designing and Conducting Mixed Methods Research*, 2nd edn, Thousand Oaks, CA: Sage.

Creswell, J., Plano Clark, V., Gutmann, M., and Hanson, W. (2003) "Advanced mixed methods research designs," in A. Tashakkori and C. Teddlie (eds) *Handbook of Mixed Methods in Social & Behavioral Research*, Thousand Oaks, CA: Sage, 209–240.

Davies, G., Chun, R., and Kamins, M. (2010) "Reputation gaps and the performance of service organizations," *Strategic Management Journal*, 31: 530–46.

Denscombe, M. (2008) "Communities of practice. A research paradigm for the mixed methods approach," *Journal of Mixed Methods Research*, 2: 270–283.

Duncan, R. (1979) "Qualitative research methods in strategic management," In D. Schendel and C. Hofer (eds) *Strategic Management. A New View of Business Policy and Planning*, Boston: Little, Brown and Company, 424–447.

Dyer, J. and Hatch, N. (2006) "Relation-specific capabilities and barriers to knowledge transfers: Creating advantage through network relationships," *Strategic Management Journal*, 27: 701–19.

Edmondson, A. C. and McManus, S. E. (2007) "Methodological fit in management field research," *Academy of Management Review*, 32: 1155–79.

Elbanna, S. and Child, J. (2007) "Influences on strategic decision effectiveness: Development and test of an integrative model," *Strategic Management Journal*, 28: 431–53.

Gibbert, M., Ruigrok, W., and Wicki, B. (2008) "What passes as a rigorous case study?," *Strategic Management Journal*, 29: 1465–74.

Greene, J. (2007) *Mixed Methods in Social Inquiry*, San Francisco: Jossey-Bass.

Greene, J., Caracelli, V., and Graham, W. (1989) "Toward a conceptual framework for mixed-method evaluation designs," *Educational Evaluation and Policy Analysis*, 11: 255–74.

Hanson, W., Creswell, J. W., Plano Clark, V. L., Petska, K., and Creswell, J. D. (2005) "Mixed methods research designs in counseling psychology," *Journal of Counseling Psychology*, 52: 224–35.

Hatten, K. J. (1979) "Quantitative research methods in strategic management," in D. Schendel and C. Hofer (eds) *Strategic Management. A New View of Business Policy and Planning*, Boston: Little, Brown and Company, 448–467.

Hitt, M. A., Gimeno, J., and Hoskisson, R. (1998) "Current and future research methods in strategic management," *Organizational Research Methods*, 1: 6–44.

Hoskisson, R., Hitt, M., Wan, W., and Yiu, D. (1999) "Theory and research in strategic management: Swings of a pendulum," *Journal of Management*, 25: 417–56.

Ivankova, N., Creswell, J., and Stick, S. (2006) "Using mixed-methods sequential explanatory design: From theory to practice," *Field Methods*, 18: 3–20.

Jick, T. (1979) "Mixing qualitative and quantitative methods: triangulation in action," *Administrative Science Quarterly*, 24: 602–11.

Johnson, B. and Onwuegbuzie, A. (2004) "Mixed methods research: A research paradigm whose time has come," *Educational Researcher*, 33: 14–26.

Johnson, B., Onwuegbuzie, A., and Turner, L. (2007) "Toward a definition of mixed methods research," *Journal of Mixed Methods Research*, 1: 112–33.

Johnson, B. and Turner, L. (2003) "Data collection strategies in mixed methods research," in A. Tashakkori and C. Teddlie (eds), *Handbook of Mixed Methods in Social & Behavioral Research*, Thousand Oaks, CA: Sage, 297–319.

Ketchen, D. J., Boyd, B. K., and Bergh, D. D. (2008) "Research methodology in strategic management: Past accomplishments and future challenges," *Organizational Research Methods*, 11: 643–58.

Mertens, D. (2005) *Research and Evaluation in Education and Psychology: Integrating Diversity with Quantitative, Qualitative and Mixed Methods*, 2nd edn, Thousand Oaks, CA: Sage.

Molina-Azorin, J. F. (2007) "Mixed methods in strategy research: Applications and implications in the resource-based view," in D. Ketchen and D. Bergh (eds) *Research Methodology in Strategy and Management*, Vol. 4, Oxford: Elsevier, 37–73.

Molina-Azorin, J. F. (2011) "The use and added value of mixed methods in management research," *Journal of Mixed Methods Research*, 5: 7–24.

Molina-Azorin, J. F. (2012) "Mixed methods research in strategic management: Impact and applications," *Organizational Research Methods*, 15: 33–56.

Morgan, D. (1998) "Practical strategies for combining qualitative and quantitative methods: Applications to health research," *Qualitative Health Research*, 8: 362–76.

Morse, J. (1991) "Approaches to qualitative-quantitative methodological triangulation," *Nursing Research*, 40: 120–3.

Morse, J. and Niehaus, L. (2009) *Mixed Method Design: Principles and Procedures*, Walnut Creek, CA: Left Coast Press.

Niglas, K. (2004) *The Combined Use of Qualitative and Quantitative Methods in Educational Research*, Tallinn: Tallinn Pedagogical University Press.

O'Cathain, A., Murphy, E., and Nicholl, J. (2008) "The quality of mixed methods studies in health services research," *Journal of Health Services and Research Policy*, 13: 92–8.

Phelan, S., Ferreira, M., and Salvador, R. (2002) "The first twenty years of the *Strategic Management Journal*," *Strategic Management Journal*, 23: 1161–8.

Plano Clark, V. (2010) "The adoption and practice of mixed methods: US trends in federally funded health-related research," *Qualitative Inquiry*, 16: 428–40.

Plano Clark, V. and Creswell, J. (2008) *The Mixed Methods Reader*, Thousand Oaks, CA: Sage.

Priem, R. and Butler, J. (2001) "Is the resource-based 'view' a useful perspective for strategic management research?," *Academy of Management Review*, 26: 22–40.

Ridder, H. G., Hoon, C., and McCandless, A. (2009) "The theoretical contribution of case study research to the field of strategy and management," in D. Ketchen and D. Bergh (eds) *Research Methodology in Strategy and Management*, Vol. 5, Bingley, UK: Emerald, 137–175.

Ridenour, C. and Newman, I. (2008) *Mixed Methods Research. Exploring the Interactive Continuum*, Carbondale, IL: Southern Illinois University Press.

Rossman, G. and Wilson, B. (1985) "Numbers and words: Combining quantitative and qualitative methods in a single large-scale evaluation study," *Evaluation Review*, 9: 627–43.

Rouse, M. and Daellenbach, U. (1999) "Rethinking research methods for the resource-based perspective: Isolating sources of sustainable competitive advantage," *Strategic Management Journal*, 20: 487–94.

Sharma, S. and Vredenburg, H. (1998) "Proactive corporate environmental strategy and the development of competitively valuable organizational capabilities," *Strategic Management Journal*, 19: 729–53.

Summer, C. E., Bettis, R. A., Duhaime, I. H., Grant, J. H., Hambrick, D. C., Snow, C. C., and Zeithaml, C. P. (1990) "Doctoral education in the field of business policy and strategy," *Journal of Management*, 16: 361–98.

Tashakkori, A. and Teddlie, C. (1998) *Mixed Methodology: Combining Qualitative and Quantitative Approaches*, Thousand Oaks, CA: Sage.

Tashakkori, A. and Teddlie, C. (eds) (2003) *Handbook of Mixed Methods in Social & Behavioral Research*, Thousand Oaks, CA: Sage.

Tashakkori, A. and Teddlie, C. (eds) (2010) *Handbook of Mixed Methods in Social & Behavioral Research*, 2nd edn, Thousand Oaks, CA: Sage.

Teddlie, C. and Tashakkori, A. (2003) "Major issues and controversies in the use of mixed methods in the social and behavioral sciences," in A. Tashakkori and C. Teddlie (eds) *Handbook of Mixed Methods in Social & Behavioral Research*, Thousand Oaks, CA: Sage, 3–50.

Teddlie, C. and Tashakkori, A. (2006) "A general typology of research designs featuring mixed methods," *Research in the Schools*, 13: 12–28.

Teddlie, C. and Tashakkori, A. (2009) *Foundations of Mixed Methods Research: Integrating Quantitative and Qualitative Approaches in the Social and Behavioral Sciences*, Thousand Oaks, CA: Sage.

Tripsas, M. (1997) "Unraveling the process of creative destruction: Complementary assets and incumbent survival in the typesetter industry," *Strategic Management Journal*, 18 (Summer Special Issue): 119–42.

14

CONCLUSION

Organizing the future by reconnecting with the past – methodological challenges in strategic management research

Maria Cristina Cinici and Giovanni Battista Dagnino

Prologue

Compared to other relevant areas of investigation in the social sciences, strategic management is a relatively young field of study that has progressively advanced towards maturity since its inception in the 1960s (Furrer *et al.*, 2008; Herrmann, 2005; Guerras-Martin *et al.*, 2014). As we have seen in the introductory chapter of this book, its genesis actually dates back to the first part of the 1960s, when a triad of groundbreaking contributors, Alfred Chandler (1962), Igor Ansoff (1965) and Ken Andrews (1971), collectively laid the foundations to establish it as an autonomous discipline (Rumelt *et al.*, 1994). Since its infancy, the status of strategic management has undoubtedly evolved considerably, turning it into a widely recognized field in the management studies domain (Hoskisson *et al.*, 1999; Pettigrew *et al.*, 2002).

Since the 1990s, strategic management's progress towards maturity has featured an improvement in the quantity of theories and in the depth of research issues (Scandura and Williams, 2000). The listing of company's "best practices" in the 1960s has given way to the thorough dissection of various research issues, such as firm competition and cooperation, resources and capabilities, diversification, internationalization and globalization, strategic leadership, strategic entrepreneurship, the relationship between knowledge, learning, and innovation, corporate social responsibility, and behavioral strategy, just to mention a few.

The use of an ample array of more sophisticated research methods has closely accompanied strategic management's journey towards maturity (Herrmann, 2005). This is a condition that has arguably fueled the rapid growth of strategic management as a field of study. Since the 1980s, statistic and econometric methods started to supersede traditional single case study analyses when early strategic management scholars decided to adopt them in their search to secure their work a broader scientific recognition (for more detail see the introductory chapter of this book). Therefore, we ask: to what extent the most commonly used research methods have favored the development of particular theories and constructs in strategic management, whilst contributing to the fading of others?

In the effort of systematizing the evolution of strategic management, research has unveiled a number of features that are fundamental to the development of strategic management. Specifically, scholars have advanced a historical analysis of the intellectual streams underlying the evolution of the field (Rumelt *et al.*, 1994; Hoskisson *et al.*, 1999), documented changes in the diversity and content of the articles published by the *Strategic Management Journal* in its first two decades of existence (Phelan *et al.*, 2002), explained the development of strategic management from an evolutionary perspective on the basis of the triad variation, selection, and retention (Herrmann, 2005), identified and analyzed the tensions between the internal and external sub-domains of strategic management research, as well as the tensions between the macro and micro levels of analysis (Guerras-Martin *et al.*, 2014), and observed the evolution of the strategic management paradigms as an history of incomplete dominances (see Chapter 2). Actually, by doing so they have managed to underscore that some theories and approaches have been imported in strategic management from industrial economics (e.g. the structure-conduct-performance paradigm), institutional economics (e.g. transaction cost economics), and unorthodox economics (e.g. the evolutionary approach), while others are the outcome of developments that, far from being exogenous, are to be deemed endogenous to the strategy field (e.g. the resource-based view and the knowledge-based view of the firm) (Nerur *et al.*, 2008).

A recent stream of research used scientometric techniques to scrutinize the intellectual structure of strategic management and its evolution. Scholars initiated to dig deeper, respectively, in the collective identity of strategic management (Nag *et al.*, 2007), the evolution of strategic management subfields (Furrer *et al.*, 2008), the intellectual structure and the more influential papers and authors (Ramos-Rodriguez and Ruiz-Navarro, 2004; Nerur *et al.*, 2008), the structure and development of the international strategic management community (Ronda-Pupo and Guerras-Martin, 2010), and its methodological shortcomings (Boyd *et al.*, 2005).

We build on the above arguments to draw our reader's attention on the extent to which research methods have actually influenced the mellowness process of strategic management. In the effort to understand this condition, we anchor our research in the extant tradition aimed to inspect the unfolding of theories and the inception research methods in strategic management (Hoskisson *et al.*, 1999; Herrmann, 2005; Ketchen *et al.*, 2008).

The remainder of this chapter is partitioned in two sections both guided by the emphasis on the benefits that over time new research methods (some of them have been discussed earlier in this book) usually convey to the evolution of strategic management. On this ground, the second section shall inspect how research methods have influenced the evolution of strategic management research, while the third shall feature how research methods are likely to affect the future evolution of strategic management investigation.

How research methods have influenced the evolution of strategic management

The image of strategic management evolution as a pendulum swinging from the analysis of success factors residing either inside or outside the firm domain was popularized by Hoskisson *et al.* (1999). According to these influential authors, the beginnings of strategic management can be traced in the 1960s, when Alfred Chandler's *Strategy and Structure* (1962), Igor Ansoff's *Corporate Strategy* (1965), and the Harvard Business School MBA textbook, *Business Policy: Text and Cases* (Learned *et al.*, 1965),[1] initially provided a definition of strategy.

Actually, as previously pinpointed in this chapter, the scholarly advancement of strategic management from the solely practice-oriented business policy to a more cherished academic field in management studies occurred at the time when the field moved from the normative, inductive case-based studies and the rough-and-ready toolkits timely provided by consulting firms (such as the BCG and the McKinsey matrixes and the experience curve), that had typified its early history, to the widespread use of statistic and econometric techniques borrowed from industrial organization economics.[2] In those days, business policy researchers began to perform large sample studies containing substantial recollection of secondary data (especially PIMS studies and Compustat database).

On the one hand, we acknowledge that this unambiguous methodological choice has contributed to turn the field in one dominated by four perspectives that have extensively influenced its course from the 1980s all through the 1990s to the year 2000 (Nerur *et al.*, 2008). At that time, in fact, Michael Porter's industrial organizational economics, Oliver Williamson's institutional economics, Henry Mintzberg's process school, and Jeffrey Pfeffer's power/resource dependence school turned to be the prevailing ones in the strategy field. On the other side, while statistic and econometric methods have contributed to confer strategic management the much-needed methodological rigor and precision in measurement, in time they also revealed hardly suitable for operationalizing constructs and theories that had appeared in the very early days of business policy and planning. This was the case of the *behavioral theory* of the firm (March and Simon, 1958; Cyert and March, 1963), where firm behavior, far from being conceived as hyper-rational profit maximizing, is seen as goal-seeking and behaviorally satisfying in a number of utility dimensions. This was also the case of *contingency theory* (Lawrence and Lorsch, 1967), that had advanced the idea of fit, alignment, and matching organizational assets and resources. These approaches actually require the use of research methods that are different from the ones used in traditional empirical research performed in strategy: for instance, field experiments (Harrison and List, 2004; Chatterji *et al.*, forthcoming) and computer simulations (Hughes *et al.*, 2012). In the current practice of research, absent a received strategic management proclivity towards their use, these methods are usually imported from experimental economics and applied psychology.

The analysis of the intellectual structure of the strategic management field over the period 1980–2000 performed by Ramos-Rodriguez and Ruiz-Navarro (2004) has supplied evidence that, after the vast impact of a few books in the early part of the field's history (especially the already mentioned Chandler-Ansoff-Andrews triplet), as well as Michael Porter's work unmatched impact, the resource-based view of the firm (Barney, 1991; Peteraf, 1993) started blasting the field in the mid 1990s, thereby rapidly turning into an endogenously generated dominant perspective. Theoretical developments in this vein have clearly featured the dramatic drift from focusing on industrial environment to centering on the firm's internal features, such as resources, competences, and capabilities.

After an initial emphasis on static approaches, the work of resource-base researchers initiated to deal with more dynamic, integrative perspectives, which necessarily involve discussing issues such as entrepreneurship, innovation, and strategic decision-making (Teece *et al.*, 1997; Mitchell *et al.*, 2011). More recently, strategic management has also begun to incorporate perspectives that include the micro-analytical levels, such as human interactions, effort and talent (Campbell *et al.*, 2012; Wright *et al.*, 2014), and the macro-analytical level, such as the study of the role of institutions and institutional contexts (Peng *et al.*, 2009).

How research methods will (likely) influence the future evolution of strategic management

At this point, we have reasons to believe that empirical and also conceptual developments in the strategic management field are (and are to be) no better than the research methods used to produce them. Given this contention, as the field advances in the 2010s, research methods ought to advance either. And as much as research methods advance as the field advances.

Actually, from what we have seen heretofore, methods have conventionally contributed to push the strategic management field forward in two major waves. The former has emerged especially in the 1980s and 1990s, when a new wave of soundness and rigor turned out as a dramatic requisite to warrant strategic management research broad scholarly appreciation. The rigor at hand was also prerequisite to test the new emerging theories (e.g. the resource-based view and the knowledge-based view of the firm) and constructs (e.g. resources, capabilities, and knowledge). The latter has started surfacing roughly a decade ago and requires an additional flow of research methods that are more appropriate to detect the value of emerging phenomena (e.g. strategic human capital) and levels of analysis (micro and macro and their multiple connections). At this time, we can therefore posit that there is impending *circular loop* between strategy theory, constructs, and methods: since they are strictly interrelated, they might hence be self-sustaining or, if poorly used and applied, self-destroying to one another.

In this sub-section, while we are fully aware that we are not fortune-tellers endowed with a crystal ball to predict the next wave of development in research methods, we shall attempt to advance some arguments potentially capable to spur dialogue on research methods' impact in upcoming strategic management evolution. In doing so, we take into account three key issues related to research methods' impact on strategic management: (a) the possibility that research methods stimulate creativity within and across strategic management subfield; (b) the possibility that research methods inspire cross-fertilizations with other disciplines and research areas; and (c) the possibility that methods are going to contribute to bridge the gap between academia and business practice.

Research methods will stimulate creativity within and across strategic management subfields

First, we contend that the use of unusual or unconventional research methods in strategic management will likely stimulate the most inventive scholars to shaken up and reshape the core of strategic management so as to turn it into a field increasingly devoted to the study of firm and interfirm dynamics (Teece, 2011; Capasso *et al.*, 2014; Chen and Miller, 2015). This means that, drawing on accumulated knowledge, the most imaginative researchers will be the ones to take on their backs developing a stream of new ideas and theories in strategy. This condition may in turn encourage creativity in research design, in raising and tackling novel research questions, and in using a combination of novel data sources as well. We pinpoint to the application of such intriguing methods discussed earlier such as multilevel models (Chapter 3), multi-indicator approaches (Chapter 11), semiotic analysis (Chapter 7), neuroscientific methods (Chapter 10), and qualitative comparative analysis (Chapter 9). In this view, the new methods (or the imaginative amalgamation of existing ones) might enable researchers to fruitfully deal with an array of important questions that lie at the very heart of strategic management so as to initiate a fertile flow of fully-fledged achievements.

Our idea is that this condition will encourage "junior scholars" to embrace new methods, and more "senior scholars" to recognize the value of those methods, so as to push the junior scholars forward in this direction. In other words, we favor allowing young students and scholars a wider berth in research issues and methods in such a way that they may have the chance to exploit the inventiveness that youngsters are naturally endowed with. At the same time, we acknowledge that we need to be cautious in adopting new methods: actually, the non-critical, mechanical adoption of a new method with little or no tradition in strategic management may call scholars to deal with arduous challenges as well. In fact, the new method may not fit well the scrutiny of a specific strategy field's or subfield's issue or phenomena, as well as challenge their fundamental research epistemological assumptions.

Research methods will favor cross-fertilization among strategic management and other disciplines

Second, by drawing constructs and insights from other disciplines, looking at new or original research methods has the potential to enlarge strategy audience.

Methods borrowed from unorthodox and institutional economics, finance, sociology, applied psychology, anthropology, economic geography, marketing, and history may have the potential to shed new light on unfolding phenomena in strategic management. While we recognize that differences in researchers' training background may affect their design choices, we also argue that these differences bear the prospect of adding good value. Collaborative research will definitely favor cross-fertilization of different thoughts and thinking in building theory, as well as in the practice of empirical research when different perspectives and methods are juxtaposed, hybridized, and utilized as complementary tools. In fact, firm problematic situations are often fragmented, have no clear boundary, and therefore increasingly require the use of integrative approaches (Jemison, 1981). This position aligns with the conviction that academic research is active within a community of scholarship where mutually held assumptions are deployed to create "conversations" (Latour, 1987).

On this ground, we hence suggest that, in their research projects strategic management scholars should explore in more depth the potential of such methods as laboratory experiments, behavioral simulations, and quasi-experiments. These methods would be helpful in rigorously testing the relations hypothesized in their theoretical frameworks. Since such research designs usually fall outside the training typically imparted in strategic management Ph.D. programs, here we see a handful of opportunities for activating collaborations between strategic management scholars and scholars in other methodologically complementary fields, such as unorthodox economics, economic psychology, organizational behavior, and applied psychology, where these investigation designs are the mainstream.

Research methods will contribute to bridge the gap between academics and practitioners

Finally, we believe that the adoption of a range of new research methods will bestow greater chances not only to perform more reliable and rigorous research outcomes, but also to craft answers that are more relevant to practice. This would contribute to fill the gap between academia and the world of practice. Actually, we ought to immediately recognize that management researchers' have debated about the need of research-rigor, or methodological soundness, vis-à-vis its (ir)relevance to practitioners (or the rigor-relevance gap). This is a rather long-standing issue in management dating back to some decades ago (Vermeulen, 2005; Gulati, 2007).

The debate above revolves around the condition that, while strategic management academic careers are essentially built on the publication of a stream of articles in premier scholarly journals, these articles have literally very little or no reverberation in the world of practitioners. The debate is thus apparent in the organizational structure of the journals in which strategic management scholars are called to publish their research effort: while the majority of them are labeled as "scholarly" journals (since they now account for over 160, counting only the ones that are listed in ISI-Web of Science recognition record, it is almost impossible to report even a quarter of them here), instead only a few of them are classified as "practitioner-oriented" journals (e.g. *California Management Review*, *Harvard Business Review*, *McKinsey Quarterly*, and *MIT-Sloan Management Review*).

Actually, the importance and reliability of the responses that strategic management research is able to supply to business problems are two very strictly interconnected issues. In fact, the impact and relevance of strategic management studies depends upon the appropriateness and rigor of the research methods chosen (Hitt *et al.*, 2004). Design choices about data sources, empirical techniques, data analysis, data checks, and so on, may dramatically affect the research outcomes, as well as the kind of conclusions that are eventually drawn. An option that strategic management researchers have (reported in Chapter 12) is to look at the way research is conducted in such long-established fields as medicine and law. While inquiry in the social sciences pursues the goal of achieving *truth*, thereby generally translating it in printed propositions (and possibly testing them), inquiry of most traditional academic disciplines and professions, such as medicine and law, pursues the goal of achieving *effectiveness of action*. If we wish future strategic management research to acquire relevance and impactful awareness on practitioners (i.e. consultants, managers, and entrepreneurs), we ought to reflect attentively whether it is the case to carry on research not only in the manner that is customary to social sciences, but also in other ways, such as in the manner that is customary to traditional professional disciplines. This might be a way for strategic management scholarship to accomplish not only simple truth, but compelling human wellbeing improving "transformational truth" (Oliver, 2010).[3]

Notes

1   Actually, Kenneth Andrews is the one who is credited to have writen the "text" part of the Harvard textbook *Business Policy: Text and Cases* (Leaned *et al.*, 1965). A few years later, the same Andrews managed to rework his initial writing and published them in an autonomous book titled *The Concept of Corporate Strategy* (1971).
2   Three concurrent watershed events signposted the inception of strategic management per se (Nerur *et al.*, 2008) (actually, we recall that earlier the area was termed as business policy or business planning): the two books, respectively, by Schendel and Hofer (1979), and Michael Porter (1980), and the launching of the *Strategic Management Journal* in 1980. Schendel and Hofer deserve the merit of providing the state-of-the-art of strategy at the time, as well of setting its research agenda for roughly the next two decades. Porter's *Competitive Strategy* drew managerial attention on the importance of industry attractiveness when choosing a firm strategy. Last but not least, the *Strategic Management Journal* offered for the first time individuals engaged in strategic management inquiry and teaching an invaluable intellectual forum to engage in robust and vigorous dialogue within the newly forming scholarly community, as well as cutting across the scholarly and the business practice communities.
3   "Scholarship, to me, is the ancient and noble pursuit of transformational truth. It is grounded in an imperative to improve the human condition through understanding and through new ways of looking at ourselves and the physical world of which we are a part" (Oliver, 2010: 27).

References

Ansoff, H. I. (1965). *Corporate Strategy*. New York: McGraw-Hill.

Barney, J. B. (1991). Firm Resources and Sustained Competitive Advantage. *Journal of Management*, 17(1): 99–120.

Bascle, G. (2008). Controlling for Endogeneity with Instrumental Variables in Strategic Management Research. *Strategic Organization*, 6(3): 285–328.

Boyd, B.K., Gove S., and Hitt, M.A. (2005). Construct Measurement in Strategic Management Research: Illusion or Reality?. *Strategic Management Journal*, 26(3): 239–257.

Campbell, B., Coff, R., and Kryscynski, D. (2012). Re-thinking Competitive Advantage from Human Capital. *Academy of Management Review*, (37): 376–395.

Capasso, A., Dagnino, G. B., King, D., and Tienari, J. (2014) The Strategic Management of Dynamic Growth. *Call for Papers: Long Range Planning Special Issue*.

Chatterji, A., Findley, M. G., Jensen, N. M., Meier, S., and Nielson, D. L. (forthcoming). Field Experiments in Strategy Research. *Strategic Management Journal*.

Chen, M-J. and Miller, D. (2015) Reconceptualizing Competitive Dynamics: A Multidimensional Framework. *Strategic Management Journal*, 36(5): 758–775.

Cyert, R. M. and March, J. G. (1963). *A Behavioral Theory of the Firm*. Englewood Cliffs, NJ: Prentice-Hall.

Furrer O., Thomas, H., and Goussevskaia, A. (2008). The Structure and Evolution of the Strategic Management Field: A Content Analysis of 26 Years of Strategic Management Research. *International Journal of Management Reviews*, 10(1): 1–23.

Guerras-Martín, L. A., Madhok, A., and Montoro-Sánchez, A. (2014). The Evolution of Strategic Management Research: Recent Trends and Current Directions. *BRQ Business Research Quarterly*, 17(2): 69–76.

Gulati, R. (2007) Tent Poles, Tribalism, and Boundary Spanning: The Rigor-Relevance Debate in Management Research. *Academy of Management Review*, 50(4): 775–782.

Hamilton, B. H. and Nickerson, J. A. (2003). Correcting for Endogeneity in Strategic Management Research. *Strategic Organization*, 1(1): 51–78.

Harrison, G. W. and List, J. A. (2004). Field Experiments. *Journal of Economic Literature*, 47: 1009–1055.

Herrmann, P. (2005). Evolution of Strategic Management: The Need for New Dominant Designs. *International Journal of Management Reviews*, 7(2): 111–130.

Hitt, M.A., Boyd, B.K., and Li, D. (2004). The State of Strategic Management Research and a Vision of the Future, in Ketchen, D. J. and Bergh D. D. (eds) *Research Methodology in Strategy and Management*, Vol. 1, Bingley, UK: Emerald Group Publishing Limited, 1–31.

Hoskisson, R. E., Hitt, M. A., Wan, W. P., and Yiu, D. (1999). Theory and Research in Strategic Management: Swings of a Pendulum. *Journal of Management*, 25(3): 417–456.

Hughes, H. P. N., Clegg, C. W., Robinson, M. A., and Crowder, R. M. (2012). Agent-based Modelling and Simulation: The Potential Contribution to Organizational Psychology. *Journal of Occupational and Organizational Psychology*, 85(3): 487–502.

Jemison, D. B. (1981). The Importance of an Integrative Approach to Strategic Management Research. *Academy of Management Review*, 6(4): 601–608.

Ketchen, D. J., Boyd, B. K., and Bergh, D. D. (2008). Research methodology in strategic management: Past accomplishments and future challenges. *Organizational Research Methods*, 11(4): 643–658.

Latour B. (1987). *Science in Action: How to Follow Scientists and Engineers through Society*. Cambridge, MA: Harvard University Press.

Lawrence, P. R. and Lorsch, J. W. (1967). Differentiation and integration in complex organizations. *Administrative Science Quarterly*, 12(1): 1–47.

Learned, E. P., Christensen, C. R., Andrews, K. R., and Guth, W. D. (1965). *Business Policy: Text and Case*. Homewood, IL: Irwin.

March J. C. and Simon, H. A. (1958) *Organizations*. New York: John Wiley and Sons Inc.

Mitchell. J. R., Shepherd, D. A., and Sharfman, M. P. (2011). Erratic Strategic Decisions: When and Why Managers are Inconsistent in Strategic Decision Making. *Strategic Management Journal*, 32(7): 683–704.

Nag, R., Hambrick, D. C., and Chen, M. J. (2007). What is Strategic Management, Really? Inductive Derivation of a Consensus Definition of the Field. *Strategic Management Journal*, 28(9): 935–955.

Nerur, S. P., Rasheed, A. A., and Natarajan, V. (2008). The Intellectual Structure of the Strategic Management Field: An Author Co Citation Analysis. *Strategic Management Journal*, 29(3): 319–336.

Oliver, C. (2010). The Goals of Scholarship. *Journal of Management Inquiry*, 19: 26–32.

Peng, M. W., Sun, S. L., Pinkham, B., and Chen, H. (2009). The Institution-Based View as a Third Leg for a Strategy Tripod. *Academy of Management Perspectives*, 23(3): 63–81.

Peteraf, M. A. (1993). The Cornerstones of Competitive Advantage: A Resource Based View. *Strategic Management Journal*, 14(3): 179–191.

Pettigrew, A. M., Thomas, H., and Whittington, R. (eds). (2002). *Handbook of Strategy and Management*. Sage.

Phelan, S. E., Ferreira, M., and Salvador, R. (2002). The First Twenty Years of the *Strategic Management Journal*. *Strategic Management Journal*, 23(12): 1161–1168.

Ramos-Rodríguez, A. R. and Ruíz Navarro, J. (2004). Changes in the intellectual structure of strategic management research: A bibliometric study of the Strategic Management Journal, 1980–2000. *Strategic Management Journal*, 25(10): 981–1004.

Ronda-Pupo, G. A. and Guerras-Martín, L.Á. (2010). Dynamics of the Scientific Community Network within the Strategic Management Field Through the *Strategic Management Journal* 1980–2009: The Role of Cooperation. *Scientometrics*, 85(3): 821–848.

Rumelt, R. P., Schendel, D. E., and Teece, D. J. (1994) *Fundamental Issues in Strategy, A Research Agenda*. Boston: Harvard Business Press.

Scandura, T. A., Williams, E. A. (2000). Research Methodology in Management: Current Practices, Trends, and Implications for Future Research. *Academy of Management Journal*, 43(6): 1248–1264.

Teece, D. J., Pisano, G., and Shuen, A. (1997). Dynamic Capabilities and Strategic Management. *Strategic Management Journal*, 18(7): 509–533.

Teece, D. J. (2011). *Dynamic Capabilities and Strategic Management: Organizing for Innovation and Growth*. Oxford: Oxford University Press.

Vermeulen, F. (2005). On Rigor and Relevance: Fostering Dialectic Progress in Management Research. *Academy of Management Journal*, 48(6): 978–982.

Wright, P., Coff, R., and Moliterno, T. (2014). Strategic Human Capital: Crossing the Great Divide. *Journal of Management*, (40): 353–370.

INDEX